W9-BDU-726

ALICE GUY BLACHÉ:
LOST VISIONARY OF THE CINEMA

Women Make Cinema

Series Editors: Pam Cook, University of Southampton
Ginette Vincendeau, University of Warwick

Women Make Cinema is a ground-breaking series dedicated to celebrating the contribution of women to all aspects of film-making throughout the world. Until recently feminist criticism has focused on the exclusion of women from mainstream cinema, emphasizing the relatively small number of women directors and their restricted opportunities. *Women Make Cinema* assesses the historical impact of women as both producers and consumers of cinematic images. As stars, directors, scriptwriters, editors, producers, designers, critics and audiences, they have exerted a powerful influence on world cinema. This series opens up this hidden history, giving women a central place in the development of cinema.

Already available:

Heroines without Heroes: Reconstructing Female and National Identities in European Cinema, 1945-51, edited by Ulrike Sieglohr

Cinema and the Second Sex: Women's Filmmaking in France in the 1980s and 1990s, by Carrie Tarr with Brigitte Rollet

Forthcoming:

Simone Signoret, by Susan Hayward

Also of interest from Continuum:

Gaslight Melodrama, by Guy Barefoot
Batman Unmasked, by Will Brooker
Women in British Cinema, by Sue Harper
Oscar® Fever, by Emmanuel Levy
Stars and Stardom in French Cinema, by Ginette Vincendeau

ALICE GUY BLACHÉ

Lost Visionary of the Cinema

Alison McMahan

Continuum
NEW YORK • LONDON

2002

The Continuum International Publishing Group Inc
370 Lexington Avenue, New York, NY 10017

The Continuum International Publishing Group Ltd
The Tower Building, 11 York Road, London SE1 7NX

www.continuumbooks.com

Printed in the United States of America

Library of Congress Cataloging-in-Publication Data

McMahan, Alison.
    Alice Guy Blaché: Lost Visionary of the Cinema / Alison McMahan.
      p. cm.
    Includes bibliographical references and index.
    ISBN 0-8264-5158-6 (alk. paper)
    1. Guy, Alice, 1873–1968. 2. Motion picture producers and
directors—France—Biography. I. Title.
    PN1998.3.G89 M39 2002
    791.43'0233'092—dc21
    [B]   2001047720

CONTENTS

Acknowledgments

THIS BOOK WAS ten years in the making. It started out as a doctoral thesis at the Union Institute, and benefitted greatly from the academic support of my doctoral committee: Susan Amussen, Mary Sheerin, Anthony Slide, Richard Abel, Antonia Lant, Anne Will, Carol DeBoer-Langworthy and Victor Bachy.

Alice Guy's family was incredibly generous in its participation. Roberta Blaché, Alice Guy Blaché's daughter-in-law, let me look through Guy Blaché's documents, letters and mementos, as well as shared her personal memories with me. Her daughter, Addrienne Channing, Adrienne's husband Bob, Guy's other grandaughter, Régine Blaché Bolton, and Gabriel Allignet, Guy Blaché's nephew, all shared their memories of Alice Guy with me and often let me look at family documents.

A book like this is impossible without the help of archivists. I am particularly grateful to Marianne Chanel, the curator of the Musée Gaumont, who opened all the files in her archives, helped me cut through red tape, gave me free(!) access to the photocopier, made sure I got the slides I ordered before I went home and allowed me to look through materials that were being organized for an exhibit and were technically off-limits. She also introduced me to Mr. Allignet. Graham Melville at the National Film and Television Archive in London did many of the same things Marianne did, and brought to it his own interest in early cinema. He also put me in touch with scholars working in related areas. I am also grateful to Elaine Burrows and her staff at the BFI. Rosemary Haines and Madeline Katz at the Motion Picture Division of the Library of Congress were generous with their time, assistance and expertise, as were Paolo Cherchi Usai and his staff at the George Eastman House, Christopher Horak at the Stadtmuseum in Munich and Charles Silver and Ron Maggliozzi at the Museum of Modern Art in New York. Sabine Lenk, then at the Cinémathèque Royale de Belgique, started what has become a beautiful friendship by responding to my first letter of inquiry with an incredibly detailed answer filled with names and addresses. Once we met in Brussels, she then introduced me to Jeanine Baj and together we identified one of the films in the Alan Roberts collection. Since then Sabine, Frank Kessler and Martin Loiperdinger have helped me greatly with their comments, encouragement and friendship. I am extremely grateful to Serge Bromberg of Red Lobster Films in Paris for access to films in his collection and information about them. Madeleine Bernstorff, an independent organizer of film retrospectives and art exhibits on women artists in Germany helped me make appointments and see films in Munich and Berlin and introduced me to the curators of various archives, also translating for me when necessary. Louise Anderson, the organizer of the Symposium on early women filmmakers at the Museum of the Moving Image in London did her job with competence and grace, helped me when the films I wanted to screen as part of my presentation were lost and managed to get a copy of *Cupid and the Comet* from Munich so that we could screen it. Christian Delage selected me as part of the Gaumont Centenary research team giving me access to the Gaumont files at the Cinémathèque Francaise, where Laurent Mannoni was very helpful. Jessica Rossner at Kino Video in New York has been extremely supportive and helpful.

I am also very grateful Nico de Klerk and Nicoline Witte and the entire staff at the Nederlands Filmmuseum in Amsterdam, for all their support for me and my Early Film History students while I was teaching at the University of Amsterdam. I am especially grateful to my MA and doctorandus students in Film History at the University of Amsterdam from 1997 to 2001, for eager participation in my courses and their frequent insights. I thank the Film and Television Studies program and Professor Elsaesser for making it possible for my students to program their own early film shows at the Nederland Filmmuseum and for their overall support of work in early cinema. I also thank my co-teachers for the Film History courses, Andre Waardenburg and Franca Jonquière. I owe a debt of gratitude to the Archimedia program in Europe, its organizers and participants.

I owe an infinite debt to Marquise Lepage, the National Film Board of Canada director who hired me as a researcher and later line producer on her documentary about Guy Blaché, thus making all of her findings accessible to me and allowing me to see some of the Guy Blaché films that I otherwise would not have seen until much later or not at all. Ms. Lepage also introduced me to Roberta Blaché.

Joan Simon provided tremendous encouragement to me, for my project as a whole, and especially for pushing me to continue with the work and turn my dissertation into a book. Ms. Simon has almost single handedly raised the money to preserve many of the rapidly decomposing Guy films.

I am extremely grateful to Claire Dupré La Tour, Malte Hagener, Sabine Lenk and Rolland Westreich for their assistance in interpreting German and French materials.

My research has especially benefitted from previous work by Anthony Slide, Felicity Sparrow, Victor Bachy and Richard Abel.

I would like to thank Richard Abel, Rick Altman, Mieke Bal, Ivo Blom, François de la Bretèque, Marco Bertozzi, Warren Buckland, Edwin Carels, Richard Crangle, Claire Dupré La Tour, Elizabeth Ezra, Annete Förster, André Gaudreault, Frank Kessler, Richard Koszarski, Sandy Flitterman-Lewis, Sabine Lenk, Martin Loiperdinger, Charlie Musser, Dominique Nasta, Richard Porton, Catherine Preston, Jan Olson, Simon Popple, Vanessa Thoulmin, Anthony Slide, Chris Straayer, William Urrichio, Eva Warth, Michiel Wedel, Alan Williams, and Sasha Vojkovic for reading parts of the manuscript at different stages and providing insights and comments or for their extra insights given at conferences.

Parts of this book were given as papers at the following conferences: DOMITOR Conference New York (1994) Paris (1996) and Washington, D.C. (1998); Congrès Lumière, Lyons, June 1995; the Columbia Series Seminar, Columbia University in New York, 1995; "Prima dell 'Autore, Spettacolo Cinematografico, testo, autorialita dalle origini agli anni Trenta Conference sponsored by the University of Bologna in Udine, Italy March 1996; The *Back in the Saddle Conference*, University of Utrecht, July 1997; the SCS Conference in San Diego, April 1998 and Washington DC, 2001; the Technologies of the Moving Image Conference, Stockholm University, December 1998; the Visual Delights Conference, Sheffield University, June 1999; the Gender and Early Cinema conference, University of Utrecht, October 1999; the Spectacular Europe 3 Conference in Warwick, UK, March 2000; the Archimedia 2000 Conference in Brussels and 2001 in Amsterdam. I benefitted greatly from the stimulating environment provided at these conferences. I am also grateful to the organizers of the Silent Pioneer Day at the Museum of the Moving Image, London June 1995, especially Louise Anderson; to the organizers of the Festival des Films de Femmes, Créteil (Paris) of

1994 and 1995; to the ArTable session organizers of 1995; to the organizers of the Cinematrix Film Festival, Hampstead, England, 1996, and the *Silence, elles tournent* Film Festival, Montreal, and American Museum of the Moving Image, NY, April 1998; to the Theater Institut Nederlands, Amsterdam, January 1999; to Olga Schubart and the other organizers of the Women's Film Festival of Loulé, Portugal, June 2000, and to the American Movie Channel. I am extremely grateful to the Giornate del Cinema Ritrovato in Pordenone (now Sacile), Italy, for the opportunity they provide year after to year to see large numbers of hard to find silent films and discuss them with other archivists and film scholars.

The process of converting thesis into a book was greatly edited by my wonderful series editors, Pam Cook and Ginette Vincendeau, who gave me much needed encouragement many times when my courage flagged. My assistant and friend Sytske van Hasselt did an incredible job scanning the images and in numerous other ways helping with the preparation of the manuscript. A thanks is also owed to my student Chiara Zappia for her help with some last minute research.

I am extremely fortunate to have David Barker as a publisher at Continuum—every writer should be so lucky!

A project like this one is impossible to see through to the end without the support of friends. I owe special thanks to Marco Bertozzi, Claire Dupré La Tour, Sara Gross, Sytske van Hasselt, Marquise Lepage, Joan Simon, Al and Yvette Marrin, Graham Melville, Richard Porton, Sasha Vojkovic, Anne Will, Alan Williams, and most of all to Roberta Blaché.

Personal thanks are owed to Steven Bluestone with whom I share the task of raising our wonderful child. A big thanks is also owed to my daughter Ruth, who followed her mother all around Europe and other times waited at home while I did the research. There aren't enough words to thank Warren Buckland, whose support, both critical and personal, was instrumental in helping me turn a Ph.D. dissertation into this book.

Dedication

THIS PROJECT WOULD never have been started, let alone finished, without the financial and moral support provided by my father, D. Bruce McMahan. This book is dedicated to him.

It is also dedicated to Roberta Blaché who, sadly, did not live to see it completed. She is sorely missed.

Alice Guy Blaché (seated) and her daughter-in-law Roberta Blaché

List of Illustrations

Key Dates in the Life of Alice Guy Blaché

1873   Alice Guy's French parents, Mariette and Émile Guy, live in Santiago, Chile, but Guy's mother travels to Paris to give birth to her fifth child. Guy is raised by her grandmother in Switzerland until she is three or four years old.

1877 (approx.)   Her mother comes to collect her daughter and takes her home to Santiago. In Santiago, Guy meets her father for the first time.

1879 (approx.)   Her father brings her back to France and enrolls her in the boarding school where two of her older sisters are already studying.

1884 (approx.)   Her father's bookstore chain is forced to bankruptcy by a series of violent earthquakes, fires, and thefts. Her parents return to France and her older sisters quickly marry. Guy is transferred to a cheaper boarding school. Her brother dies after a long illness, and her father dies soon after.

1893   Guy has trained as a typist and stenographer and gets her first job as a secretary for a company that sells varnishing products.

1894   Guy is hired by Léon Gaumont, the "second-in-command" to work for Felix Richard's still-photography company. Soon after, Richard loses a patent suit and is forced to go out of business. Léon Gaumont buys the inventory and starts his own company, taking Guy with him. Guy is present when Georges Demenÿ demonstrates his *phonoscope* and offers Gaumont the patent for his *biographe*, a 60mm. motion picture camera.

March 22, 1895   Gaumont and Guy are invited by the Lumière brothers to witness a demonstration of their *cinématographe*, a 35mm. motion picture camera, at the *Société d'encouragement à l'industrie nationale*. Guy persuades Gaumont to let her use the Gaumont camera to direct a story film.

1896   Guy writes, produces and directs *La Fée aux choux* (The Cabbage Fairy).

1897   Gaumont makes Guy head of film production, a post she holds until 1906.

1902   Gaumont demonstrates his *chronophone*, a synchronized sound-system.

1902–1906   Guy directs over 100 *phonoscènes*, films made for the *chronophone*.

1906   Herbert Blaché, a Gaumont manager, is assigned to serve as Guy's cameraman on *Mireille*. Later, Guy is sent to Berlin to oversee demonstrations of the chronophone and assist Blaché with sales.

Christmas Day, 1906   Blaché and Guy are officially engaged. Guy is 33, Blaché is 24.

Spring, 1907   Guy and Blaché marry. Gaumont sends Blaché to the U.S. to promote a chronophone franchise. Guy resigns from her position to accompany her husband to the U.S.

1907   The Blachés spend nine months in Cleveland working with investors to promote a chronophone franchise. The effort is unsuccessful.

1908   Gaumont hires Herbert Blaché to manage his studio in Flushing, New York, for the production of *phonoscènes* in English. Lois Weber is among the performers hired, and she is later given the opportunity to direct *phonoscènes* herself.

1908   Guy gives birth to her daughter, Simone.

1910   Tempted by the underused Gaumont studio in Flushing, New York, Guy creates her own company, Solax, and rents the Gaumont studio space. Her early films are melodramas and westerns.

1911   Guy gives birth to her son, Reginald.

1912   Solax is so successful that Guy builds a studio in Fort Lee New Jersey, said to cost over $100,000. Solax produces two one-reelers (10–15 minute films) a week and develops a stable of stars. Guy writes and directs at least half of these films and oversees all production. Her rate of production equals that of D.W. Griffith, working at Biograph just a few miles away.

1912   Gaumont has a falling out with George Kleine, a member of the Motion Picture Patents Company and his U.S. distributor. Gaumont moves over from the "licensed" side of distribution to join the ranks of the independents.

March 1, 1913 *Dick Whittington and His Cat* is released. With a length of three reels (45 minutes), a $35,000 budget and elaborate staging (including burning a boat) and costuming, it is Guy's most ambitious Solax project.

June 1913 Blaché's contract with Gaumont expires and Guy makes him president of Solax so that she can concentrate on writing and directing. After three months, Blaché resigns and starts his own film company, Blaché Features. Blaché Features uses Solax's plant, inventory and actors, making the two companies hardly distinguishable for a few months. Blaché Features' production eventually supersedes Solax production, so that by 1914, Solax is virtually defunct.

August 1913–August 1914 Blaché and Guy alternate producing and directing longer films (three and four reels) for Blaché features.

1914–1916 The market now demands feature-length films (five reels or more). The Blachés join Popular Plays and Players, a production coalition which produces features for distributors such as Metro, Pathé, and World Film Corporation. These films are shot in the former Solax Studio in Fort Lee, which still belongs to the Blachés.

1916 The Blachés are dissatisfied with their distribution arrangement and decide to part ways with Popular Plays and Players. As the U.S. Amusement Corporation, they produce feature films and make their own distribution deals with the same distributors who bought the films from Popular Plays and Players. Guy directs seven features, including *The Ocean Waif*.

1917 The former Solax studio is now rented out to other companies, starting with Apollo Pictures. At age 44, Guy has an excellent reputation as a film director but her last few films have not been commercially successful. Blaché, who is 35, is enjoying the attention of young actresses. In the fall of 1917, Simone, age nine, and Reginald, age five, contract rougeola and become seriously ill. Blaché sends his family to the healthier environment of North Carolina, where Guy cares for her children and takes part in the war effort by volunteering for the Red Cross while her husband continues to manage business in Fort Lee.

1918   Blaché finds his wife a job directing *The Great Adventure* for Pathé Players. The film, a comedy, is commercially successful.

1918   Blaché moves to Hollywood with one of his actresses. Guy gives up her house in Fort Lee and moves into an apartment in New York City.

1919   Léonce Perret hires Guy to write and direct *Tarnished Reputations*, offering her $2,000 for six weeks of work. The film takes ten weeks to make and in the process Guy contracts Spanish influenza, which kills four of her colleagues. Blaché, passing through New York, is alarmed by her condition and invites her to join him in California.

1920   Guy moves into a small bungalow in Los Angeles with her children. Blaché does not live with them, but hires Guy as his directing assistant on *The Brat* and *Stronger than Death*, both starring Alla Nazimova. A few months later Guy is called back to Fort Lee to oversee the auction of the Solax properties. In the middle of bankruptcy arrangements, a polio epidemic sweeps the Northeast and Guy, imitating her friends the Capellanis, flees with her children to Canada. *Tarnished Reputations* opens March 14, 1920. It is Guy's last film.

1922   Bankruptcy proceedings are finished and the Blachés are divorced. Guy (now calling herself Alice Guy Blaché) returns with her children to France.

1922–1927   Guy's efforts to work in the French film industry, including the Gaumont Studio in Nice, do not bear fruit. She returns to the U.S. in 1927 to try to find copies of her films to use to find work. She finds none, even at the Library of Congress where some of them were copyrighted. When the silent film era ends in 1929, it becomes clear that she will not make films again. She becomes financially dependent on her children, especially her daughter, Simone.

1930   Léon Gaumont publishes a history of the Gaumont company which does not mention any of the film production before 1907. Guy embarks on a deferential letter writing campaign to correct his omissions. Gaumont agrees to add to his document and corrects the manuscript himself, but it remains unpublished on his death in 1946.

1937   Guy's son, Reginald, returns to the U.S. Simone and Guy move to Paris, where Simone's work prospects are better. Guy supplements her daughter's meager income by writing children's stories and novelizations of films for women's magazines.

1940   Simone Blaché begins her career working for U.S. embassies in Europe. Guy follows her daughter on various assignments, first in Vichy (1940), then Geneva (1941–1947).

1947   Guy makes guest speaker appearances at high schools and women's clubs in Switzerland. The success of these informal appearances leads her to write her *Memoirs*.

1947–1952   Simone and Guy live in Washington D.C. In Georgetown, Guy begins to seriously work on her memoirs and filmography, and renews the search for her films. She begins a correspondence with Louis Gaumont, Léon Gaumont's son.

December 8, 1954   Louis Gaumont gives a speech in Paris on "Madame Alice Guy Blaché, the First Woman Filmmaker" whom, he says, "has been unjustly forgotten." Film historians such as Jean Mitry, Georges Sadoul, René Jeanne and Charles Ford begin to take notice of her.

1955   Guy is awarded the Légion d'Honneur, France's highest non-military honor.

March 16, 1957   Guy is honored in a Cinémathèque Française ceremony which goes unnoticed by the press.

1958   Simone is transferred to the U.S. embassy in Brussels.

1963   Victor Bachy, the professor who initiated the academic study of cinema in Belgium, meets Guy by accident and begins researching her work.

1965   Guy and her daughter move to New Jersey.

March 24, 1968   Guy dies in a nursing home in New Jersey, at the age of 95.

1976   Guy's *Mémoires* is published in French, with a filmography by Francis Lacassin.

1986   Guy's *Memoirs* is published in English, edited by Anthony Slide, translated by Roberta and Simone Blaché.

1994 Victor Bachy's *Alice Guy-Blaché: La Première femme cinéaste du monde* is published.

1995 *The Lost Garden: The Life and Work of Alice Guy Blaché, The World's First Woman Filmmaker*, a one-hour documentary directed by Marquise Lepage, National Film Board of Canada is released.

2000 Sections on Alice Guy are part of two documentaries on early women filmmakers, one produced by TMC and one by AMC in the United States. Opening of the Alice Guy Archive at the Museum of Modern Art.

Introduction:
The Search for Alice Guy[1]

I HAD TO invent Alice Guy before I could find her.

I was a filmmaker before I was a film scholar. In the late 1980's, as I wrote my scripts, I began to ask myself questions about the representation of women in the media. Many works have critiqued or deconstructed the representations of women in male-authored texts and in texts by a few well-known female filmmakers such as Dorothy Arzner and Ida Lupino. Although not an experimental filmmaker myself, I was not insensitive to the discourse of the late sixties and seventies, mostly promoted by experimental women filmmakers, that films addressing women would have to be constructed in a filmic "language" different from that for films that came out of the dominant culture. This included films by women who were token members of that culture. But would female filmmakers, removed from the economic and stylistic influence of Hollywood, necessarily come up with a cinematic language of their own? And if so, what would that language look like?

What I decided to do was to find a woman filmmaker who had produced a large body of films outside of the Hollywood system. In other words, if I was really going to make films myself using a feminist filmic language, the first thing I needed was a role model. Before I even embarked on my search for her I drew a profile of what this role model might be like. I knew that alternative modes to the dominant cinema proliferated in the first two decades of film history, so perhaps I would find her there, a woman filmmaker making films before 1913. It even occurred to me that I would be more likely to find her in Europe than in the U.S. because that would put her at a further remove from what became classical Hollywood narrative. What I was looking for was a female filmmaker who had a large measure of control over her production, someone who had left behind a substantial body of work. This would then be material for my narratological analysis.

I thought I would find at least a dozen female filmmakers working in that period, and there were a few. But in the end, there was only one woman who produced a consistent body of work

Figure 1. Alice in white feather hat

before Lois Weber started directing English-language *phonoscènes* at the Gaumont Flushing Studio in 1908.[2] This woman, of course, was Alice Guy, later known as Alice Guy Blaché.

Guy's career is fascinating from various perspectives. Her career lasted much longer than those of her contemporaries who also began in 1896: the Lumière brothers had ceased producing films by 1905, Georges Méliès by 1912, Edison by 1917. Even Romeo Bossetti, one of her trainees, ceased working as a director mid-1910s, although he returned as a character actor after the First World War.

The length of Guy's career is a testament to her ability to adapt in order to meet the changing demands of the industry. It is also a testament to her ability to fulfill various roles. From the available evidence it seems that she was almost solely responsible for every detail that appeared in front of the camera in the films she made at the Gaumont Company before the film studio was built in 1905.[3] The ideas for the films originated from her; she scouted the area around Paris tirelessly for locations; she herself went out searching for props and costumes and made many of the costumes herself; she roped her friends into playing parts, hired set designers, and acted in films herself. At Solax, the film production company and studio that she owned and operated in Flushing, and then in Fort Lee from 1910 to 1914, she had complete control over every film, from scripting to art direction to editing, and directed the majority of them herself. She directed approximately 1000 films and produced many more. Of these, slightly more than 100 survive. In this book I focus on these surviving films, especially the ones she directed.

Attribution, however, is a challenge generally, and especially for the films she made at Gaumont. Given the length and breadth of Guy's career and the variety of roles she played within the industry, how is one to approach the body of films labeled as "hers"? Indeed, which films do we say are hers—the films she wrote, the films she directed, the films she produced, or all of the above? My search through the archives was long and expensive because the archives defined a "Guy" film as one she had directed. Even if I asked to see all of the Solax films in a particular collection, for example, I was given only the films already attributed to Guy as a director. Twice I had to return to two archives to see other Solax films in their collection that they had not told me about.

Most efforts to attribute the earliest Gaumont films to a particular director are met with considerable controversy. I discuss these controversies in the appropriate chapters of this book (especially One, Three and Six). In some cases the Gaumont Company has attributed specific films to Guy (*La Vie du Christ, Madame a des envies*, and most of the *phonoscènes*, for example). In other cases, I have found documents with evidence that she directed it, or stylistic earmarks that made me think a film might be hers. The basis for the attribution of each film is discussed in the section of the book covering that film.

Though Guy was not recognized in credits in her French films (early films carried no credits, and until 1912 there was no copyright process for film scripts), she did receive plenty of official recognition in the form of awards. In January of 1907 for example, she received the Palmes Académiques as "Directrice de théâtre" as the title "metteur-en-scène" (director) had not yet been coined. She also regularly received awards at the *Exposition Universelle*'s (World Expositions) where Gaumont films had an important presence, which means that her contribution was officially recognized by the Gaumont

Figure 2. Beaux Arts Academy Medal, front

Figure 3. Beaux Arts Academy Medal, back

Figure 4. Silver Medal from the *Exposition Universelle* in Milan, 1906

Company (who nominated her for the awards) as well as the award judges and juries. Her awards include *Diplôme de collaboratrice* (Award to collaborator) at the *Exposition Universelle* in Paris in 1900 and again at the *Exposition Universelle* in Lille in 1903. She received gold medals at the *Exposition Universelle* in St. Louis 1904, *the Exposition Universelle* in Liege in 1905, and the *Exposition Universelle* in Milan in 1906.

Whether Guy *directed* every film made at Gaumont until 1905 or not, we know that she did *produce* them. According to her memoirs, until the glass-house Gaumont studio was built in 1905 she was pretty much left alone to shoulder all the responsibilities of production, writing, and directing the Gaumont story-films. In the rest of this introduction I describe how I went about finding, identifying, and working for the preservation of Guy's films. I contextualize this study of her work within other ongoing research into early film history. Finally, the introduction ends with an account of how Guy ended up as the first woman filmmaker.

The Search for the Films and Documentation

THE FIRST STEP in this study was to find the surviving films. Guy herself had conducted an intensive search at various archives for her own films, first in 1927 and again throughout the fifties, both times without success. At the time of her death in 1968, she believed that most of her films had already been lost, except for three that Gerhard Lamprecht had found in Berlin in 1958. When I began this study in 1992, about 40 films were known to exist. As a result of the efforts of many archivists and others like myself, the number now hovers at 110 (some in need of preservation), only two of which are feature length, from at least twenty two that she directed. A third feature, *The Empress* (U.S. Amusement Corp., 1917), lies unpreserved at the Cinémathèque Française. The research for this project required that I travel from archive to archive all over the U.S. and Europe. It took almost ten years. The story of my search is itself of interest, because it was alternately aided or hampered by how I, or others, conceptualized early cinema and the authorship of early filmmakers. Since these issues are theoretically important, I have interspersed accounts of my search with my account of Guy's career and the analysis of her films.

In this search I was aided by many people. I have done my best to mention everyone in the acknowledgements. Future researchers will have the benefit of Joan Simon's and Steve Higgin's efforts to create an Alice Guy Archive at the Museum of Modern Art in New York. This archive will include documents: specifically the Roberta Blaché Collection, which was carefully watched over by Guy's daughter, Simone, and then by her daughter in law, Roberta Blaché.

This project was designed to fill a gap because there was no independently written biography or book length critical analysis of Alice Guy or her work when I began my search. General historical texts mention her only in passing or don't mention her at all.[4]

Others discuss her, but their work is controversial.[5] Some of these controversies are addressed in this book, especially in Chapters One, Three and Six. Henri Langlois published an article entitled "French Cinema: Origins"[6] which mentions Guy's assistant Victorin Jasset by name, as well as Georges Méliès and Ferdinand Zecca, and mentions the titles of several Guy films, without ever mentioning Guy herself, even though Langlois personally invited Guy to a ceremony in her honor at the Cinémathèque Française in 1957. Charles

Figure 5. Alice in her writing smock

Ford, Gerald Peary, and Francis Lacassin all wrote articles about her, some of them based on interviews.[7]

Guy's memoirs were first published in French[8] in 1976. The first English version was published without the introductory chapter as *The Memoirs of Alice Guy Blaché* (1986), translated by Roberta and Simone Blaché, daughter-in-law and daughter of Alice Guy, and edited by Anthony Slide. Scarecrow Press released a new paperback version of the *Memoirs* in May of 1996 that included the missing chapter.[9] In either language, the autobiography is tantalizing in what it leaves out. The memoirs inspired a flurry of articles, most notably by Victor Bachy, Jean Mitry, Jacques Deslandes, Francis Lacassin, and Marc Wanamaker.[10] Slide included a chapter on Guy in his book *Early Women Directors*[11] and the chapter on Guy was reprinted in Richard Dyer MacCann's book, *The First Filmmakers*.[12]

In French, Jovette Marchessault's paper on Guy was published in a Canadian anthology on experimental theater,[13] Émile Breton included a chapter on Guy in his book *Femmes d'images*,[14] and Bachy's paper on why Guy was forgotten, as well as the transcript of his interview with Guy herself from the early sixties, were published in the anthology *Les Premiers ans du cinéma français*.[15] The autobiography also led to some retrospectives, most notably at the Festival des Films de Femmes at Créteil (near Paris) in 1994, as well as the retrospective at the Museum of Modern Art in 1985. The work also received the attention of feminists, especially authors of survey texts that focus on women filmmakers.[16] These books tended to rely on the autobiography and some articles in *Motion Picture World*, as well as on Lisa Viscenzi's master's thesis on Guy Blaché's Solax years (Columbia University).[17] As a result of these articles and of a handful of partial retrospectives of Guy Blaché's work organized both in France and the U.S., she is now being regularly included in general history texts.[18]

Victor Bachy then made giant strides in filling the gaps in the autobiography with his book *Alice Guy Blaché: La Première femme cinéaste du monde* (1993).[19] He established a very complete list of films that Guy worked on, but not without attracting much controversy. To a large extent, I have re-done Bachy's research and attempted to resolve the most pressing questions.

Others attempted to fill this gap with documentary films.[20] Anthony Slide, to whom this study owes much, made *The Silent Feminists*.[21] A portion of this film is devoted to Guy and includes an interview with her daughter, Simone. Nicole-Lise Bernheim made a short documentary in the late seventies that presented the basic facts of Guy's life.[22] Other documentaries are listed in the appendix. The best documentary on Alice Guy is still *The Lost Garden*, directed by Marquise Lepage for the National Film Board of Canada in 1994. This film successfully combines biography and film history, and makes a large selection of Guy's films accessible to a general viewer.

Documentaries such as *The Lost Garden* have helped make Guy and her work better known; but even so, a series of myths about her life and work persist. Each chapter in this book is built around one of these controversies. I have taken pains to debunk these myths and clarify the real issues that the myths obscure. Anyone who has heard of Alice Guy at all has probably heard that she was the first woman filmmaker and that she might have made the first fiction film, a claim that has generated considerable debate (see Chapter 1).[23] Even if those who question Guy's role in the development of narrative cinema were to remain unconvinced by the case I make here, there is no question that she played a key role in early sound film production, as she directed over 100 synchronized sound films between 1902 and 1906. Yet this part of her story is almost never mentioned (see Chapter 2). Europeans may have seen the movie *Elle voulait faire du cinéma*, which postulates that she and her boss, Léon Gaumont, had an affair. I deal with this and other issues relating to the difficulties she had in maintaining her job at Gaumont in Chapter 3.[24] Americans have probably read the general historical texts that lay the blame for the demise of Solax, her American studio, at the feet of her husband, Herbert Blaché; I argue against it in Chapter 4. The demise of Solax is also attributed to "Alice Guy losing her touch" or not being able to make the transition to features; I counter this in Chapter 5. Finally, in Chapter 6 I try to answer my original question: what does Alice Guy have to say to viewers today? Was she a feminist? Are feminist readings of her films possible once we adjust to the language of early cinema? Can she, in fact, serve as a guide for feminist filmmakers, and are her films a fertile ground for theoretical analysis?

The myths and controversies surrounding Alice Guy's life have had two effects: they make Guy look like a victim, especially with the loss of her historical record, the blame for which is often laid at the feet of various (male) historians;[25] the myths have also seduced us into overlooking her work. At the homage to Alice Guy held as part of the Films de femmes Festival in Créteil in 1994, it became clear that even for feminists, Guy's films have taken second place to the historical and emotional value of her personal achievements. This is partly because only slightly more than 100 of the approximately 1000 films that she directed still exist, and almost half of these have been found only recently. Her films are spread out in archives all over the world. Not all of them are available for viewing even to scholars, and many of them are in desperate need of conservation and preservation.

My goals in this book are to carefully examine some of these "well-known truths" about Guy and sort out, as much as possible, fact from fiction, as well as to summarize, analyze and critique what remains of her work. My principal aim is to make her films more intelligible to modern viewers. In the process, I hope to shed some new light on the birth of cinema and the beginning of the visual culture in which we live today.

This book is partly a product of the movement that started at the 34th annual conference of the International Federation of Film Archives (FIAF) held in Brighton in 1978. FIAF was set up in 1935 to serve the world community of film archives; the purpose of the annual conference is to bring together archivists from all over the world and study specific aspects of world cinema which are not well documented or researched. The original mission of the 1978 conference was to view and discuss fiction films made between 1900 and 1906.[26]

The importance of this mammoth effort to view the films cannot be underestimated. The work of film historians previous to the Brighton Conference of 1978, especially film historians writing on early cinema, was engaged with documents as many films had not yet been found and archived, or if archived, not yet preserved, or if preserved, not yet correctly identified. By putting such an emphasis on film viewing and film screening, a new approach to film history was born. The emphasis on films made between 1900 and 1906 matched the new interest among film historians: historically speaking, this was almost virgin terrain, unexplored and untheorized. A love-affair between academe and early cinema was begun, and, partly as a result of the Brighton Conference, key advances in how film history is theorized were made by historians working on early cinema, those who wrote from 1978 to the present day.

Decisions and observations made at Brighton and immediately after influenced the course of future research for almost two decades. For example, though the conference organizers had chosen to focus on fiction films, non-fiction films dominated the market during this period. The focus on fiction led to a later over-emphasis which is only now being corrected. (Many developments in fiction films came out of non-fiction films.) Also, most of the films brought to Brighton from the U.S. were produced by Edison and Biograph (where D.W. Griffith started out as a director), even though films produced by Pathé Frères dominated the U.S. market until 1907. A further contrast is that most non-fiction films were shot on location, and fiction films on sets, until around 1905; the choice to focus on fiction led to a focus on sets. Furthermore, the decision to focus on fiction was not an easy one to put into practice: were "fake" newsreels (re-stagings of newsworthy events) fiction or non-fiction? (The organizers decided they were fiction.) And what about a film that recorded a vaudeville act, were they fiction or non-fiction? (It was decided they were fiction, because up until 1904 almost all films produced were designed for inclusion in a vaudeville program.)

Many of the papers given at Brighton, and papers inspired by Brighton, grew into books by scholars such as Richard Abel, Ben Brewster, Noël Burch, André Gaudreault, Sandy Flitterman-Lewis, Tom Gunning, Miriam Hansen, Judith Mayne, Charles Musser, Barry Salt, and Janet Staiger. Thomas Elsasesser's anthology, *Space,*

Frame, Narrative[27] reprinted some of the papers given at Brighton and added others.

Writing 13 years after Brighton, Gunning tried to sum up the effect the conference had on the participants:

> I think that for many of us, our experience with early cinema began with something we just could not understand… the aspect of early film that exerted a magnetizing effect on me at first encounter was how little I understood what was happening on the screen. Processes that had become automatic for most film viewing—getting a joke, identifying a genre, or even such fundamental phenomenological acts as understanding spatio-temporal relations or knowing where to look in the film frame—loomed for me as uncertain ventures in early cinema.[28]

The astonishment felt by Gunning and others led to a wealth of scholarship that revolutionized how all film history is written, not just early film history. And by 1992, when Gunning wrote that follow-up article, he was also able to point to areas that at that time had not been addressed: actuality filmaking; the cinema of the 1890s; the role of genre in early cinema; narrative modes of one-reel film; the contrast between national cinemas (many countries produced early cinema, and all of these needed to be studied, not just US, UK and France which were prioritized in Brighton); and finally, the interconnections between all the cinemas.

Much work has been done in the decade since Gunning wrote that article. Scholars all over the world are recovering the earliest cinema history of their own regions. Genre analysis proceeds apace, most notably on genres like the western. The cinema of the 1890s and pre-cinema has been carefully examined, especially by French scholars such as Laurent Mannoni. And some scholars such as Richard Abel (especially in *The Red Rooster Scare*) are looking at the relationships between countries. Even that most difficult area for early cinema—reception—is currently being studied by scholars such as Judith Thissen, Ben Singer, Shelley Stamp, and Kay Sloane.

Gunning's 1992 list of work still to be done left out some key aspects: though some feminist analysis had been done, most notably by Linda Williams and more recently by Constance Balides, much work remains, and female filmmakers, whether directors, producers, writers, or editors, or working in exhibition, all have stories remaining to be told.[29] In addition, work by filmmakers of color, immigrant filmmakers working in foreign countries, etc. has been conspicuously left out until fairly recently; four recent books on Oscar Micheaux (see my discussion in Chapter 4) have begun to fill the gap and encouraged other writers such as Anna Everett, Jacqueline Stewart, Elizabeth Ezra and this writer to focus on race production and representation in the U.S. and Europe before 1915. Some work, most notably by Alison Griffiths, has been done on colonial film; but much more work is needed. Animation and early sound films have also been neglected, though some work has been done by Rick Altman and Donald Crafton.

Another legacy of Brighton was a new and almost unprecedented level of cooperation between film scholars and film archivists. Without the collaboration of archivists from all over the world and the increased access to films that the era after Brighton provided, this book could never have been written.

Alice Guy's early years

How DID GUY come to be a film director at all, years before other women took on directing?

When Alice Guy was born on July 1, 1873, her father, Émile Guy, who was French, owned a chain of bookstores in Santiago, Chile. Guy's mother made the sea voyage to France so that Guy, her fifth child, would be "properly French." Guy was born in Saint-Mandé, then a Parisian suburb near the Bois de Vincennes.

Information about Guy's childhood is sketchy. In her autobiography she explains that many French people went to South America "in order to rebuild a fortune much shaken by the Revolution." Among these were the aunt and uncle of Guy's mother, Marie. These relatives, having made their fortune, returned to France for a visit and noticed that their niece, Marie, was beautiful and charming and offered to help her marry well by matchmaking her with another member of the French expatriate community in Chile, Émile Guy. In an arrangement typical of the day, Alice Guy's mother was taken as a teenager out of the strict convent where she had been educated, and suddenly married to Émile Guy on a ship bound for South America. Once there, she resolved to help her husband with his book business and to perform philanthropic services in the Chilean community.[30]

When Guy was born, her mother was twenty-six years old and already had numerous children. How many exactly is not quite clear; Guy mentions "brothers" in the plural in her *Memoirs*, and later mentions the early death of her oldest brother at the age of seventeen, of a rheumatic heart. The other brother is not mentioned again. More information is available on Guy's sisters, in order of age: Julia, Henriette and Marguerite. Julia never married, though Gabriel Allignet indicated that she had a love affair with "a Corsican," and died in a convent in Lyon. Henriette (b. 1872, d. 1939) married and had one child, Yvonne, the mother of Christiane and Gabriel Allignet. Guy's nephew Gabriel went into the film business (as an animator) and became friends with Alice Guy after she retired from film directing.[31]

Then there was Marguerite, who died at the age of twenty-five, and finally, Alice. Apparently, Guy's mother only took the trouble to make the seven-week sea voyage to France with Alice, her fifth child. Roberta Blaché, Alice Guy's daughter-in-law, who knew Guy intimately at the end of her life, told me how Guy would recount with glee a kind of "family legend": Marie, Guy's mother, took the precaution of going to France to give birth to her fifth child because she had been having an affair with one of the Chilean *vaqueros* on the hacienda. If the child was not Émile Guy's this could have been obvious at the birth, so it was prudent to give birth far away from prying eyes. When pressed to confirm or dispute this story, Alice Guy would simply shrug, with a twinkle in her eyes. There is no accurate way now to confirm nor dispute this story, but the fact that Guy chose to tell it herself in her later years gives us an idea of her sense of humor.

However, the circumstances of her birth make it seem unlikely. As soon as each of the Guy children reached the age of six, they were sent to Jesuit boarding schools in Europe "to receive the only education judged proper at the time,"[32] as Guy put it. When her older brother and three sisters were ill or had a school holiday, they took refuge with her maternal grandmother, who lived in Switzerland. Guy's childhood differed slightly from that of her siblings because her mother and father went to Paris where Marie gave birth to her. Guy's father returned to Santiago immediately and Guy's mother followed a few months later, leaving her baby in the care of her mother in Switzerland. Guy remembered her three years with her grandmother fondly, and claimed that her parents' "abandonment" of her "did her no harm." The abandonment, however, was not permanent, as four years later Marie returned to take her baby back to Chile. This was traumatizing, as by then Alice Guy had completely forgotten her.[33] She was distracted from her loss by the ship itself, and in her memoirs vividly recounts many of the sights she saw, especially the passage through the walls of ice at the Strait of Magellan. As usual her mother suffered greatly from seasickness and could hardly walk when she got off the ship. Upon arriving in Valparaiso, Guy met her father for the first time:

> The cabin-boy... conducted me to my mother whom I found, to my profound astonishment, in the arms of a tall gentleman who kissed her repeatedly and then examined her with care: "The voyage has tired you my poor Marie," he said, "you don't look well."... My father... for the gentleman with the Gallic moustache was my father... seemed to notice me for the first time. He drew me near him and looked long at me.
>
> "She resembles you, Marie," he said at last, embracing me.[34]

So from age four to age six Alice Guy lived on the Guy hacienda in Valparaiso, Chile. Again, for this part of her life, the only information we have comes from the *Memoirs*. She specifically says that she did not see much of her parents, as her father was engaged in his business and her mother in her social and charitable duties. She was entrusted to the care of a Chilean nanny named Conchita, and spent every day with her, even Sunday, following her from the laundry room to the market, to mass, to the cliffs on Sunday afternoon where Conchita socialized with her friends as they pounded flour for empanadas on the rocks, and all over the hacienda. She slept in a hanging willow basket and learned to speak Spanish.

When she turned six, it was her father and not her mother who took her back to France. Apparently this turn of events was associated with some kind of trouble, either in her parents' marriage or in her father's business, as she remembers her father being distressed and unapproachable throughout the trip. Upon arrival he enrolled her at the Convent of the Sacred Heart, at Viry on the Swiss border, where her three sisters were also enrolled. The contrast with her previous life could not have been greater. The convent was dark and gloomy, the order strict. Meals were eaten in silence while a sermon was read to them, punishments like kneeling for hours with arms crossed was meted out for the smallest offense. The only relief were the times when she was sick (she suffered often from tonsilitis) and had to spend a week with her grandmother.

Guy remembered her six years at this convent as "years of imprisonment," but she also said: "But the Sisters were not cruel. The Order was a strict one for them, also. The superior, a very great lady, wished to make us into strong, accomplished women, capable of conducting themselves correctly in any rank of society. To that end she employed the means of that era… We enjoyed, however, my sisters and I, a certain favor: we four were the protégées of Monseigneur Merlinod, then Bishop of Geneva, and family friends."[35]

The "imprisonment" ended when Guy was twelve. In her memoirs, she runs through the pain of those years quickly and briefly:

> A series of catastrophes put an end to our imprisonment. In Chile violent earthquakes, fire and theft ruined my parents. My father returned alone to France. He gathered up with him my brother and two eldest sisters and we, my last sister and I, were placed in a less expensive convent at Ferney, in the ancient chateau of Voltaire, properly exorcised. Who knows if his shade did not wander sometime in the garden or the rooms, listening with irony to our lessons.…

> The death of my eldest brother, carried off at seventeen by a rheumatic heart, brought my mother back to France and reunited us all in Paris, in living conditions very different from those we had known. My eldest sister entered l'École normale, the two others were hastily married. I finished my studies in a little class on the rue Cardinet, while my father died at fifty-one, more broken by sorrow than by illness. I remained alone with my mother, who had never until then had to occupy herself with the realities of life.

> However, he had kept several friends. Thanks to them, my mother was named director of the Mutualité Maternelle, a society created by the textile unions to aid needy women workers entering on maternity, social security being nonexistent in those days.… Thinking that contact with true misery could only be healthful for me, my mother took me with her to aid her in her work. My debut was difficult. I was to perfection the little white goose of the period. A bit of a snob, I felt the suburban people to be a different class of being. A few visits sufficed to waken my sympathy, my pity, often my admiration.[36]

This brief and stoic description of catastrophe piled on personal tragedy shows that Guy had learned the lessons taught in the strict convents very well.

Unfortunately, their troubles were not over. A disagreement with the management ended Madame Guy's employment at the Mutualité after only a few months. But they had a new friend, the Secretary General of the Syndicate, nephew of the foundress of the convent where she had been educated. He was seventy years old and Alice, seventeen, but she found herself "perfectly charmed by him." It was this friend who suggested that Guy study typing and stenography, new "sciences" at the time. Guy learned rapidly, and her teacher soon found her a job at a varnishing factory. The job was meant to be temporary from the beginning, a way of polishing her skills. At this job Guy experienced sexual harassment for the first time. She was the only female in the building, and one of her male colleagues felt free to shower her with coarse language and innuendo. Guy stood up for herself, but then the man complained to management that she was harassing him. Guy stood her ground with the management as well, and strangely enough she and her harasser ended up becoming friends!

In March of 1895,[37] her old stenography professor informed her of a better position that might be suitable for her. And so at twenty-one Guy found herself knocking at the door of Le Comptoir général de photographie, a company that produced still photography and optical equipment owned by Felix Richard. A young inventor named Léon Gaumont was second-in-command and interviewed Guy for the secretarial position they had open. According to Guy's *Memoirs*, after reading her recommendation he said:

> "The recommendation is excellent, but this post is important. I fear, Mademoiselle, that you may be too young."
> All my hopes crumbled.
> "But Sir, I pleaded, "I'll get over that."
> He looked at me again, amused.
> "Alas, that's true," he said, "you shall get over it. Well, let's try."[38]

The "try" went well and Alice Guy got the job. She described her job conditions as follows:

> In front of one of the windows giving on the avenue of the Opera, a little table was placed for me, with a typewriter. I was

surrounded by a screen. An electric bell linked me to the office of the directors, and, from eight in the morning until eight at night, six days per week, I had to answer the imperious bell-summons from the directorial desk.[39]

Jules and Félix Richard had taken over their father's precision-tool company in 1877, and in 1882 re-organized it as Richard Frères, with a capital base of 60,000 French francs. Also in 1882, three other businessmen (Perrichont and the Picard brothers) started a boutique to sell photographic equipment at 57 rue Saint-Roch.

November 29, 1891, the Richard brothers decided to end their business collaboration. Félix sold his rights to his brother for 300,000 French francs, and agreed not to create or work for any kind of competing company. But Félix took his cash and bought the photographic company from Perrichont and the Picard brothers. He immediately began selling the *photo-jumelle* camera invented by Carpentier, the engineer who would later manufacture the *cinématographes* for the Lumières.

On October 5, 1893, the Paris Court found Félix Richard in violation of his non-competition agreement and forbade him to continue with his photographic boutique or to promote Carpentier's *photo-jumelle*. Léon Gaumont, who had been an apprentice of Carpentier's, went to work for Félix Richard sometime in 1893. Félix Richard appealed, but the decision was re-affirmed on the 28th of May of 1895. Once Richard found he had to retire from the business, he convinced his second-in-command to buy the company from him for 50,000 French francs. Gaumont didn't think the company was worth that much, but Richard assured him (falsely, as it later turned out) that he would have exclusive rights to Carpentier's *photo-jumelle*. Gaumont bought the company on July 6, 1895. On August 10, 1895, Gaumont's Company, L. Gaumont et Cie, was established.[40] According to Guy's memoirs, this occurred a few months after she came to work for the company as a secretary. When Gaumont bought the business and turned it into L. Gaumont et Cie., Guy remained as a trusted employee (her position was roughly what we would call an office manager today). And so she was in an enviable position to witness and participate in the birth of the industries of motion that characterized the 20th century: aviation, studies of human and animal locomotion, and cinema, all three of which were closely linked in their development.

1 THE BIRTH OF
   FILM NARRATIVE

> The impetus for this book stems from one little-known fact:
> the first director of a story-film in history was a woman, and to
> this day, even with significant persuasive evidence, historians
> either insist it isn't true, or else belittle the magnitude and the
> effect of her contribution.[1]

> Alice Guy... The World's first woman director and possibly the
> first director of either sex to bring a story-film to the screen...
> Her first film... preceded Méliès' story-films by a few months,
> according to several authoritative French historians, although
> others claim that the film wasn't made until 1900 or even later.[2]

THE ABOVE COMMENTS from Ally Acker and Ephraim Katz sum up
a decades-long controversy over who directed the first fiction
film. The certainty that Guy was not given credit for directing the first
fiction-film by misogynistic male historians usually goes hand-in-hand
with the original historical question of how and when film began,
adding a further layer of murkiness to an already difficult problem.

Controversies of such long standing usually indicate that conflicting historical and theoretical approaches are being used in a debate
and that the differences between these approaches are blurred,
whether deliberately or accidentally. In this chapter, I will answer the
question: did Alice Guy direct the first fiction-film? However, the
answer is not a simple yes or no. First of all, we need to understand
what we mean when we say *a* film. Then, we need to clarify what
we mean by *fiction* film. Finally, we need to sift carefully through
archival evidence in order to settle questions of dates and production.
It is only in this way that we can then say with confidence what Alice
Guy did and did not do, why her work is important, regardless of
whether she directed the first film or not, and why her story should
be told.

To begin with, we have to define what we mean when we talk
about a film. Today the answer seems obvious, at least as long as
digital technologies are left out of the equation. But when Alice Guy
got her first job with a still photography company, film as we know

it had not yet been invented. Even as she began to make her first films, controversy swirled over what kind of beast these new motion pictures would be, whether their real purpose would be an extension of still photography, a tool for motion studies and other sciences, an accidental spin-off of aerodynamics, or a combination of all of the above. In order to really understand the various discourses surrounding the birth of cinema and the first filmmakers, we need to look at each of these elements in turn.

The Birth of Cinema: Photography[3]

THE HISTORY OF the cinema can be read as part of the industrial drive to mechanization. This drive can be recognized in the relationship between the technological development of the cinematograph (as the first motion picture cameras were called) and the development of flying machines, particularly in France. In some cases the same inventors worked on both. In order to understand the social transformation that Alice Guy was witnessing from her secretarial desk, it is useful for us to pause and take stock of the social and scientific milieu in which photography was being perfected and cinema was developing.

Looking back, we notice that the people of ideas who concerned themselves with the development of photography and projection often also concerned themselves with the development of aerodynamics. This combination of interest in spectatorship, projection of images, and flight characterized many men of science of the day. Many were more successful at combining their interests in photography and flight than our first example, Gaspard-Felix Tournachon, born in Paris in 1820. In the 1830s he took on the nickname Nadar, under which he published stories, essays, and caricatures. He turned to photography in the 1850s and was one of the first to practice photography as an art and not only for scientific study.[4] In 1857, he made his first ascent in a hot-air balloon. Later he began to go up in balloons with his photographic equipment to take pictures. (Taking pictures from hot air balloons and other flying devices was so common that Frédéric Dillaye, in his famous manual of instructions for photographers, spent several pages describing the proper way to attach a camera to the basket of a hot air balloon and to a kite.[5])

Nadar loved the hot-air balloon and its silent ride, but was soon frustrated by the difficulties he encountered navigating it. After studying the motion of kites, birds, projectiles, and his favorite example, a worker who soaked his sponge in water before tossing it up to his colleague on a scaffold, Nadar concluded that controlled aerial navigation required the flying body to be heavier than air. So, along with Baron Taylor and Jules Verne, he formed the *Société d'encouragement pour la locomotion aérienne au moyen d'appareils plus lourds que l'air* (Society for the Encouragement of Aerial Locomotion by Means of Machines Heavier than Air). The purpose of this society was to bring together men with the ideas and raise enough money to fund the construction of their flying machines, especially a helicopter. To raise the level of public awareness of flight and funds to build a helicopter, Nadar decided to build a gigantic balloon, the *Géant*. Completed in October 1863, it was forty-five meters in circumference and could carry over a dozen passengers in a two-tiered basket. Nadar made five ascensions in the big balloon between 1863 and 1867 and wrote two books about his experiences.[6]

Predictably, the *Géant* sucked up whatever profits Nadar's photography studio could churn out. The financial "encouragement" to build helicopters never materialized either.[7] Although he never gave up his dream of flight, Nadar had to focus on his photography again, and on January 7, 1887, found himself giving a demonstration of positive and negative photographic papers developed in 1884 by George Eastman and W.H. Walker to the *Société française de photographie*, a session at which Marey was present.

Such scientific demonstrations enable us to trace the links between photography and flight. One key demonstration occurred in 1873 when Pierre-Jules Cesar Janssen demonstrated his photographic rifle, based on Plateau's phenakistiscope, to the Academy of Sciences. (Marey was also present at this demonstration.) Janssen was an astronomer and part of a team that was travelling to Japan in 1874 to witness the passage of Venus across the face of the sun, an event that only occurs twice each century. He spent two years preparing a photographic device to register the event. The "rifle" registered images on a light sensitive wheel. His second version was able to register 48 images in 72 seconds and succeeded in taking the pictures he wanted of Venus crossing the face of the sun. These images enabled him to prove one of his theories, that the solar corona was in fact an attribute of the sun itself and not an effect of looking at the sun through the Earth's atmosphere. Janssen's rifle was used to photograph solar eclipses for many years.[8]

The Birth of Cinema: Motion Studies

IN 1868, ÉTIENNE-JULES MAREY[9], a celebrated physiologist in Paris, wrote: "[in the human body] movement is the most important act, to which end all bodily functions cooperate."[10] Marey dedicated his life to the study of human and animal locomotion and along with his associate, Georges Demenÿ, was one of the theoretical constructors of the modern concept of physical education. In 1876 an exposition of *appareils chronographiques* (chronographic devices: *chrono* for time, *graphic* for writing: capturing the movements in time with graphs) was held in London and Marey's devices made up a large exhibit.

His eventual move to the use of photography to study a flying body was partly inspired by Janssen. What Marey was after, like Leonardo Da Vinci before him, "was above all to make the world visible; only thus, he believed, could it be measured, and only through measurement could it be truly known. Marey's world was the world of motion in all its forms, its conquest was his greatest achievement... Marey was primarily interested in a visual description of human motion—the walk, the run, the jump, and so on—and the forces at work in their execution."[11]

The Birth of Cinema: Aerodynamics

IF WE CONSIDER the Webster's dictionary definition of aerodynamics as "the branch of dynamics that treats the motion of air and other gaseous fluids and the forces acting on bodies in motion relative to such fluids,"[12] the areas of overlap with motion studies become apparent. Both sciences are interested in forces that are not immediately visible to the human eye, and both problems were addressed in the 19th century by the same people or by different people who met in the same venues, that is, these learned societies.

The aerodynamicists had their own societies as well. Here is a quote from a report of the aeronautical society in 1868:

> With respect to the abstruse question of mechanical flight, it may be stated that we are still ignorant of the rudimentary prin-

ciples which should form the basis and rules for construction. No one has yet ventured to give a correct experimental definition of the primary laws and amount of power consumed in the flight of birds; neither, on the other hand, has any tangible evidence been brought forward to show that mechanical flight is an impossibility for man... We are equally ignorant of the force of the wind exerted on the surfaces of various sizes, forms, and degrees of inclination; these are generally *assumed* on the mathematical laws of the resolution of forces...[13]

What this quote makes clear is that although much theoretical work had been done—in fact, most of the mathematical theories needed for flight had already been developed—the would-be airplane builders still had no clear idea on how to accomplish their goal.

The idea that was popular in most aerodynamic circles was the concept of the ornithopter, or a flying device modeled on birds. On the other hand, as noted, some favored the idea of a rotating blade that would screw upwards, as in a helicopter. Great minds like Da Vinci and Otto Lilienthal favored ornithopters; and in order to build one, it was necessary to study the flight of birds.

Such studies had already been attempted, including graphic studies by Marey in 1869 and 1870 in which he produced line tracings from the flights of harnessed birds. His results were published in the journal *La Nature*, edited by photographer Gaston Tissandier, who had written a book on aerial locomotion himself.[14]

The Birth of Cinema: The Helicopter

IN 1872, ALPHONSE PENAUD, one of the unsung heroes of aerodynamics, cooperated with Marey to build a mechanical bird (Marey had previously built a mechanical insect). It is not clear how successful this model was, but apparently more work was needed, because in December of 1873, Penaud made a presentation to the *Société française de navigation aérienne* (French Society for Aerial Navigation) that both praised Marey's work to that point and offered suggestions on how it could be improved. Specifically, Penaud suggested that instead of recording the flight of birds graphically, they should be photographed. He then reminded Marey of the presentation Janssen had made of his photographic rifle just a few months earlier. Though Penaud claimed to know nothing about photography, he also foresaw that this device would need something like a

Maltese Cross.[15] Other engineers present (Villeneuve and Armengaud) made suggestions which Marey would end up applying almost ten years later.

In the meantime, Penaud gave up on ornithopters and designed a helicopter, which he patented in 1876. He spent four years trying to raise the money to build one without success, and in despair committed suicide in 1880 at the age of thirty.

Penaud's influence on Marey was long-lasting in two ways. Marey did end up building the photographic gun, a key step toward the development of the motion picture camera. But he had to wait a few years for Janssen to give him his rifle and the permission to improve upon it, and a few more years to overcome his own reluctance to abandon his graphic devices. Finally the sight of Muybridge's photographs of Leland Stanford's racehorse encouraged him to continue. He applied for a grant to further his studies of motion and in 1883 was awarded money to erect a building on his *Station physiologique*, his center for the study of locomotion. He greatly relied on his associate, Georges Demenÿ, to run the Station and continue the experiments during the six months he spent every year in Naples. Demenÿ ran the *Station physiologique* for Marey for over ten years. He began as Marey's worshipful acolyte and gradually emerged as a scientist and inventor in his own right.

When Marey witnessed Nadar's demonstration of the Eastman Kodak film, it had a great influence on his own work. Up until then, he had used single large fixed plates where a series of images would all be imprinted; the overlap in these images made it difficult to decipher the motions he wished to study. But on October 29, 1888 he presented the *chronophotographe sur bande mobile*, a motion-picture camera which could register up to 20 images a second. Because the roll of paper was not perforated, it was not possible to make the images equidistant, thus making it unreliable in the capture and projection of true motion picture images. Marey was not concerned about this because his interest was the study of locomotion and not motion picture projection. By 1890, celluloid,[16] commercialized by George Eastman, had become widely available. Marey patented his camera for use with celluloid on October 3, 1890.

Marey and Demenÿ then began to produce motion pictures in earnest, always with the purpose of studying locomotion. Unlike Muybridge, Marey—ever sensitive to public opinion—avoided photographing women; most of his films feature nude male athletes going through various athletic moves such as jumping, leaping, using a baton, etc., though one film was made of ocean waves.

Until 1892 Marey studied his images of locomotion by cutting them out and then attaching them equidistantly inside a zoetrope. By May of 1892 he began to feel the need for real projection, and began to work on a *projecteur chronophotographique* in earnest. By November of 1892, many of his colleagues considered the projector he developed to have resolved the problems of projecting movement. However, Marey's projector, like his camera, did not use a perforated-film system, which made it difficult to assure a steady movement. Emile Reynaud, the magician and showman, projected bands of animated drawings joined on perforated strips of leather at the Musée Grevin. Other inventors, like the Lumières, resolved this problem by perforating the celluloid.

It is interesting to note the role played by "pre-cinematic" optical toys in the development of motion studies and cinematography. Plateau's phenakistiscope influenced Janssen's photographic rifle. The "projecting phenakistiscope" or zoetrope, inspired the design of Emile Reynauld's praxinoscope. Reynauld used his praxinoscope to display early animated films in his *Projections Lumineuses*, seen by many over 1200 performances at the Musée Grévin in Paris from 1892 to 1900. Muybridge's series of images of the horse galloping were published in the form of zoetrope strips in popular magazines for readers to cut out and re-play at home. In other words, these pre- or proto- cinematic devices played a role in the motion studies which led to flight as well as reconfiguring the spectator as a point of view within the field of the moving image.

Motion Pictures for Motion Studies

DEMENŸ CONTINUED TO work on the improvement of his master's inventions. He was also eager to commercialize them.

In 1893 Demenÿ produced his own series of films entitled *La Psychologie de la Prestidigitation* ("The Psychology of the Magic Act"). He invited the most famous magicians of his day to be filmed at the station: Méliès, Dickson, Arnould, and Raynaly.[17] Unfortunately, Méliès did not agree to be "chronophotographed," but the request might have influenced later developments in his career.

By 1889, Demenÿ had become much more self-assured. He no longer needed to consult with Marey when he wrote his papers and was eager to assert his own ideas. The relationship between the two men began to suffer. However, Marey recognized that Demenÿ was coming into his own and encouraged him to speak at conferences, publish papers under his own by-line, and work on his own inventions. Demenÿ was also named "Laboratory Chief" of the *Station physiologique*.

In 1891, the Musée Grévin, a wax museum which had been exhibiting Émile Reynaud's *Théâtre Optique* since 1888, invited Marey to give a theatrical demonstration of some of his films with his newly developed projector. There is no record of Marey's reply, but his reluctance to commercialize his invention had been a source of strife between him and Demenÿ for some time. In July of 1891, however, Demenÿ gave a demonstration of his *phonoscope* at the Musée Grévin.[18]

The phonoscope was a projector designed to reproduce the living manner of a subject as s/he pronounced short phrases. (One film shows Demenÿ himself saying "Vive la France"). The images were taken with Marey's *chronophotographe* and then laboriously transferred to a glass disc, from which they could be observed through the phonoscope peephole or projected. Demenÿ also gave some thought to synchronizing his phonoscope images with a phonograph but apparently never actually did so. His original intention was to use the device to teach deaf-mutes how to speak, but he also hoped to commercialize it ("How many people would be happy if they could even for one moment revisit the living features of a lost loved one!"). Demenÿ exhibited the phonoscope alongside devices invented by Janssen and Marey at the *Exposition Internationale* on April 20, 1892, and received a great deal of press attention.

However, since the phonoscope could not stand on its own without a *chronophotographe* to record the images in the first place, Demenÿ could not market his phonoscope without Marey's cooperation. The relationship between the two men had eroded and Marey, upset at the attention Demenÿ was getting from the press and disappointed at the failure of his own (admittedly minimal) efforts to commercialize the *chronophotographe*, refused to cooperate. Demenÿ went ahead and founded *La Société générale du phonoscope, portraits vivants et tableaux animés* ("The General Phonoscope Company for Living Portraits and Animated Tableaux")[19] to exploit his invention in partnership with Ludwig Stollwerck, a German industrialist, and François Henry Lavanchy Clark, a Swiss businessman. Demenÿ tried to interest Marey in his company but Marey responded by firing him from his position at the *Station physiologique.*

Marey, cognizant that his *chronophotographe* was necessary for the success of the *phonoscope*, re-patented it in June of 1893. But Demenÿ got around the problem by patenting his own "camera chronophotographique," which was the camera of Marey's design with one improvement: by using an oval-shaped reel, the film could be unwound in a more regular manner. This solution was not completely satisfactory, as the speed varied as the film unwound, but it solved the problem of dealing with Marey.

In 1894, Demenÿ patented an improvement to his mechanism, a cam that ensured a more even movement of the film through the motion picture camera. The cam remained in use in motion picture cameras until 1910, as it was adopted by Thomas Armat in 1895, making it possible for him to project Edison's films[20] and was used by the first cinematographic cameras developed by Gaumont with Demenÿ's cooperation in 1895. By approaching Gaumont and cooperating with him in the development of a motion-picture camera and projector, Demenÿ crossed over from developing devices to study movement to developing cameras to project movement.

Demenÿ's first visit was actually to the Comptoir général de photographie, headed by Félix Richard, in January of 1895, just after Demenÿ had tried to interest the Lumière brothers in his devices without success. Alice Guy recalled Demenÿ's first visit to Gaumont's office in her memoirs:

> ...we received the visit of a very amiable and young savant, Georges Demenÿ, nervous, well-bred. His knowledge seemed unlimited: music, special mathematics, mechanics and physics, anatomy, he was a professor of physical education at the School of Arts et Métiers....[21]

> ...I first met Georges Demenÿ, then aide to Marey, when he came to present a camera, the phonoscope. This camera was composed of a wooden box containing two discs, one in glass, bearing the images, and the other in cardboard, pierced with eye-holes and serving as a shutter.

> Georges Demenÿ said, "I have made an instrument specially intended to give the illusion of the motions of speaking and of facial movement. I have named it the *phonoscope* ...recalling its

parentage in the phonograph that causes one to hear the voice, and the other causing one to see it on the lips. The apparatus has the quality of being transparent to light, and of letting one see images in a time span so short that the flow is invisible to the eye."[22]

Though everyone present was impressed with the *phonoscope*, the lawsuit between the Richard brothers prevented any action from being taken. Demenÿ appealed to Gaumont himself in July of 1895, just as Gaumont had bought Richard's company and had discovered that he did not, in fact, have the right to promote the Carpentier *photo-jumelle*. After consulting with his principal stockholders, Gustave Eiffel and Joseph Vallot, Gaumont signed a contract with Demenÿ on August 22, 1895.

Gaumont purchased the rights to Demenÿ's patents for the *phonoscope* (patented in 1891) and the *biographe* (patented in 1893). Demenÿ's patent of October 10, 1893 became the basis for the Gaumont 60mm. camera, also called a *chronophotographe*, which was perfected in the first few months of 1896.[23] According to Alice Guy's memoirs[24] it was during this period, sometime before May of 1896, that she wrote, produced and directed her first fiction film. She does not specify which camera she used, but it is most likely that she used the Demenÿ-Gaumont 60mm. camera.[25]

Until 1906 or so, most films produced were actuality films. In their "realistic" reproduction of life, these actualities could be said to epitomize Marey and Demenÿ's drive to study motion. That paradigm remains with us today, in the form of the instant football replay and of surveillance cameras that pretend to tell us if a crime has been committed or not.

A few people like Georges Hatot at the Lumière Company and Alice Guy at Gaumont, began to shift the paradigm away from motion studies and towards the fiction film.

Fiction Film

A STRONG FRIENDSHIP existed between Léon Gaumont and Antoine and Louis Lumière, although they were also business competitors. Their two businesses had much in common. All three were scientists and industrialists, and they approached film production from the point-of-view of inventors and businessmen. In addition, they shared an almost life-long business relationship with Jules Carpentier, an engineer and an inventor in his own right.

Carpentier had begun to know Gaumont at a series of lectures on astronomy and in 1881 hired the sixteen-year-old autodidact to work in his factory, where Gaumont remained for nine years.[26] It was typical of Gaumont that he maintained a close relationship with Carpentier for the rest of his life. He fought to promote Carpentier's photo-jumelle camera and continuously wrote to his former mentor for advice during his early years at the Comptoir de la Photographie. They were still friends in 1924 when Gaumont became an officer for the Légion d'Honneur.

Gaumont, Carpentier and Georges Demenÿ[27] as well as Alice Guy,[28] were among those invited to witness the demonstration of the Lumière *cinématographe* on March 22, 1895, for the *Société d'encouragement pour l'industrie nationale à Paris*. (However, apparently Demenÿ was not able to attend.[29]) Carpentier, "seduced by the invention of the Lumière brothers… put his workshop at the disposal of the great inventors of Lyons."[30] The Lumières accepted Carpentier's offer to build *cinématographes*. Carpentier also designed a *Défileur Carpentier-Lumière* that allowed longer bands of film to pass through the camera.[31]

By the time of the March 22, 1895 screening, Gaumont and the Lumière brothers were already "two old friends."[32] The fact that Gaumont was working on a competing motion-picture camera/projector did not interfere with this relationship at all. Gaumont even bought all of his raw film stock from Victor Planchon, who was developing better film stocks for the Lumières and whose factory was next to theirs in Lyons.

It was the equipment that held Léon Gaumont's attention at that March 22nd screening; but Alice Guy was fascinated by the medium itself. As she tells it:

> But Gaumont, like Lumière, was especially interested in solving mechanical problems. It was one more camera to put at the disposition of his clients. The educational and entertainment values of motion pictures seemed not to have caught his attention. Nevertheless, there had been created, in the ruelle des Sonneries, a little laboratory for the development and printing

of short "shots": parades, railroad stations, portraits of the laboratory personnel, which served as demonstration films but were both brief and repetitious…. I thought that one might do better than these demonstration films. Gathering my courage, I timidly proposed to Gaumont that I might write one or two little scenes and have a few friends perform in them. If the future development of motion pictures had been foreseen at this time, I should never have obtained his consent. My youth, my inexperience, my sex, all conspired against me. I did receive permission, however, on this express condition that this would not interfere with my secretarial duties.[33]

In none of the correspondence I have read did Alice Guy claim to be the first director of a fiction film; whenever that claim was made on her behalf she was quick to point out that *L'Arroseur arrosé*, the first fiction film made by the Lumière brothers, came first.

However, the account in her memoirs can be *read* as if she considered herself the first fiction film maker, and many scholars, especially feminist scholars, have interpreted what she said to mean that she was the first. The account in her memoirs is influenced by the fact that when she first saw a demonstration of the Lumière *cinématographe* only the *Sortie d'usine (Workers Leaving the Factory)*, a nonfiction film, was shown. It is possible that as of March 22, 1895, *l'Arroseur arrosé*, generally considered to be the first narrative film, had not yet been made.

Partly as a result of the successful projection of a series of films for a paying public by the Lumières in December of 1896, Gaumont realized that further exploitation of Demenÿ's *phonoscope* and *Bioscope* would not be profitable, as neither of these devices were suitable for projection. Many other inventors and industrialists were jumping into the fray with devices for filming and projection. Gaumont encharged his employee, Decaux, to build a camera that could also serve as a projector for 60mm. film which produced a 58mm. frame after it was perforated. On May 6, 1896, Gaumont signed a contract with Demenÿ indicating that the 60mm. Demenÿ camera would manufactured for sale. According to Mannoni, Gaumont at this point had an idea of opening film theatres himself, to screen films produced by the Gaumont Company and Demenÿ.[34] If Gaumont recognized the value of projecting films for paying audiences by May of 1896, then the conversation that Guy retells where he gave her permission to try out some her ideas for stories on film, which he never would have done if he had foreseen the importance of cinema, must have taken place before that date.

So Who Made the First Fiction Film?

As WE HAVE seen, Alice Guy saw her first Lumière film on March 22, 1895. Méliès saw the first public Lumière screening at the Grand Café des Capucins on December 28, 1895, where *L'Arroseur arrosé* was screened. Immediately after the screening, Méliès offered Antoine Lumière (Lumière *père*) 10,000 francs for a *cinématographe*. M. Thomas, the head of the Musée Grévin, offered the Lumières 20,000 francs. M. Lallemand, director of the Folies Bergères, offered 50,000 francs: "M. Lumière replied with great good humor that the secret of this device is not for sale and that he planned to exploit it himself."[35] Not to be dissuaded, Méliès went to London in February of 1896 where he bought a Bioscope, a motion-picture camera developed by William Paul. In April, he used this camera/projector to screen Kinetoscope films produced by Paul and Edison at his Théâtre Robert-Houdin. In May, he returned to London and bought some Eastman unperforated celluloid film stock, which he cut into strips and had perforated by a mechanic named Lapipe. In May or June, he shot his first 20m. film.

So, if we take Alice Guy's word for it, she made her first fiction film before Méliès made his; but since *L'Arroseur arrosé* was made and publicly screened before either of them made their films the debate over whether Guy or Méliès was the first fiction film director is moot.

To be fair to historians, it must be noted that many of them *did* take Alice Guy's word for it (most notably, Anthony Slide, Victor Bachy, René Jeanne, and Charles Ford) and accepted that a) *La Fée aux choux* was her first film and b) she wrote, produced and directed it before May of 1896. Francis Lacassin at first also took Guy's word for it, but later reversed himself in *Pour une contre-histoire du cinéma*.[36] His argument is that it appears as no. 379 in the Gaumont catalogue (issued in 1901). Since film no. 397 is an actuality reel recording a mayor's meeting and banquet presided over by French President Loubet, which took place, according to contemporary press reports, on September 22, 1900, Lacassin argues *La Fée aux choux* must have been made the same year. However, other early film historians, such as Aldo Bernadini, writing on Pathé, and Jean Mitry, have pointed out that the earliest film catalogues cannot be relied upon for establishing chronology. Victor Bachy points out that other Gaumont films from the same catalogue, such as *Baignade de chevaux à la caserne*, (no. 377), *Promenade des animaux au jardin d'acclimatation* (no. 378), and *Baignade dans le grand bain* (no. 380) all seem to be "escapees" from a series of *Vues animées* ("animated images") shot in 1896, or at the latest, 1897.[37]

An early film, which I have tentatively identified as #2042 *Les Joueurs de cartes*,[38] lends some credence to Bachy's argument. Although the Sieurin films are on 35mm., the only description that I have found in the Gaumont catalogues to match *Les Joueurs de cartes* is actually from a list of 15mm. films (with their own separate numbering system; the 35mm. films didn't get up to 2042 until 1908 or later). *Les Joueurs de cartes* is an example of a Gaumont film from this period that originated in one format and was then re-printed or re-made in another, a process which was not acknowledged in the catalogues. The process of copying was also applied to the Gaumont 58mm. films; at least one, listed as number 7 in Mannoni's reconstituted list, *Avenue de l'Opéra (Walking Backwards)* also appears in the Sieurin French Collection. So, though *Fée aux choux* does not appear in a Gaumont Catalogue before 1900, and though it is not among the suriving 58mm. films, there is still a strong possibility that Guy directed it for the Gaumont 58mm. camera. Laurent Mannoni argues heatedly against this possibility, but on the very next page he attributes the direction of some of the 58mm. films, especially those of the dancers from the Moulin Rouge to Demenÿ, while at the same time admitting that he has no documentation to support this attribution.[39]

Lacassin also thought it unlikely that Gaumont would have started full-fledged production before he started mass-production of his own film projector in 1898. This projector was designed to screen films shot on the Lumière *cinématographe*, a 35mm. camera, after he had given up on commercializing his own 60mm. camera based on Demenÿ's patents.

In this, Lacassin might be correct: Gaumont might not have decided to invest seriously in film production before he had equipment to sell that would justify it. But it makes sense that as the Gaumont-Demenÿ 60mm. camera was tinkered with and perfected films were made with it, and it was not immediately clear to anyone that the Gaumont-Demenÿ camera, with its larger negative and therefore higher image quality, would not win out over the Lumière camera in the marketplace or at least find a market share among the still-photographers and scientists who already made up the bulk of the Gaumont clientele. The "biographe" used 60mm. film that was non-perforated, and results weren't as reliable as the results obtained with perforated film. Therefore, in April of 1896, Gaumont unveiled another camera based on Demenÿ's design with improvements by Léopold Decaux.[40] Note that the date of the unveiling of this camera coincides with the date that Guy gives for making her first version of *La Fée aux choux*. Further evidence that the camera was being used regularly comes from an unexpected source: on May 23, 1896, *La France automobile*, a newsletter for motorists, mentions that Gaumont filmed the departure of an automobile parade from the Porte Maillot in Paris with a Demenÿ camera.[41] (This film still exists and was shown as part of the Gaumont exhibit at the Palais de Chaillot in the Spring of 1995.) Mannoni notes that the Gaumont catalogue for the 58mm. films lists around 150 films made. *La Fée aux choux* does not appear on this list, which Mannoni accepts as definitive proof that Guy did not make this film in 1896[42] but, as we have seen, the catalogue listings are unreliable. Of the 150 made, about 30 remain: nine in the George Eastman House collection, which Paolo Cherchi Usai is currently preserving; more in the National Film and Television Archive in Bradford (Slade collection); at the Cinémathèque Française (Will Day collection), and in the Service des Archives du film de Bois d'Arcy (Vivié collection and others).[43] Only one of these films had been preserved in time for this study: *La Biche au bois*, ("The doe of the forest"), shot by Jacques Ducom in the summer of 1896 and screened for the public for the first time on November 14, 1896.[44]

Biche is a ballet from a popular *féerie* performed at the Châtelet, *La Biche au bois ou Le Royaume des fées* by the brothers Théodore and Hippolyte Cogniard. The film was made so that it could be inserted into further performances of the play. It was shot on a stage on the roof of the Chatelet and hand-colored; in other words, it has much in common with *La Fée aux choux*. The contract between Léon Gaumont and Edmond Floury, the technical director of the Chatelet, still exists.[45] The existence of *Biche* lends credence to Guy's claims for her own film. With a demonstration film like *La Fée aux choux* it would have been easier for Gaumont to win such a contract with the Chatelet.

In addition to shooting *Lu Biche au bois*, Jacques Ducom was an assistant projectionist for the historic Lumière screening on December 28, 1895. In his book *Le cinéma scientifique et industriel*, published in 1911, he recalls some early encounters between Demenÿ and Gaumont:

> In 1893 we went often to visit M. Demenÿ, at the Villa Chaptal, 17, in Levallois-Perret. M. Demenÿ had a modest but well-equipped laboratory where we made music, as he was also a gifted musician. Demenÿ's invention was the talk of the scientific and photographic circles, and a stream of visitors went through the Villa Chaptal. Among them was M. Gaumont, his financial backers, and M. Lumière. They were searching for the best practical way to launch the new invention in France and how to make the best of it from an industrial point of view.
>
> After numerous such encounters it was M. Gaumont who acquired the right to exploit M. Demenÿ's patents. The Lumières, father and sons, preferred to research their own projection system. The registration claw, which is proprietary to the Lumières, was developed by them around mid-1894. The first Lumière experiments were done on bonds of photographic paper that were perforated at the same time the picture was taken.[46]

By May of 1897, it was clear that the 35mm. cameras developed by the Lumières and Edison were more marketable than Gaumont's 60mm. camera. In an issue of *La Mise au point*, the Gaumont sale catalogue dated that same month, four of the 60mm. films attributed to Guy are listed as 35mm. films, which means they had been remade or reprinted.[47] *La Fée aux choux* first appeared in the earliest available complete Gaumont film catalogue, published in July 1901. Of the 500 films listed it was the only one with any kind of qualifier: "*Très Gros Succès*" (A Great Success) in bold capital letters. This meant that not only was the film commercially successful, but that it had been around for a while.

Alice Guy's First Fiction Films

WHAT GUY DESCRIBED as "demonstration films, but also brief and repetitious," were the earliest Gaumont *actualités*, or actuality films, films of notable events such as parades of the newly-invented automobiles or lifestyle scenes of people engaged in leisurely activities. Actualities were filmed by various workers from the laboratory, cameramen who had a franchise-type arrangement with Gaumont, and as we have seen, by Gaumont himself. Of the Gaumont films from this period that still exist, the three films in Barcelona (Spain), are among the oldest: *Le Pêcheur dans le torrent* (Gaumont 1896 or 1897), *Baignade dans le torrent* (Gaumont 1897) and *Retour des champs* (1899-1900). *Pêcheur* is a gag scene in the tradition of *Arroseur arrosé*: a man is fishing; two playful bathers push him into the rushing water. The entertainment lies in watching him struggle in the water. This could be described as a narrative film. It was probably made by a cameraman who had been assigned to film something like *Baignade dans le torrent*, which simply shows swimmers frolicking in the rushing water. Given the similarity of the settings, these two films could have been shot in the same location on the same day. The film labeled *Retour des champs* was probably *Le Laboureur*.[48] Although the Arxiu de Catalunya credits these films to Guy, it is more likely that they were filmed by various workers from the laboratory, cameramen, or by Gaumont himself.

Among the oldest surviving films of Alice Guy's in existence are the fifteen films discovered in 1999 by a junk dealer who was clearing out an old house in Charente-Maritime in France. In the bottom of a cupboard was a large collection of nitrate films, which he quickly sold to two film collectors. The collectors divided the films between them and immediately burnt about half of the films because of their advanced state of decomposition (decomposing nitrate is highly flammable and poses a fire hazard; however we can only dream of what we might have learnt from this footage). The collectors then found that they couldn't project the rest because the film had shrunk and needed to be preserved. So they took the films to Serge Bromberg at Red Lobster Archives in Paris. Mr. Bromberg was able to identify all of the films. Thirty of them were early Méliès films and thirty were Gaumont films. Bromberg attributed fifteen of these to Alice Guy. *Ballet Libella* (1897) is a beautiful hand colored film showing two women, one in a fairy costume, preparing to dance and then dancing. *Danse du papillon* (1897) and *Danse fleur de lotus* (1897) are typical of the earliest Gaumont films, both serpentine dances and beautifully hand colored. Films at this stage were produced more for the purpose of selling the camera equipment; the films showed off what the camera could do and were sometimes included with the sale of the camera, in the same way that computers are bundled with software today.

Chez le magnétiseur (1898), *Scène d'escamotage* (1898), and *L'Utilité des rayons X* (1898) show that Guy was impressed by Méliès' trick films and was making her own as well. However, Guy's "themes" such as crossdressing (explored more thoroughly in Chapter Six) can already be seen here. *Escamotage* shows a magician change a woman into a monkey (a man in a monkey suit). Though this was probably part of a pre-existing act, it is interesting in relation to the themes of some of the other films: *Magnétiseur* shows a mesmerist hypnotising a woman, then using a magnetic force to remove her clothes and reveal the fact that the woman is actually a man. *Rayons X* also appears to be a pre-existing vaudeville routine. A man in drag and costumed as if he were pregnant enters a gate posted "Entrance to Paris" where he is questioned by customs police. Though s/he appears innocent s/he is x-rayed to reveal a pregnant belly full of contraband; the man is stripped and all the contraband removed, using a stop-motion technique. *La Petite Magicienne* (1900) is special because it features a girl as the magician, whereas in the world of Méliès, magicians were always male.

In her *Memoirs*, Guy listed the names of all the prominent people who used photography and whom she assisted when she started out as a secretary at Richard's photographic equipment and supply company.[49] Writers like Émile Zola, numerous statesmen, scientists studying the motion of the stars or the function of the body, and engineers like Eiffel, aeronauts like Andrée, and aviators like Santos Dumont, all relied on Guy's assistance in using the Gaumont motion picture equipment for scientific purposes. This meant that Guy, probably without realizing it, was in a front row seat to witness one of the greatest social transformations of recent memory: the drive to mechanization. Some of her earliest films were parodies of the scientific films that she helped the scientists produce. For example, *Chirurgie fin de siècle* (1900) shows a team of surgeons amputating a man's limb, but they are hopelessly inept, and take off the wrong limb, then take off an arm, then mix up the various limbs and the action ends with mayhem; like most of the other films in this group, this could have been a pre-existing vaudeville routine. The rest of the films, such as *Guillaume Tell (1900)* (probably performed by the clowns Plic and Pluc), and *Faust et Mephistophélès (1903)*, showcase famous scenes from well known narratives, such as the moment when William Tell shoots an apple off his son's head (from Rossini's

opera) or the seduction of Faust by the Devil as portrayed in Gou-
nod's opera. *Intervention malencontreuse (1902)* is a slapstick ren-
dition of domestic strife. A couple enter fighting and the man begins
to throw dishes. A concierge (man dressed as a woman) enters and
begins to beat up the man with her broom; the woman gets into the
fight as well. *Les Chiens savants (1902)*, is actually two films back
to back; what is interesting is that the dog trainer is female and her
assistant is a man in black face. Clearly the act was filmed without
much alteration for the camera. This film and *Les Malabars (1902)*
were types of actuality films, as Guy had faithfully recorded two
vaudeville acts: one a woman with her trained dogs and the second,
a team of African acrobats going through their routine that had
probably toured France after having a run in the Paris Exposition.
Although some of these films, such as *Intervention, Magnétiseur,
Rayons X*, and *Chirurgie*, contain a narrative, if they were film versions of existing vaudeville acts, they could also be considered a
type of actuality. As with the Lumière films, the line between narrative and actuality, between fiction and non-fiction, could be very
blurry, as it can still be today.

According to Guy, her first fiction film was shot on a makeshift
stage set up on the concrete patio behind the Gaumont laboratories
in Belleville. I was recently able to document the tentative identification of a version of this film by Jan Olsson and Tom Gunning.[50]
The process of identification of this and other films shows how
many people and how much effort it takes to properly identify an
early film.

In July of 1996, Professor Jan Olsson of Stockholm University
was doing research at the Cinémathèque Royale in Brussels and told
Sabine Lenk, an archivist and expert in film preservation about a reel
of early films recently preserved by the Swedish Film Institute that
he thought might be Gaumont films. Lenk was able to confirm his
assumption based on his description of the black sprocket holes,
typical of Gaumont during its ELGÉ period [the first "brand" for the
company was the phonetic sound for Léon Gaumont's initial, (E)L
G(É)]. She then asked him what was on this film, and he mentioned
a lady pulling babies out of cabbages. Sabine remembered my search
and put me in touch with Professor Olsson, who invited me to
Stockholm to see what was known as the Sieurin French Film
Collection.[51]

Alice Guy's First Film: *The Cabbage Fairy*

THE SIEURIN COLLECTION is a marvelous treasure: 17 or more Gaumont films (some of these films appear to be two or more short films from a series joined together) from the very beginning of the company's activity. The films were purchased, along with a Gaumont camera/projector, by Emil Sieurin, a young Swedish engineer, at the turn of the century. One of Sieurin's first jobs was working for a mining/brick company in Höganäs, in the south of Sweden, where he made films on work and leisure subjects. Some of the films Sieurin made also survive in the Sieurin Swedish collection. The films I discuss here are from the Sieurin French collection. The French collection was deposited at the Teknisha museet (science museum) in the late twenties. From the late thirties the museum housed the embryonic national film archive. The archive was transferred to the Swedish Film Institute in the sixties, and the Sieurin collection was probably part of that transfer.[52]

The Sieurin French films are equally divided between *actualités* and narrative films. Some of the *actualités* show people at work and other every day activities; almost half of them are footage of the 1900 *Exposition Internationale* in Paris. Eight of the Sieurin films are narrative films; most of these are shot on a stage. In some of these films, such as the one I have identified as *Chez le photographe*, it is clear that this stage is a concrete patio.

I attribute all of the narrative films in the Sieurin collection to Alice Guy as director as well as producer for several reasons. For one, since we know she made *La Fée aux choux*, it seems likely that the other films from the same period, produced in a similar manner, are also hers. On this basis, I attribute all of the films that are clearly shot on the concrete patio to her (*Les Joueurs de cartes*, *Chez le photographe*, *L'Aveugle fin de siècle*, *Chez le maréchal-ferrant*, *Chapellerie et Charcuterie mécaniques*, *L'Hiver: danse de la neige*). The other narrative films that were shot on a location (which could have simply been around the corner of the laboratory building) contained plot elements or gags that Guy reused again later in films that the Gaumont company has attributed to her or that appear in Solax films. For example, the plot of *La Concierge* is repeated almost exactly in *Dick Whittington and His Cat* (Solax, 1913). The absentminded absinthe drinker in *La Bonne Absinthe* reappears in *Madame a des Envies* and the fighting card players reappear in *Les Fils du*

Figure 6. Alice Guy's first film, *La Fée aux choux*

Figure 7. *Danse de la neige*

garde chasse (both Gaumont 1906). These plot elements were taken from Lumière comic films, and indirectly, from the vaudeville stage. I use this same reasoning for attributing *Les Dernières Cartouches* and *Surprise d'une maison au petit jour* to Alice Guy, as their plot and stage business is echoed in *La Fiancée du volontaire* (Gaumont 1906). When Guy reuses elements from these early films years later, she repeats the visual approach to the gag (or piece of dramatic business) as well as the gag itself.

In addition, of course, Guy claimed (and I have found no evidence to the contrary in any of the Gaumont documentation) that she directed all of the narrative films made at Gaumont until 1905, the year the glass-roofed studio was completed and production was significantly increased.

According to Guy, the first film she made for Gaumont was *La Fée aux choux*. Until we had positively identified this film in August of 1996, we could only surmise what it was like based on Guy's account and her 1902 remake of the film, *Sage-femme de première classe*. The distinction between the two was so blurry that stills from *Sage-femme* have often been identified in books and in documentaries as stills from *Fée aux choux*. However, the two films are quite different. *Sage-femme* has three actors in it: Yvonne and Germaine Mugnier-Serand playing the fairy and the wife, and Guy herself playing the husband, wearing a kind of Pierrot outfit. There is a clearly defined plot: the husband convinces his wife to buy a baby from the fairy, the wife has a hard time choosing one, but after examining eight babies she finally does, and her husband pays for it. The story of *Sage-femme* is told in two shots, and a complete scene is played out in each shot. The first shot ends when the all three actors pass through the door in the garden wall, and the entire action of opening the door and passing through it is repeated in the next shot. *Sage-femme* is clearly a narrative film.

By contrast, the Sieurin 35mm. version of *La Fée aux choux*, made between 1897 and 1900, falls purely into the realm of cinema of attractions. This film is 20-meters long (one minute) and takes place on a single set, a cabbage patch (the same painted and cut-out cabbages were used in *Sage-femme*). The fairy, played by Yvonne Mugnier-Serand, Guy's friend and later her secretary, comes forward. She wears a very low-cut, diaphanous white dress with flowers around the collar that further highlight her cleavage. She leans her ear toward the cabbages, then pulls out a baby, and sets it on the floor. She repeats this action with a second baby. A third baby turns out to be a doll, which she puts back behind its cabbage as if it weren't ready yet. Then she curtsies deeply. This movement, like most of her movements, further displays her erotic charms.

In order to make *La Fée aux choux*, (and the other films she shot on the concrete patio in Belleville), Guy went to the office on the rue

St-Roch (in the center of Paris) at eight a.m., did a long morning's work, then went to the Buttes Chaumont lab (on the outskirts of Paris) on the trolley. Here she spent four hours working on her film, returned to the office at four-thirty in the afternoon and worked until ten or eleven at night. This film was so successful that it sold eighty copies and had to be remade at least twice, as the original prints disintegrated.[53]

How Alice Guy Learned to be a Filmmaker

AFTER *LA FÉE aux choux,* it appears that Guy learned filmmaking by remaking a large number of the Lumières' fiction films, including *L'Arroseur arrosé* (directed by Louis Lumière), which she remade in early 1898.[54] In the Sieurin French Collection there is also *Chapellerie et Charcuterie mécaniques,* which shows two men feeding things into a machine that spews out men's hats from one end and sausages from another. This film is clearly a remake of Louis Lumière's *Char-cuterie mécanique*[55] which shows four men throwing a live pig into a "machine" (basically, a large garbage bin) and having sausages and hams come out the other end. Guy's *Chez le photographe* shows a man who goes to have his picture taken and then resists the painstaking process of being photographed; it is a remake of Louis Lumière's *Photographe*[56]. Today we would consider such direct copying to be plagiarism but at the time it was standard industry practice. By imitating the Lumière fiction films, Alice Guy was following the procedure of the Gaumont cameraman who shot *actualités*; many of the earliest Gaumont documentary scenes are also close copies of their Lumière predecessors. But for Guy, the fiction films produced by the Lumière company were also her film school.[57]

As models, Guy seemed to favor fiction films—*Vues comiques* and *Vues historiques*—directed by Georges Hatot for the Lumières.[58] Many of her "remakes" even had the same titles as Hatot's original films, such as *Colleur d'affiches* ("The Poster Hangers"),[59] *Les Der-nières Cartouches* ("The Last Bullets"),[60] and *Surprise d'une maison au petit jour* ("House Ambushed at Dawn").[61]

Other films that Alice Guy made for Gaumont may not have the same titles as their Lumière models, but they are almost exact copies nonetheless. And so the Lumière *Le Cocher Endormi* ("The Sleep-ing Carriage Driver") in which a sleeping carriage-driver's horse is replaced by a toy horse becomes the Gaumont *Cocher de fiacre en-dormi*[62] in which the horse is replaced with a donkey; Hatot's *Faust: Apparition de Méphistophélès* becomes *Faust et Méphistophélès*;[63] and

Figure 8. *Surprise d'une maison au petit jour*

Figure 9. *Surprise d'une maison au petit jour*

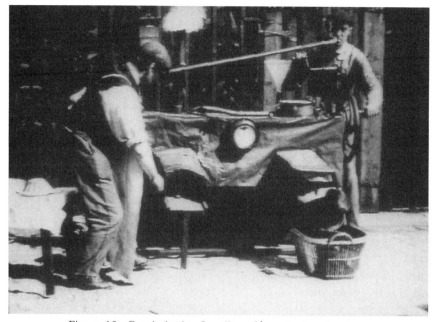

Figure 10. Guy imitating Lumière: *Charcuterie mécanique*

Figure 11. *Chez le photographe*

most interesting of all, the Hatot's *Poursuite sur les toits* ("Pursuit Across the Rooftops", with sets by Jambon) becomes the Gaumont *Les Cambrioleurs* ("The Burglars").[64]

Alan Williams has stated that "...at least once Guy bought an entire set of used scene backgrounds from a theatre that had no more use for them, and then figured out ways to employ them in her films."[65] In the case of *Les Cambrioleurs* it is clear that Guy bought the backdrop for *Poursuite sur les Toits* from the Lumières, or perhaps from Jambon himself,[66] and then proceeded, with only the slightest alterations, to remake the film *using the Lumière set*. Until I compared the prints of each film in the Cinémathèque Royale de Belgique Collection, several scholars were absolutely convinced that there was only one film, the Lumière film. Comparison of the two films prints was complicated by the fact that the Lumière/Hatot film, part of a compilation reel, was printed flipped, as can be determined by the reversed identification number 85910 that was painted on the front set piece of the tiled roof.

A close examination of both films showed that the main set piece in the rear is exactly the same. The front piece of stage scenery, a tiled roof, is different, and the Gaumont version has a window added to this part of the set. The action in both films is almost identical: both take advantage of the dumb waiter shaft to give us

Figure 12. *Les Cambrioleurs*—Gaumont, 1898

a sharp break between a two dimensional effect (the white walls of the shaft can be "read" as a flat wall onscreen) and a three dimensional effect (when the first robber drops down the shaft we realize we are looking at a three dimensional space). The moment in the Gaumont film is almost identical, except the extra trapdoor was also used at the same time. Both films show a woman throwing water out the window; the Lumière film shows a real woman and the Gaumont film, as was Alice Guy's custom when acrobatics were involved, shows a man wearing a wig and women's clothing. The police are depicted slightly differently: the Lumière policemen have the more modern-looking pillbox-type hats and the Gaumont policemen are clearly from another era with their tri-cornered, Napoleonic-style hats. This might also explain why after following the Lumière film action by action the Gaumont film differs in the end by having the robbers get the better of the cops.[67]

Les Cambrioleurs was probably not the only film for which Guy borrowed or bought scenery from the Lumières. In both the Lumière version and the Gaumont version of Les Dernières Cartouches, there is an identical door with broken window panes set on the screen's right frame.

Guy did not stop with simply remaking Lumière films. As she grew and developed as a filmmaker, she began to work from her own original scripts and later from the scripts a young journalist named Louis Feuillade wrote for her. But even in her later films, we occasionally see images that are clearly inspired by Lumière films or at least Lumière film topics. For example, the Lumières made a series of films about nannies and soldiers (not all directed by Hatot): Bonne d'enfants et Cuirassier[68], Bonne d'enfants et Soldat[69], Nounou et Soldats (directed by Hatot)[70], La Nourrice et les Deux soldats[71] and La Nourrice et les Soldats amoureux[72] (directed by Hatot). In 1904, Guy made a film entitled Militaire et Nourrice[73] in which three soldiers compete for the attention of a nursemaid; the nursemaid tricks the soldiers of lower rank into watching her young charge while she flirts with the ranking officer. Two years later, Guy made a film entitled La Hiérarchie dans l'amour ("Rank in Love"),[74] which I recently identified among the Gaumont prints at the National Film and Television Archive in London. In this film, four soldiers of progressively higher rank take turns courting a young housekeeper in a park.[75]

Guy's 1906 film *Le Matelas alcoolique* ("The Drunken Matt-ress")[76] seems to owe at least a passing allegiance to the Lumière *Querelle de matelassières* ("The Quarrel of the Mattress-makers")[77] and her *Cakewalk de la pendule*[78] to the Lumière series of cake-walk films, starting with *Le Cakewalk au nouveau cirque*.[79] The last one no longer exists, but catalogue descriptions indicate that in-camera superimpositions were used to have life-sized figures and miniature figures in the same frame. This shows that in addition to imitating the Lumière films, Guy was also aware of and imitating the trick films of Méliès. She would have been aware of the magician's Théâtre Robert Houdin because Antoine Lumière, the father of the famous brothers, had a photography studio directly above the theatre, and the relationship between the Lumières and the Gaumont Com-pany was very close.

The cordial relationship that existed between Léon Gaumont and the Lumière brothers extended to a significant influence over film topics, film content, and film form without the kind of intrigues that later characterized the competition between Gaumont and Pathé (see Chapter Three). It seems impossible that Guy could have copied so many of Hatot's films (and other Lumière films), let alone used the same sets, without having some contact with Hatot himself. I have not found any documentation, such as letters between Guy and Hatot, in the Gaumont Archive or in Roberta Blaché's collection of papers to support this hypothesis.

However, in the correspondence between Guy and Louis Gau-mont there are three letters that mention Hatot. First, Louis Gaumont sent Guy a copy of the Gaumont 1899 catalogue with the request that she identify the films that she had directed. Guy noticed the photographs from a film entitled *La Vie du Christ* that was listed there and remarked with horror that those images were not from her film. She reminded Gaumont that her film (made in 1906) had sets designed by Menessier based on the paintings by Tissot. In his reply, Louis Gaumont said that the film in the 1899 catalogue was prob-ably the film by Georges Hatot, who had made a Passion film the same year.

My comparison of the images in the 1899 catalogue and images from the Hatot film in *Auguste et Louis Lumière: Les 1000 pre-miers films* leads me to agree with Louis Gaumont. Hatot's film, as advertised in the Lumière catalogue, had 13 scenes, and the film in the Gaumont catalogue only had eleven. However, this could mean that certain scenes that were shot on the same set (around the set with the three crosses) could have been combined to make one longer scene.

This confusion might be part of the reason why Sadoul credited Guy's 1906 *Vie du Christ* to "Jasset... with the assistance of Georges Hatot."[80] Jasset *was* in charge of what today would be called second-unit directing on Guy's 1906 *Vie du Christ* (he directed the exteriors and managed the crowds of extras). But there was no mention anywhere else of Hatot having anything to do with the 1906 film, or with any other Gaumont production for that matter.

The fact that Louis Gaumont assumed that if the film was not Guy's, it had to be Hatot's, indicates that the Gaumont company, in addition to distributing its own films, was also buying films from the Lumières for distribution and listing them in the Gaumont catalogue. This was an amazing business relationship between two companies that were otherwise competitors, and it showed that Léon Gaumont and the Lumières had a deep friendship that superceded the rivalry that might have been engendered by business.

The Lumières and Gaumont had similar philosophical views and values. They were unabashedly members of the turn-of-the-century bourgeoisie, with what would today be considered "right-wing" or "conservative" politics and a paternalistic attitude toward their employees. In effect, the bourgeois family structure seems to have been their model for business relationships. This approach worked fairly well in France, where such familiarity could be regarded as an early, non-aggresive form of "networking"; but proved disastrous when each company tried to break into the United States. Only Pathé, with its more aggressive approach and greater financial resources, was able to establish a real foothold in the United States.

The friendship between Léon Gaumont and Louis Lumière in particular lasted until the end of Lumière's life. They corresponded regularly, as did Léon Gaumont and Antoine Lumière, although this correspondence was more perfunctory and essentially limited to medical resource topics of interest to both men. In 1918 Gaumont refused to support a committee put together to honor the late Georges Demenÿ because he felt that the committee's claim that Demenÿ had invented the *chronophotographe* before the Lumière's invented their *cinématographe* was unfair and inaccurate.[81] In 1934, Léon Gaumont actively defended the historical precedence of the Lumière camera over Messter's camera (which Louis Lumière claimed was a copy of the Lumière *cinématographe*)[82] and in August of 1930, he even attempted to re-create and re-film *Arrivée d'un train à La Ciotat* for the thirty-fifth anniversary of cinema—a project that never reached completion.[83]

Gaumont also visited Louis Lumière at the Lumière vacation home for about a week every summer. Lumière filmed one of their fishing trips with a home movie camera and sent it to Gaumont with the following letter, which serves as a fitting final commentary on the lifelong business relationship and friendship between the two men:

> April 4, 1937
> My dear Léon
>   Here are some bits of film that I shot during our last fishing trip. They aren't that great—please be indulgent of a neophyte!
> Cordially
> Louis Lumière.

In spite of the close relationship between Gaumont film production and Lumière film production, it would be a mistake to ascribe too much weight to the influence of the Lumière films on Guy and Gaumont in general. For one thing, Gaumont was not unique in imitating Lumière films—everyone else did too, including Edison[84] and Méliès[85] and the Lumière films were not the sole source of influence. As I describe in more detail in Chapter Six, Guy was well aware of Méliès' output. It is also clear from at least one film with us from this period, *Chez le maréchal-ferrant* ("Horseshoeing scene"), that Guy was aware of Edison's production as well. This is one of the most curious films from the Sieurin French collection. It is staged on the concrete patio, disguised with a backdrop. In the foreground, two men are shoeing a huge workhorse. One man struggles to hold the horse's hoof up and occasionally glances at the camera surreptitiously. In the background, another man pounds away at an anvil. Halfway through the scene a tiny girl—no more than three or four years old—walks across the middle ground, clutching a large doll in her arms, glancing fearfully at the horse. This film falls into the category of cinema of attractions: it was made to show off the spectacle of the working men; and the shirtless man pounding away at the anvil certainly delivers.

At first glance, one would call the film an *actualité* showing men at work. But like the earliest Edison kinetoscopes which had to be shot inside Edison's studio, the Black Mariah, this scene of work has been staged. Why stage a work scene like this when Gaumont cameramen had already made hundreds of films of people at work at their worksite locations? The Lumières even have their own versions of these films, *Forgerons* and *Maréchal-ferrant* both credited to Louis Lumière.[86] Both of these films were shot on location. Guy seemed to have been aware of them, because her two men shoeing horses were moved into the foreground (the Lumière figures were in the background) and had the man holding the horse's hoof to be shod squarely facing the camera. This leads me to believe that she was aware of the value of close-up effects almost from the beginning, though she used them intermittently.

Though Guy was surely aware of the Lumière horseshoeing and blacksmithing scenes, my hypothesis is that her *Maréchal-ferrant* owes a more direct debt to two Edison films, *Blacksmith Scene* and *Horseshoeing Scene*. *Blacksmith Scene*, according to Charles Musser, was made before May of 1893 by Dickson and Heise and was one of the first of the films shot in the Black Mariah to have a commercial life. The film shows three men working around an anvil, stopping to pass around a bottle of beer, then resuming work. Musser described *Horseshoeing Scene*, made in 1894, as a "simple variation of *Blacksmithing Scene*." Musser used these scenes as a departure point for discussing the male homosocial nature of the amusement world and the emphasis on masculine daily work life in Edison's films. It took at least a few months for the makers of the Edison kinetoscope films to realize that female patrons were also drawn to the kinetoscope and that the "masculine appeal needed to be tempered." Additional "non-offensive" subjects also became necessary when "more provocative selections" met with censorship.[87]

Guy was surely as conscious of the masculine-dominated work-environment (especially since she herself worked in one) and the male address in cinema in its earliest period as the audience for the Edison kinetoscopes were. Could that explain the insertion of a little girl, holding a baby doll no less, in a film that so clearly parodies the genre of male workplace films? Could it also explain her "privileging of female characters," as Richard Abel has described it, in films such as *Le Maréchal-ferrant* or *La Vie du Christ* that were generally seen as being about men?

Alice Guy, Cinematic Storyteller

FOR FEMINISTS WHO liked to view *Sage-femme* and let it stand in for *Fée aux choux*, *Choux*'s eroticism and lack of narrative might be disappointing. It's important to see *Choux* in its context. What is key here is that a comparison of *Choux* and *Sage-femme* demonstrate that by 1902, Guy had made the transition to narrative cinema, although many elements from the cinema of attractions are still present in her Gaumont films. The rest of this chapter is devoted to the films she made during her cinema of attractions period (up to 1902) and to later films that show her transition from the cinema of attractions to narrative cinema.

Gunning himself, who, along with André Gaudreault, coined the term "cinema of attractions" (based on a usage of Eisenstein's)[88] pointed out that "although different from the fascination in storytelling exploited by the cinema from the time of Griffith, it is not necessarily opposed to it. In fact the cinema of attractions does not disappear with the dominance of narrative, but rather goes underground, both into certain avant-garde practices and as a component of narrative films, more evident in some genres (e.g. the musical) than in others."[89] Gunning's key argument is that cinema of attractions films set up a different relationship to the spectator as compared to narrative films after 1906 primarily by not maintaining the fourth wall. "The cinema of attractions expends little energy creating characters with psychological motivations or individual personality... it was precisely the exhibitionist quality of [film] that made it attractive.... its freedom from the creation of a diegesis, its accent on direct stimulation... the period from 1907 to about 1913 represents the true *narrativization* of the cinema"[90]

But many films made before 1906 exhibit a "narrative mode"[91]—this is true of a full third of the Lumière films, for example. To account for these, instead of a narrator, Gaudreault posits a "monstrator." He defines two levels of narrativity that correspond to the "two articulations of the double mobility, which is cinema's characteristic: the mobility of the subjects represented (made possible by the sequence of photographs) and the mobility of the spatio-temporal segments (made possible by the sequence of shots)."[92] Accordingly, single-shot films only demonstrate the first level of narration: "the film [*L'Arroseur arrosé*] shows no sign of any intervention by the narrator (whose discourse, or narration, comes from the articulation between shots.)"[93]

Both Charles Musser and Edward Branigan have argued against this position at length. Specifically, Musser says:

> Although juxtaposing shots is certainly an important way for a narrating presence to assert itself, such a narrational voice would seem to be at work even with one-shot actuality films. The choice of subject matter, camera position and the framing of the picture, the decision to show this moment and not some other—to start at moment x and stop at moment y—all imply the presence of a narrator who is telling us what to see, what to look for, and from what perspective.[94]

Musser argues that the term "cinema of attractions" applies to a strand of pre-1903 cinema, to films shown in vaudeville houses that were "brief and often non-narrative, emphasizing variety and display." But it clearly does not apply to all cinema before 1903.[95] Musser points out that the opposition between attractions and narrative is somewhat forced—is the narrative in Méliès' *A Trip to the Moon* the slender hook on which to hang a series of visual pleasures or are the film's little spectacles the raw material out of which the narrative is constructed?[96] He also points out that Edwin Porter's *The Gay Shoe Clerk*, which Gunning argues is an attraction film because of the close-up of the lady's calf, is a narrative film because separate spaces of awareness are constructed for lovers and chaperone, and the fourth wall is maintained.[97] However, though he sees the cinema of narrative integration as well in place by 1904-1906 (instead of 1906-1909, as Gunning argues), Musser continues to use the multi-shot film as the basis for the definition of the cinema of narrative integration.[98]

It seems clear that the "cinema of narrative integration" existed from the very beginning of cinema; certainly it is present in single-shot films. I have three arguments to support this claim: 1) that elements of the *mise-en-scène* of single-shot films can serve the same function as editing, such as the use of staging in depth or off-screen space; 2) that certain single-shot films do display a passage of time; and 3) that character development is clearly evident. The Cinema of Attractions theory was developed to account for a more limited body of early films than we have available today and primarily in relationship to the trick films of Méliès. However, Elizabeth Ezra has shown that even these films can be categorized as narratives, using modern definitions of the term.[99] What follows is an analysis of Alice Guy's earliest films along similar lines.

One of the characteristics of cinema of attractions films are their "nowness," their lack of temporal unfolding, which can only be achieved through continuity editing.[100] In keeping with this argument, Gaudreault's monstrator shows us the story in the present time. This leads Branigan to ask the following questions, especially about the monstrator theory:

> What exactly does the camera record: an actor, or a character who is already fictional, or both? Does monstration include set design, composing the image, anticipatory camera movements, performance, and sound? Is off-screen space simply what is not being shown at present, or is it space which has been witheld in the telling of the event? Does the sound of a door opening off-screen tell us, or show us, the door?[101]

In a footnote to this passage, Branigan adds:

> The theoretical status of what is "off screen" at any given moment is a concrete test of how a theory conceives the general problem of *presence and absence* which, in turn, is at the center of any explanation of representational, or symbolic activity. When can it be said that something is no longer present, not there, at an end, no longer causally effective? Is the answer: we no longer see or hear it? Or, when we no longer believe it to be present? Or, when we no longer have sufficient justification to believe it to be present?[102]

Off-screen space is used in various ways in the films of the Sieurin French Collection. In *La Bonne Absinthe,* the waiter chases the drunkard offscreen and then returns, but the couple seated at the table watch him and laugh at the drunkard's punishment, so we know what is off-screen is still present to them. However, in *L'Aveugle fin de siècle* and *La Concierge,* once a character goes off-screen, s/he is assumed to be no longer present. The first film is staged on a proscenium stage with a scenery (painted flats) of trees that define what Noël Burch has called the sixth type of off-screen space;[103] in this case, a place to hide behind the park bench. A beggar wearing a sign that says "blind out of necessity" and carrying a begging cup is led by his seeing-eye-dog to the bench where he sits and begs. A policeman enters, pulls him by the arm and pulls him off screen left. While they are away a "bourgeois" man enters from the rear of the stage, sits on the bench and falls asleep. The beggar returns, takes the sleeping man's hat and valuables, replaces them with his sign, and exits. The policeman enters from the left, takes the sleeping man to be the beggar and begins to harangue him. The beggar, this time as if he had been lying in wait behind the scenery depicting trees, re-emerges to laugh at the hapless napper, as do other characters from the film.

La Concierge is more sophisticated in its use of off-screen space. Now the setting is a real location, the sidewalk in front of a door marked "concierge." The concierge is sweeping the sidewalk when a man enters from screen left and inquires about the price of a room. Apparently the cost is more than what he has with him because he exits screen left again. While she is alone she takes snuff and then goes inside. Some children enter from screen left and ring her doorbell, then run off-screen left again. She comes out of her door and makes it clear that when she gets her hand on those kids she'll.... She goes back inside, and now the would-be lodger enters screen left and rings her doorbell, then turns his back to the door, removes his hat and scratches his head—a gesture that leaves him very

Figure 13. *La Concierge*

vulnerable to the bucket of water the concierge douses him with before she realizes that this time the doorbell ringer was not the children! The two begin to argue on the sidewalk, much to the amusement of the children who have re-entered from screen left and other onlookers who have entered from screen right.

Both films end with all characters re-entering to laugh at the joke in a variation of the apotheosis ending of the *Féeries*,[104] but while the narrative part of the film is underway off-screen, space is treated as "not present" for the most part. (The exceptions, of course, are the moments when the beggar steps behind the trees to wait for the sleeper to get into trouble and when the concierge steps inside her doorway; these offscreen spaces are contained by the on-screen *mise-en-scène*.) Each entrance and exit marks a temporal progression in the action and a new psychological space for the main character, whose key traits are chronicled with each action (the beggar is shown to be industrious in his vagrancy, then harassed, then clever and strategic in his response to his harassment; the concierge is shown to be hard-working, sharp-tempered, addicted to snuff but finally not without a sense of humor). Both films, made before 1900, depict off-screen space as related to on-screen space much as two shots relate to each other. The spaces indicated as off-screen are potentially on-screen. In a multi-shot film, they would have been represented with a separate shot.

When a film uses off-screen space in this way, we can no longer categorize it a "cinema of attractions;" the on-screen space no longer exists as a pure spectacle, but in relation to off-screen space. By allowing single shot films that can be narrativized, we can also begin to address the issue of focalization (how a character becomes the source of our knowledge of a causal chain).

The First Dramatic Close-Up?

IN THE REST of this chapter, I will show how Guy made the transition from the cinema of attractions to a more narrative cinema as she was also refining the forms of her address. Her response to the male homosocial aspects of the films she had imitated could be described as a desire to emphasize that women also worked and played in the world alongside men. Beyond that, she began to articulate a female address, a layer of messages aimed at women, mostly in the form of satire of heterosexual relations. Of the films that survive, the

Figure 14. *Madame a des envies*

Figure 15. *Madame a des envies*

earliest to show this is *Sage-femme de première classe*. *Madame a des Envies* (Gaumont 1906) could also be seen as a third in a series that begins with *Sage-femme* and *Fée aux choux*.

Madame a des envies ("Madam Has Her Cravings") is similar to other early Guy films based on a stereotype or bit of "folk wisdom." In this case, "pregnant women have cravings which they cannot resist." In these films, Guy expresses a satirical view of the conventions that defined permissible behavior in heterosexual relations. This satirical attitude is playful in a film like *Sage-femme*, brazen in *Envies*. But for Guy, *Envies* also represents a tremendous advance in narrative continuity.

Like Cecil Hepworth's *Rescue by Rover*, made not long before, *Envies* relies on a series of real locations to establish its narrative continuity. *Envies* improves on *Rover* by making a woman the driving force from one location to the next, rather than a dog, and emphasizing this with a series of dramatic close-ups.

The close-ups in *Madame a des envies* dramatically emphasize the subversive theme of the story. The allusions to fellatio make the film lascivious, but the woman's subjectivity[105] stands in strong contrast to Georges Méliès' or later Victorin Jasset's reliance on the female nude as a source of spectacle. Compare the woman in *Envies* to the women who "eroticize the firmament,"[106] in the 1907 Méliès film *L'Eclipse du soleil en pleine lune*. These women, dressed in leotards and gossamer veils, dangle from stars and planets, drift across the sky, or find themselves rocked lecherously between an old man from Saturn and a soldier from a nearby star. The close-ups of *Envies* can also be compared to the close-ups of the faces of the Sun and Moon as they have an erotic encounter (during an "eclipse") in their expressions.

The close-ups in *Envies* are not so close that we are allowed to forget the woman's very pregnant state; her condition and the way she is swathed in nun-like drapery add a layer of satire to what would otherwise be simply voyeuristic, like the vignetted close-up of a woman's ankle in Edison's *The Gay Shoe Clerk*. Guy used a narrative strategy similar to that of *Envies* in *La Hiérarchie dans L'amour*, in which a series of soldiers court a nursemaid (for full analysis of the latter film, see Chapter Six).

Envies may represent the first time narrative had been structured around close-ups in films. [It is possible Guy did something similar in the drama *La Première Cigarette* (Gaumont 1904) which no longer exists.] The close-ups in *Envies* are an extension of "comic gag"

Figure 16. Giving birth in a cabbage patch in *Madame a des envies*

films, single-shot films where an actor is shown in medium or close shot, and the fun of the film consists of the grimaces of the actor. These were comic versions of the melodramatic convict films, the cinematic equivalent to mug shots, in which convicts would grimace in order to make themselves less recognizable in pictures which required long exposures. The Pathé films starring Dranem, *Ma tante* made in 1900 and *Man Eating Pomegranates* made in 1903, are both examples of this kind of comic film. Guy herself made at least one film of this type, *Horribles Grimaces* in 1898.

The next industry development in the use of close-ups was to use a single non-diegetic close-up (i.e., it did not form part of the narrative world of the film) as an ending or beginning of the film, such as the close-up of the bandit that is the emblematic shot for *The Great Train Robbery*.[107] Burch points out that these close-ups replaced the "primitive medium close-up" (such as the close-ups in *Envies*) and:

> ...either set up the concern of the film (at the beginning of *Rescue by Rover* the baby is asleep, watched over by the dog) or give

it closure (at the end of *How a British Bulldog Saved the Union Jack* (Walturdaw Company, U.K. 1906) the dog is filmed from close to with the flag between its teeth) or its joke (at the end of *Le Bailleur* 'The Yawner' Pathé, 1907, the protagonist's irrepressible yawning, the sole source of the film's humor, breaks a strap that has been fastened around his jaws, in close-up.)[108]

Guy used such close-ups in both the closing and the opening of *La Course à la saucisse* (Gaumont 1906), a farcical imitation of *Rescue by Rover*, and possibly a source of inspiration for *British Bulldog*. Again, male actors are dressed as female characters when those characters are called upon to perform acrobatics; a large crowd pursues a dog that has stolen a long chain of sausages. In the process, much property, including food, livestock, dairy products and the work of a mattress-stuffer and the papered hoops of a group of acrobats (another trope in Guy films), is destroyed by the dog and the crowd that pursues it. The plot is resolved when a hunter shoots at the dog, frightening him into dropping most of the sausages, which the people in the crowd then proceed to eat as just reward for their laborious chase. But none of these earlier uses matches Guy's achievement in *Envies*: to completely structure a narrative that alternates between long shots (in which the pregnant woman steals a succession of phallic objects) and close-ups (in which we watch her consume the phallic objects with evident delight).

Although *Envies* represented a narrative advance, it was not really imitated. It is possible that the film was not well distributed, or perhaps the "erotic" content limited its possible venues. This might explain why the use of close-ups in *Envies* has so rarely been discussed.

For many years, D.W. Griffith was credited for the first dramatic use of a close-up, based on Linda Arvidson's account in her book *When the Movies Were Young*,[109] which claimed that D.W. Griffith's first use of the dramatic close-up came in his film *After Many Years* (Biograph, 1908). In fact the shot described is almost a long shot of Florence Lawrence, although we only see her shoulders and head because the rest of her is blocked by a hedge. She is also framed on one side by a pillar, giving the image a vignetted effect (using the camera aperture or a masque to put a black round or square shadow around the face as a way of calling attention to it).

Guy experimented with vignettes also, at least in her *phonoscènes* (see Chapter 2). In *L'Âne récalcitrant*, she also had a wagon pull up a little close to the camera about halfway through a scene. But she appeared to abandon these approaches quickly in favor of simply moving the camera closer to the actors in order to get a closer shot.

Edison also released *The Whole Dam Family and the Dam Dog* (May, 1905) which, according to Charles Musser, "took postcard caricatures and realized them in a series of facial expression films.[110] In each new scene of this film, we see another member of the "Dam" family, vignetted by an elaborate frame that is built up high around the bottom side so that only the head and shoulders of the sitter are seen. However, the camera is still quite far away from the sitters; if the frame were not there, and if the sitters were not sitting down, we would be able to see to their knees. Guy was surely aware of this film when she made *Envies*; she improved on the Edison film by removing the frame (the vignette) and moving the camera closer for the close-up effect.

One film that might have been inspired by *Envies* is *Mrs. Wilson's Countenance* (U.S., Vitagraph, 1910). My information on the film comes from *Moving Picture World*, which includes a picture of Mrs. Wilson's face in its "inane" mode, and which is clearly a close-up, as we define close-up today (head and shoulders). The reviewer in *Moving Picture World* characterizes the close-ups thus:

> *Wilson's Wife's Countenance* (Vitagraph): The man who has sometimes been transfixed by an icy stare will appreciate the beginning of this picture. Here is a face as immobile as a stone. No matter what is done, it does not change. But a cure is begun, and through a long series of grimaces it is restored to normal flexibility and expression. The last glimpse is natural and pleasing, and represents the work of a powerful restorative administered by a despairing husband.[111]

Clearly, this is no feminist comedy, or even an erotic one; the assumption at work here is that a husband is entitled to see his wife's smiling face whenever he looks at her.[112]

It seems safe to say that the Vitagraph production team that made this film had learned the lesson of using close-ups dramatically, possibly even from *Envies*. (I have found records of some of Guy's 1906 Gaumont films being distributed in the U.S. one or two years later, but none for *Envies*). But unlike *Envies*, which delights audiences of both sexes, *Mrs. Wilson's Countenance* seems to be a joke for men only.

Romeo Bossetti, one of Guy's trainees, probably had *Envies* in mind when he made *Le Tic* (Gaumont 1908), about a peasant woman who goes to Paris for her honeymoon, where her uncontrollable winking makes men think she is inviting them to make a pass at her, much to her husband's chagrin. In 1908, Bossetti also made *Une dame vraiment bien*, which does not use close-ups but uses the same woman-moving-through-real-locations plot structure. The story is about a pretty well-dressed, woman[113] out for her constitutional.

She creates havoc wherever she goes because the men she passes by get completely disrupted in their work when they stop to admire her. She is completely oblivious to the effect she has. Finally two policemen cover her with their cloaks and escort her home, and even they are overcome with admiration for her. Though Bossetti had mastered the visual narrative form, for him, the visual spectacle of the woman was the driving energy of these films, but the subjectivity belonged to the male characters that react to her and follow her. This is a far cry from the woman in *Envies*, who is both subject and spectacle at the same time.

Alice Guy, though not the first person to make a fiction film, was among the first to make the transition from the cinema of attractions to narrative cinema, and that earlier than previously supposed. She was among the first to put the close-up of the human face to dramatic use. If this were all that there was to be learned from exhuming and studying her films, it would be enough. But the surprise in the package of Alice Guy's early work is the in-joke, elbow-in-our-ribs feeling we get when we look at her films and see her own satirical gaze looking back at us.

So far we have seen that Alice Guy was a pioneer of early narrative development. During the next phase of her career, from 1902 to 1907, she continued to work on narrative development, as we shall see in Chapter Three. At that same time, she produced and directed synchronized sound films for the Gaumont Company, the topic of the next chapter.

2 SOUND REWRITES SILENTS: ALICE GUY AND THE GAUMONT CHRONOPHONE

THE SECOND MOST commonly asked question about Alice Guy's life and career is: why did Alice Guy's film manufacturing concern, the Solax Company, cease producing in 1914? The usual assumption is that Solax went bankrupt at that time. It was not actually the case. In 1914, the company merged with another concern; the physical plant was sold as part of bankruptcy proceedings in 1920.

Various authors, film historians and feminists among them, lay the blame for the demise of Solax on her husband, Herbert Blaché.[1] The myth runs something like this: Alice Guy was the first woman to have her own studio company and studio plant, and all of her films were very successful, but the company went bankrupt because her husband would rather ruin the company than let his wife outshine him and Alice loved him so much that she let him do it. Herbert's guilt is "proven" by the fact that he left Alice Guy in New York in 1918 and went to Hollywood in the company of one of his actresses.

The answer to the puzzle is much more complex, and in the end, more salacious, more full of action and colorful characters than anything the rumor mill could cook up. And it began and ended with the Gaumont Chronophone.

I discovered this connection almost by accident. I had not set out to prove or disprove Herbert's guilt or innocence—that didn't seem possible. All I wanted to do was find out something about the chronophone, Gaumont's system for producing early synchronized sound films between 1902 and 1913, because Alice Guy had directed so many of them—over one hundred. In the process, I found the answers to one of the mysteries of Alice Guy's career. I also found myself forced to re-evaluate one of the "grand narratives" of early cinema: the idea that silent cinema came first, and synchronized sound cinema came belatedly after, and that sound has always been a modest handmaiden to the film-image queen.

My search for answers led me to focus on a set of discs. Paul Spehr, of the Library of Congress, had alerted me to the existence of one hundred or more of them, mostly 16-inch but also some ten- or twelve-inch, in the Motion Picture, Broadcasting and Recorded Sound Division of the Library of Congress. The collection was purchased within the last twenty years from a private collector,[2] but remained unprocessed.

At first glance the nature of the discs seemed quite obvious: most of them were in record sleeves that read: "The Chronophone: Pictures that Sing and Talk." The sleeves had a hole in the center which allowed us to read a paper label affixed to the disc. The label read: "Chronophone-Gaumont Patent, Gaumont Co, New York" and then blank spaces were left for the title and the performing artist's name. Most interesting of all, a blank space was left next to the word "start," and then a blank space for the title of the song. So it would appear that there was no mystery here after all; these discs were not simply phonographic recordings, they were actually parts of films—early sound films, and the blank space next to "start" often filled in with "first note" or "first word" showed us how the manufacturers communicated with the eventual projectionist and told him how to maintain synchronization between phonograph and film.

I have chosen the term "early sound films" (rather than the more common "early sound experiments") to represent a variety of production and exhibition practices. In the first instance, films such as those made for the Gaumont Chronophone and for similar systems, had sound recorded first and the picture shot as the actors lip-synched to their own playback. During exhibition, the image projector was "slaved" to the phonograph players. The term could also be extended to include music films such as those made for the Beck System in Germany, in which the orchestra played along, following the direction of an orchestra conductor visually recorded in the corner of the film. Finally, "early sound films" include films which had live sound accompaniment in the form of a piano player, sound effects artist, or narrator.

It seemed strange to me that these Gaumont discs were in the Recorded Sound Division and not the Motion Picture Division. To me, they were soundtracks for films, half of a single entity, and they should have been archived with the movies upstairs. But the solution to the library's cataloguing problem was not so simple. Because, on examining the discs more closely, I saw that an original label was often visible under the Gaumont paper label, and this original label revealed that almost all of these discs were commercial recordings from companies, mostly Victor, but also Cameo, Red Label, Zonophone, and Pathé Odéon.

Using the record matrix numbers, we have established that most of these records dated from 1907 to 1913—the peak years of the Gaumont Chronophone in the U.S.

The two overlapping labels on each disc symbolized their identity crisis. In fact, someone had attempted to scratch off some of the Gaumont paper labels, in the process destroying valuable information about the disc's role in a film production. This conflict, between the view of the discs as 78's with some musical numbers, popular songs, opera arias and dance music, and the view of the discs as movie soundtracks, represents a big problem in our current conception of early cinema history—the problem of image versus sound.

Obviously the man to consult in any such conflict is Rick Altman, who wrote:

> If cinema could be defined solely from the standpoint of the image, then it might make sense to base a definition entirely on the image apparatus. Seen in this manner, cinema has for a century followed a more or less straight-line trajectory. An entirely different figure appears—zigzagging and indirect—when we take sound into account.[3]

Altman published these lines in 1992, and some additional work has appeared in response to his challenge, including his own essay, "The Silence of the Silents," published in *Musical Quarterly*.[4] Quite a lot of primary research is underway, but it usually takes the form of one researcher finding out everything there is to know about one early sound system. What is lacking is a critical and historical reassessment of the results of this research. It is my argument that once the so-called early synchronized sound 'experiments' are taken into full consideration, the history of silent cinema will have to be completely rewritten.

Sound Rewrites Periodization

THE CLASSICAL PERIODIZATION of film history is one of the first historical givens that needs to be altered. I use Thompson and Bordwell's here:

1880s–1904	Invention and early years (also known as Cinema of Attractions)
1905–1912	International Expansion (also known as the transition to narrative cinema)
1913–1919	Early "classic period"
1920–1925	Late Silent era
1926–1945	The Development of Sound[5]

If we add sound to this picture, this is what an early periodization might look like:

1894	William Kennedy Dickson produces the so-called "Dickson Experimental Sound Film" at the Edison Co.
1896	Messter synchronizes music to his "Biorama."[6]
1900	Three separate talking film exhibits are shown at the Paris Exposition: the Phono-Cinéma-Théâtre, the Théâtrescope, and the Phonorama.
1901	Gaumont takes out his first chronophone patent, which owes a debt of inspiration to Edison's kinetoscope coupling and the work of M. Baron.
1902	First Gaumont chronophone demonstration.
1903	Messter presents his "Biophon"—a cinematograph-phonograph coupling that the Gaumont Company considered to be a plagiarization of the Gaumont system—on August 29, 1903, in the Apollo Theatre in Berlin.
1905	Construction of Gaumont Chronophone studio.
1906	Frely, working for Gaumont, invents the first microphone connected to an electromagnetic signal for recording the human voice. This device is not patented in order to preserve the Gaumont company's competitive edge.
1908	Gaumont considers the problems of post-synchronization and amplification to be solved. Construction of a *chronophone* studio in the U.S. is begun.[7]
1907–1908	Peak years for Messter's Tonbilder in Germany.
1910	Chronophone films are seen by thousands of spectators.
1912	Gaumont gives up on English language chronophone production.
1913	After one last concerted sales effort, Gaumont pulls out of the U.S. altogether. At about the same time, Messter pulls out of Tonbilder production.

Let's start at the beginning of this new periodization of film history with the oldest synchronized sound film known to exist, the "Dickson Experimental Sound Film." The film was made in late 1894 or early 1895, perhaps even earlier. The image part of the film has been known to cinema scholars and archivists for many years, but in spite of the film's name, no one was really sure if it ever really had a soundtrack.

A wax cylinder was discovered during an inventory at the Edison National Historic site in 1960 that was labelled "Dickson Violin." Because the image was kept at the Library of Congress in Washington D.C. and the soundtrack was at the Edison National Historic Site in New Jersey, it took a very long time to put the two back together. The preservation effort was produced by Rick Schmidlin, who worked with Jerry Fabris of the Edison National Historic Site and Walter Murch of Skywalker Sound. First, a crack in the wax cylinder had to be repaired. Then laser technology was used to lift the sound which had to be resynchronized to the image as the thump caused by the repaired crack was edited out. The result was the music of Dickson's violin as he played an air from Pietro Mascagni's "Cavalleria Rusticana" with the sound of the dancing men's feet on the wooden platform, in perfect sync. The total cost of preservation was over 300,000 U.S. dollars, which was paid for by Skywalker Sound, a George Lucas company. The film will not be commercially available.[8] At the time of this writing, it was rumored that Lucas might use it as a logo for his company.

The successful preservation of the *Dickson Experimental Sound Film* reminds us of Edison's famous statement of 1887:

> ...that it was possible to devise an instrument which should do for the eye what the phonograph does for the ear, and that by a combination of the two all motion and sound could be recorded and reproduced simultaneously.[9]

The *Dickson Experimental Sound Film* shows that this statement is not simply typical Edison hyperbole. However, Edison's vision of recording synchronized sound films seemed to end there, at least until 1908 or 1909. And although Dickson succeeded in recording the sound and image of his film simultaneously, it is doubtful that the film was ever shown synchronized. The post-synchronized sound films such as the phonoscènes made for the Gaumont chronophone on the other hand, were recorded and filmed separately, but were exhibited regularly, properly synchronized, to paying audiences. And the chronophone was not the only one; in the U.S., there was the Cameraphone, the Cort-Kitsee Device, and the Synchronophone. In England, there was the Cinematophone, the Vivaphone, and most successful of all, the Animatophone, developed in 1910 from Thomassin's Simplex Kinematograph Synchroniser. Mismanagement forced the Animatophone Company out of business in 1911.[10] In Germany, there was Messter's *biophon*; Alfred Dusker produced a *Cinephon*; Karl Geeyr built the *Ton-biograph* for the company Deutsche Mutoskop und Biograph GmbH; and Guido Seeber developed the *Seeberophon* and later used Messter's *synchronophon* as a technical model for the German Bioscop. According to Michael Wedel, after the demise of Messter's *Tonbilder*, synchronised music films continued to be produced in Germany from 1914 to 1929 on the Beck system, the Lloyd-Lachman device, and the Notofilm system.[11]

The proliferation of devices was matched by placid expectation in the editorials; for example, from around 1906 to the mid 1910s, *The Moving Picture World* discussed widespread synchronized sound film production and distribution as if it were just over the horizon, an inevitable and natural occurrence. In the public's mind, it also appeared to be just a matter of time. Everyone seemed to be waiting for the right system to be developed by the right inventor and then commercialized by the right company. Writers for the trade press recognized that implementing the changes necessary for synchronized sound exhibition would require a large capital base. As Alan Williams has noted, "until the Vitaphone, in fact, the history of sound filmmaking is the history of repeated failure, not of technology, but of marketing."[12]

All we remember now is this "failure of marketing," and this blind spot in our memory has led to a blind spot in our history. What we need to think about instead is at least twenty years (from the mid-1890s to the mid-teens, and other early sound systems continued well into the 20s, after Gaumont and Messter gave up) of uninterrupted, commercially successful, internationally distributed, early sound practice.

Alice Guy was a key figure in early sound film practice. Of the 150 or so phonoscènes produced at Gaumont between 1902 and 1906, she directed over 100. And because the chronophone played a key role in Alice Guy's career and in her personal life, it is impossible to give her work serious consideration without confronting the issue raised by early synchronized sound production in general. This consideration begins with a basic question:

A Poor Man's Sound Cinema?

WHEN WE START with a periodization like the Bordwell and Thompson model, we accept a concept of the early cinema as almost equivalent to a "cinema of attractions," characterized by its lack of cause-effect narration, lack of character focalization, lack of montage and closure, its emphasis on gags and spectacle, shallow staging, frontal performance and direct audience address, including theatrical entrances and exits and such theatrical practices as bowing. But if we re-tell the history of cinema in light of synchronized sound, would it not be more logical to claim that the cinema of attractions—these spectacle films without a soundtrack—were really a poor man's sound cinema? In other words, could we argue that there was no cinema of attractions period at all? What if the attractions aesthetic was just one stylistic option in a sound cinema that was imperfectly mechanized?

My inspiration for this concept is Alan Williams' article "Historical and Theoretical Issues in the Coming of Recorded Sound to the Cinema."[13] Williams' basic argument is against Bazin's concept of an ever-increasing drive for realism in the cinema that was accomplished by adding sound and color. Instead, Williams argues:

> If there was an evolutionary pressure at work in cinema history which eventually culminated in the general adoption of synchronized recorded sound, this trend arguably has little to do with demand, the sphere of consumption, and much to do with the logic of industrial production. For what the triumph of Warner Bros.' Vitaphone finally accomplished was to complete a process begun long before: the progressive mechanization of the cinematographic spectacle. Years before the 1895 debut of the Lumière Cinématographe, Emile Reynaud's Optical Theatre projected moving images (painted, not photographed) onto a screen. The Lumière apparatus did not immediately drive this competition out of business but did exert considerable economic pressure, because Reynaud's spectacle was *incompletely mechanized*. Not only were his images painted rather than photographed (thus taking much time and skill to produce), but each projection was in the fullest sense a performance.[14]

Knowing what we do now about the proliferation of post-synchronized sound experiments from the turn of the century on, it is not a great leap to apply Williams' argument for the increased mechanization of spectacle[15] to sound. Which is to say that vaudeville acts like Little Tich's,[16] dances, magic acts like the earliest of Méliès', and gag films, were all meant to be read as sound films without the sound. They coexisted in a system of production and exhibition practice right along with post-synchronized sound films, often made by the same production companies, often featuring the same artists.[17]

To begin with, a certain type of "attractions" films—those that most resemble filmed vaudeville acts—and early synchronized sound films shared the same aesthetic. Consider the *phonoscènes* made for the Gaumont chronophone: these were usually filmed versions of opera performances or of single songs by a singer from the café-concerts. They were shot proscenium style, with the camera taking the point of view of a spectator in the center of an auditorium, between five and ten rows back. The performers were mostly seen in long shot, that is, from head to toe, and much of the stage and backdrop were included in the frame. In rare cases, the camera was moved a little closer so that the performer was seen from ankle to head, although much of the backdrop was still visible. And on very rare occasions, the performer was shot in a medium shot or even a medium close-up. Occasionally, some kind of vignette was used to produce a close-up effect.

In other words, if post-synchronized sound films and many of the cinema of attractions films are compared to each other, especially "attractions" films whose diegesis clearly calls for sound, then it becomes clear that the only difference between the two types of films is the origin of their soundtracks: either mechanized or not-mechanized.

In her paper at the Colloque de Cerisy-La-Salle on Georges Méliès, Isabelle Raynauld was struck by "the noise these films made... all of these exploding engines, bubbling magic potions, shouts of surprise, giant clocks ringing midnight, ringing bells, the visual sonority of the musical notes in *Le Mélomane* or the cacophony of musical instruments in *L'Homme-orchestre*."[18] She calls these representations of sound effects that are indicated within the diegesis of the film "sound events" (*événement sonore*), and defines them as a sound shown on the screen, such as the devil ringing the bells in *Le Diable au couvent*, which has a direct effect on the narrative, by making people run to church for mass. Not surprisingly, "sound events" can be further subdivided into dialogue, sound effects, and music. Raynauld based her analysis on a viewing of 170 of Méliès' films and found that 60 of them "contained an intrigue based on an argument and/or a sound event."[19]

It seems possible to argue that Méliès, knowing he had the resources of the Théâtre Robert Houdin at his disposal, including musical accompaniment and live sound effects, designed a large proportion of his films with such sound accompaniment in mind. And yet, the same films would be released to other exhibition venues, which may or may not have similar resources at their disposal.

Dance films are another fertile terrain for exploring this issue. A careful examination of various early Gaumont catalogues,[20] shows that about one-quarter of the total Gaumont output up to 1901 were dance films. It seems clear, as Abel points out, that Gaumont was looking to establish a market niche of its own as competition increased. By 1898, Méliès had claimed the genre of "transformation" films or "fantastical scenes" as his own.[21] Though Gaumont could not compete with Méliès when it came to *Féeries*, Alice Guy apparently was in charge of making films that featured a "sound event"— a dance—prominently, and by hiring dancers from the Olympia and the Opéra, at least one of whom was also hired by Méliès, which, as Abel noted, "...obviously raises questions about the context of their exhibition. One would like to know, for instance, if such films were read and received differently, depending on whether they were screened in the music halls or fairs..."[22] In music halls and in vaudeville theatres, the principal exhibition spaces of the day, these films would have had a musical accompaniment.

The earliest Gaumont dance film still in existence is in the Red Lobster Films collection in Paris, already mentioned in Chapter 1. *Ballet Libella* (1897) is a beautiful hand colored film showing two women, one in a fairy costume, preparing to dance and then beginning to dance, while the second woman watches her with an intense gaze. Neither woman appears to be a professional dancer. On the other hand, in *Danse du papillon* (1897) and *Danse fleur de lotus* (1897) both women are "Loïe Fuller" type dancers, performing what were known as "serpentine" dances, in which the emphasis is on the swirling material of the dancer's costume; the costumes here are intricately decorated, which makes the dancer's task harder, as she must swirl the cloth in such a way that the patterns are displayed to best effect.[23,24]

The Sieurin French Collection *L'Hiver: danse de la neige* (Winter: Snow Dance)[25] shows a woman dancing on a stage, dressed in a ballerina costume with a white, feathery cloak or wings. As she moves, she emerges slowly from the cloak; her emergence apparently causes feathery snowflakes to fall, and the dancer revels in them. As differentiated from the Loïe Fuller genre of films (and most of the other dance films in the Gaumont catalogue where the names of the performers are prominently featured), the dancer does not seem to be a professional. The film is an example of the cinema of attractions aesthetic, designed to give pleasure with movement and with sight of the titillating (by fin-de-siècle standards) and exposed female figure; but it is hard to imagine it being exhibited without music. Now, let us compare these films to the synchronized sound films produced by the Gaumont Company.

Synchronized Sound Production at Gaumont

GAUMONT FIRST TRIED to synchronize a cinematograph and a phonograph in 1900. Others had attempted it before him; for example, Clément Maurice introduced his *Phono-Cinéma-Théâtre* at the Paris Exposition of 1900. Maurice made films with Sarah Bernhardt, Coquelin, Réjane, the dancer Cléo de Mérode and the tenor Henri Cossira. And Felix Mesguich, one of the Lumière camera operators, also showed a *Cinéma parlant et chantant* at the Paris Exposition. Mesguich later worked with August Baron on talking pictures.[26] Their efforts influenced Gaumont in the development of the *chronophone*.

Gaumont took out his first sound patent on July 11, 1901. The patent described an electrical coupling between cinematograph and phonograph. Both machines were driven by two coupled electrical motors, with the phonograph determining the speed.[27] Gaumont himself said that his first effort was simply a variation of Edison's kinetoscope coupling.[28] This system, though presented publicly on September 12, 1902, was not very reliable; the coupling was affected by vibrations and jerks in the cinematograph.[29] Gaumont assigned his employees, Laudet and Frély, to work on the problems of sound volume and electrical sound recording. As a result of their efforts, Gaumont patented a sound amplifier in 1905 which became the *chronomégaphone*.[30] In 1906 Frély invented the first microphone connected to an electromagnetic pencil for recording. It was not patented in order to protect the secret of the device's function and preserve the company's competitive edge.[31]

The first *chronophone* sales were made in April of 1904. The system was exhibited in London for the first time on November 21, 1904.[32] On November 7, 1902, Gaumont made a presentation to the *Société Française de Photographie* of a synchronization system he had devised with the assistance of M. Decaux (he also acknowledged his debt to the patents filed by M. Baron). Three scenes were shown: first, Gaumont himself demonstrating his "Block-note 4 1/2 x 6" camera and explaining how it worked; naturally, the first synchronized sound film was a commercial. The other two films were dances performed in synchronization with the music played by the phonograph—one a "gypsy dance" and the other a *gavotte*.[33]

A system that joined the two machines with cables soon proved to be impractical, as the projector and the phonograph in a theatrical situation had to be quite a long distance from each other. So, an electrical transmission was designed:

> A dynamo with a split circuit was connected to the phonograph and its speed adjusted to the normal speed of the latter. The dynamo was connected with the projector drive motor through a rheostat mounted on the projector base. If both units were started at the same time, they ran in perfect synchronism.[34]

As of this date, Gaumont considered the problem of synchronization solved. The problem of amplification took more years of research, but on February 21, 1908, he presented the *chronophone mixte*, which had "perfect synchronism and with which the problem of amplification was definitively solved."[35]

Gaumont might have thought that he had solved the problem of amplification, but once the device was installed in theaters, problems cropped up consistently. Different solutions were tried: first, the use of a large horn on the phonograph; later the *chambres de résonance* (resonating chambers); and still later, the use of compressed air. According to Léon Gaumont, the compressed air system was already being used to project sound films to "thousands of spectators" in 1910.[36] In this variation, the control panel for the two devices (called "the orchestra conductor" in the Gaumont sales catalogue) and the cinematograph were "joined by telephone cable."[37]

Figure 17. Ad for the Gaumont Chronophone from
The Moving Picture World, 1910

On May 24, 1913, *The Moving Picture World* noted:

A Forty-Five Minute Talking Picture

At the Gaumont Palace Hippodrome in Paris, a few days ago, there was exhibited a speaking film running forty-five minutes. This is by far the longest talking picture ever thrown on the screen. The photoplay was taken from a famous French farce and was witnessed by nearly eight thousand people, the extreme capacity of the house. The dialogue was distinctly heard in the farthest corners of the auditorium without appearing unduly amplified to those in the pit. The Paris Daily papers gave the Gaumont talking pictures from four inches to three-quarters of a column next morning and described the entertainment as a revolution in the cinematographic art. Speaking photoplays running from twenty to thirty minutes are now being shown nightly by means of the Gaumont improved chronophone in the Gaumont Palace Hippodrome.[38]

Figure 18. Alice Guy (silhouetted figure on right) directing a synchronized sound film in the Gaumont Chronophone Studio in Paris, 1906

This suggests that Gaumont's claims in his company history are accurate. According to Guy, some of the *phonoscènes* she shot in Spain, of Spanish dancers, were projected at the Hippodrome "when that great theater became the Gaumont Palace for the first demonstration of talking pictures."[39]

In addition to amplification, there was the problem of recording sound. The optimal distance for recording the human voice was 50 centimeters, though an orchestra could be picked up by a microphone a few meters away. So the first problem to be resolved was the recording of the voice.

Initially, this problem was resolved by recording the voice first. The phonograph with the voice recording was then placed behind the motion picture camera while various takes of the singer were filmed as s/he sang along with her or his own recorded performance. "It was simple enough after that to start the two machines at the same time and have a synchronized performance," said Gaumont.[40]

In the documentary film clip that we have of Alice Guy directing a *phonoscène*, we see this process at work: Guy starts up the phonograph (with a double horn) and watches the dance troupe (for a scene from *Mignon*) go through its steps. Next to her, a still photographer is taking pictures and the motion picture cameraman is waiting for the rehearsals to be complete so he can film the performance.

According to Guy,[41] she never had anything to do with the sound part of the *phonoscène* recordings. She received the already-recorded wax cylinders and rehearsed the actors until they could perform a movement that matched the recording.

The whole procedure was extremely tricky and it did not take much to throw it out of sync. The system lent itself best to song and dance performances and, as F. Honoré pointed out in *Établissements*, "songs with a certain kind of movement, because the difficulty for an actor to repeat a verbal performance exactly as he did it down to the second is obvious."[42]

Alice Guy shot the first of her numerous *phonoscènes* on the concrete terrace behind the labs at Belleville, where she had shot the first version of *La Fée aux choux*. She did not have to work on the concrete terrace for long. Soon after, Gaumont built his glasshouse film studio in Belleville; he also built two studios for the filming of *phonoscènes*.[43] Guy described the process she went through for making the films and the kinds of acts she put on film:

> I was in charge of the cinematographic part of the repertoire and thus filmed the Mante sisters, very fashionable popular dancers at that time; Rose Caron of the Opéra, with her singing class. With Mmes Mathieu-Luce and Marguerite Care of the Opéra-Comique, Mlle Bourgeois and others, we recorded *Faust*, *Mignon*, *Carmen*, *Les Dragons de Villars*, *Mireille* and many others. The Café-Concert itself was made to contribute, with Mayol, Dranem, Polin, Fragson and many others.
>
> I have often been forced to admire the courage of the artists and their professional loyalty... Mme. Mathieu-Luce was singing the air from *Mignon* "Connais-tu le pays?" She went straight to the end, smiling, but when the camera stopped, she fainted. She had placed her bare foot on a burning ember fallen from an arc lamp, and had endured the burn rather than interrupt the filming.[44]

Not all celebrity artists were as "professionally loyal" as Mathieu-Luce. Guy also engaged the opera singer Caruso, who agreed to make several chronophonic scenes of some of his best- known arias. The date was set and Guy commissioned the well-known and very expensive set decorator Jambon to make ten backdrops.

> On the agreed date, I sent one of my assistants to find the great star in one of the company's first automobiles (a Panhard and Levassor), but he answered that he had thought it over and that with his name, he could not reasonably be expected to demean himself to this degree. Which proves that a good voice is not always the sign of an excellent education.[45]

To date, I have not been able to find a precise description of the Gaumont *chronophone* studio. However, Richard Koszarski looked up the construction permit application for the Gaumont Flushing studio which was designed for the filming of English language phonoscènes.[46] According to these records, there were two studio buildings: one a frame and glass structure, built sometime before 1909, with a roughly hexagonal shape and skylight over the entire area; the other a brick building for "taking photographs and developing films." The dimensions for the latter were 35'6" x 65'0" with an elevation from the curb of 29', and it had a skylight.[47]

Aesthetics of the Sound Films

WHAT DO THE *phonoscènes* look (and sound) like?

Compared to what viewers of the optical sound era are used to, they do not stay synchronized very well. However, it is hard to tell how well these films were synchronized when originally screened and how many of the errors in synchronization are due to the manner in which they were preserved. The length of the films was limited by the size of the phonographic discs: twelve-inch discs, the largest American standard, ran for just five minutes, while the standard ten-inch disc ran three to four minutes. There were also two-minute and four-minute cylinders.

Generally, the actors in the *phonoscènes* maintain theatrical tradition and look out into the distance, not acknowledging the presence of the camera while they are performing, not making eye-contact with the cinematic spectator, although in *Ce que c'est qu'un drapeau*, M. Dana is clearly nervous, and glancing toward someone behind the camera who is giving him directions before his number starts. He sings without moving his body and without making any gestures with his hands, but his face registers some of the emotions indicated by the song: he looks up at the "flag" proudly, he smiles during triumphant musical passages. But when he is not actively singing, he drops out of character—his face becomes still and impassive while he waits for the instrumental transition to end and for his turn to sing to come again.

Mayol, in *Questions indiscrètes*, walks on stage from screen left after the music begins. When he is framed in a medium shot, he stops and bows; all of this time, he is "out of character," he is a generic performer in a tuxedo. Then he starts to sing, and he is transformed. The song is a flirtatious conversation between a man and a woman. The generic costume allows Mayol to "be" each of the characters in turn; although he doesn't move around on the stage, he has a lot of body movements to indicate which character he is playing at a given moment. His gestures are a combination of theatrical pantomime (to go with the dialogue) and caricatured behavioural gestures, like putting his hands on his hips, elbows out, and swaying saucily from side to side when he is playing the coquettish girl. Once he begins to sing, he remains in character for the entirety of the song, until he has sung all of the lyrics. Although the music is still playing, he then drops out of character and reverts to his persona, gives us a goodbye smile, and backs off the stage in a half-bow, so that he has made his exit by the time the instrumental music has finished playing.

The combination of pantomime gestures and caricatural gestures are the most striking element of Mayol's performance. In the extant *phonoscènes* of Dranem there is an even richer combination of personas in each *phonoscène*. Dranem was a very energetic performer, moving around the entire stage, combining whole body language with pantomime and caricature. Although he wore the same "bum" or "clown" costume in each of his films, he had a different prop (a bucket, a poncho, a vegetable) in each one. He enters the stage already in character. One persona is that of the "narrator" who sings a few lines of the song that explains the situation. He then plays one or more characters; in one song, he simulates two people walking, by depicting each character with a different set of caricatured gestures and pantomimed dialogue. When there is an instrumental, he reverts to the "narrator" persona, with a smile or frown that passes judgement on the behaviour of the "characters." When the song ends, he exits the frame, either in his "narrator" persona or as one of the characters, and then re-enters the frame after the music is over, now out of character, and bows.

By 1907 chronophone productions had moved out of sets and onto real locations, as the next extant film attests, *Anna, qu'est-ce que tu attends?* (known in England as *Let's All Go Down to the Strand*).[48] The film starts with the singer, Fragson, already in character and with the business of the film (packing for a picnic) underway. The scene is shot at a location, in front of a country cottage, and then for the second tableaux, at a sylvan riverside setting. Fragson's character gathers his children and sings "Anna, what's keeping you?" to his wife, who is so detail-conscious that it is almost impossible for her to leave. In the second tableaux he continues his song as the children and wife continue with farcical (and silent) business.

Why weren't more *phonoscènes* made on location? A possible answer would be tradition and cost. It might have been hard to get away from stage practices, especially for the actors, and location shooting was more time-consuming.

A script in the Bibliothèque Nationale showed that the ability of the camera to change things was being used by 1908 in promotional films for the *chronophone* itself. The script was a silly poem in rhyme apparently meant to be presented by a single character. After a great many extravagant claims were made for the device, the script indicated that the character underwent "a complete change of voice and physiognomy;" indicating that the camera was stopped and one actor was substituted for another. The script was then wrapped up with a wistful goodbye and an apology for any failings of the system.

Guy herself shot monologues and scenes as *phonoscènes* in 1906. Unfortunately, none of these remain, but there is another script, from a film made later, in the Bibliothèque Nationale, entitled *Le Voyage sentimental* (Gaumont 1909), that shows a husband and wife on the phone with each other; the husband in a telephone booth, the wife in an elegant bedroom setting. This suggests that either a split staging or a split screen was used.

The wife is off on a cure, and this is their daily phone call. She claims that she misses him and she is lonely; he reminds her that she has her (male) cousin to keep her company, and in fact, he finds her cousin rather over-attentive and he fears the cousin is out to seduce her. The wife tells him his fears are groundless; meanwhile the cousin himself has appeared and is embracing, kissing and caressing the wife. When the wife tells the husband she is going to send him a kiss through the phone, it is actually the sound of the cousin kissing the wife that the husband hears. The cousin's attention gets more and more passionate, and after saying goodbye to her husband "because it is time for her to undress for her massage," she drops the phone without replacing it properly, leaving the husband free to listen, and react, to all the sounds of her passionate love-making with her cousin.[49] These two scripts show that the *phonoscènes* were starting to rely more and more on dialogue.

The *phonoscènes* also influenced the making of silent films. Though still "silent," they showed a new consciousness of sound. A wonderful example of this is *Les Débuts d'un grand ténor* (Gaumont 1907), a film I identified in the NFTVA collection (known there as *Eine Tenorstimme*). It is still not possible to attribute the film to a director, but the whole purpose of the film is to make fun of *phonoscènes*. A silent film making fun of talking films! The story begins in the Gaumont *Chronophone* production office, where a tenor applies for a position. When asked to sing, his voice turns out to be so powerful that it literally blows away everything in the room. The singer is thrown out of the office, but he finds a telephone and calls them up again, and his voice through the telephone also has the effect of a powerful wind. Finally he is arrested by the police, who are hard-put to keep him and his voice under control.

When Guy was making films for Solax, she made silent film versions of many of the operas that she had staged as *phonoscènes*. She also showed a heightened consciousness of music in such films as *His Mother's Hymn* (Solax, 1911), in which a woman plays a specific hymn on the organ which leads her prodigal son back to her (this film is discussed further in Chapter Four). *Canned Harmony* (Solax, 1912), like *Les Débuts d'un grand ténor*, shows the separation of sound from instrument. The comedy comes from an actor impersonating a famous violinist with the assistance of a phonograph hidden under a table. As a result of this impersonation, he is able to win the hand of his beloved from her musician father, but on their wedding day his best friend thinks it would be a great joke to start up the phonograph again. However, by then the hero is safely married to his beloved, so father agrees to make the best of it.

It is possible that in addition to a thematic influence, the *phonoscènes* encouraged Guy to reconsider her actors' performances. For the talking pictures, she was restaging vaudeville and operatic

Figure 19. *Canned Harmony*—Solax, 1912. The music for Billy Quirk's
violin is provided by the phonograph hidden under the table

acts that relied heavily on what Roberta Pearson has called the
"Histrionic Code:"

> The histrionic code is, in a sense, reflexive, referring always to
> the theatrical event rather than to the outside world. Until the
> second half of the nineteenth century, most English and American
> actors in most theatres performed in a self-conscious theatrical
> fashion, ostentatiously playing a role rather than pretending to
> be another person.... Performers, audiences and critics all knew
> that a theatrical presentation was an artificial construct meant
> to bear little resemblance to any off-stage reality... the pleasure
> derived not from participating in an illusion but from witnessing
> a virtuoso performance.... At times the audience would demand
> the reenactment of entire scenes, displaying a particular fondness
> for the repetition of heartrending, pitiful deaths.[50]

A Frenchman, François Delsarte, even wrote a manual for these
emotional gestures, and the Delsarte system was promoted in the

United States by Steele Mackay. These gestures were not "words but phrases," such as "resolution or conviction: fist clenched in air, brought down sharply to side of body," and "feminine distress: hand to cheek or hands on both sides of face."[51] In *Eloquent Gestures*, Pearson outlines the transition made in the Biograph films from the histrionic code to the "verisimilar code," in which a more accu-

Figure 20. Ad for the Gaumont Chronophone from
The Moving Picture World

Figure 21. M. Dana performing a cabaret song in a *phonoscène* directed by Alice Guy

rate representation of emotional reality (as emotional reality was defined in 1913) gradually took precedence.

Guy also appeared to be conscious of the difference between the histrionic code and the verisimilar code; it is my hypothesis that she became conscious of this difference while directing deliberately theatrical *phonoscènes* at the same time that she was also directing silent films on location. At her Solax studio, she even had a large banner that said "Be Natural" hanging on the back of the studio wall. The banner impressed many studio visitors, such as Leon Smith, an actor who visited the Solax studio in 1914. He compared this command to the usual instruction given to actors, "pose for the camera." Smith credited this advice (as a young, inexperienced actor, he took it quite to heart) for helping him get started on a fifty-year acting career.[52] But the results Guy achieved with such instructions to her actors in the early Solax films were mixed. Some, like Lee Beggs, were never able to lift their performances out of the histrionic code; others, like Marion Swayne and Darwin Karr, seem much more natural and, to contemporary viewers, more modern. Still others, such as Mrs. Hurley, played a range of styles, from the deliberately histrionically coded *Old Love and New* (Solax, 1912) to the more verisimilar *Roads Lead Home* (Solax, 1913). Chapter Three discusses the performing styles in the melodramas that Guy made for Gaumont in 1906, at the same time that she was producing the *phonoscènes*.

The Effect of Sound Films on Guy's Career

AS MENTIONED AT the beginning of this chapter, one of the most overlooked aspects of Guy's career was the way the development of the *chronophone* and Guy's work were intertwined. Without the *chronophone*, Guy and Blaché might not have had the chance to pursue their relationship. Without the *chronophone*, there would have been no Solax Company, and without the *chronophone* there would have been no Solax studio. But these details are not widely known. When the *chronophone* is mentioned at all, it is noted that Guy directed over 100 *phonoscènes*, long before optical sound synchronization. But the real extent of the relationship between Gaumont's *chronophone* production and Guy's career has not been understood.

To begin with, the *chronophone* played a kind of matchmaker role in her relationship with Blaché. Guy first met Herbert Blaché-Bolton while preparing for the filming of *Mireille*, (a film in which she also acted in). Her usual cameraman, Anatole Thiberville (who was still working as a cameraman for Gaumont in the 1930s) was tired and unwell:

> Gaumont decided that Herbert Blaché should take his place, which would permit him to familiarize himself with the function of the motion-picture camera.[53] He accepted without enthusiasm. Later he told me that he had never met a woman who was at first so cold, so distant as I. No doubt he was right. Still young, in a job where I had to give proof of authority, I avoided all familiarity. With my personal friends, Feuillade among others, for whom I felt a great sympathy, I recovered my true personality. My youth and gaiety quickly regained the upper hand.[54]

When the two met in 1906, Guy was 33 and Blaché 24. Scenes for *Mireille* were shot in Camargue, a village bullfight was staged, and the crew crossed the Rhone in the moonlight. The toreador Machaquito was filmed in the bullfight rings at Nimes, and he ded-

Figure 22. Machaquito, the bullfighter, in Nîmes, 1906

icated his kill to Guy. It was during this shoot that Guy and Blaché fell in love.

When the negative of *Mireille*, shot at great expense in the Camargue, was developed and discovered to be overexposed and full of scratches, it was not the cameraman, Herbert Blaché, who was blamed (although it appears he never shot a film for Gaumont again). Guy, in a letter to the Marquise de Baroncelli, blamed the unreliable cameras themselves.[55] This seemed likely enough, since Guy told of the highly experienced Thiberville having similar problems with the equipment while they were shooting both silent and sound films in Spain, rendering many of the films made there unusable.[56] Bernard Bastide, who edited the *Archives* collection of historical documents on films shot on the lands of the Baroncelli's, including *Mireille*, fantasized in a footnote that Guy "imagined" the flashing on the negative of *Mireille* to cover up for Blaché, whom she married soon afterwards. His support for this theory was that Guy made some *phonoscènes* with songs from *Mireille*; his assumption was that these songs were what was salvaged from the location shoot. However, stills from the Gaumont Catalogue showed that the *phonoscènes* of *Mireille* were shot on a stage.[57]

Toward the end of her life, Guy recounted the story of filming *Mireille* to Victor Bachy. In spite of her post-divorce bitterness towards Blaché, never in her memoirs or in other documents that I have seen, did she put the blame for the damaged film on him. Whenever she spoke of this trip, she remembered the time in the moonlight, crossing the Rhone, the toreador Machaquito. She kept photographs of these events for the rest of her life.

When the filming of *Mireille* ended, Blaché returned to his post as manager of Gaumont's German affiliate in Berlin. Guy "did not expect to see Herbert Blaché again. But we are only the toys of destiny."[58]

It was the *chronophone* itself, in the end, that enabled their romance to continue:

> Hardly a few weeks had passed when many of our German clients complained of the difficulties they had in assuring the delicate interaction of the two elements of the chronophone to obtain a perfect synchronization.
>
> Gaumont, kept in Paris by important business, spoke of delegating me to Berlin. I objected that I knew neither the country nor the language. "That doesn't matter, you know Blaché, don't you? He will accompany you and serve as interpreter."[59]

When Guy returned to Paris, Blaché followed her soon after, bringing with him his own father who made a formal request to Guy's family for her hand. Thus it was that on Christmas day in 1906, Alice Guy and Herbert Blaché were officially engaged.

What was Gaumont doing with the *chronophone* in Germany? At first, he attempted to market it outright, although his *phonoscènes* were in French (a handful of *phonoscènes* in German were filmed in Berlin). To promote the *chronophone* in Berlin meant competing with Oskar Messter, the German equivalent of Gaumont himself in Germany.

As early as 1896, Messter had exhibited "Bioramas" with a phonograph playing *Unter den Linden* accompanied by "living images," not "just any accompaniment" but a very precise series of pieces to match the images. Messter also worked on a cinematograph-phonograph coupling device (from various letters in the Gaumont archives at the Cinémathèque Française, the general opinion over at Gaumont was that he completely plagiarized the Gaumont system) and presented it as the "Biophon" on the 29th of August, 1903 in the Apollo Theater in Berlin. A journalist described the program:

> The Phonograph stood directly under the screen which left the lower third of the wall uncovered. From its horn came a joyous dance tune. We had just sat down on the chairs which filled the entire room facing the screen and the phonograph when the electric light went out. Lifesize on the screen appeared one of the beloved serpentine dancers who went through her motions as precisely to the beat of the music as we were accustomed to seeing at the Variété theaters. We were tempted to believe there was really a human being of flesh and blood up there dancing for us, if it had not been for the skin color of the dancer which was the same as her costume—white as the screen was before. The picture ended, the room lit up again, short pause, and then the phonograph came in again with a belligerent march. The screen lit up again too and accompanied by the tune "Hohen-friedverger Marsch' we saw the loafers of the guard parading towards us, umbrella or stick held like a gun in their arms. And the crowd thickened, the music was approaching! Yes, it was the drum-major and then we saw the marching band behind the drums and the pipes![60]

Both Messter and Gaumont had patents on their inventions. Messter's sound productions sold well as long as he maintained his technical advantage over other filmmakers in Germany. He owned his own chain of theaters in Berlin and in other German cities. By 1913, he had sold 500 Biophon projectors to other exhibitors. This ensured him a regular outlet for his films, which sold at a much higher price than silent films: one meter of sound film cost 2 1/2 German marks, not counting the costs of the records, which after a few projections became unusable and had to be replaced. At that time, silent movies cost 1.60 German marks and 1.20 German marks, depending on whether the film was in color or in black and white. Older programs were even cheaper.

Martin Loiperdinger credited the sound film with a very important role in establishing stable theaters in Germany, a trend that started in 1905 as sound films were shown as part of a program of vaudeville acts.[61]

For his sound films, Messter hired only the best from opera and theater and hired opera directors to make the films. For a few years, Messter put all of his resources into the *Tonbilder*, which represented 83% of his company's production in 1907 and 90% in 1908. Other German film producers started their own production of *Tonbilders* and put together machines to record and play these films, comparable to those of Messter and Gaumont. Alfred Dusker produced a *Cinephon*; Karl Geeyr built the *Ton-Biograph* for the company Deutsche Mutoskop und Biograph GmbH; Guido Seeber developed the *Seeberophon* and later used Messter's synchrophon as a technical model for the German Bioscope. He continued the work of the *Tonbilder* and shot *Synchroscope-Tonbilder* films with highly imaginative special effects. Soon a dozen machines were competing in Germany, bringing comparable results with very similar technical solutions.

The strong competition brought about drastic price drops for *Tonbilder*. Many vendors produced films more cheaply than Messter, taking advantage of the essential playback system of the *Tonbild* recording; they used records from known singers but left the sync-singing to cheaper actors. Messter, who took out more than 35 patents for the *Tonbild* alone between 1903 and 1908, fought back with a heavy advertising campaign against the imitators and sued Alfred Duskes, the Deutsche Mutoslop und Biograph GmbH, and other competitors. Cinema owners using machines other than Messter's were threatened with judicial action. This strategy was quickly abandoned, since it was counter-productive to sue the theater owners whose machines presented a potential outlet for Messter *Tonbilder* production, whatever their origin. In a conciliatory tone, Messter announced:

> We are still prepared for the owners of *Synchroscope* or of a *Duskes Cinephon* to contact us directly, and ready to contribute. We wish to make every effort to clear up the judicial aspect as soon as possible, and to agree to provisional continued use of their devices.[62]

Though Messter won his suit against the other vendors, the *Tonbilder* bonanza was over. In 1908, Messter produced forty Tonbuilder and eight silent films and in 1909, only three new *Tonbuilder* and ten silent films.[63]

Because it was difficult to market French *phonoscènes* in Germany and German ones in France, Messter and Gaumont came to a gentlemen's agreement: Gaumont did not ship his *phonoscènes* to Germany, and Messter stayed out of France. The machines were sold by both manufacturers and also offered together under one combined brand called the Gaumont-Messter Chronophon-Biophon. It was Blaché's (and for a short time, Guy's) job to maximize these sales.

Such a civilized arrangement worked for Gaumont with Messter in Germany, but he had much less luck in the United States.

In 1911, Gaumont wrote to his son, Charles:

> I have completed one more trip to the USA and Canada, I have thought long and hard, and I have reached this conclusion: the USA is truly a country for business, and for cinema in particular. I want you to spend a few months here so that you may understand this new life which allows for *large* ideas and which shows the world of business in a new light. There is no place for sentiment anywhere and in everything a single desire: to be better and stronger than your neighbor and to get the better of him as soon as the occasion arises.[64]

Gaumont's entry into the United States was his *chronophone*. He had demonstrated his system at the London Hippodrome in 1907, where it caught the attention of members of the Motion Pictures Patent Company, who licensed it for distribution in the United States. Gaumont's initial venture in the United States was to send one of his managers, Herbert Blaché, to Cleveland to try to establish a *chronophone* franchise with backing from some American investors. Since Guy and Blaché had just married, Guy retired from her position of eleven years at Gaumont and accompanied her husband to the United States in February or March of 1907.

Although the Motion Pictures Patents Company had originally expressed interest in the *chronophone*, Edison's chief counsel, Frank L. Dyer, was opposed to it, as is reflected in a letter Edison sent to Dyer on February 24, 1909:

> I had the pleasure yesterday of seeing a very good performance by means of the chronophone, although one or two false starts were made before it could be made to work. Afterwards Messrs Gaumont and Blaché talked for a long time going over all of the old reasons why they should be licensed so far as the chronophone was concerned. Blaché practically admitted that whether or not Gaumont will abide by his contracts with Kleine depends

on the vote of the Manufacturers on the chronophone tomorrow. Mr. Kleine is to be here, and Gaumont gave me to understand, would bring the matter up.

So far as I could see, there is little to fear in the way of competition from this chronophone, and possibly some advantage in the fact that the Licensed Manufacturers have such a device to offer to exhibitors. I was under the impression that you really did not care whether or not the chronophone is licensed, but Mr. Berst informed me over the phone today that you were unalterably opposed to it. Will you please let me know by wire tomorrow how you wish to have your opinion expressed and your vote cast in the matter?[65]

In tandem with his chronophone license, Gaumont entered into a contract with George Kleine to distribute Gaumont silent films in the United States. Gaumont also entered into a separate agreement with the Edison Manufacturing Company to strike prints from Edison negatives for sale abroad, and the Edison company provided Gaumont with the same service in the United States. Correspondence between the two companies indicates that Gaumont continued to lobby for direct membership in the Motion Picture Patents Company without success.[66]

When Gaumont sent Blaché (and his new wife) to Cleveland in early 1907, Blaché was not going as an official Gaumont employee. A pair of American businessmen had bought the American rights to the Gaumont chronophone, and Blaché went in as a kind of marketing partner, with the aim of creating a franchise.[67] For the eight months that Guy and Blaché were in Cleveland, they tried to exploit the chronophone. Guy helped her husband in spite of her pregnancy and the birth of her first child.

Blaché was not actually getting a salary. The couple lived off her dowry and his savings, and these ran out after nine months. At that point the investors went bankrupt, so Blaché and Guy went to Flushing, New York, and Blaché asked Gaumont for work at the newly constructed Flushing studio. Gaumont had spent at least $20,000 converting it into a studio for *chronophone* film production.[68] (Possibly a lot of that investment was for the equipment that would enable the plant to produce 50,000 feet of positive film a day, which was designed for Gaumont uses and for hire.[69]) In October, the *chronophone* was exhibited to the public and reviewed by the *New York Dramatic Mirror*:

Gaumont Talking Pictures

The Gaumont Chronophone, a machine for producing moving pictures and talking machine records in combination, is now in use at the Unique Theatre, Fourteenth Street. Owing probably to the fact that the talking machine must be located at the side of the stage in this house, instead of back of the curtain, the picture curtain being fixed to a solid wall, the illusion of talking pictures is wholly destroyed. The records, also, are somewhat feeble, although they appear to be perfectly synchronized with the films. The subjects last week included Harry Lauder in three songs, "Stop Your Ticklin', Jock," "We Parted on the Shore," and "Awaken, O." Other songs by various vaudeville singers were: "Smarty," "Peek-a-Boo," "Harrigan," "Home-Boy," "A.B.C.'s of the U.S.A.," "The Right Church, But the Wrong Pew," "Make Believe," and others.[70]

By November the company announced in *The New York Dramatic Mirror* that they had over 139 chronophone subjects in English, mostly popular songs by various vaudeville singers with titles like "Cuddle Up a Little Closer," and "I'm Afraid to Come Home in the Dark." Phonoscènes were shown regularly at the People's theatre and the Unique in New York and toured New England in the fall of 1908.[71]

Guy gave birth to her first child, Simone, in 1908, and to her son Reginald on June 26, 1912. She mentions assisting her husband with marketing the *chronophone* in Cleveland, but there was no mention of her directing *phonoscènes* at the Gaumont Flushing Studio.[72]

Lois Weber, an actress and gospel singer, was hired to act for the American Gaumont Chronophones (in 1907 or 1908). Guy credited both her husband and herself with giving Weber her start.[73] From performing, Weber and her husband, Phillip Smalley, went on to scripting and directing a *phonoscène* in English, which became the beginning of Weber's long film career. Although it was most likely that Guy herself had nothing to do with hiring Weber, it stands to reason that the precedent Guy had set with her husband and the Gaumont company probably made it easier for these men to give Weber her chance.

Though the Motion Picture Patents Company as a group had licensed the Gaumont Chronophone, opposition to it at the Edison Company continued to grow. As early as May of 1908, one of his exhibitors in Los Angeles sent Edison a telegram saying, "Can't you

Figure 23. Alice—the exhausted mother

prevent Gaumont Pictures running here under talking picture?" and an answer handwritten on the margin says, "Probably yes."[74] By 1910, *The Moving Picture World* reported:

The Truth of the Gaumont Rumors

FOR SOME TIME there have been repeated and conflicting rumors circulated as to which of the three opposing camps would market the Gaumont product. Both the Independent factions claimed it openly, but George Kleine, who has held the contract for years, preserved his usualy Sphinx-like silence. We are assured that he will continue to market the films of the Gaumont Company, of Paris, as usual, which should set at rest the minds of the licensed exchanges and exhibitors. But the business of the Gaumont Company, of New York (located at Flushing, N.Y), which has been managed from its inception by Mr. Herbert Blache (sic), has now been purchased outright by him and will have no connection whatever with the Gaumont Company of Paris. The purchase includes, of course, all of the American and Canadian rights of the Gaumont Chronophone, which department of the business will now be fostered. It having been reported that Gaumont-American film would be produced in the Flushing plant... they have no immediate intention of doing so.[75]

However, Gaumont managed to maintain his business arrangement with George Kleine until January of 1912.[76]

In addition to Edison's opposition, the *chronophone* had its own problems. The system was expensive to install, lacked the necessary amplification and rarely remained synchronized for long periods of time. By 1910, Gaumont abandoned *chronophone* production in the United States, but he continued to refine the system in France. On February 17, 1911,[77] Gaumont presented nine *phonoscènes* in Paris,[78] all of which required very precise synchronization, such as a lecture by d'Arsonval. It made a very favorable impression on Gaumont's fellow inventors and scientists, who made up the membership of the *Société de la photographie*. (The lecture by Mr. d'Arsonval was also presented to the *Académie des Sciences* on December 27, 1910.)

Buoyed by this success, Gaumont returned to New York with a "new and improved" *chronophone* in 1913. The program, a combination of chronochromes (the Gaumont color process, a predecessor to Technicolor) and *phonoscènes*, was shown at the 39th

Street Theatre in June of 1913 and advertised as "First time in America."[79] But the exhibitors had long memories, and now the field was populated with talking picture systems, including the Cameraphone and Edison's new and improved Kinetophone, as described by *The Moving Picture World*.[80] This article was "the first to gain any considerable recognition in America." Now that Edison had his own system to push and the backing of the other members of the MPPC, Gaumont found the doors to doing business in the U.S. effectively closed to him.

Gaumont was slow to lose his faith in his *chronophone* system. He promoted it tirelessly for over twenty years, from the first presentation in 1902 to June 15, 1922, when he gave a public demonstration of the improvements in the Gaumont Theater. The press responded to this latter demonstration enthusiastically. However, in 1925, the Gaumont Company formed a partnership with the Danish Electrical Fono Films[81] company that represented Peterson and Poulsen to exploit a double band system called "Gaumont, Peterson & Poulsen." Their research resulted in the projection of the first synchronized feature film in France, Marcel Vandal's *L'Eau du Nil* ("The Waters of the Nile") on October 13, 1928. However, the double-band system was not commercially feasible and was abandoned in favor of optical sound, in which the Gaumont Company invested heavily from 1929 on. Léon Gaumont himself retired in August of 1929. It seems fitting that he should have retired when the silent era was clearly over and the synchronized sound system he had championed for twenty years was finally retired from the ring.

The Chronophone in the U.S.

THAT IS THE story of the *chronophone* in Europe. Let us return to developments in the United States.

When she first arrived in New York after the failure in Cleveland, Guy was apparently content to tend to her newborn daughter. As time passed, however, she noticed that the Flushing studio was little used, and, as she put it, "the temptation was too strong. I resolved to rent it and try making a few films."[82] In October of 1910, she formed her own company, Solax, to produce silent films at the Gaumont Flushing studio that would then be distributed by Gaumont.

When Gaumont abandoned *chronophone* production in the United States in 1910, he still had the expensive Flushing plant on his hands. According to articles in *The Moving Picture World* (see quote above), he sold the plant to Herbert Blaché, but it is not clear if this sale ever took place. It is hard to see where Blaché would have gotten the funds, as his nine months without a salary had wiped out his resources. Whatever the arrangement was, the Blachés took over the plant and started up the Solax Company. According to *The Moving Picture World*, Herbert Blaché was the "presiding spirit," George A. Magie was the business manager, and Alice Guy Blaché was in charge of film production.[83] At the same time, Herbert Blaché continued to manage Gaumont's interests in the U.S.

Wheeler Winston Dixon[84] has repeated Marc Wanamaker's statement[85] that both Herbert and Léon Gaumont refused to invest in Guy's Solax Company. It seems quite apparent that Blaché was totally behind his wife's efforts, although until 1913 he continued to manage the Flushing Studio (now the distribution base for Gaumont's silent films) as well. Léon Gaumont might not have invested money, but he did provide distribution, as a handful of the first Solax films[86] were distributed along with the Gaumont films. Solax films also went to Paris to be developed, edited, and titled, which might explain why some of the English inter-titles had a noticeably French flavor. Additionally, Gaumont must have bought Guy's Gaumont shares back from her (as a Gaumont employee, she had been part of a profit

Figure 24. Alice (left) and Herbert (standing in front) with friends

sharing program), and it was from the sale of these shares that Guy came up with $50,000 in start-up funds for Solax.[87]

The distribution arrangement with Gaumont worked well for both parties. Gaumont had gotten rid of the Flushing studio, which was something of a white elephant for him when he cut back on U.S. chronophone production. However, Gaumont's distribution arrangements with the Motion Picture Patents Company (MPPC) were tenuous, with considerable rancor from 1909 on. Gaumont never succeeded in joining the MPPC, and in early 1912, he and George Kleine had a falling out and Gaumont joined the ranks of the independents, who did not receive him graciously.

While Gaumont was dealing with these problems, Solax was doing incredibly well, soon producing two one-reelers a week. Léon Gaumont felt that if Solax was so successful, then the U.S. Gaumont branch, which shared the same plant, should be doing equally well or better. The person caught in the middle of this was Herbert Blaché, whom Gaumont reproached for mismanaging the Gaumont plant both directly and indirectly, in the press. The Blaché's response was two-fold: first, they made sure that Herbert's name would not be associated with Solax in the press, and second, from April of 1911 to 1914, the Solax films were to be distributed by Eclipse, a French film manufacturing company with a world-wide distribution network and a branch in New York.

In the U.S. the Solax films were distributed by the Motion Picture Distributing and Sales Company, a distribution outlet for independents formed in response to the Motion Picture Patents Company. Although there apparently was no rupture between Guy and Gaumont, there was some indication that Gaumont and Herbert Blaché had a falling out. Gaumont felt that Blaché had cheated him on some business deals. He only refered to this indirectly in the letters he and Guy exchanged when both were aged, but Guy picked up on the reference and vehemently protested that Blaché was always an honest businessman (there was some implication that perhaps he was not the best businessman, but he was honest). Guy also reminded Gaumont that Blaché had advised him again and again to pull out of the MPPC and open his own chain of film theaters in the United States.[88] As Richard Abel has pointed out, this would have been impractical, as even Pathé, with its greater financial base, did not attempt it.[89] Gaumont referred repeatedly to the money he invested in the Flushing Studio and then lost because the MPPC had blocked him from exploiting the *chronophone*. In any case, he felt that further investment in the United States would be throwing good money after bad.[90]

In mid-1912, the Motion Picture Distributing and Sales Company split into various factions out of which emerged The Sales Company, The Mutual Film Corporation, and Universal. The division showed that the coalition of Independents was too brittle to cope with the mounting stress caused by a tightening market and the strain of dealing with the litigation for patent infringement of the MPPC. Although Solax joined the Sales Company, the outlook for profit-making was considerably less brighter than it had been in 1910. It could not have happened at a worse time: Guy had just invested everything she had and accumulated huge debts to build the $100,000 Solax Studio in Fort Lee. Construction on the studio was not even complete when she lost her access to wide distribution outlets, just as Gaumont lost his access to licensed distribution. Solax's experience as an independent company that first had MPPC-sanctioned distribution and then was forced to resort to independent distribution outlets is also unique in the history of this period. The change that occurred in mid-1912 would have a disastrous effect on the fortunes of the Solax Company.

3 The Growth of Narrative: Alice Guy's Silent Film Production at Gaumont, 1902–1907

IN CHAPTER ONE, I described the controversy over whether Alice Guy had actually made *La Fée aux choux* when she said she did. For those who accepted Lacassin's argument that *Choux* dated from around 1900 (which Lacassin himself later rescinded)[1] it opened the way for every claim that Alice Guy had ever made about her career to be discredited by former colleagues, competitors, and later film historians. In this study, I have worked painstakingly to document every claim that Guy made about her own work, and it surprised even myself how much of what she wrote when she was in her eighties was completely accurate. In this chapter, I will examine, confirm or refute (sometimes both at once!) the most well-known claims by the naysayers. I will also show how the narrative developments that Alice Guy pioneered at the Gaumont Company were imitated (often not very well) by Pathé. Since the Pathé films were more widely distributed than the Gaumont films, this meant that Alice Guy's influence, her emphasis on character perspective and psychological development, spread far and wide. Because Pathé films are more numerous and more accessible for study, many theories of narrative development rely primarily on a study of Pathé films. These will have to be modified once the early Gaumont films—most of which were directed by Alice Guy or produced under her supervision—are taken into account.

Gaumont: Pathé's Narrative Role Model

IN CHAPTER ONE, I demonstrated how Guy trained herself as a filmmaker by copying, sometimes quite precisely, the Lumière fiction films, especially those produced by Georges Hatot. Once films became longer than twenty meters (one minute of running time) and were no longer used solely for the purposes of demonstrating equipments to clients, such plagiarism was no longer economically or ethically acceptable. And yet plagiarism was rampant. All the film companies imitated each other, sometimes paying actors to serve as spies for them:

> Competition was hard. We were protected by no laws. The extras, employed indifferently by all the studios, served as spies, which obliged us to race to finish first.[2]

> However, other companies were formed and the extras they employed irregularly came to offer us their services. We would engage them and they, naturally, would then hurry to tell our competitors about our activities. It was thus that *La Guérite* appeared simultaneously in the catalogues of both Gaumont and Pathé. When I protested to the latter company I was answered that this was fair warfare and we had only to do the same.[3]

Guy's film, *La Guérite*, was also listed in the Gaumont catalogue as *Douaniers et Contrebandiers* (Gaumont, August 1905). It is described as a comedy, based on the opera *Carmen*: Spanish smugglers wish to cross the frontier, but a soldier stands in their way. Beautiful Carmencita seduces the soldier, and persuades him to make love to her in the sentry box which they have laid down on its side. A supervising officer surprises them and turns the sentry box right side up. He is also charmed by the young lady, but once she knows her friends have crossed the border she escapes from both of them.

Unfortunately, this film no longer seems to exist. The Pathé imitation was entitled *Douanier séduit* (Pathé August 1906). The plot was identical. It also appears to no longer exist.

Another pair of identical films, made by Pathé and Gaumont in 1906, were both entitled *Le Pendu*. Of the Gaumont film (Gaumont Catalogue no. 1562) all that appears to survive is the scenario in the Bibliothèque Nationale collection. In the Gaumont version, a pair of newlyweds are enjoying themselves on the sofa, while the wife's mother sits aside and feels neglected. She goes to her own room, finds her phonograph, and brings it into the living room and plays it loudly. The husband gets annoyed by this, but when he reproaches his mother-in-law his wife scolds him until finally he is run out of the house. In despair, he decides to hang himself. A pair of lovers sees him hanging in the forest, still flailing. Instead of trying to help him, they ask help of other passersby in the forest, who go looking for a policeman, who comes and look at the still-flailing man then goes back and looks for his superior officers. Before someone finally cuts the rope, a photographer takes a photograph. Finally, the man is cut down, now apparently quite lifeless, when his wife and mother-in-law turn up. The wife's sobs have no effect, but the mother-in-law cranks up the phonograph again which gets the dead man up on his feet and scurrying away.

The Pathé version of *Le Pendu* stars Max Linder. Linder comes courting a young lady with flowers; she likes him, but the parents send him away. The girl would not disobey her parents, so he leaves the flowers sadly on the doorstep. Outside the gate, he takes out a gun and tries to shoot himself, but lacks the courage, so he goes into the forest and hangs himself. A man digging for truffles finds him and gets a policeman, who comes and looks at the flailing man, then gets a cavalry officer, who searches for another cavalry officer, who looks at the still-flailing man and goes to the village to get a doctor. The doctor tells two servants with a ladder to follow him and finally the man is cut down. His sweetheart and her parents arrive on the scene; she throws herself on him to no effect, but a nearby cyclist manages to pump him back to life with his bicycle pump, and this time, the parents agree to the marriage.

It seems clear that the Pathé version is later: it is more romantic but also less farcical. By making the people who should be helping into officials of progressively higher rank, a satirical criticism of institutional bureaucracies is built into the plot. Such improvements are one sign of a remake. What remains the same is the hilarious suspense of watching the hanging man flail around as no one seems to be able to help him. Unfortunately, the original Gaumont film is not available for a closer analysis.

For the next three cases, all the films still exist, facilitating comparison. The first is *Le Matelas alcoolique* (Gaumont Catalogue no. 1550, November-December 1906). Pathé remade this film as *Le Matelas de la mariée*, (directed by Charles Lucien Lépine, December 1906). The films have an almost identical plot. A couple needs a mattress restuffed, and a female mattress-mender takes it away. She sets it up outside, slices open the mattress, and begins to work. In time she feels the need for refreshment and goes into a local bar. Meanwhile, a drunkard stumbles along, finds the mattress inviting, and settles into it, completely disappearing into the stuffing. The mattress-mender returns and sews him up into the mattress. She then tries to return it to its owners, but finds that the mattress has taken on a life of its own. It rolls her down a hill, leads her to fall off a bridge, pulls her into a pit, and so on. Finally she gets it to its owners, who quickly make up the bed, only to find that their sleep is interrupted by the mattress's violent shaking. All ends well when the mattress is sliced open again and the drunkard is released.

It seems apparent that the Gaumont is the original. The Pathé copy is not very literal, but it is also an improvement in various respects: the pacing is quicker, and the owners of the mattress are on their wedding night, shown in a medium long shot, so that the comic potential in their eagerness to get to bed is fully exploited, whereas the Gaumont version has a much older couple shot in a very long shot. However, this emphasis takes away the main issue which is the expression of the mattress-mender's forbidden desires.

In her autobiography, Guy wrote a detailed account of how she got the idea for the Gaumont version of this film. In spite of this account, Frédérique Moreau and Henri Bousquet have argued that this film was directed by Romeo Bossetti.[4] It is possible that Guy claimed authorship because she wrote the scenario, and then assigned Bossetti to direct it. But since Bossetti played the drunk in the film and presumably spent most of the shooting time inside the mattress, it is hard to imagine him directing the film at the same time.

Guy's explanation of how she got the idea for the film leaves very little room for doubt:

> Searching for a setting for a film... I [saw] a mattress-maker had installed her frame for stretching the canvas. She finished filling it with wool which she had just carded. For I know not what reason, she left her work and went away for a few minutes. Almost at once a drunk arrived, climbed the mound and rested in contemplation before the half-finished mattress.[5]

It must also be noted that the Lumières made several comic scenes involving mattress-menders that could have served as inspiration for this film. And the idea was also the subject of cartoons, as shown in Donald Crafton's book on Emil Cohl.[6] Comparison of how both companies treated the same theme, and the fact that the Pathé is a close imitation of the Gaumont film, supports Alan Williams' statement that:

> We will never know for certain, but it was presumably Alice Guy who created and nurtured the mood of excitement and sheer

aesthetic pleasure that one senses in so many prewar Gaumont films, including the ones made after her departure from the Paris studio. It is this, finally, which distinguishes the larger and more profitable Pathé film operation from the smaller one founded by Léon Gaumont and shaped by Alice Guy: the people at the latter company took more risks, had more joy in their work. Ideologically, Pathé Frères was far more liberal (Gaumont, Guy and later Feuillade all had pronounced right-wing leanings); humanely, the Gaumont company was the more liberated, its films ultimately more liberating.[7]

In the Gaumont film, the mattress, a symbol of matrimony as well as sex, is removed from the domestic sphere as depicted by a very sketchy bedroom set. Once out in the field it is possessed by the most appropriate symbol of the irrepressible and aggressive spirit of the street: a drunkard.

Although Guy originally intended the mattress's opponent to be a male porter, the film is much funnier and more satirical when it is the female mattress-mender. Though the character is played by a man in drag, in keeping with industry practice when stuntwork was required, the source of humor is the same: a woman must call upon half a dozen men in various public places as she wrestles with her runaway symbol of desire and domesticity. Ironically, after failing to get any real assistance from all those men on the street, it is the (female) building concierge who helps the mattress-mender resolve the problem by giving her a tool with which to slit open the mattress, releasing her animus (to put it in Jungian terms). Only then do the police arrive and cart both the drunk and the mattress-mender to jail, where, one presumes, the mattress-mender and her runaway desires will be tamed.

In her autobiography, Guy recounts how this film brought her her first taste of fame. The Greniers, a vaudeville family, had rented the film and invited her to appear at the first screening. After the peals of laughter had died down, they presented her to the audience—one of the few times this occurred during her Gaumont career.[8]

Drunkards, such as the one in *Matelas alcoolique*, represent the irrepressible and destructive social elements usually found on the street. Poachers often served the same function for films set in the countryside in many early Gaumont films (and in films by Pathé as well), as can be seen in the next pair of films I have found for comparison. These two films show that Pathé often imitated Gaumont films shot-for-shot. These are Gaumont's *Le Fils du garde-chasse* (August 1906) and Pathé's *La Revanche de l'enfant* (January 1907).

The Gaumont story begins with a gamekeeper about to go out on his rounds. He prepares his rifle and kisses his wife and two sons goodbye. In the woods, he catches two poachers red-handed and chases them. After a prolonged chase, the poachers cross a plank that bridges an abyss, but when the gamekeeper follows they upend the plank so that he falls to his death. The boy has followed his father and witnesses the murder. He runs back to his mother and gives her the news. Her scene of mourning is staged like a pietà scene (imitating Catholic imagery of the Virgin Mary in mourning at the foot of the cross or with the dead Christ in her arms), a visual signature of Guy's. The boy spots the two poachers and follows them to a bar, where he hides under a table while they drink and flirt with the waitress. He then attacks them, which brings the police, and another chase ensues. One poacher is shot down by the police, the other falls to his death in the same abyss where the gamekeeper meets his fate.

Figure 25. *La Revanche de l'enfant*, a Pathé copy of
Alice Guy's film *Le Fils du garde-chasse*

Pathé copied this film almost shot-for-shot in *La Revanche de l'enfant*.[9] The Pathé film is faster paced; the actors are not given the time to emote like in the Gaumont film. There are some minor differences: the boy is younger than the boy in the Gaumont film, and he has a little sister instead of a little brother. As Richard Abel pointed out, the ending in the Pathé film seems rather forced.[10] Instead of ending with the boy achieving revenge at the edge of the abyss where his father met his death as the Gaumont film does, a kind of coda is added when the mother throws herself over the body of her dead husband at the foot of the precipice. Perhaps the most significant difference is that in the Pathé film the boy strikes the poacher with a knife (before the gendarme arrives), while in the Gaumont film the boy simply makes the poacher so anxious that he loses his footing and falls to his death. It seems clear, in this case, that all the Pathé changes are motivated to punch-up the drama of particular scenes in their copy of a film that was already successful for Gaumont; in the process the unity of character and narrative is weakened.

Hunters and gamekeepers were also recurring characters in early Gaumont films, with the gamekeepers representing honor and order. The deep-focus in *Le Fils du garde-chasse* and the use of the landscape was characteristic of Guy's visual aesthetic, also apparent in *La Passion* (Gaumont, 1906), her masterpiece of the Gaumont period. The actress who played the mother in *Le Fils du garde-chasse* was the same actress who led Gaumont to the forefront of narrative development when Alice Guy staged her in a series of dramatic close-ups that propelled the narrative in *Madame a des envies* (Gaumont, 1906). By copying the film so closely, Pathé was borrowing Guy's visual signatures in order to improve their own films.

The next pair of films I have for comparison are Gaumont's *La Marâtre* (September, 1906) directed by Alice Guy and Pathé's *Mauvaise Mère* (November-December, 1906). Guy's film begins in the home of a simple workman, in great disorder since he is a widower with a young son. A neighbor comes in with her small daughter and sets everything right. Apparently he has hired her to do this, because he pays her at the end of the scene. In the next scene, we see the woman in her own home, which is so well kept that it appears luxurious compared to the widower's. She primps at a mirror, then hastily starts ironing when she hears a knock at the door. The father comes in, gives her flowers, and she flirts with him as she pulls the petals off a flower, "he loves me, he loves me not." When she finishes—he does love her—he proposes and hands her a ring. She reminds him that she has a child, and he reminds her that he has a child. She agrees to marry him and they shake hands. When he leaves, she admires her ring with joy.

In the next tableaux, they are seen living in his cramped quarters. After the father goes to work, the stepmother shows her true colors, abusing the boy while favoring her own child. Even when the father returns, the boy has trouble getting his father's attention; when the father notices he is crying, the stepmother says she had to punish him. The boy gets a reprieve when his father sends him for tobacco.

The next scene is the only exterior shot in the film: the boy goes to the cemetery and weeps over his mother's grave. However, it is not his mother who saves him, but a constable who pulls him up and hauls him to the police station. The police station is a set, but it is clearly a public space, with the Chief of Police enthroned behind his desk and flanked by several attendants. (Similar police stations would be a staple of Guy's Solax films.) The father comes in and tells the police that his boy has disappeared. The police says they have a boy matching the description and the father looks very relieved. The boy is brought in and his bruises revealed. The father takes his son home and shows the woman the bruises; she turns away from the sight in shame, which infuriates him, so he throws her on the floor and is about to beat her when the boy steps between them. She jumps up and tries to embrace her husband, but he picks up her child and throws both of them out of the door. The father sits down and pulls the boy on his lap, with no sign of regret for the departed wife. The last line of the script reads: "Having found each other again, father and son embrace." This line reinforces the theme of the film, that the primary bond is between father and son and not between father and wife.

Pathé copied this film very faithfully in *La Mauvaise Mère* (Pathé 1906). In the Pathé version the woman comes in to clean, but she is not paid for her cleaning services. Her daughter is also slightly older than the daughter in the Gaumont films. But the action of the film is the same: the father is sewing a pair of his son's pants while the boy sleeps, the woman comes in, finishes the sewing, sweeps the room, and cleans the dishes. All the while (unlike in the Gaumont film, where she was merely efficient) she is flirting with him. And she makes a point of kissing the sleeping boy goodbye with a great show of affection, a bit of conniving missing from the Gaumont version.

The second scene is her home, which is not so different from his. She primps, irons, he comes in, he gives her flowers, she plays "he loves me, he loves me not," he proposes, gives her a ring, they embrace and then shake hands. A difference with this couple is that it seems to be a more romantic attraction and less a relationship of convenience as in the Gaumont film.

In the third scene, they are living together in a new home, which is still a poor one. She feeds breakfast to her husband and to the boy, who looks silent and sullen. After the man leaves she beats the boy, then coddles her own child.

We see a brief transition scene as the boy leaves school with a fellow student. He tells his friend how his stepmother beats him. The other boy's mother comes to get him and leaves. (This scene is a departure from the Gaumont original.)

At the house, the minute the boy comes in the door, the woman starts beating him. The father comes in and sees the boy crying, and she says he needed to be punished. The father sends him out for cigarettes. After the boy leaves, the father starts coddling the girl, much to the stepmother's delight, a detail also missing from the Gaumont version.

In another departure from the Gaumont original, the boy returns and, unable to bring himself to go inside, leaves the cigarettes on the doorstep, then goes to the cemetery. In the cemetery he weeps over his mother's grave, and a policeman comes and leads him away, as in the original.

In the police station, the policeman brings the boy and his bruises are revealed. The policeman who found him is sent out with the boy's jacket. In another departure from the original, the policeman goes to the construction site where the father is working and shows the man the boy's jacket so that the man will follow him. Back at the police station, the boy's bruises are revealed to the father, who pays little attention to the boy but swears to the police officers that he will correct the problem.

Back at home, father walks in and shows the woman the boy's bruises; she turns away. The man lunges at her, but the boy steps between them. The father pushes the boy away, then gets the little girl and thrusts her and her mother out the door. Then he sits in his armchair and hangs his head, already saddened by what he has done. Meanwhile, the boy sits in a corner, completely ignored. He approaches his father tentatively, kneels at his feet. Gradually the father realizes he is there and pulls the boy onto his lap. Finally the boy is getting some affection, but the father stops to shake his fist at the door the woman left through.

In his paper given at the DOMITOR[11] Conference in Paris in 1996, Tom Gunning pointed out that the Pathé film did not privilege any one character. For Gunning, the film appeared to be about the boy whom the stepmother abused but at the end, the focus shifted to the father when he tried to beat his wife in retaliation. Gunning saw this as evidence of the retarded state of filmic narrative in France, compared to the unity of Griffith's Biograph films just two years later.

Gunning's reading shows the dangers of privileging the Pathé films as representative of the period and also shows the need for making Gaumont films more accessible to scholars.

The difference between the Pathé and the Gaumont film seem to come from a desire on the part of the filmmakers at Pathé to make the ending more dramatic. Many of the Pathé changes can be seen as improvements: the flirting between the man and the woman justifies the marriage and also the father's blindness to his son's torture; the woman's efforts to keep her abuse a secret make it easier for us to believe he did not notice it. Her conniving also clearly marks her out as the villain. Having the police go looking for the father seems more logical than the Gaumont plot where the father arrives looking for his son, but it also takes the focus off the boy. Instead, what this story is about is the relationship between a man and his second wife. In the Gaumont film, the father is clearly depicted as culpable, and expresses grief and guilt to his son at the end of the film; but the Pathé film makes the woman the entire source of the problem, and the man's desire for the woman is what gets him into trouble.

The Gaumont film clearly focuses on the boy as principal character throughout the film. Almost the entire narrative, except for the scene where his father proposes, is told from his point of view. Even the moment when the father attempts to beat the stepmother is simply the set-up to enable the boy to stop the beating and show his stepmother the kind of mercy she never showed him. Although Guy tells the film with fewer scenes and with staged tableaux, the emphasis on the boy and his relationship to his father is clear. Guy seems to take it for granted that a stepmother is automatically bad for a child, and so the blame is laid at the feet of the father for remarrying at all. By shifting the focus on the relationship between husband and wife, the Pathé film emphasizes that remarrying was not the father's problem but choosing his mate poorly. But the filmmakers at Pathé were not committed enough to their version of the film, and so their film ended up with a mix of the original and the new, and character coherency was lost as a result. And yet character coherency—the emphasis on one character's psychological perspective—was Alice Guy's innovation, even if her Pathé imitators did not recognize it for what it was. In other words, though Guy did not direct the first fiction film, she greatly advanced the practice of psychological narrative in the cinema.

The Problems of Attribution

THAT PATHÉ LOOKED up to Gaumont films for material in this way also lends support to William's statement that though Pathé was better capitalized, the filmmakers at Gaumont were more inspired. But how was Pathé able to make such close copies of these films? Guy blamed the extras who worked for both companies. However, plagiarizing films was not the work of actors but directors, even if they relied on actors for information. In this case it would mean Ferdinand Zecca. And yet, it was to Zecca himself that Guy probably complained about Pathé's plagiarism, as he had worked for her briefly.

Ferdinand Zecca (1864-1947) was an entertainer of the Café-Concert when Charles Pathé hired him to perform songs and monologues to be recorded for the phonograph in 1899. In 1900, Zecca was put in charge of the Pathé exhibit at the *Exposition Universelle*, and there Charles Pathé asked him if he was interested in assisting him in the production of story films. Zecca agreed, and within a few weeks was put in charge of film production, a position he essentially retained until he retired in 1939.[12]

Just as Guy started out by imitating Lumière films, Zecca started out by imitating English trick films and comedies. Although he is now better known as the father of the "naturalistic story film" (also known as "low life and crime melodrama,") he at first thought the *féeries*, or fairy-tale films, had the most commercial potential. This was not a surprising conclusion, since Georges Méliès, whom Zecca also freely imitated, was having great commercial success with just these types of films, featuring fairies, magicians, magic tricks (mostly dependent on stops for their effects), and elaborate sets. Zecca himself directed a series of these films, and remembered his 1901 work, *Sept châteaux du diable* (The Devil's Seven Castles) with special fondness.[13] By 1904 this relationship was reversed, and Méliès began imitating Zecca's melodramas as the popularity of the *féeries* faded.[14]

This switch-over in Zecca's choice of subject matter confirms Alan Williams' statement that "unlike the Lumière and Méliès operations, Pathé Frères was not doomed by any maladaptive compulsion to repeat film subjects, or other commercial strategies, once their profit potential began to decline."[15] In addition to copying from other film manufacturers, Zecca adapted material from other media: "music hall skits, soft-core postcard pornography, dance, sports, biblical illustration, dirty stories."[16] Other filmmakers, including Alice Guy, did the same, but Zecca did it systematically, mixed things up, and then his imitations were imitated in turn. It is fairly impossible, then, to really ascertain what idea was original to whom; but by comparing films that Pathé copied from Gaumont, we can isolate one strand in narrative development.

As noted above, Pathé-Frères was much more aggressive in terms of developing markets for its films than Gaumont was. Pathé built its first glass-house studio in 1902; Gaumont in 1905, (by which time Pathé had already built two more). Charles Pathé was much more of a risk-taker than Gaumont, and had the funds to try everything and anything (from a successful phonograph business). From 1900 to 1939, except for one break, Zecca was the fulcrum through which every kind of cultural influence went in and many kinds of films came out.

In 1904, according to Francis Lacassin, Alice Guy stumbled across Ferdinand Zecca in the streets of La Villette, selling soap door-to-door, and wetting it so that it would weigh more. Moved, Guy immediately hired him as her assistant (up until this moment, according to her memoirs, she had none).[17] In addition to assisting her with several films, Zecca also directed several films himself, most notably *Les Méfaits d'une tête de veau* (The misdeeds of a Calf's Head), one of Gaumont's greatest successes. Ironically, this is one of the few early Gaumont films directly attributed to Alice Guy, by one of her other assistants, Etienne Arnaud.[18] Guy herself always refuted this attribution and credited Zecca. It is easy to understand Arnaud's mistake, as he did not come to work for Guy at Gaumont himself until two years after Zecca had been there; by the time Arnaud was hired,

Zecca had resolved his problems with Pathé and had returned to work there, and Guy was again solely in charge of film production at Gaumont.

The attribution of *Les Méfaits d'une tête de veau* is further complicated by the fact that a film of that title was listed in the Gaumont 1901 catalogue, but Zecca apparently was not "rescued" and hired by Guy until 1904. Again, the explanation is simple: an earlier version of the film was made in 1901, and then remade by Zecca in 1904. However, Guy attributed the 1901 version to Zecca. (See footnote 4 on page 304). It appears that Gaumont commonly remade successful films, especially comic films, as shorter and longer versions of the same titles that appear throughout the catalogues. For example, Arnaud's *Un coup de vent*, the first film Arnaud directed and first script Feuillade wrote for Gaumont in 1906, could have been a remake of two comic films featuring clowns entitled *Les Chapeaux I* and *Les Chapeaux II* listed in the 1903 catalogue. There also appears to have been two versions of *Les Petits coupeurs du bois vert* and *Le Déménagement de la cloche de bois*. It seems likely that Guy simply showed her assistants the shorter versions and gave them the assignment to produce a longer, expanded version. This was a practice she carried over to the United States, since in her Fort Lee studio she made longer, more elaborate versions of some of the films she had made for Gaumont (most notably *Les Résultats du féminisme*, see Chapter Six).

In the Gaumont filmography she put together for *Gaumont: 90 ans de cinéma*,[19] Frédérique Moreau credited Zecca with directing *Les Méfaits d'une tête de veau*, which was listed in the 1901 catalogue, and pointed out the discrepancy between Guy's account that she hired Zecca in 1904 and the listing of the film title in the 1901 catalogue. However, the 1901 film was listed as being only 22 meters long, which would take about a minute and a half to play. The Zecca film, which still exists, is at least 100 meters long and takes over 10 minutes to play. In addition, the plot of the Zecca film is about a man who sits down to eat at an outdoor cafe, is served a head of veal (literally, a calf's head) which affixes itself to his head. As he goes running down the street in his efforts to get the calf's head off of his own head, he creates pandemonium, and a large crowd begins to follow him, until finally he manages to get the head off. The film fits squarely into the genre of chase films, and is a very good example of that.

The description of the 1901 film in the catalogue, however is quite different:

> A calf's head escapes from the plate where it's been set and hangs itself back up on a nail. The butcher puts it back on the plate and cleans it with rage. The enchanted head then sets itself on the butcher's shoulders, while the butcher's head takes the place of the calf's head on the center of the plate. The calf's head, having become the butcher, takes revenge by scraping away at the butcher's head on the plate, half suffocating it with parsley and then taking the pot the butcher was washing the calf's head in earlier and forcibly pressing it down on the butcher's skull.[20]

The film is listed as "a comedy of transformations" and is clearly a *féerie* in the genre of Méliès' films (by 1901 Méliès had made several films where his head magically appeared in places it did not belong).[21] Unless Zecca worked for her in 1901 instead of 1904, this version of the film is clearly attributable to Alice Guy.

Henri Gallet's name also emerges in accounts of cross-feeding between Gaumont and Pathé. According to Sadoul, he was hired as Guy's first assistant sometime in 1904, having previously worked as *bonimenteur* or film narrator in Montmartre.[22] Sadoul interviewed Gallet in the forties, when Alice Guy was living outside of France. Gallet claimed to have directed a variety of films that Guy attributed to herself, including *La Fée aux choux*, which he said was made in 1904. (As we have seen in Chapter One, this is clearly not true, as the first two versions of *Fée aux choux* were made before 1900, and *Sage-femme*, the second remake, in 1902.) Gallet also accused Zecca of plagiarizing his films. At the same time, he was accused by Gaumont of being a stool-pigeon for Pathé. He was fired from Gaumont in 1905 and became the manager of a theater. Guy vehemently denied that Gallet had directed any films for Gaumont; she claimed not to remember him at all, but admitted he could have worked there as an extra.[23] The fact that Gallet left Gaumont under difficult circumstances and that he never made another film again, in addition to the fact that several of his claims were easily disproved, cast doubt on all of his claims.

One thing that does ring true is the accusation of Pathé's plagiarization. The very drive that made Pathé so successful also made it starved for story product, while Gaumont's smaller size, more compressed working conditions and Guy's emphasis on story gave the company the advantage in the area of narrative development. About this period, Abel has said: "For the mass production and marketing that Pathé pioneered between 1904 and 1907 coincided with the waning of the cinema of attractions and the emergence of an increasingly narrativized cinema."[24] Abel gives a brilliant analysis of the transition from the cinema of attractions to a narrative cinema and uses examples from various French film companies, not just Pathé. However, it seems clear that the transition to a more narrativized cinema was well underway at Gaumont before 1904; much of this was due to the way Gaumont's films, especially those by Guy, focused on, and developed empathy for, a single character, with a resulting clarity and forcefulness in the narrative.

The Development of Point of View Sequences

HOW THIS NARRATIVE unity evolved can be traced in the development of point of view sequences in each company. André Gaudreault and others have shown that point of view sequences in early cinema consisted of two-shot sequences: a shot where we see the character looking and the shot of what he sees.[25] What was seen in point of view shots in early films was usually a spectacle typical of the cinema of attractions aesthetic.

In the shift to narrative, point of view sequences changed. Instead of two shots, they now have three: the looking shot, the shot of what is seen (also called a point-of-view shot), and the reaction shot, which classically consists of a tighter version of the looking shot.

Precursors to the three-shot point of view sequence can be found in many early films, especially films where characters look through keyholes or into ocular devices such as a microscope (see for example Emil Cohl's *Les Joyeux Microbes* (Gaumont 1909), *Les Locataires d'à-côté* (Gaumont 1909) and *Le Miroir magique* (Gaumont 1909). The reactions of these characters are then shown in the long shot; the audience reads their reaction in their body language, and not on their face.

The earliest close-ups were included in films for their spectacle value. Close-ups of characters at the end of the film, or emblematic shots, were used for closure and to conflate the identity of actor and character.

A certain type of emblematic shot also served as precursors to the classical reaction shot (and hence to the latter use of the close-up for character empathy and identification). Two examples can be seen in Pathé's film called *La Peine du talion* (February 1906) and the Gaumont film, directed by Alice Guy, called *Madame a des envies* (1906).

The Pathé film is about a butterfly collector who is brought to judgement by the butterfly fairies. His punishment is that he will be pinned to a rock in the same way that he pinned butterflies into boxes; he is to learn remorse by suffering the pain he inflicted on the butterflies. The pinned man is filmed from the ceiling. From that angle—an angle that does not match the shots before or after it—we can see that he is lying on a wooden stage, and no effort is made to conceal that fact, although the scene is ostensibly taking place in the woods. Since we see the man from head to foot as he flails like a bug, the shot is not a close up, but it does eliminate all extraneous detail—such as the woodland stage setting—that would take attention away from his emotional reaction to his predicament. Similar shots were common in Passion films, usually a medium shot of Christ after he was flogged and labelled *Ecce Homo*. See for example Zecca's *La Passion*, 1907, or a medium long-shot of Veronica holding up her veil, as in Guy's *La Passion* (Gaumont 1906).

The close-ups in *Madame a des envies* are related to this type of reaction shot. The woman sees the sugar stick, craves it, steals it, and then there is a cut to a close-up that serves the same function as the shot of the pinned man in *La Peine du talion*: we watch her enjoyment of her prize, depicted through amusing facial contortions as she sucks on the phallic sugar stick in a very suggestive manner. The shot is a medium close-up, or bust-shot, but unlike the earlier emblematic shots, the actor does not make eye contact with us, she remains sealed behind her fourth wall, securely enclosed in her own diegetic world.

And as with the Pathé film, no effort has been made to match the neutral backdrop in this shot to the actual location where the establishing shot was filmed. It would not have been so difficult to move in for a close-up on location, but instead, the actor was apparently filmed in the studio.

Alan Williams has pointed out the "noticeable visual conflict [that] arises between the backdrop in one scene and location shooting in another, and sometimes also between one backdrop and the next." This conflict between set and location is visible to some extent in Guy's *La Passion*, and even more so in her Gaumont melodramas.

Williams labeled the characteristic mismatch between set and location a characteristic of the Gaumont company's house style, along with heavy reliance on locations and an art direction that was "less refined, but generally also more flexible and expressive" than Pathé's. Williams credits Guy with originating the prevalence of location shooting: "Guy was the first producer/director methodically to scout for locations, and she often made up a film story to fit a visually interesting location or event".[26]

I believe that the mismatch between backgrounds when it came to reaction shots and the original location or stage settings for the master scene was deliberate, a "subjective insert" as Elizabeth Ezra[27] has labelled it. Such shots provide a way of pausing the forward movement of the plot in order to allow the audience to fully empathize with the reaction of the character. The close-ups in *Envies* are a particularly good example of this.

Richard Abel notes that Pathé pioneered mass production and marketing between 1904 and 1907. The transition to mass production coincided with the transition from the cinema of attractions to an increasingly narrativized cinema. Other scholars (such as Noël Burch, Barry Salt and Kristin Thompson) have posited a binary model of film practice from a "primitive" to a "classical" cinema. Still other scholars (Tom Gunning, André Gaudreault, Ben Brewster, Charles Musser and Thomas Elsaesser) posit a tripartite model, which includes "a transitional period distinct from, while sharing characteristics with, both the cinema of attractions and the later classical narrative cinema."[28]

Abel categorizes the period of transition into four different models of transformation which he sees as having developed during this period "to negotiate between the competing interests of spectacle attractions and those of spatial contiguity, temporal linearity, and narrative continuity."[29] The four models are: the *Bricolage* model, the Comic Chase model, the Erotic model, and the Compound model.[30] *Bricolage* films combine fiction footage with *actualité* footage or two genres or two distinct visual approaches. The most well known of these is Pathé's *Un tour du monde d'un policier* (1906), in which staged scenes of a detective chasing a thief around the world are intercut with Pathé travel film footage.

Comic chase films worked on a model of "repetition with slight variation" to quote both Abel and Musser.[31] "Rather than accumulate a variety of elements around a unifying action or theme, [comic chase films] constructed a synthetic space through a series of loosely linked shots in which one character was pursued by another (or else a whole bunch of others), each of which repeatedly moved into and out of one frame after another in a continuous line of action."[32] The most well known example of this type of film is Pathé's *La Course à la perruque*, (1906), in which some boys attach a balloon to an old woman's hat; the hat floats away, taking her wig with it, which starts a chase all over Paris. *Grève des bonnes* (Pathé 1906) and Guy's *La Glu* (1906), both discussed in detail in Chapter 6, also fall into this category. A further example is Gaumont's *Un Coup de vent* (1906), in which a man chases his hat all over various humorous obstacles. Abel notes that there is no reason that the man should finally catch his hat at the moment he does, on a coal heap, except it allows for a final racist gag when the man is black-faced by the soot.

Abel's third model of transformation is usually used in erotic films, and often involving voyeurism and point-of-view sequences, (in this reference, POV sequences have two shots) that may have evolved from the *cabinet* or peep show popular in French houses of prostitution.[33] Pathé's *Un Coup d'œuil par étage* (1904) is a good example: the concierge of an apartment building pretends to be dusting and delivering mail, but actually he is stopping to peer into the keyhole of the apartment on each floor. What he sees are three unrelated scenes (each scene is a one-shot Pathé film of earlier vintage; one of them is Dranem in *Ma tante*). After gazing through each keyhole, the character reacts by stepping up to the camera and miming what he has just seen. Through the fourth keyhole he sees a young man struggling to put out a fire, and the rest of the film becomes a chase-narrative about putting out the fire.

The bust-shots, or reaction shots, in *Madame a des envies* also fit into this model. The magnification quality of the bust-shot has a comparable effect to the POV spectacle-shots that the peeping-Tom characters of these Pathé films were treated with; except now the peeping Tom character is eliminated. For Guy, there is no reason for a character to mediate between the audience and the spectacle of the woman practicing fellatio on various phallic objects. The reaction of the peeping Tom character is also eliminated; in its place we have the pure enjoyment of the woman herself, who is both spectacle and subject of the film, all at once.

Abel's fourth model of the transition from attraction to narrative is the compound model, typical of dramatic and realist films. "The compound model depended on contiguous changes in framing or camera position—whether through camera movement or through cutting to a different perspective of either the same space or else an adjacent space... [these frame changes] became narrativized or remotivated through a continuous flow of action, not only to construct a synthetic, diegetic space for that action, but also to elicit, suspend, and fulfill narrative expectations... [the] story now served as the dominant principle of organization."[34] Abel then goes on to list and analyze a series of examples, most of which involve a patriarchal plot: the protection and preservation of a man's property, or his honor, or the honor of his family. Pathé's *La Revanche de l'enfant* is among these.[35] Abel praises the use of deep-space in the Pathé film and notes how the act of listening forwards the plot (the gamekeeper stops to listen and hears the poachers before he sees them, for example). He also critiques the awkwardness of certain moments, such as the grand-guignol ending in which the narrative focus suddenly switches from the boy to his mother who throws herself over her husband's body. But as I described above, the deep-space and the listening aspects of the film were copied from Guy's film, *Le Fils du garde-chasse*, while the difference in ending can be accounted for as an attempt to improve on the Gaumont ending by sensationalizing it. I would also classify Guy's *La Fiancée du volontaire*, (Gaumont 1906) as an example of Abel's compound model. This film (discussed further below) has very advanced character development for the period and compares well to many similar melodramas made in the mid-1910s.

The Influence of Alice Guy

ZECCA'S WAS NOT the only career that Guy had an influence on. She also trained Arnaud, Feuillade, Menessier, and Jasset. Alan Williams credits Guy with creating the Gaumont "house-style" and with

> developing and training a team of filmmakers who would be, quite simply, the best in the business, including perhaps most notably her successor as head of production at the company, the great Louis Feuillade. But if Feuillade, and others of the new generation which came to prominence around 1907–08, achieved greatness, it was by standing, as it were, on the shoulders of Alice Guy.[36]

In her memoirs, Guy said that having Zecca as her assistant for just a few weeks made her realize how badly she needed one. She began with Arnaud and then Louis Feuillade, whom she trained as writers and directors, and the set designer Henri Menessier and his assistant Ben Carré, both of whom later followed her to the United States.[37] In 1905, she hired Victorin Jasset, who had worked as a stage-director of large spectacles at the Hippodrome. Jasset directed the exteriors of the Gaumont version of *La Passion* (1906) and was also in charge of the crowd scenes (the film had a cast of 300). Having all of those extras get their orders from Jasset probably contributed to the film being credited to him for many years. However, it is one of the few films that Gaumont attributed to Guy from the beginning. According to Guy, she was introduced as the film's director when it was screened for the *Société de photographie de Paris*. She pointed out that the bulletin of that showing attributed the film to her: "Fortunately for me, as many persons tried to take credit for that work." Slide noted in a footnote to that remark that this was "presumably a reference to Georges Sadoul's crediting the film ...to Jasset... with the assistance of Georges Hatot."[38]

The idea that Alice Guy had only received, and continued to retain, her post as head of production at Gaumont because she was Léon Gaumont's mistress started with Jasset. Again, the source for this claim needs to be examined. Jasset was a flamboyant character, full of life and verve, and a womanizer. This went against the grain of both Guy, his boss, and Gaumont himself. The last straw came when Jasset was accused of statutory rape by one of the Gaumont extras. Guy fired him on the spot, and when Jasset appealed to Gaumont, Gaumont upheld her decision. This event did not hurt Jasset's career at all: he went on to make films for the Eclipse Company and then to pioneer the development of serials at Éclair. An exhaustive survey of all the extant correspondance between Guy and Gaumont, and interviews with Alice Guy's daughter, Simone Blaché, and her daughter-in-law, Roberta Blaché, show no indication whatsoever that a love affair between Guy and Gaumont ever existed. In addition, Alan Williams has pointed out that though Léon Gaumont could easily have kept a mistress, he was too conscious of appearances, and too conservative to pick her from among his employees.[39]

It seems clear, however, that Gaumont supported Guy's tenure at his company from beginning to end, and continued to support her when she was running the Solax Company as an independent producer on the Gaumont Flushing studio "lot." Gaumont acted this way towards most of his employees, many of whom worked for his company throughout their entire professional lives. Though Guy could count on Gaumont's support, she was not universally popular with her colleagues. In her memoirs, she recounts how she stopped the casting director, Vincent Denizot, from claiming a percentage from the actors' weekly salaries, and how he tried to get revenge by having a gypsy harass her on a set for a film about gypsies.[40] She also recounts how the head of the set shops, René Decaux, cut up the flats painstakingly painted for *La Passion* in order to wrap the set-shop pipes and prevent them from freezing. The rivalry between Decaux and Guy must have been intense: Decaux wanted to direct films, and did direct some phonoscènes (while Guy was in Spain with Anatole Thiberville making phonoscènes there). The fact that Decaux made no more films after that indicates that he was probably not very good at it. However, he was a close friend of Gaumont's. So Gaumont probably found it difficult to mediate in this case. The sets for *La Passion* were replicated in just ten days "as the disgusted employees sincerely wanted to make up for [Decaux's] action."[41] This was not the only time Decaux would use such methods to disrupt Guy's production. The cost overrun on *La Passion* meant that Guy had to give an account to the Gaumont board of directors, and it was suggested that she was no longer up to the job of running Gaumont's film production. However, the president of the board, Gustave Eiffel, took her side, and she remained in her post.[42]

The Miracle Films

DURING HER 11-YEAR tenure as head of film production for Gaumont, Guy regularly produced a certain kind of film that I have dubbed "the miracle film," because a miracle in keeping with Catholic faith or folklore was always at the center of the story. Guy only produced these Catholic films for Gaumont, although a connection or evolution can be traced between these "miracle films" and some of the fairy tales and dramas she produced for Solax.

The "miracle films" could be comedies, fairy-tales (about Santa Claus, for example) or serious films, like the Passion plays, but they all have one thing in common: they revolve around some article of Catholic faith or folklore. In every film, some kind of miracle is the center event of the plot; Guy sometimes threw everything she knew about plot structure or character consistency out the window in the service of this "miracle."

Few of these films still exist, but from the catalogue it appears that she made at least one or two a year. Many of these "miracle films" have a Christmas setting or focus on a Christmas event. The surviving film of this type is *Le Noël de M. le curé* (The Parish Priest's Christmas) 1906, 128 meters, about a parish priest who realizes he needs a statue of the infant Jesus for his Church crèche, but his congregation is too poor to afford the asking price of the local statuary dealer. The priest returns to his church and sets up an empty manger in front of the altar; this seems a little redundant since the altar figure is a life-size statue of the Virgin Mary holding an infant Jesus. But the parishioners arrive and kneel down around the empty crèche, and their faith is rewarded when two angels appear, and the Virgin Mary comes to life and hands the statue she is holding to the priest who lays it in the manger at her feet.

Le Noël de M. le curé is the only surviving film of this type found to date, but there are a handful of similar scripts in the Gaumont scenario collection at the Bibliothèque Nationale. *L'Enfant Jésus du curé* is the script title of the film that became *Le Noël de M. le curé*. It is interesting to note that the film corresponds exactly to the script, except for the change in the title. There is no way to be sure that this is the shooting script, and not a script made after the fact for the purposes of registration. Apparently, in 1906, some kind of registry for scenarios was developed, a voluntary deposit of scenarios (since the flammable nitrate films would be too dangerous for the Bibliothèque to store alongside its other documents), which was the source for the Bibliothèque Nationale's scripts. This registry was a counterpart to the paper print collection at the Library of Congress, which was started in 1896.[43]

Some of the more elaborate scripts have detailed character lists and indicated the need for hard-to-find props, which gives the impression that these were all shooting scripts. If that is the case, then generally speaking, the scripts were followed very closely in 1906 and 1907, judging from the few films from this period that are still extant.

The script for *Comment Yannick fut à la messe de minuit*[44] shows a rustic teenager trying to get to midnight mass but being waylaid by elves who force him to dance a strenuous ballet with them; finally, by making a sign of the cross he escapes them. When he calls on St. Yves and St. Anne, his call is answered by the appearance of angels. They place the now unconscious Yvannick onto a carriage shaped like a swan and draw him to the church, where he wakes up alone just in time for mass.

Figure 26. *Le Noël de M. le curé*—Gaumont, 1906. The parish priest cannot afford to buy a statue for the crèche

Figure 27. *Le Noël de M. le curé*—Gaumont, 1906. The Virgin's statue hands him her baby for the crèche

Le Noël du pauvre hère[45] is about a starving artist in his garret who has no fireplace in front of which to set his shoes (the Christmas custom in France is to set shoes instead of stockings in front of the chimney), so he draws one on his wall; the next morning, he is rewarded with a brand new pair of shoes. *Le Bonhomme Noël* which in the catalogue is listed as *Les Lunettes du père Noël* (St. Nick's Spectacles), is a very elaborate film with a variety of sets. The story begins with St. Nick having a drink with St. Peter up in heaven and leaving his spectacles on the table. Then he gets in his sled and starts delivering gifts, but his near-sightedness causes him to give everyone the wrong thing, so that the little girl gets the tin soldiers meant for the little boy, the boy gets the irons meant for the little girl, the "demi-mondaine" or high-class call girl gets the live rabbit meant for the cook and the amputee gets the pair of pants meant for the old dandy. St. Nick happens upon a couple of thieves, and tosses them down the chimney of the local police officer. Then he spies a very sick indigent child and showers him with gifts, clothes, medicine, and food. Finally, once his sled is empty, with a gesture he makes the right gifts fly up the wrong chimney and down into the correct one.

Apparently most of these films were aimed at children and appear to have been made to serve seasonal market demands. Guy did not make this kind of film when she opened her own studio in the United States, (although she did produce other fairy tale films, most notably *Dick Whittington and His Cat,* Solax 1913) which further indicates that they were made to satisfy some marketing niche and not as an expression of her own Catholicism.

However, much later in her life, when her film producing days were over and she was obliged to make a living as best as she could, she again tried her hand at writing stories of this type. Her nephew, Gabriel Allignet, a graphic artist, even illustrated one of these stories for her, but apparently none of these stories were published. Roberta Blaché said that Guy was more of a "cultural" Catholic than a truly pious one.[46] In the many years that Roberta Blaché knew Guy, often living within just a few miles of her if not in the same house, she only saw her go to mass once, and that was a formal occasion. Guy's daughter, Simone, buried her mother in a Catholic cemetery. She was not above referring to herself as a "Christian" when it suited her, as when, at age 90, she re-affirmed the veracity of all the claims she made for herself as a filmmaker in her memoirs in an interview with Victor Bachy.[47] It is interesting to bear all this in mind as we consider *La Passion* (Gaumont 1906).

Her film *La Passion ou la Vie de Notre Seigneur Jésus-Christ* (The Passion or the Life of Our Lord Jesus Christ), 660 meters, with 300 extras and 25 hauntingly beautiful sets designed by Menessier, is her masterpiece from the Gaumont period. It does not suffer from the excess or inconsistencies that appear in the lighter films made for children. Although miracles are often still the focus of each tableaux, now her depiction of her character's internal struggle has become quite sophisticated. Her *Passion* differs in many significant ways from the established genre of passion plays, notably in the "insistence on privileging women in relation to Jesus" as Richard Abel points out.[48] As he and others have noted, three of the miracles represented involve women, and some are miracles not usually depicted in other passion plays. Even when she stages an obligatory scene like the Nativity or the Crucifixion, she focuses on the Virgin Mary and other female characters as much as possible. Although this film, with its self-sufficient tableaux that could be sold individually

Figure 28. *La Passion*: the baby Jesus sleeps

represented a return to an earlier form of cinematic narrative, certain moments stand out for their complex characterization.

One of the most striking of these scenes is the tableaux for the Last Supper. Judas approaches Jesus as if he wishes to speak, and suddenly Jesus is transformed into a vision of what he will look like after his death and resurrection, with his wounds, the crown of thorns, and a host of angels. The vision frightens Judas and sends him scurrying off to carry out his betrayal, although he seems to accept his ordained destiny against his will. Once he leaves, Jesus becomes himself again and continues serving food to his other disciples, who seem to have noticed nothing. The scene is a masterful expression of Judas' dilemma: to not betray Jesus and therefore prevent salvation for the rest of humanity, or betray him, let him save the world, but be damned himself.

Visually, the film is based on gouaches painted by Tissot for an illustrated Bible, and even bears the same title as his illustrated life of Christ, *La Vie de notre Seigneur Jésus-Christ*. About the Tissot Bible, Guy said: "At the 1900 Exposition, Tissot had published a very beautiful bible illustrated after the sketches he had made in the Holy Land. It was ideal documentation, for decors, costumes, and even local customs... we had to drape each costume from the documents in the work of Tissot."[49]

Jacques Joseph Tissot was a successful salon painter and "dandified boulevardier"[50] in Paris in the 1860s who relocated to London during the 1870s. It was there that he anglicized his name to James Tissot. When he returned to France in 1882, he found his style of painting was out of favor. However, Tissot was swept up in the Catholic Revival of the fin-de-siècle—a combination of biblically based fundamentalism and spiritualism—and converted to Catholicism after seeing a vision in the church of Saint Sulpice. After his conversion, Tissot made two pilgrimages to the Holy Land, where he amassed a wealth of data, much of it indiscriminate, in the form of notes, sketches and photographs, of what life was "really like" in the Holy Land. He then returned to his studio in Paris, where he painted 365 gouaches and made over 100 sketches on the life of Christ. (Later, he would do much the same for stories from the Old Testament.) He then used his sketches and photographs as the basis for his "intuition"—he would go into a trance and then start painting scenes from the life of Christ. For images of biblical Jews, he used the faces of Yemenites he had sketched in Palestine, but for the Romans he drew on the faces of Parisian waiters. His Bible was published in French in 1896, (Alice Guy purchased a copy of it in 1900) and was an instant success. The paintings themselves were exhibited twice in Paris, once in London, and toured the United States and Canada (the entire collection was purchased by the Brooklyn Museum through public subscription). Streams of people viewed these images with hushed reverence, often dropping onto their knees to pray in front of one and then proceeded to the next image still on their knees.

Side-by-side with his claims that the images were a result of "intuition" or divinely inspired, Tissot highlighted the fact that topographically they were very exact. It is apparently this fidelity to topographical realism that inspired Alice Guy to use Tissot's Bible as the visual inspiration for her *La Passion*; in her memoirs she also noted that she hired two Jesuits "recently returned from a pilgrimage to the Holy Land"[51] as consultants on the film.

As Herbert Reynolds has pointed out in his paper on how the film *From the Manger to the Cross* (Kalem 1911) was inspired by the Tissot Bible:

> The book's division into five sections (The Holy Childhood, the Ministry, Holy Week, The Passion, The Ressurrection) already begins to suggest a five-act dramatic structure, or perhaps a five reel feature such as the one made by Kalem.... Moreover, Tissot's Bible would be a kind of preliminary script and storyboard, because in putting it together Tissot assembled a single chronological narrative by matching a few verses from one or two gospels to each of his paintings....[52]

Although Reynolds dismisses Guy's *La Passion*, it seems clear that the Kalem film took Guy's idea a step further: instead of painting sets that were based on Tissot's images, an attempt was made to duplicate Tissot's images on location.

Guy's version of *La Passion* stands out visually for Menessier's often breathtaking sets. In contrast with Zecca's *La Passion* made at Pathé the same year, Guy designed her film to emphasize the use of deep focus and to have movement filling the frame along diagonal lines. Although Jasset was in charge of directing the exteriors, it was clear that Guy had a comprehensive plan for the entire film, as the lines of movement and use of deep focus stood out whether the tableaux was set on a stage with painted flats or whether it was on-location.

For the sets, Tissot's paintings have been copied quite literally in some cases, such as in the setting for the Last Supper or the scene known as "Ecce Homo;" other times, only visual motifs were borrowed. For example, the brick archway in the Nativity scene is actually taken from Tissot's painting *The Flight to Egypt.*

Pathé's catalogue boasted that "each of our scenes has its own special decor." This was exaggerated, but Pathé's trompe l'œil backdrops were so elaborate as to give the impression of being at least as important as the film's plot.[53] Guy's backdrops were simpler, but there was often a thematic relationship between her use of interiors (usually depicted on sets) and exteriors (usually locations). The expressiveness of Guy's films comes from the degree to which she manipulates exterior and interior spaces to express how she thought about domestic and public spheres. The domestic sphere, usually depicted by a set, is a world run by women: orderly, safe, and filled with flowers—or at least a floral patterned wallpaper. The public sphere is dominated by men, although women are there too: it is often threatening, violent and disorganized. In the farces like *Madame a des envies*, the traditional hierarchy between the two spheres (and by extension between the sexes) is turned upside down. Although Guy was a royalist with right-wing leanings, she delighted in making films that showed authority being challenged, whether it was wives challenging their husbands or, as in the case of *Les Maçons* (Gaumont, 1906), workers challenging their bosses.

In her melodramas such as *L'Enfant de la barricade* (Gaumont 1906), the distinction between domestic and private spheres was treated more straightforwardly. *Barricade* is a melodrama shot in seven scenes. The only set is an interior, a very flowery depiction of a domestic space shared by the elderly mother and her teenage son. Through the doorway, a backdrop depicting a street is visible, and in the first scene the boy notices soldiers running past. He looks for any excuse to get outside and finally seizes an empty milk bottle. His mother fearfully lets him go.

Outside, the boy sees a group of people building a barricade. In spite of their warnings, he climbs over it and walks around the corner, only to see workmen trade shots with cavalry soldiers (the event depicted is the failed Commune uprising of 1871) and then run for the safety of the barricade, followed by the boy. The cavalry kills most of the rebels, then lines up the remainder in front of a firing squad, including the boy, who had picked up a rifle but had not used it. The boy shows his milk bottle to the commander and begs for a reprieve so that he can finish his errand. His wish granted, he returns to the interior set, leaves the milk with his mother, kisses her tenderly several times, and returns to his position in the firing squad lineup! This time his mother has follows him, and with her pleading, she wins the boy a permanent reprieve.

The film is a remake of an episode from a dramatic poem of Victor Hugo's. Although not her finest script, *La Barricade* does illustrate the way Guy thought about the domestic and public spheres. A child leaves the domestic sphere before he is ready; he is allowed to return because the mother, who rules the home, and the commander, who rules the street, agree that he is not yet prepared for the public arena and its consequences.

This is not to say that Guy always depicted the home as safe. In *La Marâtre* (discussed above) the plot of *La Barricade* is almost exactly reversed. The workman's home is in great disorder until the stepmother brings in an (ostensibly) organizing and harmonious influence. In this film, the policemen enthroned behind their huge, tall desks, are the real providers of order and harmony.

Both *Envies* and *La Marâtre* deal with characters who find domesticity lacking. The wife in *Envies* is not happy with her husband, so she takes to the street in pursuit of a phallic substitute; the man in *La Marâtre* cannot run his home unaided, so he brings home the first woman who will pick up after him.

One of the lessons of *La Marâtre* is that we cannot always divide Guy's vision of domestic space and public space along gender lines. In *La Fiancée du volontaire* (Gaumont, 1906), the two kinds of spaces—the public spaces of the warrior and the domestic spaces of women—come into direct conflict. The *volontaire* takes a tearful leave of his fiancée before enlisting. We see him kissing her goodbye in a warm, wallpapered sitting room, and then she waves to him from a garden full of flowers. Later we see him besieged inside a house (the set is reminiscent of the painting *Les Dernières Cartouches*, which as we have seen in Chapter One, was the Lumières' inspiration for a film of the same title, which Guy copied in 1898). In a scene full of carefully choreographed technical effects, the room is slowly destroyed by gunfire from without: first the windows are shot out, a portion of the ceiling falls in, the credenza falls over

Figure 29. A *tour de force* of special effects as the room is destroyed
around the soldiers in *La Fiancée du volontaire*

Figure 30. The enemy promises to deliver the ring in
La Fiancée du volontaire

Figure 31. Rescuing the wounded from the battlefield in
La Fiancée du volontaire

and the dishes break all over the floor, and finally chunks of plaster fall from the walls and ceiling as the soldier is fatally wounded. He entrusts the man who shot him with a ring for his fiancée. The enemy soldier is later wounded himself and taken, by coincidence, to the fiancée's home, and through the ring, she realizes who he is. Now she must choose between killing him (by not giving him his medicine) or forgiving him, which she does.

The plot device of a man relying on a woman's forgiveness for sustenance would return many times in the Solax melodramas, where the noble and forgiving women effectively take the place of the Virgin Mary and the ministering angels who disappeared from Guy's films after she went to the United States.

For both soldiers in *La Fiancée du volontaire*, to be accepted by women in women's domestic spaces is tantamount to staying alive. Women are pedestalized as the sources of life in Guy's Gaumont melodramas, but they must choose to play this role, as opposed to the stepmother in *La Marâtre*. The heroines of Guy's comedies go a step further and run out into the street, the public space, in pursuit of their own desires. Guy combined the symbolic way of handling internal conflict and her habit of pitting the private and the public spheres in a comic film made that same year, *Le Matelas alcoolique*.

The advances in narrative that are discussed here using Pathé and Gaumont as specific examples were part of an industry-wide process. In the United States, the period from 1904 to 1908 saw the transition from travelling exhibitors to the rise of film exchanges (exchangemen bought films from manufacturers and then rented them to exhibitors, much like how a video store operates today). This new, steady supply of films led to the development of permanent cinemas, also called the nickelodeons. Films continued on vaudeville programs during this period, especially in Europe where Guy was making films, but the nickelodeon boom firmly established movies as a new form of mass entertainment and brought about a demand for a steady supply of quality films. Story films were the preferred product and began to replace non-narrative actualities as the most popular genre. According to Gunning, "Film chases and other action-based narratives appeared that mediated between the cinema of attractions and the cinema of narrative integration that dominated Griffith's period."[54]

After 1907, the American and the French cinemas began to influence each other in a much more direct manner. Unwittingly (at that moment Guy thought her career was over), Guy's migration to the United States in 1907 matched a major transition in the film industry from an emphasis on French product to an emphasis on American product. Although France continued to dominate the film market until 1914, the American style of filmmaking was becoming more important. In addition, American audiences were becoming somewhat resistant to French product. By moving to the United States, Guy was following the direction of the industry itself. We must now follow her there in order to continue our analysis of her work.

4 SOLAX: AN AMERICAN FILM COMPANY

FROM 1910 TO 1914, Guy Blaché owned and ran her own studio, the Solax Company. Not only did she own and run the production company but she had over 50% ownership of the entire physical plant—film stage, set construction shop, film processing plant, and so on. At first, she rented the Gaumont Chronophone studio and added some set buildings and other property (which included a small western hotel, country store and saloon, a small park and a lake) to the Gaumont Flushing Plant.[1] Later, as her rate of production increased and her limited access to the Gaumont studio was insufficient, she built a new Solax studio on Lemoyne Avenue in Fort Lee, New Jersey. So far, she is the only woman in film history to have actually owned her own studio plant. A popular myth is that Solax ceased to exist as a film manufacturer in 1914, and Guy went bankrupt in 1920, because Herbert Blaché's sense of competition with his wife, and his desire to promote himself over her, led to company failure. In this chapter I will dispel that myth and show how the fortunes of the Solax Company and the Gaumont Company were inextricably linked even when Guy was no longer a Gaumont employee. In the process I will give a new and much needed perspective on the relationships between the three types of film companies in Fort Lee (the licensed, the independent and the foreign), using the Solax plant as the unifying thread.

Solax Studio on Congress Street, Flushing, NY

GUY DIRECTED THE first films at Solax by herself, but soon hired other directors to work under her supervision. One of them was Mr. Wilbert Melville who was described by *The Moving Picture News*[2] as the "managing director" of the Solax Company. Melville was credited with the idea of having a regular release of military pictures (which began with *Across the Mexican Line* on April 28th, though this particular film was probably directed by Guy, as it had been announced before the military series was announced), and he also wrote and directed "practically all of them." We can therefore credit him with the direction of most of the military films released from May 12, 1911, onwards. The fact that Melville had been a Captain in the Spanish American War lent credibility to the Solax claim for accuracy in the military depictions. It was Melville's military connections that enabled Solax to film for three weeks at Fort Meyer, Virginia,[3] with the cooperation of Colonel Joseph Gerard, commander of the 10th Calvary. The *Moving Picture News* credited the direction of the Fort Meyer military films to Wilbert Melville, specifically *The Mascot of Troop C, An Enlisted Man's Honor,* and *The Stampede*.[4] The *News* also credited Captain Warren Dean, the commander of Troop "C" for his acting ability and for writing two of the scenarios (one of these may have been *The Altered Message,* which features a character named Captain Dean).

Solax stock actor Romaine Fielding was complimented for his ability as a crack shot, owing to his three years at the Shattuck Military Academy in Faribault, Minnesota, and his later membership in California's first signal corps.[5]

Guy supervised Melville closely, and press photographs show them together on the set, often on horseback. Another article entitled "Madame Alice Blache (sic), President of the Solax Company" indicated that Guy herself was not continuously on the set, but she went around giving advice to the directors, though the writer also noted that she personally directed many of the films herself and "edited" all of the scripts. One of these military films directed by Alice Guy was probably *Greater Love Hath no Man* (the unrequited lover was played by Romaine Fielding), which had minimal use of the cavalry and ended with a classic Guy pietà tableaux.

Solax's success with the Fort Meyer films led to the company being commissioned by the Sales Company to produce a special feature film on the mobilization of the Atlantic Squadron on the Hudson River in New York, which consisted of 102 fighting vessels, 22 destroyers, 16 torpedo boats, 39 battleships, 4 gunboats with oil tanks, and miscellaneous other fighting craft.[6] Mention of Wilbert Melville disappeared from the press around August 1911. He is mentioned in *The Moving Picture World* two years later, in an article entitled "Studio Efficiency: Scientific Management as Applied to the Lubin Western Branch by Wilbert Melville."[7] This article praised Melville's efficient reorganization of the Lubin Western Studio in Los Angeles, with individual directors working with their own property men, and an efficient organization of studio buildings. In the article Melville claimed "the beginning of this system was laid a number of years ago when he reorganized the Solax Studio and was manager of it." It seemed more likely that Melville learned a great deal from Alice Guy Blaché, clearly described in other articles as the one in charge of the reorganization of Solax at the time it took place, but chose not to mention her. The remark also shows he must have worked at Solax until at least December of 1911, as the studio was reorganized from September to December.

This reorganization started with a trip the Blachés took to Europe. On July 26, 1911, the *Moving Picture News* announced that Herbert Blaché and Alice Guy had sailed for a two-month trip to Europe on the Kronprinzessin Cecilie, where "they look forward to meeting their many friends in all the big European cities, where they are both well known."[8] The couple spent part of this time hiking in the Swiss Alps with friends. However, part of the trip was devoted to business, as the *News* noted in the announcement of Herbert Blaché's return on the same ship on September 12th. The article specified that he spent his time in Europe pursuing new avenues for the Gaumont Chronophone, while Madame Blaché "brings fresh ideas [for the Solax Company Productions] back with her from Paris."[9] One of these ideas would be the plot and setting for *The Violin Maker of Nuremberg*, inspired by the couple's visit to that city.[10]

In the issue of *The Moving Picture News* dated September 23rd, an article announced the "reorganization of the Solax company." This included new personnel in its stock company and the fact that a new director would soon be hired, though no name was given.[11] The first step in this plan was to hire Darwin Karr, a comedian with fourteen years experience on the stage, including Broadway. "The engagement of Darwin Karr is the consummation of only one of the big plans which Madame Alice Blache (sic), the president of the company, at this time has under advisement," said *The Moving Picture News*. The next step, according to the same blurb, would be to hire a good comedy scriptwriter.[12]

The same issue carried an announcement of the hiring of H.Z. Levine as a publicity manager for Solax,[13] and an announcement that Solax would then be releasing three films a week. The addition of the third weekly release was, however, later postponed to December 24th.[14]

On December 9th, a long feature article in the *News* announced that the Solax company would be building a new plant in Fort Lee, New Jersey, described as follows:

Twelve lots of ground have been purchased.... comprising almost an acre; on this will be constructed a building 62 x 62. This building will be two and three stories. On the lower floor will be the offices of the company, on the second in all probability will be the dressing room, and the third floor will serve possibly as a scene room. To one side of the above-mentioned department, but still within the dimensions of the building proper, will be the glass studio, which will be splendid and spacious, affording ample room for the setting of the scenes. "Deep pictures," said Mr. Magie, "are what we are after."[15]

George A. Magie was the treasurer of Solax, and "represented that concern to the Sales Company." He also helped organize the Film Supply Company. According to the *World*, he was a native of New York but had been educated in France. A career in railroad management, which enabled him to travel around the world (including two years in London to build its "underground railroad"), was interrupted by illness, during which he became aware of motion pictures, which eventually led him to Solax.[16] He left Solax in 1913 to found his own film manufacturing company, the Pilot Company. However, this was not a successful venture, as just a few months later he went to work for Universal.

The same article that announced the studio included notice of the addition of Marion Swayne to the Solax stock company. Although Miss Swayne was "very young," she already had two seasons' experience in stock and on the K. and P. Circuit. At the end of the first year, she would leave Solax to play in summer stock, but would return because "she likes the pictures and Madame Blaché's organization."[17] Other stock members listed were Mr. Gladden James, Miss Fanny Simpson, Mr. P.C. Foy, his wife Mrs. Magda Foy and their child, Little Magda Foy, dubbed "The Solax Kid", and Blanche Cornwall. Also listed were the two Solax directors, Edward Warren and Edgar Lewis.[18] An article in the *News* on December 16 profiled Lee Beggs, aged 40, a rotund "character comedian," with twenty-five years' experience in the theatre and in vaudeville. Finally, the "famous Pathe (sic) and Biograph Star", Billy Quirck, was added to the Solax ensemble. Quirck was best known for his comedy roles, especially the "Billy" series for Pathé and the "Muggsy" series for Biograph. At 35, he had four years of screen acting and more years of working on the stage behind him. Alice Guy told the *News*: "We are making an emphatic effort to organize a perfect comedy stock company. We want to be known as the best comedy producers in the business."[19]

Dramatic productions were not neglected, as on February 3, 1912, the *News* announced that Solax had hired "Handsome Mace Greenleaf," formerly of Reliance and the legitimate stage, who would be doing dramatic leads.[20] He played Dr. Headley in *Falling Leaves*, amongst other roles. In April of 1912 he accepted a contract with the Lubin Company, but never made a film with them as he suddenly died of typhoid pneumonia.[21] The company was rounded out with Mrs. Hurley, an experienced older screen actress, in 1912 and Joseph Levering, a leading-man type with experience on the stage, in 1913.

All of the above show clearly that a carefully planned expansion was underway. On September 7, 1912, *The Moving Picture World* carried a humourous article describing the move of the Solax studio from Flushing to Fort Lee, which made it clear that Flushing locals had been enriched by the fact that their studio rented their homes (at least the front porches) as locations and brought a lot of business to local merchants. Darwin Karr was specifically mentioned as an actor who was widely admired.

On September 21, 1912, *The Moving Picture World* carried a two-page article describing "The New Solax Plant: A Modern Structure Representing the Last Word in Moving Picture Plant Architecture."[22] The article made it clear that the efficient layout of the studio was entirely planned by Herbert Blaché and Alice Guy, with much emphasis placed on how related departments were placed alongside one another and the grounds were landscaped to represent different types of locations to minimize the need to shoot outside the studio grounds. The studio also boasted equipment for printing and drying 20,000 feet of film a day. The spacious and airy dressing rooms, designed to keep peace among rival actors, were highly praised.

Role of the Solax Studio in the History of Studio Development

TOM GUNNING,[23] JANET STAIGER[24] and Charles Musser[25] have all attempted to break down the development of early studio production systems into particular phases determined by the mode of distribution and the changing role of the filmmaker. Since Guy's filmmaking career is the only one that spans all of the periods described, chronicling it poses a unique and particular challenge to the film historian.

Between 1906 and 1914, Guy worked in several highly contrasting modes of film production. From 1896 to 1907 she produced and directed silent films, largely without supervision; from 1902 to 1906 she directed *phonoscènes* within a rigidly hierarchical production system; and from 1910 to 1914 she headed her own studio at Solax, where she had complete control. By 1914, Solax essentially had been absorbed into Herbert Blaché's company, Blaché Features. Using the Solax plant, properties, and even some of the same actors, Guy and Blaché alternated directing a feature film every month, and sometimes hired outside directors to direct a film they had produced (for example, Capellani directed *The Red Lantern*).

From 1914 to 1917, the Blachés directed and produced films directed by others for Popular Plays and Players, a distributors' coalition for independent filmmakers. Feeling it would be more remunerative if they worked on their own, they began to produce films for their own production company, the U.S. Amusement Company. For a short period from 1916 to 1917, they produced films for the U.S. Amusement Company and Popular Plays and Players simultaneously. Guy directed six to eight films for Popular Plays and Players in three years; she directed another six for the U.S. Amusement Company in one year. After 1917, Guy became a director for hire, making films for other producers, with little control over script, location or casting. (For an in-depth discussion of Guy's transition to features, see Chapter Five.)

Janet Staiger has outlined a historical framework for studio development in the United States. She posits five successive systems of production in the American film industry from 1896 to 1920: the cameraman system of production (1896-1907); the director system (1907-1909); the director-unit system (after 1909), which developed as the manufacturers increased output; the centralized producer system (after 1914) with centralized management; the division and order of production system (from the first years through the 1920s), with the subdivision of the work.[26]

According to Staiger, the cameraman system dominated until 1907 when cameramen directed as well as operated the camera. When Guy started making films for Gaumont in 1896 she started as a director with a cameraman, Anatole Thiberville. Thiberville shot all of her films for her until he fell ill—apparently the result of exhaustion—and was replaced temporarily by Herbert Blaché on *Mireille* (Gaumont, 1906, never released). The cameraman system as

Staiger described it was used at Gaumont: individual cameramen shot the *actualités*, and some of the earliest narrative films that were shot on location may have also been made this way. But from the very beginning of her career, Guy's work practices fell into Staiger's second category of director system.

Why did Guy have a cameraman? Possibly because she started out with an emphasis on narrative with her very first film and saw her task as comparable to that of a theater director. She wrote the scenarios, hired set designers, shopped for bargain clothing to use for costumes, and persuaded friends to act. In addition, for the first few years, these tasks had to be accomplished while she continued to perform her duties as Léon Gaumont's personal secretary and probably what we would call today an office manager. The original extant correspondence in the Gaumont archives at the Cinémathèque Française shows that from September of 1895 to 1899, Guy was fully carrying out her secretarial duties, as her handwriting is everywhere visible on the drafts of letters. Various letters written by Gaumont are also shown with the name of the person the letter was addressed to in her handwriting. One letter was completely written and signed by her (to Demenÿ, dated November 26, 1896). By the end of 1899, a new hand appeared to take over. This might indicate that as her film obligations grew, her secretarial tasks were taken over by others. The existence of these letters contradict Laurent Mannoni's statement that there is no records of Alice Guy's presence at Gaumont in 1896–97 at all, even as a secretary.[27] In her memoirs, Guy noted that in order to facilitate her work, Gaumont had invited her to rent a little house he owned near the Gaumont labs in Belleville:

> It was at this epoch that Léon Gaumont, finding that I lost too much time in going to and from, offered to arrange for me a little house he owned at the bottom of the ruelle des Sonneries, behind the photographic studio, which he rented to me for a minimal sum (eight hundred francs per year, all the same). Seeing my hesitation he promised to install a bath and to have the garden cleared by the Buttes Chaumont gardener. I ended by agreeing. I was already bitten by the demon of the cinema.[28]

It is also possible that Guy did not run a camera herself because this was considered a masculine task. In addition, she did not have to select a camera or a film stock when she started because there was only one available to her—Demenÿ's 60mm. camera—until the

Lumière 35mm. camera replaced it. Thiberville probably had little to say in these matters himself, as cameras and film stock were of the highest interest to Léon Gaumont. Guy was making films to sell these cameras, after all. So Gaumont, in a kind of executive producer function, assigned her to make films for each new machine as it was developed, the same way he assigned her to make *phonoscènes* between 1902 and 1906.

Though Guy might not have turned the crank herself, she took an avid interest in photographic processes:

> [It was] thanks to the... advice and lessons of Frédéric Dillaye (technical advisor to the Gaumont establishment and author of excellent books on art photography), to the experience gained day by day, [and] to luck, that we discovered many little tricks such as: *films turned in reverse*, permitting one to take a house falling down and then reconstructed as if by magic; a person falling from a roof and jumping up spontaneously; a greedy client at the bakery, finding his bill too high, giving back intact the swallowed cakes. *Films slowed down or accelerated* by a turn of the handle, transforming peaceful passers-by into creatures seized by frenzy, or, on the contrary, sleepwalking. *Stops*, permitting one to displace an object, which in projection would seem to be animated by a supernatural life, stupefying an archeologist when his precious mummy plays in the laboratory.... *Double exposures. Fade-outs* used for visions and dreams. My faithful cameraman Anatole Thiberville (who, before becoming a cinematographer raised chickens in Bresse, if I remember) helped me with endless patience and goodwill.[29]

It is clear from the *Memoirs* that other Gaumont staff developed, fixed, dried, and sometimes hand-colored the film. However, it is also clear that Guy was well aware of everything involved in these procedures, especially what could go wrong.[30] It appears, therefore, that Guy's career passed over the cameraman system phase as Staiger described it and began immediately with the director system, which according to Staiger lasted from 1907 to 1909. Staiger herself recognizes that some film manufacturers, such as Vitagraph, first hired directors as early as 1904. By 1905, as the pace of production picked up and Gaumont invested in a glass-roof studio, she was able to hire workers:

> The role of director was complex: scenario, choice of actors, agreements with the decorators, the costumers, the furnishers.

Finally, rehearsal, stage direction, lighting. Editing, cutting and montage of the finished film was also important. I was fortunately seconded by excellent assistants.... [Louis] Feuillade, shines in the first rank in the list of early animators [an early term that was synonymous with "filmmaker"], a secretary, Yvonne Serand, who had acted in *La Fée aux choux* and later became the wife of director Arnaud who directed several comic films, and finally [Henri] Menessier the set designer whose collaboration was precious to me and who rejoined me in the United States... a casting director, [Vincent] Denizot... in 1905 Victorin Jasset.... Every Monday we discussed the week's work together. The studio became a hive of activity. Thus we made a series of comic films, pursuits, tumbles, clashes, acrobatics, what one calls slapstick. The extras were usually provided by the personnel of the workshops.[31]

The *phonoscènes* had a more hierarchical organization than the silent film production Guy carried out simultaneously. This was due to the complex and delicate nature of the equipment and the multiplicity of tasks to be carried out. This supports Musser's thesis that the film industry "...moved from the traditional craft model of the cameraman system to the complex multi-unit production of the central producer system, involving greater division of labor and hierarchy."[32] except that Musser does not see this happening in the U.S. until after 1908. At Gaumont it was well in place by 1905 at the latest. What is interesting about Gaumont is that Guy, while making silent films, was given almost free creative rein and worked on a more or less collaborative basis, while simultaneously directing *phonoscènes* in a rigid labor divided, hierarchical environment.

But since the *chronophone* apparatus and the *phonoscènes* to be projected in it were sold together as a package, Gaumont's sound production in terms of distribution, falls more into Gunning's "self-contained producers" category, even though it chronologically came later.[33] This is an example of how difficult it is to apply existing theories of studio management to early sound films, but it also shows Alice Guy's role in pioneering studio development.

Musser is careful not to call the earliest film producers "directors," but the term, as we use it today, certainly seems to apply to Guy when it came to the *phonoscènes*. For these films she was solely and specifically responsible for the performances. The performers arrived with their material, their music, their costumes and their "acts" set and mastered; what Guy did, for the most part, was to restage an operatic, cabaret or vaudeville sketch on film, without substantially altering it. Her task and the tasks of her collaborators were essentially mechanical as long as these musical numbers were simply photographed, proscenium-style, on a stage in front of a backdrop.

How could two such divergent modes of production, the collaborative and the hierarchical, co-exist under one roof? Literally, of course, they did not: the silent films were shot in the greenhouse studio, where various sets could be worked on at the same time, and sunlight was principal source of illumination. The *chronophone* studio, as we can see in the Gaumont film-clip of Guy directing a *phonoscène*, (see illustration no. 18) was much smaller and relied heavily on artificial light. Because of the requirements of sound recording and performing to playback, only one production could take place at a time. Most important of all, Léon Gaumont, contrary to his usual practice, was intensely interested in everything that had to do with the *chronophone*, which he continued to champion well into the 1920s. Musser (and Staiger) saw the "introduction of hierarchy and division of labor... [that] circumscribed the parameters within which... workers engaged in filmmaking... made decisions and the quality of their interpersonal interactions"[34] as coming about gradually in the United States after 1908. But inside the Gaumont *chronophone* studio in Paris, a more factory-like mode of production prevailed by 1905, if not earlier, which made Alice Guy a pioneer of studio management. Since so many of the men she trained, including the director, Victorin Jasset, and designers Menessier and Ben Carré, went to work at Éclair, it was clear that Guy's pioneering techniques of studio management travelled across the ocean, not just with her to Solax, but to other Fort Lee Studios, and indirectly, later, to Lubin (via Melville) and Metro.

By 1905, Guy's assistants such as Arnaud, Feuillade, Bossetti and Jasset, were assigned films to direct themselves as well as to assist Guy on larger productions as Jasset did on *Vie du Christ*. Therefore, it could be said that she was running the Gaumont studio as a director-unit system as early as 1905. When she started her own American studio, Solax, in Flushing, New York, in 1910, she directed all of the output for less than a year, then hired additional directors, Edgar Lewis, Edward Warren, and Wilbert Melville.

Each of the three directors then specialized in specific genres of films, although these specializations were not always adhered to.

Guy primarily directed comedies, romantic comedies, and elaborate costume dramas based on fairy tales or literature. The week at Solax started with a roundtable staff meeting. The copyright records meticulously reflect the roundtable method of scriptwriting, as some films reflect up to five authors, while others name only Guy herself as author. For example, *Kelly from the Emerald Isle* lists the following authors: Alice Blaché, Edward Warren, Herbert Blaché, Barney Gilmore (the star of the film), and Campbell McCullough.[35]

Ironically, Guy's later Gaumont period (1905-1907) appeared to be structured more hierarchically (the other directors, like Bossetti, Jasset and Feuillade were her "assistants" and she herself was accountable to the Board of Directors) than her Solax period. Solax had a less hierarchical structure, a more family-like environment. Guy's children visited the studio often, and her daughter Simone sometimes appeared in films, such as *The Violin Maker of Nuremberg*. Collaborators like Menessier, her set designer, were encouraged to try their hand at other tasks such as scriptwriting.

Production Design at Solax

THE USE OF depth and deep focus and the sophisticated use of space that characterized Guy's later Gaumont films, such as *La Passion*, were not so evident in the countless drawing rooms and bedrooms that were the sets depicted in the Solax films. But every now and then (for example, in *The Girl in the Armchair*, Solax, 1913), we glimpse that quality there too. Of course, in such films as *The Sewer* (2 reels, 1912) where the sets could be more fanciful, this quality is very apparent. *The Sewer* is about a band of thieves who plan to rob a philanthropist. They train a young boy against his will to break into the philanthropist's house; the man catches the boy in the act, forgives him, and lets him go with the parting gift of a half-dollar that splits open to reveal a knife blade. Later, when the thieves kidnap the man and drop him into a stone pit, the boy sneaks him the fake half-dollar so he can cut himself free. The man then makes a laborious, lonely trek through various sewer tunnels until he can get home and get justice. The story ends when he adopts the boy and his older brother.

Menessier, who had designed the sets for *La Passion* for Guy in France, also designed the sets for *The Sewer*. Guy remembered her American collaboration with Menessier in her interview with Victor Bachy many years later:

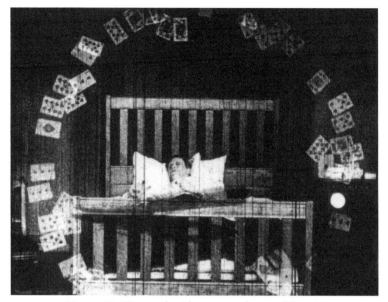

Figure 32. Haunted with remorse for gambling in
The Girl in the Armchair

Menessier was one of my best collaborators, and not only for *La Passion*. He was the son of a great theatrical set designer, but he himself was a sort of vagabond. I said to him one day: "Menessier, I have good news for you. Gaumont has agreed to give you a raise in salary." Then he said to me: "I have even better news for you. I've bought myself a little carriage. I go around from market to market and I intend to continue like that." I said, "Well, we can't force you to stay in the cinema!"

In 1907 I left for America. One fine day I was at home and I was told: "Madame, a French gentleman is here to see you." It was Menessier who came to offer me his services. He said: "Boss, tell me if you want me or not." I said, "Yes, I want you, I'll hire you." So he stayed with me [from 1911 to 1914].[36]

It was Menessier who led the rest of the Solax crew to Guy to offer to take a 50% cut in pay when Solax began to founder in 1914, a desperate measure which did not help the company stay afloat.[37] After working for Solax, Menessier went on to work with Jasset at Éclair, then designed sets for Albert Capellani while Capellani was at World, and then followed Capellani to Hollywood when Capellani began making films for Metro. He returned to France

Figure 33. Poster for *The Sewer*

Figure 34. Menessier's set for *The Sewer*

Figure 35. Darwin Karr in *The Sewer*

Figure 36. Darwin Karr in *The Sewer*

in 1920 and continued to work as an art director for French and American films until the late 1930s.

The sets Menessier created for *The Sewer* are still breath-taking today.[38] There was a new unity between the design of the set and the hero's emotional state, perhaps due to the fact that Menessier had also written the script. Menessier dug trenches around the Flushing studio for *The Sewer* and enlisted an army of specially trained rats to attack the hero (the white rats had to be painted red so they would read as gray on screen). Menessier's sewer sets are expressionistic painted flats, arranged theatrical style to create a deep-focus series of spaces that the hero struggles through. Karr, the actor, had a long sequence where he struggles alone, interacting only with the rats. The set resonates with his fear and despair as he struggles to find a way out of the endless tunnels.

The Solax Melodramas: The Forgiveness Films

GUY PRODUCED AND directed melodramas of various types, but it is possible to see a connecting thread running through all of them.

Peter Brooks points out the connection between melodrama and the French Revolution:

> This is the epistemological moment which it illustrates and to which it contributes: the moment that symbolically, and really, marks the final liquidation of the traditional Sacred and its representative institutions (Church and Monarch), the shattering of the myth of Christendom, the dissolution of an organic and hierarchically cohesive society, and the invalidation of the literary forms—tragedy, comedy of manners—that depended on such a society.
>
> Melodrama does not simply represent a "fall" from tragedy, but a response to the loss of the tragic vision. It comes into being in a world where the traditional imperatives of truth and ethics have been violently thrown into question.... [It] becomes the principal mode for uncovering, demonstrating, and making operative the essential moral universe in a post-sacred era.[39]

Guy aptly illustrates Brook's point. Perhaps because of her strict Catholic upbringing, including education in convents that were still run on rules dating back to the Middle Ages, a sense of the sacred still lingered in her French films. It is easy to see this in films like *La Passion*, which was based on the paintings of Tissot, who himself was part of the Catholic Revival movement. But it is also visible in the miracle films, in the sense of awe and wonder and the child-like (from a modern viewpoint) faith in the miraculous as part of the everyday. In the miracle films it is an angel, or Saint Nick, who appears and saves the day; but in the American melodramas it is often a wealthy, forgiving mother figure that stands in for Mary and offers saving grace to those who need forgiveness. When it was a woman who needed forgiveness, as in the features she made during the late 1910s, this forgiving mother was replaced by a patriarchal savior. She seems to have relished making films on the evils of gambling, because she returned to the subject again and again. Victor Bachy[40] says that Herbert Blaché's predilection for gambling contributed to the depredation of the couple's assets. In her memoirs, Guy does not mention gambling per se, but she does say that "Herbert played the stock market heavily and lost."[41] Another film, *A Hard Lesson* (Solax, 1912), no longer extant, had an even greater investment in special effects showing the evils of gambling:

After the night's playing, he is advised by the owner of the den that it would be hazardous for him to attempt going home alone with so much cash on his person. Chance decides to remain over night. He is shown to a room.

During the night, he not only finds that he has been trapped, but an attempt is made on his life. The panels on the wall disclose to him the eyes of a person, while his bed begins to sink gradually below the floor. Chance makes his escape, however.[42]

Gambling was not the only heinous sin for which a man would need forgiveness. The other was the neglect of his wife and home. This theme is dealt with satirically in *Burstop Holmes Murder Case* (Solax, 1913) and melodramatically in *Old Love and New* (Solax, 1912), *Roads Lead Home* (Solax, 1913), and *His Mother's Hymn* (Solax, 1911).

In *Old Love and New* Darwin Karr is forced to choose between his mother and his fiancée (he chooses his mother, of course). In this case, it is the mother who has to be forgiven for spilling tea on the elegant sweetheart. This film is interesting in its staging: when the point of view changes from the son's to the mother's, the camera also crosses the line on the axis and from thereon the action takes place in the foreground, theatrical proscenium style.

Roads Lead Home features a similar theme: when a rich woman's only son declares he will marry an actress, his mother disowns him. The son marries his sweetheart, but five years later his devotion flags in favor of playing cards at the club. Fed up, his wife leaves, taking their young daughter, but soon finds she cannot return to the stage. She becomes a servant for her husband's mother but keeps her identity concealed. When the mother is ruined she stays by her, even pawning a necklace her husband gave her when they were engaged. The necklace in the pawnshop leads the husband back to both women and all are reconciled.

Roads Lead Home fits into my loose category of "forgiveness films," but it also relates to the feature films (many of them starring Olga Petrova) that Guy directed in the late 1910s. In the feature films, the plot usually involves a Good Woman who is corrupted, and then has to recover herself to become virtuous again; that is, in alignment with middle-class mores. In *Roads Lead Home*, the actress is always a Good Woman, but is judged as bad because of her profession. The husband has the sense to recognize this, but the mother has to be enlightened. Ironically, in *Roads Lead Home,* it is the husband who goes from Good Son and Husband to Bad Son and Husband and back to Good again (after he finds the necklace, he gives up cards and throws out his gambling buddies). It is intriguing that the mother's enlightenment only comes about after her own financial ruin. In other words, her original objection to the daughter-in-law is that she is not a member of their class, but the mother's own impoverishment enables her to see her daughter-in-law's true worth.

In *His Mother's Hymn,* we have a similar mother-son relationship, this time without the sweetheart-intermediary. A young man from the country (the interior set was filmed outside amongst the trees in Flushing so that real countryside can be seen through the windows and doors) is hired as a stockbroker in the city. He takes a tearful leave of his mother, who plays her favorite hymn, "Lead Kindly Light," on her organ to see him off. After six months in the city, he takes to gambling and drinking and is seen by one of his colleagues losing all he owns, which gets him fired. Desperation sets in and he resolves to become a burglar, but the first house he robs is inhabited by an aged lady who plays "Lead Kindly Light" on her organ. This causes the would-be burglar to repent, and he kneels at her feet and returns the stolen jewels. The lady forgives him, saying she has a "lost son" herself, lends him money and helps him find a job. Back in his room, he sits on his bed, chagrined, and sees the vision (superimposed) of his own mother playing the hymn. Then he follows-up on the lead the lady gave him, does well there for a year and marries the boss' daughter, which gets him made partner. Celebrating with his new wife and her mother, they hear a burglar in the house; it is the other lady's "lost son." Our reformed young man decides to reform this "lost soul" in turn and after providing him with a new suit of clothes delivers him safely to his mother.

His Mother's Hymn could be compared to *Comment Yannick fut à la messe de minuit*: dark forces (the gambling dens) threaten to lead the young man astray but the forces of light (the mothers playing their hymns) carry the young man away from temptation.

In other words, these "forgiveness films" are direct descendants of the "miracle films" Guy made during her tenure at Gaumont; the "forgiveness films," with their focus on the family romance, are her way of adapting what worked in France for an American audience. The films starring Olga Petrova could be labelled as "fallen women films" (a label designed for melodramas that focused on the loss of female virture) but I prefer to see them as a continuation of the "forgiveness" films and therefore prefer the term "redemption" films, especially since the character in need of redemption (because he had brought about the loss of the female hero's virtue to begin with) was just as often male. (For more on this, see Chapter Five).

Class Issues in the Solax Melodramas

LIKE THE FEMALE vamps in later feature films, a Good Man could fall from grace, i.e., be led into wrongdoing, because of poverty. His salvation would be brought about first by the restoration of his good name, and second by the charitable act of a wealthy person. The female heroes of these melodramas are strangely passive compared to the women in Guy's comedies, or even compared to the women in Guy's French melodramas. To justify their lack of agency, these women are often ill to the point of death, or overwhelmed by caring for an ill person. Or the woman is not a woman at all, but a child. This child is often Magda Foy playing a boy. Dressing a girl-child of less than ten years of age as a boy would hardly seem to qualify as crossdressing, especially since the practice followed a long theatrical and pantomime tradition. Nevertheless, crossdressing in a Guy film always points to an issue of gender identity. In the comedies of crossdressing, it is feminine identity that is usually under the gaze of Guy's lens. In the melodrama, it is masculine identity. God's miraculous henchmen have disappeared from these films but in their place, we have an almost all-powerful patriarch.

In order to create a situation where a patriarch had to step in and save the day, a situation of great need was first established. In every case, the hero (whether male or female) of the film is rendered help-less, almost completely lacking in agency, by poverty (most common in the cases of male characters), a slander against his or her good name, extreme illness (most common with female characters), or the fact that the hero is a child. In the case of poverty or slander, the hero is prevented from taking action to protect himself by adherence to rigid mores: a righteous person need not defend himself, but stand-by and wait for justice in silence.

The very first film that Guy directed for Solax, *A Child's Sacrifice* (Solax, 1910), combines all of these elements. A workman is on strike, and he cannot afford to buy the medicine his wife desperately needs. The couple's little girl sells her beloved doll to a peddler to get money for medicine. The owner of the factory sees her act and buys her another doll. The girl does not forget his kindness and repays it by saving his life when the strike turns violent. This film is no longer extant, and only one publicity still remains, showing the mother in her sickbed, the child with her doll standing at the foot of the bed.

Falling Leaves (Solax, 1912), a surviving film, is very similar in tone. The sets for this film were designed by Henri Menessier; Mace Greenleaf played the doctor, Blanche Cornwall the mother, Darwin Karr her husband, Marion Swayne their daughter dying of tuberculosis, and Magda Foy played Trixie, the dying girl's little sister. The film opens by presenting us with Dr. Earl Headly in his white robe in his laboratory. Two fellow doctors, dressed in black, come to visit him and examine the cure for tuberculosis that Dr. Headly has just discovered. As each man in black flanks him, the presentation of Dr. Headly is reminiscent of the presentation of angels and saints from the miracle films of Guy's Gaumont period.

At the house of the sick girl, another doctor tells the parents that nothing is to be done, and their daughter will be dead by the time the leaves fall. Little Trixie overhears this, and that night she climbs out of bed to tie the leaves back onto the trees. Dr. Headly happens to be walking by and asks her what she is doing. When he hears Trixie's story, he asks to be introduced to her parents. Of course, his injections cure the sick girl, and he falls in love with her and decides to marry her.

The relationship of these films to the earlier miracle films can be traced through the changes in how point of view is depicted. Visions are a frequently used device, although shown in different ways. Superimpositions to reveal thoughts (and to illustrate dialogue) such as we have seen in Judas's vision scene in *La Passion* and in *His Mother's Hymn* are used in *The Thief* (Solax, 1913), *Dick Whittington and his Cat* (Solax, 1913), and *The High Cost of Living* (Solax, 1912). Precise choreography of movement of background characters is used in *The Girl in the Armchair* (Solax, 1913). And, most sophisticated of all, props were used to reflect a character's thoughts, thoughts that form a counterpoint to the dialogue as in *For the Love of the Flag* (Solax, 1912), in a manner reminiscent of theatrical practice.

The Thief communicates a character's thoughts almost entirely through a screen-within-a-screen. The film opens with two prosperous friends recalling their early days in the military, and their third friend, who is not present. Superimpositions of themselves and Colonel Spottiswoode appear; these superimpositions serve the same function as the photographs in *Old Love and New* (Solax, 1912), and since the men are looking at their yearbook, one has to wonder why an insert of a photograph was not used. From there on, the film plays out like a regular melodrama: the men send Spottiswoode an invitation to a reunion. Spottiswoode has fallen on hard times, and his daughter is gravely ill. His wife and daughter improvise a suit and shirt so that he can attend the meal, in the hopes that it will lead to employment. At the dinner, the second companion shows off a diamond pin he is giving the host as a gift. As the diamond passes from hand to hand, two menservants get into a tiff and knock the lights out. When the lights are back on the diamond is nowhere to be found, and suspicion falls on Spottiswoode. He refuses to be searched, generating more suspicion. He is allowed to leave, but his two friends follow him at a distance. When he arrives home, the host watches him through the window—the window framing the action as if the action itself were another superimposition. He discovers why Spottiswoode wouldn't be searched: he had stuffed his pockets full of food for his daughter. The host barges in, demanding to know why Spottiswoode did not tell him what his true situation was. When he is introduced to Mrs. Spottiswoode, she notices the diamond pin firmly stuck into the heel of his shoe.

The plot of *The Thief* was a common one, and many of the other film companies produced films with very similar themes at the time, although more often than not the person suspected of thievery was an innocent young working woman. Spottiswoode never does fall from virtue, although by virtue of his poverty he has fallen from social grace. Again, Guy's Catholic background seems to be manifesting itself here, as she does not make the Protestant ethic assumption that poverty is equivalent to a lack of virtue.

The High Cost of Living takes a much more politicized approach to this same theme: an old man is on trial for thievery. As he defends himself, superimpositions tell his story (the film in the present never leaves the courtroom set). He tells of hard times, of his honest, hard labor, and of circumstances and the wrong-doing of others that pushed him to steal food in desperation. At the end, he is acquitted and reunited with his family.

In his study of Oscar Micheaux, J. Ronald Greene compares the middle-class values of D.W. Griffith, based on a philosophy of white supremacy, to those of black filmmaker Oscar Micheaux, who aimed for "uplift of the Race" in his films:

> Griffith's couple [at the end of The Lonely Villa] looks like the same ideal couple one sees at the end of such Micheaux movies as Within Our Gates and that all Micheaux's films also seem to strive for. Griffith, however, was trying to hold on to the exclusive privilege that the icon had represented, whereas Micheaux was trying to force access to the middle-class life that the same icon had denied him. Both Griffith and Micheaux were hurt by the convention represented by the icon. Griffith was a victim of psychological repression... Micheaux instead worked to revise his attitudes toward the bourgeois conventions, including those of cinema that were hurting him and his ostracized group.[43]

For Micheaux, according to Green, the formation of a couple even though one member of the couple (usually, in Micheaux, the woman) does not meet all the bourgeois standards because she is "impure" (has a sexually checkered past), is an act of self-affirmation and the first step towards racial uplift. In his films, each member of the couple is an active agent, and the re-forging of the African-American couple was the foundation for economic, sexual, spiritual and social uplift.[44]

The same argument could be applied to Guy. Though she was always of middle-class outlook, the loss of her father's fortune and then of her father when she was still young led to a life of economic struggle. The economic hardship that she and her mother experienced, and the fact that she was the youngest daughter in a Catholic family, led to placing priority on work and career over marriage. When she did marry, it was to a man from a different culture, eight years younger than she was. With him, she aspired to have an equal and productive partnership, which they did have for fifteen years, though it was always Guy who was the primary breadwinner.

Though Guy did not explicitly make any theoretical statements about class, some arguments about class and gender relations can be traced in her films. In her melodramas, as we have seen, agency is attributed to both partners. Either partner can fall from grace, but the restoration of the bourgeois marriage cancels out all previous faults. And as in the films of Oscar Micheaux, these "faults" have a different value in Guy's films than they do in films made at the same time by D.W. Griffith at the Biograph studio in Fort Lee.

In Guy's melodramas where a powerful (usually maternal) female figure or a female partner who is in control of her own agency must forgive an aberrant (usually criminal) male, both manhood and womanhood are constructed in terms far different from those of mainstream cinema. What Micheaux and Guy had in common was their outsider status to mainstream cinema. Though Hollywood did not yet exist, the system of licensed film manufacturers which controlled the lucrative distribution outlets did. Independent film producers like Guy, and later, Micheaux, who had little or no control over the exhibition of their films reflected their industry standing and the drive it took them to succeed in any sense in the narratives of their films. Both prioritized redemption and retribution over rescue, citizenship over criminality, justice over vengefulness, mutuality over possessiveness. Micheaux valued hybridity over purity, but purity still mattered to him; in her melodramas of fallen women being restored to their earlier class standing, Guy demonstrated that purity, or the lack of it, had little to do with a woman's true value.

Women who are pure in Guy's films are in that state because they are too young to have reached the level of active agency or because they have been too ill to go out and live the life a real woman should live. That these women have to be saved by father figures at first appears that Guy is making the same case that Griffith makes: that the great white fathers have to protect the innocence and virtue of the young and female. A closer examination, however, shows that what is really being exacted in these films is restitution. A system where Spottiswoode's cronies become rich men, but Spottiswoode in *The Thief* can fall on hard times, calls for restitution in the form of help from his friends; the young man in *His Mother's Hymn* is rescued from his own mistake, a mistake he might not have made if his own father still lived, by another father figure, who eventually adopts him as his son-in-law. The ill older sister in *Falling Leaves* is similarly rescued by a man who has access to medicine and medical know-how that the system denies to her, just as it does to countless other ill women and children in countless other melodramas. In these films, Guy is not arguing for revolution, but for restitution, just as Micheaux would do almost a decade later.

Though Guy equated social acceptance and social status with agency in her melodramas, her westerns and dramas, especially those dealing with citizenship, dealt with similar issues in very different terms. Because Guy made numerous westerns as the genre was developing, it is necessary to give an overview of the genre itself before proceeding to the Solax westerns.

Issues of Americanization at the Solax Company: The 'Eastern Westerns'[45]

> The American Western started in artifice and pantomime in the East, found reality and a rough poetry as the industry moved west, and then deviated into myth and fiction as the star system took over. (William K. Everson)[46]

BEFORE 1912, TRADE papers used the term 'western' in a descriptive sense, as in the phrase 'Wild West dramas'. At that time, the films that today would be called 'Westerns' were known under various genre categories: military films, Indian films, sometimes even 'Western dramas' and 'Western comedies'. Apparently, the first appearance of the term 'Western' to describe a film generically appeared in *The Moving Picture World* on July 20, 1912.[47] Ironically, the westerns shot in and around Fort Lee had their heyday in 1911; by mid-1912, the western 'fad' appeared to be over. According to a variety of articles and editorials in *The Moving Picture World*, the audience became tired of them. The use of 'Jersey Scenery' especially exasperated one writer in *The New York Dramatic Mirror*.[48] A few companies kept making them, of course, but more and more of these were satires, which demonstrate that the genre, indeed, had reached maturity. Of course, the migration of film companies to California brought spectacular light and landscapes, real Indians, real bronco riders, real Mexicans and stars like Tom Mix and William S. Hart to the genre, giving it a new life by 1915.[49]

Many of the 'Eastern Westerns' were made by French film manufacturers. A careful examination of these films reveals much about the special character of these early westerns, especially about how, with their 'artifice and pantomime', they handled issues of ethnicity, race and gender identity in their films.

The earliest description of a French Western that I have found was in a British-Gaumont catalogue from 1905. The title was The *Pioneers: A Story of the Early Settlers.* It is described as "A series of Five Splendid Scenes taken in the Adirondack Wilderness." The Five tableaux appear to owe a debt of inspiration to the 'Attack on the Settler's Cabin'; plays that were routinely included in Wild West shows such as Buffalo Bill Cody's. Cody's show toured Britain and other parts of Europe often; the first tour to Britain was in honor of Queen Victoria's Golden Jubilee in 1887. The second tour began in Paris for the inauguration of the Eiffel Tower and to open the Paris Universal Exposition in 1889, where the show had a six-month run and was immensely successful.[50] Like the American film manufacturers, French filmmakers were fascinated by the myth of the American West as it was depicted in plays, paintings and dime novels.

The same catalogue lists a few other films based on novels or burlesque acts that contain what we would today call western elements. However, by 1910, the genre that showed the most western elements[51] was the military film. This was a clearly delineated genre, but through 1910 and 1911, a sub-category generally referred to as 'Western drama' or even 'Western melodrama' began to emerge from it.

Bowser refers to military films as "Civil War Films,"[52] and indeed many of these films were set in the Civil War; but some were also set in the Revolutionary War and the Mexican War or the war against the Indians. It is principally in the latter that the line between westerns and military films would blur. By 1911, the *Motion Picture World* and the *Moving Picture News* clearly advertised and described westerns and military films as classifications within a single genre; Indian dramas, on the other hand, could be released as military films or as dramas.

One of these advertisers was the Solax Company. Solax, though an independent company, had distribution through the Gaumont Co., which had access to licensed distributor status through George Kleine. Like most film manufacturers, Solax released specific genre films on specific days of the week. In April 1911, Friday became the release day for military films.

By reading through such ads, it is possible to trace the evolution of the term 'western' and 'Indian Drama' out of the military film category.

Solax produced military films every week throughout 1911 and well into 1912. A chronological examination of the films themselves can give us some idea of how the western evolved out of the military film. Not surprisingly, an overriding theme of these films is patriotism. Some were shot in military settings, such as Fort Meyer, Virginia, and the Atlantic Squadron's fighting vessels stationed on the Hudson. The opening scenes of *The Sergeant's Daughter* (Solax, 1910) showed scenes of thousands of troops embarking on a man-of-war, as well as scenes shot in the Philippines. This entire backdrop was for a love story. Unfortunately, the film no longer exists

For the Love of the Flag is a melodrama with the trappings of a military film. It exists only in nitrate form in the John E. Allen collection. Frank Roberts (Darwin Karr) is a draughtsman in a military office. He is fired after being accused of lying by a co-worker. His wife (Blanche Cornwall) is supportive but in a few months they have lost their lovely home and are living in a boarding house, where she is taking in sewing while caring for their child (Magda Foy). At one of his job interviews, a "representative of a foreign government"(Lee Beggs) overhears him describing his military experience. Beggs' character follows him out to the street and offers him a large

Figure 37. *Pietà* ending tableau from *Greater Love Hath No Man*

sum of money if he will re-draw the set-up of the fortifications now being built. Roberts would not do it, but back at home, things have gone from bad to worse; his wife's strength, which has kept him going until then, had worn out. Roberts sits down and makes the drawing. The representative enters waving around a fat wad of cash. The two men sit down to discuss the arrangement while the child plays with tin soldiers at their feet—reminding Roberts that he is betraying his country. Beggs kicks the soldiers over and the boy runs off. The men resume their negotiations but now the child runs in, wildly waving a little Stars and Stripes. This is too much for Roberts, who stuffs the cash back into Beggs' pocket. Beggs goes into a rage and takes his rage out on the child, which firms up Roberts' resolve to kick him out and tear up the drawings. Roberts' wife tells him to go back to his first job and explain what really happened, but there is no need for that, as a telegram arrives saying he has been exonerated and re-hired as head draughtsman.

For the Love of the Flag moves quickly, starting with the first moment of the first scene showing the quarrel between the draughts-men. Though Roberts is stony-faced throughout, we read his emotional state through his wife's steady emotional decline, the growing mountain of sewing, the child's tin soldiers, and the toy flag. Here, good American citizenship is measured by melodrama's yardstick. Roberts is expected to passively starve rather than betray his country, and his virtue will be rewarded by some higher source after he has been thoroughly tested.[53]

The next Solax military film is more recognizable as a western. *Greater Love Hath No Man* was released in June of 1911. Set in a Gold Rush camp, it starts with the familiar tale of two men in love with the same gun-toting woman who pans her own gold dust. When the camp supervisor, the object of the woman's affection, is threatened by Mexicans in the camp, Jake warns his rival of the danger and then defends him from the Mexicans to the death, winning himself one kiss from Florence as he dies in her arms. The military only appears in the form of a cavalry troop just in time to save the pair of lovers but too late to save Jake. Though the heroine played by Vinnie Burns, whom Guy trained as a stuntwoman, is spunky, she lacks the agency of similar characters played by the same actress in romantic comedies directed by Guy or even in other Solax Westerns such as *Two Little Rangers*. Most of the Mexicans are in blackface, and are not individuated.

Representations of Ethnicity in the Solax Films

SOME WORK HAS been done on how Native Americans are depicted in early films[54] but few scholars have looked at how Mexicans are represented. In *Greater Love*, the Mexicans are given some reason for their revolt: they believe that the camp supervisor is short-weighing their gold dust. No such justification is given in the next Solax western, *Outwitted by Horse and Lariat* (Solax, July 28, 1911)— a film I attribute to Guy, as Melville was directing military films at that moment.[55]

Vinnie Burns, who played Florence in *Greater Love Hath No Man,* the older sister in *Two Little Rangers* and the one who got friendly with a tiger in *Beasts of the Jungle,* plays the heroine that punches 'SOS' onto a leaf with her hairpin after she has been kidnapped by Mexican bandits. The bandits are played by Anglos in make-up and live in a teepee village; they agree to assist the rejected and vengeful white villain simply because that is the nature of Mexican bandits. Vinnie's lover and rescuer is played by a bronco rider, Otto Kline, who swoops down into the enemy camp and lifts her up onto his galloping horse with one arm. In her autobiography, Guy said that she and her regular actors all learned how to use the lasso from these bronco riders. She also told the *Moving Picture News* that she had not thought of making a western until she saw these bronco riders in action. This seems like a rather disingenuous remark on her part, given the high demand for westerns. Guy discovered the Cheyenne Days Company troop of cowboys on hiatus between Orpheum Circuit engagements when she was in Ft. Meyer, Va., supervising the production of some military films.[56] The Cheyenne Riders also starred in *The Girl and the Bronco Buster* (Solax, 1911) which was released July 14. What is interesting is that while complimenting her on the realism of her bronco rider, the writer for *Moving Picture World* has nothing to say about the inconsistent way in which the Mexicans were depicted. They are purely 'threat[s] to white rule, thereby requiring civilizing or brutal punishment,' as Daniel Bernardi has described it. Indians shared this threat category but were also shown as 'fetishized objects of exotic beauty, icons for a racist scopophilia'.[57] Mexicans are depicted as villainous and ignorant more often than Indians are. Only 'half-breeds' are lower than they on the social and moral scale. Female Mexican characters were more likely to be fetishized though they were usually played by Anglo actresses, as was the Mexican woman in the first of the Solax military pictures, *Across the Mexican Line*, (Solax, 1911). One reviewer described it as follows:

"Across the Mexican Line"

(Solax) This story is based upon the imbroglio in Mexico. It details a love story, coupled with the thrilling adventures of a woman spy. Apparently the Mexican general did not get the information he wanted, and the prisoner was recaptured by the American troops. The climbing of a telegraph pole and sending a message from its top is a novel stunt, which pleased the audience. The situations are also interesting.[58]

"The situation" referred to is an interracial romance (the Solax film still exists at the NFTVA, but it is unclear if it can be preserved). Some film companies went to Mexico and shot films using the Mexican war as a backdrop; Solax sent a director, cast and crew to New Mexico to shoot several films and commissioned a cameraman in Mexico to provide them with footage of the revolution. From the admittedly scarce remaining evidence, this did not seem to have changed the way Mexicans were represented.

One film that stands out is the November 1910 Pathé Frères release entitled *A Mexican Legend*. Apparently shot in the Vejas mission in Northwest Mexico, the plot focuses on a monastery attacked by Indians. Father Ignatius, the abbot, is imprisoned in a tomb. A Christ figure in a painting comes to life and leads the father out of the vault, across a river on a floating island, over a mountain to a hacienda where he enlists the help of some Mexican Vaqueros who come to the aid of the besieged monastery and expel the Indians who are now drunk with monastery wine. In this case, the Mexican setting—even the use of real, exotic locations—is all put into the service, not of a western, but of a French "miracle film" in Mexican garb. Still, the lead character is a Mexican (since the film no longer exists, we do not know if the actor was Mexican or an Anglo in blackface), which is rare for this period.

In films depicting Native Americans, the fetishization was more often applied to the male, taking advantage of his nudity. Many Indian characters were played by whites painted red and little regard was given to correct depiction of Indian customs or dress. Some

Indians complained about how they were represented and their complaints were publicized in *The Moving Picture News* and *The Moving Picture World*. In response, some companies such as Pathé American began to hire real Indians although extras were usually still played by whites in make up. Pathé American hired two Winnebago Indians, James Young Deer and Miss Redwing, who had worked for The New York Motion Picture Company, the Lubin Company and Kalem as actors. Young Deer also wrote and directed. The pair were veterans of Wild West shows and circuses, and were probably more influenced by their show business experience than their own cultural background. The Indian hero of the Wild West shows was stoic, noble and ready to sacrifice him or herself for a white colonist who had showed them some small kindness or friendship. An example of this is a film in the Netherlands Film Museum collection, *Indian Seizes Kidnapper*, (Pathé 1910).

Indians en masse were also treacherous attackers, motivated or unmotivated. Rarely was the suffering of the Indian at the hands of white colonizers shown. Most of the Indian dramas that featured all-Indian characters were usually love stories where inter-tribal warfare or feuds kept the lovers apart. Gaumont's 1912 *Cœur ardent*, directed by Jean Durand, is interesting because it is shot in southern France and all of the characters are played by French actors. The plot is about two lovers from the same tribe; the young man cannot raise the bride price to marry his love so he steals from another Indian herd. He is punished for this by being made a target for the other tribes' warriors but if he can make it to the river before they shoot him down, he will live. Since he survives bravely, he is finally able to marry the chief's daughter. The emphasis in the film is on the bloody ritual test.

Cheyenne's Bride (American Kinema 1911) shows inter-tribal warfare; at the end the disobedient daughter is tied to a wild horse and sent to die in the wilderness, but is saved at the last minute by her lover.

Not all the films focused on brutal (and mythical) tribal practices. A Pathé film known as *Indian Love* is another miracle film in Indian garb. A chief from a neighboring tribe falls in love with another chief's daughter, who then rejects his peace initiatives. The daughter pines away from thwarted love and dies, but the spirit of the Great Manitou takes pity on them and shows her lover how to use a magical grass to bring her back to life.

That westerns produced by French film manufacturers owed more to French genres than adherence to western myths is also shown in the 1910 Pathé film *Abraham Lincoln's Clemency*. In this film, Lincoln is shown forgiving a sentinel who fell asleep at his post, a common legend that was usually recounted of Napoleon Bonaparte.

Solax ceased releasing military films on a weekly basis early in 1912, a development which might have been tied to Melville's departure from the company around the same time. By 1913, westerns with a "Jersey setting" were no longer being made, with the exception of parodies. Again, a Solax film is an example. The title is *Playing Trumps*, (August 1912).[59] Billy Quirck plays suitor to Blanche Cornwall, but her attention is always diverted by the more elegant and more sophisticated entertainment offered to her by his two rivals, one played by Darwin Karr. In addition to the contrast between their cosmopolitanism and his relative simplicity, they are also both a foot taller than he is, so that they can physically overpower him when they need to get him out of the way.

Billy's winning strategy is to hire a film production company. He instructs the film director carefully. While Blanche is out on a drive with his two rivals their car breaks down. A gang of "Mexicans" (white actors in makeup) assault the car and take Blanche hostage. Billy arrives, shoots into the air, and rescues Blanche. His two rivals both react with perfect cowardice. It is their reaction which is key here, as no effort was made to conceal the fact that the Mexicans were "actors." Once Blanche is safely in Billy's arms, the actors all get up from the floor where they were playing dead and the director enters the frame and congratulates Billy on his performance. Billy and Blanche then get into the film crew's van and leave the two rivals behind. Billy's goal in the film is to show Blanche that he is better at scripting and staging his own life (or at least, his own romance) than his rivals are, and it is on this basis that he finally gets her attention. As we can see, though the western as a genre is satirized, the representation of Mexicans has hardly changed.

This discussion of early westerns made with a feminist and satirical perspective would not be complete without at least mentioning Ruth Ann Baldwin's[60] feature *49-17*, one of the earliest feature length westerns, and a satire. The story begins with a millionaire who has made his fortune in the Gold Rush of 1849. In 1917, he decides to re-live his glory days by hiring a troupe of actors to recreate a mining town experience for him. Like *Ocean Waif*, which Alice Guy directed two years earlier, *49–17* features an innocent young girl who is rescued from the sexual aggression of an older man (played by Jean Hersholt) by the younger man she loves. Here however, the love story is less the focus than the satire, as every western trope is turned on its head. There is a slight possibility that Baldwin may have been influenced by a Solax film in the making of *49 to 17*.[61] Solax released *Memories of '49* on January 26, 1912, and summarized it in *The Moving Picture News* as follows:

> A hardy old frontiersman, sitting in front of his cabin roasting a leg of lamb, dozes off and dreams of his struggles on the prairies. He lives over again the time when his father's pioneer wagon was attacked by Indians, of the time when nearly all of his relations were massacred, and of his escape and rescue.

> His whole career looms up before him and passes on in review. His boyhood on the plains, the struggles of an early manhood, his tender love affair, his marriage, his growing family and their gradual demise and finally the mists of this nightmare begin to fade away and we see the hardy old frontiersman "get a hustle on" and prepare a meal for his lonely self and his big, faithful dog.[62]

Except for Pathé Frères, the French companies rarely ventured West. When the war broke out in 1914 most of the French filmmakers returned to Europe. Guy spent the war in the United States and began making features at this time, none of which appear to have been Westerns.

Passing as American Citizens: Erasure and Masquerade after the Red Rooster Scare[63]

THOUGH IT IS hard for us to imagine it today, up until 1914 French films dominated the world film market. This was especially due to Pathé's mass of product and long reach. The audiences did not seem to have a preference for one type of film over another in the first years of the century, but American film manufacturers chaffed under the French dominance. Gradually, a movement to "make cinema American" grew in strength. In *The Red Rooster Scare: Making Cinema American 1900-1910*, Richard Abel offers a cultural history of early American cinema's nationalization, focusing on the role Pathé films played in expanding and legitimating the American cinema up to

1908 and then on how they "were repeatedly stigmatized and/or marginalized, especially in the trade press, as foreign or alien to American culture."[64] Abel focuses on how the "morally superior" American national identity was elaborated and enforced by first censoring and then barring Pathé films from US distribution. In order to survive, Pathé had to reconfigure its output aimed at American audiences and then "wrap it in the mantle of Americanization."[65]

Abel's book focuses on Pathé, but a similar process was at work at other French production companies in Fort Lee, including Gaumont and Solax, the independent "American" film company run by Alice Guy Blaché.

Abel points out that in the process of forming the cinematic American national identity, the identity of the primary nickelodeon audience—the disenfranchised recent immigrants, most of them from Eastern Europe—was also erased. In this section I will examine the measures that Solax took in order to justify its own press claims that it was an "American" film company. I will also examine two Solax films that have the issue of citizenship or ethnic identity as a theme: A Man's a Man (Solax, 1912) and The Making of An American Citizen (Solax, 1913). The former is ostensibly about anti-Semitism and the latter "against" the oppression of women, but both can be read multiplicitously (as de Lauretis uses the term) to show that Guy and her (mostly European) colleagues at Solax came up with an "American mode of address," a masquerade that tells us more about the social and economic pressures to "Americanize" than it does about what constitutes American citizenship.

The plot of The Making of An American Citizen involves a husband and wife (presumably Russian) who leave the old country and arrive at Ellis Island, then establish themselves on the Lower East Side, and still later, on a farm in the country. The husband treats his wife as a pack mule, and when she collapses from fatigue, he goes into a fury. In every scene, a representative of an all-male American Society teaches him better manners. This is a very advanced version of the 'forgiveness' films (seen in last chapter) and also an early example of a 'redemption' film, the mature form of the forgiveness film. Most of the 'redemption' films Alice Guy made were features, examined in the next chapter.

The Making of an American Citizen lends itself to a multiplicitous reading: first, the spectator is positioned as a non-immigrant or a successful (i.e., assimilated) immigrant. The assumption here is

Figure 38. The Gentile knocks over the Jew's apples in *A Man's a Man*

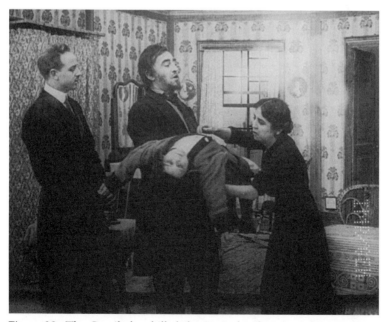

Figure 39. The Gentile has killed the Jew's daughter in *A Man's a Man*

that the viewer is male, but there are moments when the address is clearly aimed at females, such as the scene wherein the wife pokes her abusive husband, now restrained by a policeman, with the stick he had just been using to beat her—her first moment of self-assertiveness. Later in the film, religion is used as a way of internalizing the control represented earlier by the chastising 'American citizens.'[66]

It is surprising that the French producer of these films, Alice Guy, did not make more films about foreigners. Among her extant films, there is one other on cross-cultural relations: *A Man's a Man* (Solax 1912, 1 reel, George Eastman House). Generally, in films of this period, Jews are depicted as loan sharks, pawnbrokers, or peddlers. Invariably they are evil, or at best, as in *Lucky Cohen* (Lubin 1913), clever enough to have someone else take the blame for their misdeeds. Cohen is a peddler who is robbed by a tramp who takes his clothes. A mob, thinking the tramp is the Jew, attacks him and leaves him by the road, beaten. Cohen then recovers his clothes and his goods and goes happily on his way. Guy herself depicted Jews as stereotypical pawnbrokers and loansharks in other films. These roles were usually played very broadly by Lee Beggs, but in *A Man's a Man*, Beggs plays the head of the lynch mob and the Jew is played by an unknown actor. The film is reviewed in *The Moving Picture News* as follows:

A Man's a Man
(Solax)

In the Solax production of "A Man's a Man," which is to be released Friday, January 19th, a Jew is represented as a man and not as a subject of ridicule. The poor peddler, although he is wronged by a thoughtless and happy-go-lucky mixer, not only forgives but is big enough to protect the offender from mob violence.

The production shows one of the finest managed mob scenes seen on any stage. There are nearly seventy-five people in the mob and they are all good supers, all there for a purpose and strengthen the ensemble. They are led into the Jew's home to lynch a man who has run down a child. The man is in hiding in the Jew's home. Although it is his own child who has been run down, the Jew protects the offender.

There is an interesting counter-plot which brings out strongly the emotional and tensely dramatic values of the entire production.[67]

Figure 40. The Jew hides the Gentile from the lynch mob in *A Man's a Man*

Figure 41. The Jew lies to the lynch mob to protect his
daughter's killer in *A Man's a Man*

In this film, Guy seems to be conscious of the general atmosphere of anti-Semitism (on the same page as the Solax review a Gaumont film entitled *The Christian Martyrs* is heavily publicized) and tries to redress this by depicting the Jew as a complete victim. The Jew is a Lower East Side apple vendor who is first insulted, then knocked down by a rich Gentile. (When his apples spill on the sidewalk he is set upon by street urchins who steal them all.) The rich man also runs over the Jew's only child, killing her. But the child's father shelters his daughter's killer from the lynch mob that comes after him. The rich man offers him money, but the Jew refuses it. A year later both men meet at the cemetery, over the child's grave. The final title is: "A man's a man, be he Jew or Gentile."

Clearly the film does not address real issues between Jews and Gentiles but the fact that minority groups have to struggle to achieve real citizenship. This is understood by a second reviewer in the same issue of *Moving Picture News*:

A Man's a Man
(Solax)

For centuries the popular impression of the Jew has been gleaned from the material, the unrelenting and the uncompromising figure of Shylock as portrayed by Shakespeare in the "Merchant of Venice" (sic). Up to very recently, the stage Jew was the only type which furnished universal amusement. Vaudeville has had its own way of showing him and the legitimate has had its way. Burlesque has had still another way, in which it portrayed the unfortunate brethren of Israel. Although each of these branches of amusement apparently attempted to represent the Jew with fidelity, not one of them saw possibilities in showing the Jews in another way than in long whiskers, derby hat down to the ears and hands moving like the fins of a fish.

Within the last few years what has been commonly known as mirth-provoking stake Jew has been gradually disappearing from view and in his place has come the new type of Jew—the American Jew—the Jew who is doing his share in American business, society and politics. No longer are Jews being represented in the old ways, but they are showing him in his new environment, where his manhood, his sentiments and his convictions are not burlesqued, but are idealized.[68]

The same plot could easily have been recounted in the guise of an Indian drama or a race picture produced by whites. Guy actually

Figure 42. Reconciliation scene in *A Man's a Man*

did produce and direct at least one film aimed at black audiences, which in 1912, and until the fifties, saw films in segregated theatres or in segregated areas within mostly white theatres. The recent discovery of this 1912 Solax picture with an all-black cast gave me an opportunity to examine the discourse of Americanization within the context of the early race picture movement. This film, *A Fool and His Money* (Solax 1912) was discovered by David Navone, an engineer in California, when he bought a trunk from an estate sale and then discovered four reels of nitrate film locked inside it. All of them are films made in the early 1910s by French filmmakers working in Fort Lee. The fact that *A Fool and His Money* was made by an immigrant filmmaker gives us a unique opportunity to compare its modes of address with that of other films of the period that featured black characters.

To most people, the term "race pictures" means films aimed primarily at black audiences who had grown weary of the "good old darkeys" and dancing pickaninies of mainstream cinema and who were outraged by the success of D.W. Griffith's *Birth of a Nation*. These audiences could be targeted in an economically efficient way because their viewing was primarily restricted to all-black theatres that arose after the 1897 Supreme Court Ruling mandating "separate but equal" racial segregation in the U.S. Most of these theatres were clustered in the "chitlin" belt—the vaudeville houses catering to black communities in the South. In 1919 there were 300 race picture houses in the U.S.; ten years later that figure had risen to 461.[69]

About 500 race pictures were made between 1915 and 1952, with the peak of production occurring in 1921-1922. These were also Oscar Micheaux's (b. 1884, d. 1951) most successful years as a film producer (he made over forty feature length films between 1919 and 1948). Because of this, and because he was the only silent race filmmaker to make the transition to sound, he has come to emblematize the race picture movement as a whole. Micheaux's work was long neglected but recently, several books on both his novels and his films have appeared.[70]

Although it is now easier to find material on Micheaux, it is harder to get a sense of the context from which the race picture movement emerged. The first race picture producer was probably black showman William Foster who started the Foster Photoplay Company in Chicago in 1913. Foster began making films for colored audiences following the model of Hollywood genres but with all-black casts, backed with white funding.[71] At least half a dozen race picture producers operated in the Chicago area alone, as Arnold Bernstein's noted in his book *Hollywood on Lake Michigan*, but more research is clearly needed.[72]

It is almost as difficult to find information on early race audiences. *Film Daily*, which kept track of such things, did not start publishing until 1919. To understand the numbers and composition of race picture audiences in the early to mid-1910s, a more painstaking type of research will have to be done. This is what I try to do with *A Fool and His Money*.

The first mention of *A Fool and his Money* is in a full-page ad that Alice Guy's company, Solax, took out in *The Moving Picture World* on Sept 21, 1912, and it simply says "*Darktown Aristocrats* Released Friday, October 11ᵗʰ." The use of the term "Darktown" to refer to primarily black neighborhoods was apparently a common one, as the Historical Feature Film Company of Chicago, which produced two-reel comedies aimed at both white and black audiences in the mid-1910s, released a film in 1915 entitled *Money Talks in Darktown*.[73]

The Solax film was advertised rather differently in the October 5, 1912 issue of *The Moving Picture World*:

A Fool and his Money
(The new title for Darktown Aristocrats)
Released Friday, October 11th

James Russell, the Cakewalk King, is featured in this attraction. The story is a satiric comedy dealing with the pretensions of colored folks. The way they try to ape and imitate their white brothers forms the basis of the story. A negro labourer suddenly gets in possession of a lot of money and there goes the pace.[74]

Although the film has not yet been preserved and therefore cannot be viewed, David Navone constructed an ingenious device that enabled him to photograph a representative sample of frame stills, which he then put on the web.[75] When we look at the film, even in this limited way, we can see that the emphasis is not on blacks "aping their white brothers" but on what is the proper way for someone—here, a black labourer, but the argument could just as easily be applied to immigrants—to better their social and economic standing. The change in emphasis shows that the film may have been conceived by Alice Guy and her production team with a black audience in mind but that the ad copy was later crafted for *The Moving Picture World* by the Solax publicist, H.Z. Levine.

It was probably also Levine who provided *The Moving Picture World* with the following plot synopsis, which was usually based on the script (which means there are often discrepancies between plot synopsis and finished film):

A Fool and his Money

(Oct. 11th). Sam Jones is a laborer—a wielder of the white-wash brush. He is in love with Lindy Williams. Having saved up quite a little money, Sam buys some swell second-hand clothes and goes to Lindy's home. Lindy's people are quite prosperous, her father having retired from his job as "Public Porter."

Lindy is a coquettish ebony beauty and trifles with Sam's affections. She plays Sam against Bill Johnson and finally, in despair Sam retires from the field. Walking along the road beaten and despondent, Sam finds a lot of money. Now, he vows, he will show them! He buys full dress clothes and other swell duds, an automobile and jewelry. Like a peacock he begins parading himself before Lindy and his rival, and, as can be expected, coquettish Lindy transfers her affections to him. Sam makes hay while the sun shines and proposes to Lindy and basks in her smiles. After his acceptance he sends out invitations to a reception, on which occasion he plans to announce his engagement.

During the reception Bill Johnson and his pal, Slick Mr. Tighe, concoct a scheme to break Sam. They invite him to a poker game and by cleverly stacking the cards and passing aces under the table with their naked toes, Sam is relieved of his fortune. When Lindy is apprised of this she gives Sam the cold shoulder and offers her arm to Slick Mr. Tighe, the possessor of all of Sam's wealth.[76]

I do not have any documentation so far that shows Alice Guy directed the film herself—it could have also been directed by Edward Warren—but in many ways this film follows Guy's standard operating procedure: the title, like many others produced by Guy during her career, refers to some idiom or myth, in this case, "A Fool and His Money Are Soon Parted." The film is a straightforward comic rendering of this axiom. Guy made many films that depicted the evils of gambling. In this film, however, gambling is given a comic treatment.

From the stills, we can see that Sam is a dark-skinned black and Lindy is very light skinned, with long hair in Mary-Pickford type sausage curls. The main attraction of the film is Sam's transformation as he spends his money: travelling to New York, buying a suit, jewelry, and a car.

The images show that the film is a romantic comedy, and not slapstick, though some scenes, like the scene where Slick (depicted as "the rowdy town black of Reconstruction, grinning under his high hat" as Cripps describes Griffith's "favorite bugbears"[77]) cheats at cards by passing a card around the back of the table with his bare foot, are played very broadly. Still, there are no pickaninnies dancing—instead, the engagement party shows extremely well-dressed couples waltzing or foxtrotting.

The opening scene, which shows Sam in his painter's overalls hard at work, and the closing scene, showing a sadder and wiser Sam back on the job, intimate that Sam has been punished for aspiring to rise above his class. But the film also shows a sophisticated black middle-class enjoying themselves in an elegant setting. This aspect of the film caught the attention of the reviewer for *The Moving Picture World*, who said: "It's a love story with good darky comedy, human and fresh. There is a darky evening reception and dance that is something quite new. We think that it will please everywhere any pictures of darkies would be acceptable and commend it as a first rate offering."[78]

The father, who is the source of the wealth in this elegant household, is clearly described as a retired Pullman Porter—one of the few ways that black men could cross class lines, though it took long years of dedicated work. In other words, Sam is not a transgressor because he aspires to be rich and marry a rich man's daughter, but because he wants to enjoy the privileges of wealth without working long and hard for it as Lindy's Pullman Porter father did.

Who was the audience for this film? H.Z. Levine's ad copy makes it clear that in the white trade press, at least, the film was being marketed as a slapstick comedy, though the title and the stills indicate something more like a morality tale. Would Alice Guy have been aware of discourses circulating among black spectators? There is a slight possibility that she would have been acquainted with the black cultural review, *The New York Age*, which featured a weekly column on theatre, music, and film by critic Lester A. Walton. Even if she was not familiar with the *New York Age*, she would have read the reprint of his article entitled "Degeneracy in the Moving Pictures" which appeared in the *Moving Picture News* in 1909. In this article, Walton decries the representation of lynching in certain films and the use of lynching images in theatrical posters.

According to Anna Everett, several white papers were moved to endorse Walton's position and urge motion picture manufacturers to "cease giving offense to vast numbers of our population."[79]

According to Walton there were almost 1000 nickelodeons operating in the New York area in 1914. Black spectators could only sit in certain sections or attend on certain days. In addition, they might have seen films at school or in church. It seems possible that the distributor for whom this film was intended suggested a plot along these lines, that the morality tale quality of the film is Guy's interpretation of "uplift." In other words, the dream that is reflected here is the dream of assimilation, which on the industry side refers to a "long-range strategy... to submerge all class distinctions into an ostensibly homogenous culture of consumption,"[80] and a desire on the part of minorities to overcome the debilitating effects of "twoness."

Assimilation was an issue for immigrants as well as for people of color. We could see the issues of assimilation at work in the fact that Guy used a plot she might just as easily have used with white characters; but she may have felt a personal connection with the story as well. The setting, in fact, is Alice Guy's own house,[81] and the car that Sam drives is her car. Guy herself may have identified with Sam to a certain extent: she had just sold her shares, earned as an employee, in the Gaumont Company and had taken the huge risk of investing every last cent, plus taking out an additional mortgage for the second half of the needed funds, to build a new studio for the Solax Company in Fort Lee. Because this studio was not yet ready, films like *A Fool and His Money* were shot in and around the Gaumont studio in Flushing, New York, and on location (in this case, Guy's own house, at least the exteriors). The plot of the film, and the timing of its release, leads one to ask if Guy had some doubts about putting all of her hard-earned money into the studio, especially with a baby at home and another one on the way. Perhaps, she had those doubts and exorcised them by making this film.

The film appears to be the only one that Guy produced with an all-black cast. Blacks hardly appear in her extant films, and when they do, as when the white hero mistakenly proposes to a black woman in *Matrimony's Speed Limit*, (Solax 1913), they are a cause of comic revulsion for the white characters. In *Beasts of the Jungle* (3 reels, Solax, 1913) directed by Edward Warren under Guy's supervision, a pro-colonialist stance is clear: blacks are half-naked, whites are clothed; blacks live in tents, whites in wooden houses; blacks are eaten by the lion one by one, but whites remain unscathed. In her feature film *The Great Adventure* (Loew 1918), there are two racist depictions. First, in a scene where the heroine Milly, and her aunt leave their country town and get off the train at the big city, when a black porter takes their luggage, the aunt is sure that he is stealing it; Milly has to explain the system to her. Later, there is a black receptionist at the hotel who is usually asleep on the job, or clowning around in some way.

In her feature film *House of Cards* (U.S. Amusement Corporation, 1917), Guy seemed conscious of the injustice and tries to remedy it by depicting the little black boy (the only principal character who is unnamed in the press materials) as an almost blameless victim. The boy has been kidnapped by gypsies (Guy had a typically French antipathy towards gypsies, who always played the roles of "heavies" in her films) and brainwashed into doing their dirty work. He lures a little rich girl out of her home so that the gypsies can hold her for ransom, but "the girl's beauty and purity bring him to his senses" as it says in the script, and they run away together. The rest of the film shows the children working in various factories (Guy said she made the film to show the horrors of child labor) and sharing all their proceeds and hardships in perfect partnership. In the end, the boy's conversion prompted by the "pure little white girl" exonerates him from his original crime. The film does not use the black character as an opportunity to enlarge on the dialogue between blacks and whites. It is not race that causes discord, in Guy's view, but inequalities in class standing.

We can conclude, then, that for Guy, assimilation partly meant taking on the stereotypes of the adopted culture. In many ways, expressing "Americanized" views did not entail straying very far from her own biases.

At the same time, we can read some sense of identification between immigrant and disenfranchised black; at the very least, we can recognize a willingness to put Jewish characters (*A Man's a Man*), Eastern European immigrants (*The Making of an American Citizen*) and blacks (*A Fool and His Money*) at the center of melodramas that incorporate stereotypical tropes but also undercut those tropes. Such films require a multiplicitous reading and point to the need for further study of early representation of blacks and ethnic characters, early race cinema, and of how these films were received by various audiences.

5 THE FEATURE-LENGTH FILMS AND THE END OF THE SOLAX COMPANY

THE TRANSITION FROM one-reelers to feature-length films as we know them today (five reels or more) began in 1909 and 1910, when Stuart Blackton and D.W. Griffith made their first tentative multiple-reel films. In 1911, Griffith again tried to push the 900-foot standard length with his *Enoch Arden*, a longer version of his one-reeler, *After Many Years* (Biograph, 1908). A further aid to this shift was the exhibitor's practice of showing two reels from a serial together to make a longer story. As early as 1909, Vitagraph sent out *The Life of Moses* in multiple reels, one each week, and theaters held onto them, screening the multiple reels as a single feature. In 1912, Adolph Zukor distributed a three-reel French film entitled *Queen Elizabeth* starring Sarah Bernhardt (Film d'Art 1912). Other film companies began to make forays into multiple reel films, although the Motion Pictures Patent Company, which had built up an industrial system predicated on single-reel films, was firmly opposed to it. Things changed quickly though, as David Robinson has pointed out.[1]

As is well known, Biograph, in spite of Griffith's eagerness to make longer films, was slow to jump on the feature-length bandwagon. But even so, he was able to produce two five-reel films in 1913 and several three-reel films. The conflict over film length eventually encouraged Griffith to leave the company later that year.

In 1913, change came not just for Biograph, but for the industry as a whole. It was the last year that European film manufacturers were able to match the U.S. market share. The success of two Italian epics, *Quo Vadis?* and *The Last Days of Pompeii* showed that the day of the feature-length film had arrived. And yet production of one-reel films continued unabated.[2] For many scholars, 1913 is the year that cinema as we know it really came to be.[3]

Solax was quick to jump on the multiple-reel bandwagon, and so, once again, a peak moment in the career of Alice Guy matched a peak moment in the film industry as a whole: 1913 was also the height of Solax's artistic, if not financial, success. Many critics have assumed that Solax went out of business in 1914 because Guy could not make the transition from directing one-reeler films to multiple reel films, either artistically or economically. I have already dealt with the economic side of the question; now, let us look at the artistic issue.

Solax started to move toward longer productions by pushing the length-limit of one-reel films. The first of these was *The Violin Maker of Nuremberg*, released December 9, 1911, and the second *Mignon*, based on the opera, released February 2, 1912. Both films were around 1,000 feet long, twice the length of the average one-reel film. *Mignon* was timed to go with the principal musical moments of the opera, and Solax provided an orchestral arrangement to the exchanges.

The first true multiple-reel film to be produced by Solax was the three-reeler *Fra Diavolo*, directed by Guy herself (July 1912). Based on the Aubert opera which itself was based on the life of Michele Pezza (1771–1806), known as Fra Diavolo, the production cost 25,000 dollars and required 200 workers.[4] The picture called for elaborate staging and costuming. Judging from the photographs in *The Moving Picture News*, some of the costumes from *The Violin Maker of Nuremberg* were re-used. *Fra Diavolo* was Guy's first three-reeler, but she picked her plot well: in its staging, this film repeated some of the best bits of business from her previous one-reel films.

Fra Diavolo (Billy Quirck) romances Lady Allcash in order to steal her jewelry, and Lorenzo (Darwin Karr), a lieutenant of the guard who is in love with the innkeeper's daughter, Zerline (Vinnie Burns), is eager to catch Diavolo and claim the reward so he and Zerline can marry. One scene noted by reviewers[5] was the moment that Diavolo and some of his men hide in a closet in a room between the Allcashes and Zerline's. Zerline comes in and undresses, much to their delight, and then strikes a series of vain poses in front of the mirror. Lorenzo joins her, but his arrival awakens Lord and Lady Allcash, who catch them at an embarrassing moment. One of the thieves stumbles in the closet, so Diavolo quickly steps out to cover for his men as they escape. He pulls Lorenzo aside and claims to have had an assignation with Lady Allcash then and pulls Lord Allcash aside to tell him he had an assignation with Zerline. Both men find this amusing and let him go. Eventually of course, Lorenzo gets Diavolo and Zerline.[6]

In this film, Guy appears to have re-used some tried and true pieces of business: robbing a coach harkens back to one of her earliest period films for Gaumont, *L'Assassinat du courrier de Lyon* (Gaumont 1904). Zerline's scene of making faces in front of the mirror and the men making faces back (even if it is the next day) bears some similarity to the mirror scene in *His Double* (Solax, 1912). She had already used Cliffhanger Point in more than one film, most memorably in *Two Little Rangers* (Solax, 1912), in which the youngest sister forces the villain over the precipice. It is a pity that nothing appears to be left of *Fra Diavolo*. It is, however, documented by several articles in the press.

One of these press pieces took pains to describe Madame Blaché's success at directing such a great film with no compromise to her femininity:

> The time has arrived, so it would seem, when woman must take her place beside man in the majority of arts and professions in the business world. In women of the calibre of Madame Alice Blaché it has also been demonstrated that there is a possibility of their doing so without being shorn of that most desirable of womanly qualities, femininity. Like Schumann-Heink, Madame Blaché is an exemplification of a successful wifehood, motherhood and professional ability and practice.
>
> From time to time the moving picture world has been awakened to admiration by the splendid work of picture production exhibited by the feminine director of the Solax Moving Picture Company. It is not so long since *The Violin Makers of Nuremberg*, with its artistic settings and masterly action, elicited the warmest praise from the public as well as the trade. Later on came the filmed production of the opera *Mignon*, and now to demonstrate even in stronger measure the masterly capability of her hand, Auber's *Fra Diavolo* flashes upon the screen before our astonished eyes.[7]

In August of 1912, Solax released the three-reeler *Dublin Dan*, starring a well-known Irish actor named Barney Gilmore. The release of this film coincided with the move from the Flushing studio to the $100,000 glass-house studio the couple had built in Fort Lee. (According to Bachy, the company's profits were between $50,000 and $60,000 a year in 1911 and 1912; most of the profit was reinvested in the Flushing and Fort Lee studio structures.)[8]

Fragments of the second and third reels of *Dublin Dan* still exist at the NFTVA. The story was novelized in *Motion Picture Story*[9] and advertised in *The Moving Picture News* on September 7, 1912. Bachy notes that in her own papers, Guy credited the direction of this film to her husband, Herbert Blaché. No director was listed in the advertisements, and Bachy surmises that this is because Blaché was still under contract with Gaumont at that time. Blaché had assisted his wife with the direction of *Fra Diavolo* in July. If Bachy is correct, *Dublin Dan* would be the first feature film Herbert Blaché directed.[10]

However, press releases sent out from Solax itself and printed in *The Moving Picture World* credit the film to Edward Warren, along with *The Equine Spy* (Solax, 1912, 1 reel), *Beasts of the Jungle*, *Kelly from the Emerald Isle* and *Brennan of the Moor*.[11] It is possible that Blaché directed it secretly in order to protect his position at Gaumont, perhaps assisted by Warren, and then allowed Warren to take the credit. If this is the case, one could imagine that such an arrangement would have rankled, especially if it applied not just to *Dublin Dan* but *Brennan of the Moor* (Solax, Aug. 1913) and *Kelly from the Emerald Isle* (Solax, May 1913). It would go a long way toward explaining why Warren left Solax when Blaché joined it officially in June of 1913, and why just a few months later Blaché started his own company, Blaché Features, and made a point of prominently displaying his own name in all the pertinent press releases and advertisements. However, I have not seen the documentation that Bachy referred to. The retraction published by *The Moving Picture World*, crediting the films to Edward Warren after mistakenly crediting them to Guy (reprinted in its entirety on page 163), seems sufficient proof to me that Warren made these films.

According to Solax's advertising, Barney Gilmore was a well-known Irish stage actor. *Dublin Dan* was billed as an "Irish" story, with Dan as a member of the FBI chasing down a group of counterfeiters. In the process, he falls in love with Rosalie (Blanche Cornwall), the ward of the villain, whom he has to rescue from kidnappers.[12] The film has some interesting touches like an entrance to a counterfeiter's den hidden behind a painting. The visual style, especially the slow rhythm of the performances, the "early noir" quality of the depictions of the criminals show that the serials of Feuillade might have been an inspiration. One of the criminals is played by Lee Beggs, and an old woman in the group is played by Mrs. Hurley. The film has some excellent lighting set-ups and high production value and was marketed with an elaborate color poster.

Although at least two Solax one-reelers were announced and synopsized in *The Moving Picture World* every week, the production of three-reelers continued unabated throughout 1913: *Beasts of the Jungle* (3 reels, January 1913, screenplay by Guy, directed by Warren), *Dick Whittington and His Cat* (3 reels, May 1913, screenplay and directed by Guy), *Kelly From the Emerald Isle* (3 reels, May 1913, screenplay by Guy, Warren, Blaché and Gilmore himself, directed by Warren), *The Pit and the Pendulum* (3 reels, August 1913, screenplay and directed by Guy, based on the tale by E.A. Poe), *Brennan of the Moor* (3 reels, May 1913, directed by Warren).[13]

A long and detailed interview with "Madame Blaché" appeared in the May 17, 1913 issue of *The Moving Picture World*. One of the striking things about this article is that the journalist compares the Solax production—written and directed by Alice Guy—of *Dick Whittington and his Cat* to *Les Misérables*, and *Quo Vadis*. In the interview, Guy describes the preparation for two of Solax's upcoming features:

> In a talk on this subject with Madame Blaché, president and manager of production of the Solax Company, and herself the producer of features like "Fra Diavolo," "Dick Whittington and His Cat," and a few others said: "Besides an expenditure of large sums of money, the production of a feature means weeks of tedious preparation and research. Before a single foot of film was taken, "Dick Whittington and his Cat" consumed five weeks of my time and the time of my staff. Our coming feature with the famous Barney Gilmore in the leading role, "Kelly from the Emerald Isle," was produced after six weeks of preliminary work. There were consultations with the director, with Mr. Gilmore, with the author of the scenario, and with the scenic artists. After the scenario was finally in shape, it was beyond the recognition of the author. Then followed the routine work of sketching costumes for the costumers, of laying out plans and sketches of sets, of going the rounds for props and incidentals, and finishing touches. Mr. Gilmore's friends in the old country were of considerable assistance. They sent over a trunk full of stuff for atmosphere and local color. The sheebeens (country taverns of Ireland), Irish sitting-rooms, and dwellings and furnishings for those sets were secured with considerable difficulty.

There are several scenes in the production which are genuinely thrilling. In one, Kelly, and his sweetheart clinging to his neck, is seen climbing down a declivity several hundred feet deep. Another scene shows Kelly escaping death by jumping on the cow-catcher of a train going at full speed. There is also a spectacular destruction of a hut by gunpowder and dynamite.[14]

This article not only indicates that Guy was considered by the trade press as a skilled director and producer of feature-length films, it also shows that Guy was perfectly aware of every element required to make a "blockbuster": action, intrigue, exotic locations, thrills, some of which were achieved with special effects, and last but not least, stars.

The article also gives us a taste of what life was like at Solax during the height of its multiple-reel productions.

The Solax Features

BEASTS OF THE *Jungle* and *Brennan of the Moor* still exist in their entirety. Although Bachy credits *Beasts* to Guy, who might have claimed authorship because she was the sole screenwriter, *Beasts of the Jungle* was advertised as the work of director Edward Warren. Stylistically speaking, it seems consistent with other films he directed for Solax. The film was heavily advertised. For many years, feminist fans attributed the film to Guy, possibly because she appeared in the advertising with Princess, the tame tiger used in some of the scenes. Also featured in the film are an elephant, a monkey, a parrot, and a lion. Vinnie Burns starred as the young girl, Darwin Karr as her father, and Fannie Simpson as her mother. Although she does not give a film title, Guy was surely speaking of *Beasts* when she made the following comments:

> Sometimes the studio resembled a menagerie, as wild animals furnished us with excellent material. The trainer [Paul] Bourgeois[15] brought me, one day, a magnificent tigress weighing six hundred pounds. He assured me she was gentleness itself and begged me to caress her through the bars of her cage, to encourage the actors. I admit that I felt a certain hesitancy, but a director must not be a wet hen; I did the thing, and Princess received my advances very nicely, purring under the caress and rubbing against the bars like a great cat. Vinnie Burns, an eighteen-year-old actress whom I had coached, was the first to enter the cage.[16]

Figure 43. Vinnie Burns, Alice Guy's handpicked star, in *Beasts of the Jungle*

Figure 44. Vinnie Burns, with elephant, in *Beasts of the Jungle*

Beasts starts with Winnie (Vinnie Burns) as a young girl in India. She decides to go for a ride on an elephant (Paul Bourgeois played the elephant keeper), and the elephant takes her far into the woods, where she gets lost. Meanwhile, a professor sets a trap in a cabin for a tiger that he has been tracking for a long time; the tiger (Princess) falls into the trap. Winnie sees the cabin and thinks there might be someone in there who can help her, then finds herself in the cabin with the tiger. After some moments of terror, she realizes the tiger is tame and lets the tiger lead the way out of the woods. Once home, she is allowed to keep the tiger as a pet, and Princess goes with her and her family when her father's work transfers him to Africa.

In Africa, we see him supervising a team of Africans who are building a railroad. The workmen live in tents and one by one are being devoured by the "man-eater," a lion. (The strong colonialist viewpoint of this film is emphasized by a scene where the workmen dance around a fire to cast a spell that will protect them from the lion.) In the climactic scene, the lion has the white family trapped in their house; there is a split-screen shot with the family on the inside of the house and the lion on the other side of the wall. Because they have been shipped some blank cartridges by mistake, they cannot shoot the lion, so they let the lion into the house and let Princess intimidate him until he falls into the cellar. Once he is trapped in the cellar, they have no weapons with which to kill him, so they set the entire cabin on fire. By now it is night, so watching the (real) cabin burn completely is quite a spectacle. The film ends with Winnie embracing the tigress. Guy might have been thinking of the split-screen shot in *Beasts of the Jungle* when she wrote the following:

> We had no difficulty in finding builders or specialized electricians, the American studios being already, from that point of view, better equipped than our own. However, their ignorance of certain procedures really astonished me. The first time that I asked my cameraman to get a special effect (on that occasion, a man walking on the water) he told me that this was impossible. I had to insist and to guide him, step by step, to obtain a result which filled him with admiration and earned me his respect.
>
> One film where I had used a system of masks that permit printing two different views of the same image, and obtain double exposure effects, so intrigued the cameramen that they begged me to explain by what means I had achieved that result.[17]

Figure 45. The split-screen scene in *Beasts of the Jungle*

According to Bachy,[18] the film was a critical and financial success. Bachy also credits it with being the film to initiate a fad for films
featuring animals as characters, but from the ads in *The Moving
Picture World* it seems clear that animal pictures were well-established
by the time *Beasts* was made. Except for the interesting use of the
split-screen and the spectacle of the fire, the film plays very flatly. The
lion is mangy, and the sets he is in look so much like zoo enclosures
that there is no suspense at all. And once the lion is trapped in the
cellar, burning the house down seems like overkill.

Brennan of the Moor, also credited to Edward Warren, is much
more successful. Starring Barney Gilmore yet again, the film plays like
a remake of *Dublin Dan.* The visual design is much more striking,
perhaps because sets from *The Sewer* were re-used and some of the
staging of that film was imitated. The film has many similarities
with *Dublin Dan*: not just the choice of actor, but the helpless female
(not quite as helpless as the heroine from *Dublin Dan*, but almost),
the use of coaches, the trading of identities with other men in order
to penetrate a forbidden space (in this case, the ball), the pit where

the hero is imprisoned, the hidden spaces within spaces that are discovered by accident. However, *Brennan* is a marked improvement over *Dublin Dan*. More of an effort is made at characterization, beginning with the death of Brennan's father. The choice of Marion Swayne makes more sense than the shrinking Blanche Cornwall for a female action side-kick. A thrilling moment comes at the end when Brennan and Lady Betty escape from the villain by crossing a chasm on a bridge formed from the linked bodies of acrobats!

The third film produced by Solax to star Barney Gilmore was *Kelly from the Emerald Isle* (Solax 1913). *Kelly* was based on a popular play of the same title, written by Mrs. Barney Gilmore, which had already made her husband into a star. Plans to make it into a film for Gilmore were begun as soon as the actor was put under contract with Solax. Because the play was so well-known, *The Moving Picture World* did not bother to synopsize it, but it is clear from the review that it is another action-adventure in the same genre as *Dublin Dan* and *Brennan of the Moor*, with an active heroine who rescues him at least once. A famous scene shows Gilmore tied to railroad tracks as the train is bearing down on him. Blaché is nowhere mentioned in the review, but the reviewer, H.K. Judson, does note that: "We believe that all who have enjoyed it on the stage will like the picture of it very much; for Madame Blaché, producing it out of doors has been able to give convincing touches of realism, impossible before the footlights, and has also given several sensational things, like the escape of Kelly and Sheilah over the cliff, a feat that will make the audience wonder how the players dare to risk their lives."[19]

At this point, the terms "produced by" and "directed by" were often used interchangeably, as demonstrated in the retraction published the following week in *The Moving Picture World*:

Director Edward Warren Made It

In a review of the Solax feature picture, "Kelly From the Emerald Isle," published in last week's issue of *The Moving Picture World*, our reviewer credited the production of the picture to Madame Blaché. Advice from the Solax studio received to the effect that Madame Blaché did not direct the production of this excellent picture, but that the credit is due to Edward Warren, who produced *Beasts of the Jungle, Dublin Dan*, and several other Solax Features.[20]

Guy continued to produce and direct features throughout 1913: *Blood and Water* (2 reels, Solax, October, 1913), *The Rogues of Paris* (4 reels, October 1913) and *Shadows of the Moulin Rouge* (also screenwriter, 4 reels, December 1913).[21] All of these films starred Claire Whitney and Vinnie Burns (who played a crossdressing detective in *Rogues of Paris*) and all, apparently, have been lost. Of the longer films Guy made for Solax, the only one remaining is *Dick Whittington and His Cat*, arguably her masterpiece from the Solax period as well as a key turning point in both her marriage and her career.

The plot of *Dick Whittington* is based on the fairy tale: Dick, a young boy (played by Vinnie Burns dressed in a Peter Pan-like outfit) hears wondrous tales of London, where the streets are paved with gold. At night he dreams of the capital (slides are projected on the wall over Dick's sleeping head to represent his dream-visions). The next day he leaves his country home to seek his fortune in London. He fails to find work at first and is almost starving when a wealthy sea-merchant (Darwin Karr) takes him in as cook's help. The cook (Mrs. Hurley) takes an instant dislike to him and tortures him mercilessly. His garret is full of rats and he often goes without food. One day, a man on the street takes him for a beggar and gives him a coin, which he uses to buy a cat. Soon after this, little Alice, the merchant's daughter, befriends him and plays a trick on the cook to steal food for Dick. The sequence is one Guy used much earlier, in *La Concierge* (Gaumont, 1901): they tie a string to the knocker and knock the door repeatedly. While the cook answers the door they steal her dinner. The second time she answers the door, she throws a bucket of water on an unsuspecting passerby.

It is also Alice who persuades Dick to add his cat to the wares the servants send out as items for sale on the merchant's ship. En route, the boat catches fire and burns (Guy actually incinerated a real boat) and the merchant and his crew are taken prisoner by the Sultan, but released when Dick's cat proves effective against the rats that overrun the Sultan's palace.

Dick decides to go home after the cook has been particularly cruel, but hears the bells of London (seen as a superimposition over his head as he sleeps) predicting that he will be thrice Lord Mayor. Dick returns and the merchant gives him a coffer full of money. Dick gives gifts to all, including the cook, and in the last scene we see him and Alice, both now grown, getting married.

Dick Whittington is probably the best representative of a genre of films that was close to Guy's heart: fantasy period pieces with elaborate sets and costuming, usually with child-heroes and based on sources such as fairy tales (*Dick Whittington*), opera (*Fra Diavolo*), plays or novels (*The Sewer, The Pit and the Pendulum*). *The Legend of Hanging Rock* (Solax, 1912), and *The Violin Maker of Nuremberg* (Solax, 1912) are among others that appear to fit into this category. Guy designed the costumes of *Dick Whittington* herself, and cast Vinnie Burns, an actress she had carefully trained and who had starred in many of Guy's most distinctive films, as the lead. To date, it is the best preserved of Guy's later films. Bachy calls it the summit of her achievement during the Solax period,[22] the period of her career when she had total artistic control. After screening what little remains of *The Pit and the Pendulum*, the other likely contestant for the honor of Guy's best Solax film, I have to agree with him.

Herbert Blaché at Solax

SINCE THE MOVE to the new Fort Lee studio, Herbert Blaché had been more and more involved in Solax production: from his vague description as advisor, he graduated to actively producing single-reelers like *A Million Dollars* (January 1913) and assisting his wife with longer films like *Dick Whittington*. The April 5, 1913 issue of *The Moving Picture World* recounts:

> While blowing up a ship for the pictures, Mr. Herbert Blaché was severely burned by a premature explosion of a keg of gunpowder. Though painfully burned about the head and arms and now confined to his bed, the doctor's last report is very satisfactory, and we hope to see him well and about in a very short time.[23]

It might have taken weeks for Blaché to mend, but neither he nor Guy were the least discouraged by his accident. Within a month, Blaché would be sitting in the president's chair at Solax, leaving Guy to concentrate on producing and directing.

Guy also recounts this incident in her *Memoirs*:

> My husband often preferred to take a personal risk. For my film *Dick Whittington and His Cat*, in order to illustrate the sinking of the pirate ship, we had transformed a big old unused

sailboat into a magnificent caravelle [sic]. The gunpowder and the fuse to provoke the explosion being ready, my husband, arguing that women lacked the sangfroid for this, insisted on executing the task himself. But when the wind had three times extinguished the fuse, he lost patience and tossed the match directly into the powder. The blast was thunderous. I was on the opposite bank with the cameramen and some journalists amused by my anxiety. I saw my husband regain the bank in the little boat into which he had fallen back, fortunately. Worried, in spite of that, I begged my assistant to go get news of my husband. He had taken refuge in a bar, where he lost consciousness. Seriously burned on the face and hands, it took weeks for him to mend.[24]

It seems clear that at this stage the Guy-Blaché marriage was still strong. Herbert Blaché was doing his best to make himself useful on the set and Guy was still actively rooting for him. In fact, all of the accounts, taken together, make the shooting of *Dick Whittington* sound like a fondly remembered adventure. And the Solax Company never lacked for adventures! Alan Williams said:

Like so many creative people once marked by the experience of poverty (in her case, relative), Alice Guy never forgot how to economize. But she also obviously liked the *challenge* of cinema, which was even more daunting when it had to be met mainly with found materials. And she liked to be surprised, sometimes pleasantly, sometimes unpleasantly, at what she ended up doing. For Guy, cinema was a process of discovery.[25]

As an economy-minded producer, Guy organized numerous productions around her latest "found resource." She created movies for found objects like the coach at the center of *L'Assassinat du courrier de Lyon* (Gaumont, 1904). We have seen how she made a series of films for Gaumont starring the O'Mers, once she had determined their cinematic value. In 1911 she made a series of Westerns after discovering a troupe of Bronco riders. The first of these films was *Outwitted by Horse and Lariat* (Solax, 1911).

In 1913, she had a new "found" resource: rats. They first appear to harass Darwin Karr from a distance in *The Sewer*. They appear twice in *Dick Whittington*, first in Dick's garret which prompts him to get a cat, and then in the Sultan's throne room which prompts the sale of the cat for a very high price. They harass Millie in *The Ocean Waif* (5 reels, November 1916, International Film Service) when she is first "haunting" the mansion. In *Dublin Dan*, they eat through the hero's ropes, a role they reprise in *The Pit and the Pendulum* (3 reels, August 1913). One has to wonder if Menessier was particularly partial to these rats, as he was the art director for all of the films in which they appeared except for *Ocean Waif*. Guy recounts a particularly grueling adventure with the rats on the set of *The Pit and the Pendulum*:

> *The Pit and the Pendulum* of Edgar Allan Poe was a hard trial for Darwin Karr, my young leading man. We had imagined as a way to deliver him by cutting his ropes... while he lies tied to the torture rack, waiting for the fatal sweep of the knife... to confide this mission to gutter rats. The cords were copiously smeared with food to attract the rats. They fulfilled their role marvelously, but a few preferred fresh meat, [and] came sniffing at the nose of the actor and even penetrated the legs of his trousers. When at last the ropes broke he was not slow to jump to his feet, swearing there would be no retake.
>
> We had the greatest difficulty in keeping the rats from invading the studio. We had surrounded the stage with metal plates, on which they would slide and be unable to get away. They had to be destroyed on the spot. First we tossed into their midst an enormous cat, who, horrified, jumped the barrier at one bound. Then it was the turn of my little bulldog, an excellent ratter... the unhappy beast was immobilized at once by twenty or so rats who attacked him from every vantage point. We had to rescue him from his miserable situation. Finally, all the personnel took arms, cudgels, clubs, and finally, not without difficulty, we won out. We were happy to be rid of the rats, but forced to admire their courage.
>
> The film had an enormous success. I went incognito to the first showing and had great pleasure in observing the shivers and anguished sighs of the public.[26]

Rats, of course, were not the only animals used in Solax films. An assortment of zoo animals were directed by Edward Warren for *Beasts in the Jungle* has already been described. "Despite her revulsion," Guy demonstrated for an actor playing the "high priest for the temple of the serpents" in an unnamed film, how to wrap a serpent around his neck. But the rats were the only animals that made regular repeat performances.[27]

Figure 46. *The Pit and the Pendulum*

The rats in *The Pit and the Pendulum* might have been symbolic of the monks in the story. The setting is Spain during the Inquisition, the hero is Dr. Alonzo (Darwin Karr), who is in love with Isabella (Blanche Cornwall). Pedro (Fraunie Fraunholz) is also in love with Isabella. When Dr. Alonzo wins her affections, Pedro joins an order of monks who use the Inquisition as a means of furthering their own interests, and plots his revenge. He hides some jeweled icons from the monastery in Alonzo's home and frames Alonzo for the theft. Alonzo and Isabella are captured and taken to the monastery, where they are tortured. When Alonzo sees that Isabella is in danger, he confesses to the theft and is condemned to death. He is tied to a table with a slowly descending pendulum that will eventually slice him in half. However, some friendly rats chew through his bonds and he breaks free, but then the steel walls of his prison, heated until they glow red-hot, start to close in on him as the sadistic monks look on. Fortunately, Isabella arrives with soldiers and sets him free.

The first reel of this film still exists in the Library of Congress. Again, we see Menessier's beautiful sets and Guy's by then trademark elaborate costuming. Fraunholz overplays his role as the evil monk

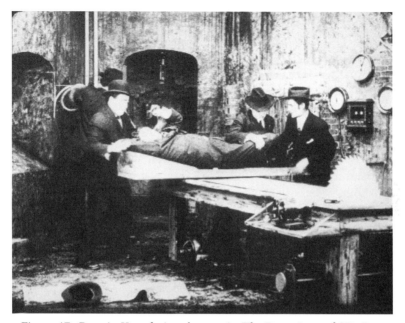

Figure 47. Darwin Karr facing the saw in *The Detective and His Dog*

but Karr and Cornwall are very natural in their scenes together. It is a pity that the great action denouement no longer seems to exist. Stills in *The Moving Picture World*[28] show that the pendulum scene was staged much more dramatically (Karr faces the audience, and his platform must have been slightly raised to give the most dramatic view) than a similar scene in *The Detective and His Dog* (1 reel, Solax, April 1912) where the hero is moving slowly toward a circular table saw. The still in the latter film shows the saw in profile and the composition of the entire scene is flat.

In June of 1913, an article appeared in *The Moving Pictures World* announcing "Herbert Blaché Joins Solax."[29] In the memoirs, Guy wrote about her husband participating more in the management of the Solax Company:

> My husband, having finished his contract with Gaumont, had taken the presidency of Solax. I abandoned the reins to him with pleasure. I never attended any of the conferences where the Sales Co. composed the programs; I would have embarrassed the men, said Herbert, who wanted to smoke their cigars and to spit at their ease while discussing business.[30]

Was etiquette really such a serious concern, or was Herbert trying to promote himself over his wife, as some scholars have stated? There were marked differences in social life between 1913 and today. The rules governing social class and daily etiquette were much stricter. The members of each class had places that were much more clearly defined. Communication between the classes and between the sexes were still formally and strictly regulated, though these rules of comportment varied widely from place to place. Given these conditions, it is hard to know the real reason why Guy did not attend these meetings.

Although Herbert Blaché was more welcome at "Sales Co." meetings than Guy was, his presidency of Solax apparently only lasted for three months, from June to August of 1913.

The August 16, 1913 issue of *The Moving Picture News* had an article about Edward Warren's departure from Solax "on good terms" (proven by the fact that Solax did the lab work for a film on the Boy Scouts that Warren produced independently). The article credits Warren with directing the following films: *The Sewer, The Equine Spy, Brennan of the Moor, Kelly of the Emerald Isle,* and *Beasts of the Jungle.*[31]

In the September 13, 1913, issue of *The Moving Picture World*, an announcement appears that Darwin Karr's two-year contract with Solax has ended and that he is now going to spend some time touring the countryside in the motor-car he had used to go visit his parents between films.[32] There is no indication why Karr, one of the key dramatic stars of Solax's successful year, did not have his contract renewed or how he parted with Solax, only that he is resting from his cinematic labors. On February 7, 1914, *The Moving Picture World* noted that Billy Quirck had joined Vitagraph. One by one, Guy appeared to be losing the people who had helped her reach her success. It would be easy to conclude, as some scholars have, that Blaché's increased presence at Solax contributed to the alienation of these key personnel, but Guy said nothing of the kind in her memoirs. As noted in Chapter 2, the causes of Solax's downfall were several, the principal one being the lack of distribution for the films after mid-1912.

On August 23, 1913, *The Moving Picture World* published a two-page ad announcing the formation of Blaché Features as well as a press release on the "Blaché American Features" that would soon be forthcoming.[33] According to the press release:

It is [Blaché's] plan to produce three-, four- and five- reel classical adaptations as well as sensational and melodramatic modern subjects. All the features will be produced under Mr. Blaché's personal direction and management with the co-operation of his talented wife. In talking about his plans for the future, Mr. Blaché said, "The demand has been very insistent for more Solax Features than the number being released. The remarkable success Solax has had with 'The Beasts of the Jungle', 'Dick Whittington and His Cat', 'Kelly from the Emerald Isle', and 'The Pit and the Pendulum', all of which were closed out for the entire country, is an indication of the demand and popularity of our productions. While Solax will continue to produce its features under the direction and supervision of Madame Blaché and my advice, I personally, however, will guide the destinies of the new brand. Our stock companies will be entirely separate and distinct as well as the other departments of our organization. In the production of our features, we expect to use some Broadway stars in the leading roles as well as the plays produced on the legitimate stage. We have made some very satisfactory arrangements in those directions and we have under preparation some very remarkable productions which will be announced shortly.

This press release actually seems to be three statements in one: first and above all, it is a declaration of independence from a man who had lived too long under the shadow of Léon Gaumont and his own wife. Second, it is interesting to note that he intends to produce exactly the kinds of films that Solax had produced so successfully: "classical adaptations" (as we have seen, Guy's specialty) as well as "melodramatic modern subjects," (Blaché's specialty, or at least, Edward Warren's). Then there is the shaky assurance that both companies will operate successfully side by side, and finally a statement about Solax's future production delivered by the "royal we" which shows that at least in Blaché's mind, the two production companies were not going to be separate at all. Clearly the time was one of great personal and business-related upheaval.

Blaché's decision to form Blaché Pictures might have been a reaction to editorials in the trade press or to what was said in those meetings. There were many editorials about how longer pictures made by bigger companies would be of higher artistic quality and would therefore sell better. So Blaché, with Blaché Features, set out to meet what he perceived to be the market demand for feature length films, based on "artistic" stories from literature and high brow theater. These films were often shot as if they were stage plays, with a proscenium approach.

Guy was listed as "vice president" of Blaché Features and the couple divided the directing work more or less equally. According to Guy's typed list, annotated in her own handwriting, the couple took turns directing one feature film a month from September 1913 until August 1914. Some of these films were advertised as Solax productions, others as Blaché Feature productions. To date, none appear to be extant. The line between the two companies became more and more indistinct, until Solax appeared to get absorbed into Blaché Features altogether.

Why didn't Guy fight for the integrity of her company? Economically speaking, things were very difficult. In one of her letters she mentions that the company was in deep financial trouble and the entire employee's body, headed by Menessier, the art director who worked for her at Gaumont and then followed her to Fort Lee, came to her on behalf of her entire staff with an offer to accept a fifty percent reduction in salary until the company got back on its feet. Solax never did get back on its feet, but this event alone testifies to the great trust and affection the Solax employees felt for their "lady boss."[34]

Why didn't Blaché try to help Solax more instead of forming Blaché Features? Actually, he did, and his response was very creative: he formed a film distribution company of his own, called The Film Supply Company of America. Its ads are laid out in an almost identical fashion to George Kleine's, whom he clearly seems to be imitating.[35]

It was a good idea, but too difficult to achieve. At the same time that Blaché was running it he was busy directing films. The Film Company seems to have merged with Mutual at the beginning of World War I, in 1914, when Gaumont, its most visible client, pulled out of the United States, as did Eclair, the U.S. branch of the French film company in Fort Lee headed by Jasset until his death in 1913.

It was at this time that the Sales Company (started by IMP and the NYMPC in 1909 in response to the formation of the MPPC by Edison and others)[36] made the offer to buy out the Blachés (as we have seen, Solax produced *the Naval Review* for the Sales Co. in 1912 and made regular contributions to its *Animated Weekly*). The offer was for $200,000 in stock and a salary of $600,000 for the two of them for five years. Solax had had a good relationship with the Sales Co., which had distributed the Solax films in the U.S. from the beginning until that moment, but the Sales Co.'s offer to pay them $200,000 *in stock* must have seemed highly suspect. After all the Blachés had only one trump card: their actual studio plant, which with its labs and costume and set building shops must have seemed to be worth much more than that. Whatever the reason, the Blachés refused the offer.

This was a mistake. The war caused a coal shortage, which meant no light and no heat, and they were competing with bigger and better funded studios in Hollywood that had much more technologically sophisticated plants. The market demanded longer and more elaborate film productions. The transition to longer films had continued, and most films were now five reels long and much higher production values were expected.

Alice Guy, Director for Hire

WITH THE TRANSITION to longer films came the transition to a centralized producer system. Films being produced by other companies at this time include Sidney Olcott's *From the Manger to the Cross*, mentioned earlier, and *Traffic in Souls* (IMP/Universal 1913). The latter was an elaborately staged, sensational melodrama about white slavery directed by George Loan Tucker. The success of *Traffic in Souls* undoubtedly prompted William Brady of the Schubert Film Manufacturing company to ask Guy to direct *The Lure* in July of 1914. Brady, as the producer, chose the script and the cast (the same cast that had performed *The Lure* in its theatrical version).[37]

The Lure was the first film Guy made for a company that had no connection to either herself or her husband and it marked the beginning of the couple's transition from heads of their own studio(s) to directors-for-hire. The film was based on a play that had been staged by a Schubert theatrical company, and their actress, Lucia Moore, re-created her lead role on screen. Several directors had refused to direct the film because of the "delicate subject matter." It is strange that censorship was truly a serious concern, as a handful of films had already been made on the topic of white slavery. In 1913, Big A produced *White Slave Traffic*, IMP produced *Traffic in Souls*, and Vitagraph produced *Traffic in Slaves*. Nevertheless, censorship was indeed a problem, as Guy recounts in her memoirs:

> I had a certain acquaintance with the subject which was of public interest, as I had met a young lawyer who was especially concerned with it and gave me some curious details about the

activities of the gangster pimps. So, I accepted on the condition that I might use the same actors who had played in the theater production.

It was agreed that if the film was accepted, all the costs of production would be divided, as well as the profits.

Once finished, the film had to be submitted to the censors. The committee, composed that day of two old maids and a priest, refused it. I appealed, objecting that a decision was only valid if taken by a committee of at least nine people. New convocation. This time the committee was more than full: twenty or twenty five persons. The chairman asked me to defend my film. I responded that I was completely ignorant of the jury's objections. The chairman then asked for a spokesperson from the jury. A young woman rose: "The subject is scabrous," she said, "and I think that only a woman could treat it with this delicacy. I think that Madame Blaché has succeeded very well." So the film passed unanimously.[38]

It is interesting that Brady, who had made a verbal agreement with Guy to split the costs and profits fifty-fifty, then renegotiated with Blaché for a flat fee of $10,000. Two months later, Guy found out that the film had made a $300,000 profit in two months! By dividing the Blachés from each other, Brady conquered. Guy remained bitter about this to the end of her life; she devotes several pages to it in her autobiography.

Unfortunately, the film of *The Lure* no longer appears to exist. From the synopsis in *The Moving Picture World*[39] it does not appear to be that different from *Traffic in Souls* (the IMP 1913 film, which is still extant). The plot of *The Lure* was as follows: Charlotte Baker is drugged by her fiancé, Paul, who is really a procurer. To find her, her family hires a famous detective, Bob Macauley, whose fiancée Sylvia works in a store. Sylvia is her invalid mother's sole source of support, but when she asks her boss for a raise she is turned down. She searches for better employment and finds a friendly woman who offers to help her. Sylvia discovers to her horror that this woman has lured her into the same prison-house of ill-repute where Charlotte is a prisoner. Bob, disguised as a workman for the gas company, visits the brothel and discovers that Sylvia is working there. He believes she has gone there of her own free will and reproaches her. When she tells him the truth he frees both her and Charlotte and turns Paul over to the authorities.

David Robinson has noted that the "widespread neurosis about 'white slavery'... suggests that the perils of young women being tricked or kidnapped into prostitution were quite real...."[40]

I prefer Janet Staiger's analysis that A Traffic in Souls (as well as other films such as A Fool There Was (Fox, 1915) and The Cheat (Famous Players-Lasky-Paramount, dir. Cecil B. De Mille, 1915)) illustrates the "possibilities for ideological activity through narrative regulation... each of these films not only describes the threat or failure of the Bad Woman, but also provides prescriptive or reformist vision for the New Woman."[41]

The white slavery films appear to have been a social response to the movement for political enfranchisement of women that was making itself felt throughout the U.S. and Europe, especially in Britain. In June of 1913, 35-year-old Emily Davison, a well-known Suffragist, was killed after rushing onto the Derby course and snatching the bridle of Anmer, the King's horse, which struck her with its chest and then turned a complete somersault. All of this happened in full view of the King and Queen and the film cameras of several film companies, including Pathé and Gaumont's. Davison, who had tried to kill herself for the cause once before, martyred herself to protest women's disenfranchisement. Her funeral procession was prohibited by the police but still got a record turnout, with hundreds of women dressed in suffragist colors. Gaumont distributed a film of her deathfall that was publicized in The Moving Picture World in July of 1913.[42] Her funeral was also filmed by various newsreels.[43]

American suffragists were generally less militant than their British sisters, though they were sometimes accused of arson, among other things.[44] Even so, they succeeded in getting the vote by 1919. As a French citizen, Guy could not vote for another twenty years, a difference that she must have felt quite keenly.

Guy took the job of making The Lure with the understanding that she was going to make a film that would raise consciousness about how young women got sucked into white slavery. The key difference between her film and Traffic in Souls is that the Good Woman of Traffic in Souls (Older Sister) is never corrupted—she is not even in the brothel long enough to change her clothes—and her virtue is never in doubt; in The Lure, Sylvia's virtue is also never questioned, although she apparently resides and works in the brothel for some time. What matters to Guy is what kind of woman the heroine believes herself to be, rather that what kind of woman she appears to be.

Figure 48. *Tarnished Reputations*, or *A Soul Adrift*—1920

Figure 49. *Tarnished Reputations*, or *A Soul Adrift*—1920

The theme of a Good Woman corrupted, who then takes her first available chance to be virtuous again returns in *The Heart of a Painted Woman* (5 reels, Popular Plays and Players, 1915). *My Madonna* (5 reels, Popular Plays and Players, 1915) tells almost the same story as *The Heart of a Painted Woman*. But in this case the woman remains virtuous throughout while her lover is corrupted. This redemption plot recalls the one-reel "forgiveness films" discussed in the last chapter. Young women models corrupted by their painters is a persistent theme in these years; one has to wonder if these artists' models are stand-ins for aspiring "photoplayers."[45]

Staiger says about *The Cheat* (Paramount 1915, directed by Cecil B. De Mille) that:

> *The Cheat* is the most prescient of what would become a preferred method for narrating. Rather than split the New Woman and the Woman Gone Astray into two entities, creating an older-style melodramatic opposition of characters in which one of the other wins or loses, having a character transform herself from a Bad Woman to a Good Woman has great moral and social force (and is more in tune with the new melodramatic-realist aesthetics). Preferably, this Bad Woman cannot have more than teetered on the brink of impure behavior, but in any event her recognition of the right way to act saves her and her family. Thus, internal regulation (in continuity with Protestant religion as well as the new self-help ethos) is favored over external regulation (prohibition and punishment for transgressions) and the audience can have a happy ending.[46]

As we have seen in *The Lure*, Sylvia's "internal regulation" never allows her to become a truly Bad Woman, but she appears to make the transformation from Good Woman, to Bad, and back to Good again in the eyes of her lover. By exonerating Sylvia from blame (in *Traffic in Souls* it is Little Sister's boredom with her job and thirst for adventure that get her into trouble) *The Lure*, as its title indicates, points back at the other player in the prostitution dynamic: the man.

Guy made *The Lure* in July of 1914. Since the economic return from the picture had been slight, she and Blaché had to find another way to make films and have them distributed.

They were not the only ones to feel the effects of the incredible upheaval in the American film industry. Production and distribution companies were formed, merged, and split, or else they left for the West Coast or disappeared. Again, Blaché's answer to the crisis was to found a new company, the U.S. Amusement Corporation, which was inaugurated in September of 1914 with a capital of $500,000. Directors of the company included Madame Alice Blaché, Joseph M. Shear, Charles D. Lithgow, Joseph Borries, Henri Menessier and Jules E. Brulatour. According to the *Moving Picture World,* an addition of a printing and developing plant was being made to the Solax studio as well as dressing rooms and offices and Herbert Blaché would be in charge of the expanded plant.[47] The first film to be produced by the new company was announced as *The Chimes,* starring the English actor Mr. Tom Terris "and his Charles Dickens' Associate Players."[48] The *Moving Picture World* noted that Solax and Blaché Features would continue to offer two four-reel photodramas a month, as in the past, while the United States Amusement Corporation "will present only large special productions at intervals." Now that Herbert was in charge of two companies, each with its own large cash base, the balance of power between the couple shifted in his favor.

But distribution was still the big problem. Without the support of either the MPPC or the Sales Co, Blaché set out to create his own network, by sending his representative, Burton Garrett, (formerly of the Sales Co.) to open exchanges in Des Moines and Indianapolis. Though *The Moving Picture World* reported success on March 28, 1914 and April 25, 1914, the fact was that the Blachés were juggling three production companies, a studio and film processing plant, and trying to manage their own distribution. In other words, Herbert Blaché was making an attempt at vertical integration which even Pathé had avoided, which shows how desperate Blaché was to keep control of his own—and his wife's—economic and artistic destinies.

Not surprisingly, the effort failed. With Guy's consent they allied themselves with a newly-formed production company called Popular Plays and Players, where they were well received.[49] Apparently Blaché thought the alliance would finally give him some security, as in June of 1916 he offered $1,000 for any scenario the United States Amusement Corporation could produce as part of its alliance with Popular Plays and Players.[50] The Blaché's contribution to Popular Plays and Players was significant enough that in October of 1915 *The Moving Picture World* referred to the (former) Solax Studio as "the Popular Plays and Players studios at Fort Lee" and noted *My Madonna* and *Barbara Frietchie*, had been shot there.[51]

Along with some other small production companies, Popular Plays and Players was part of a coalition called ALCO (the Al came from Al Lichtman, the co-founder and liaison, and the CO stood for Company). Al Lichtman and the journalist Walter Hoff Seeley joined forces with the up-and-coming Louis B. Mayer to form a powerful film exhibition circuit of their own. Seeley wanted to limit their releases to theaters in cities of 200,000 residents or more. Each theater owner was to buy films sight unseen at the highest justifiable price in return for exclusive rights for that city. After a week's run, the film would not be shown again in that city for six months, but would play in smaller towns, distributed through ALCO exchanges. The scripts, casting and all other credits of these "quality films" would be approved by Seeley and Lichtman. Companies that would be producing these quality pictures included All-Star Feature Company, California Motion Picture Corporation, Favorite Players Film Co., Excelsior Feature Film Co., Tiffany Film Corporation, B.A. Rolfe, and Popular Plays and Players. Distribution centers were set up in twenty cities. The first film was released on October 1, 1914. Films were released at the rate of one per week. Lichtman left the corporation in November of 1914 and bankruptcy proceedings began in early 1915.[52]

Mayer and Richard Rowland, a Pittsburgh multi-millionaire who had been one of ALCO's investors, managed somehow to survive ALCO without going completely bankrupt. Mayer managed to convince Rowland to form another company, Metro Pictures, (later to be the first initial in MGM), with Mayer as secretary and president of the New England Branch and Rowland as President.[53] The main impetus behind the formation of Metro Pictures was to avoid being swallowed up by Paramount, Mutual or Universal. Producers that joined Metro Pictures (and gave Metro creative control) were Columbia, Quality Pictures Corporation, Dreyda, Rolfe, and Popular Plays and Players. From the time it was founded in August 1914 to its disappearance in 1917, Popular Plays and Players produced 33 feature films; Blaché and Guy each directed six of these.

What did this mean for Guy? After years of running her own show she was now a director working for hire. She was given a fixed budget and told what kind of film to make, who to cast in it, and who would be on her crew. But she was still working out of her own studio (formerly the Solax Studio) in Fort Lee and often was still able to cast actors who had worked with her in Solax films, such as Vinnie Burns.

Starring Olga Petrova

IT WAS FOR Popular Plays and Players that Guy directed Olga Petrova in *The Tigress* (4 reels, December 1914, screenplay and directed by Guy, distributed by ALCO), *The Heart of a Painted Woman* (5 reels, April 1915, screenplay and directed by Guy, Metro), *The Vampire*, (5 reels, August 1915, adapted and directed by Guy, Metro), *My Madonna*, (5 reels, October 1915, adapted and directed by Guy, Metro), and *What Will People Say?* (5 reels, January 1916, adapted and directed by Alice Guy, Metro).

Petrova was born Muriel Harding in Wales and became well-known as a stage actress. On a tour of South Africa she fell in love with Boris Petroff, but she refused to marry him because she wished to continue with her career and retain her independence. (Years later, at the height of her film career she married Dr. James Stewart, a proctologist, in New York). After the African tour she changed her name to Olga Petrova and began to affect a Russian accent. Under this name she became very well-known. In 1914 she went to the U.S., where after some mixed success on the stage she began to act in films. The first of these was *The Tigress*. The film added Petrova to the list of actors that Guy made into film stars, as we can see from the review in *Variety*:

> Olga Petrova is featured in the melodrama, making her screen debut. The subject is highly melodramatic. It starts with the military execution of Stella's husband and progresses from that promising beginning to international intrigue involving the shelling of a foreign warship by the big coast defense guns at Sandy Hook. The feature has a plentitude of thrills, capital acting throughout, particularly on the part of Mme Petrova, who is disclosed as a cinema artist of a good deal of power, and finally a quantity of highly effective studio work.... The warship is also used in several extremely beautiful marine views with exceptionally fine photographic and light effects. The lights are skillfully handled throughout. This is particularly true of the prison scenes. The tricky use of massed shadows and a curious yellow tone to the figures go a long way to secure the "creepy"

Figure 50. Olga Petrova (born Muriel Harding)

atmosphere the director aimed at. The figures move about in a shadowy way except when they come into the foreground, when their faces and figures grip attention by the way they stand out. This part of the picture is grim and a little depressing, but from first to last action never for an instant lags and interest is nailed until the finish. The story is unusually clear for a picturised play.[54]

The second film Guy directed starring Olga Petrova, *Heart of a Painted Woman*, was not quite so well received, though Guy's original script was highly praised:

...this picture is another argument in favor of the scenario-picture in preference to the stage-play or printed-story feature film... Though "The Painted Woman"... has a couple of spots that are not convincing partially because of the situations and direction, the remainder is quite a strong dramatic, very well put on and ended at the 81st Street Theatre Tuesday evening to applause.... The playing company is quite well balanced and prevents an acting blight. Miss Petrova gives a much better performance on the screen than she has ever given on the stage. Mayhaps this is obligatory through an enforced naturalness to some extent before the camera, and Miss Petrova is silent on the screen, not having her assumed accent for hindrance. Her brunette type is also a good subject for the photographer... There is a bad fall by a poor souse on the stairs that should have been retaken at the time it was made, and the prison scene is not properly staged, for good detail, but countered against these is the direction as a whole that can retain continued interest, bring out suspense in working up to climaxes and use the camera excellently in every way, with an exception or two. This picture has an idea from Griffith's "Avenging Consience" and a photographic play from "Cabiria", but "the Painted Woman" also has a good title and is a first class dramatic feature.[55]

Petrova was paid $1,000 a week for her role in *The Tigress*, and $1,500 a week for her other roles.[56]

Guy described Petrova as "difficult to direct."[57] In a letter to Anthony Slide, written in the late seventies, Petrova described Guy's directing style as follows:

Rehearsals started. In the first scene, as in all succeeding ones, Madame Blaché outlined vocally what each episode was with action, words appropriate to the situation. If the first or second rehearsal pleased her, even though a player might intentionally or not alter her instructions, as long as they did not hurt the scene, even possibly improve it, she would allow this to pass. If not she would rehearse and rehearse until they did before calling camera. When she had cause to correct a player, she would do this courteously, and in my case, which was more than often, she might resort to her native tongue. This gentle gesture touched me deeply, softened any embarrassment I might feel. After all the scenes were set for the day had been shot, the close-ups followed.... These concluded, Madame looked, and was, tired. But during rehearsals and shooting she never lost her dignity or poise. She wore a silken glove, but she would have been perfectly capable of using a mailed fist if she considered it necessary. This I never saw her do, either on the first day nor any other day while she directed me. She never bellowed through the megaphone as I was told many another director was wont to do. She obtained her results earning the respect and obedience of her artists. In the four succeeding pictures she never deviated from these methods.[58]

Except for *The Tigress*, which was an action story, the films starring Petrova followed the same narrative logic as *The Lure*, but with plenty of intrigue (international espionage and the Battleship Wyoming return in *The Vampire*, though not to the same degree as in *The Tigress*). As the logline on Metro's advertising for *The Vampire* declared: "In which the regeneration of a woman, more sinned against than sinning, is beautifully depicted." (For further analysis of *The Vampire*, see below). Petrova enjoyed making these films and said she had parted from Madame Blaché with regret when Guy had to honor other directing contracts.[59]

After appearing in five films directed by Alice Guy, Petrova went on to star in a series of films for Popular Plays and Players. In a note in her personal papers Alice Guy lists these films, among others,[60] as having been jointly made by herself and her Herbert Blaché. By "jointly made" she must mean the production planning, as all of these films were scripted and directed by others. Most of these films were made in 1916; (for a full list, see the filmography of Guy's American films.).

Petrova starred in two other films for Popular Plays and Players which Guy did not list as co-produced with her husband: *The Waiting Soul*, (5 reels, scr. Aaron Hoffman, dir. Burton L. King, March 1917) and *The Soul of a Magdalene*, (5 reels, scr. L. Case Russell, dir. Burton L. King, May 1917.) All of these films are melodramas with a certain amount of action, but unlike the films of Alice Guy, the action is always carried out by male characters, while the heroines played by Olga Petrova stood by and suffered, waited, and loved faithfully. The emphasis on "heart interest"[61] in the stories of Aaron Hoffman almost always poorly reviewed, while Olga Petrova's story for *Black Butterfly* was really condemned. More and more Petrova was critiqued for "posing" and even for overemphasizing her profile![62] Petrova was surely referring to these latter films (and the reviews) when she describes her response when Popular Plays and Players approached her to do more films:

The work itself, outside of exterior scenes, which I liked, the weary waiting around, the heat thrown out by the huge, unprotected klieg lights, which often melted one's makeup, blistered one's skin, made one's hair so brittle that is cracked and fell out, might well be classed under the category of sweated labor. Worst of all were the major or minor attacks of klieg eyes.... Added to these disadvantages of moving pictures were the results achieved. The stories and the characters in the stories that I had played were to me unreal and unconvincing. So-called vampire roles were as antipathetic as were those of ladies who sold their honor to pay for their mother's operation or to put brother Jack through law school. Worst of all were the simple, weak-brained, weak-armed maidens who were led astray in their innocence or in spite of their half-hearted struggles to escape from one or more lascivious gents bent on their undoing.

Since my first pictures, I had seen and learned something more of "the movies." I knew now that there was place on the screen for an infinite variety of entertainers and entertainment. There was a place for the intelligent, resourceful, self-supporting woman, as there was for the vampire, the magdalene, the betrayed innocent, the sweet and ringleted ingénue. There were, not to be too carping or too snooty, better directors, better productions, than those I had been associated with.[63]

The "better directors, better productions," might have been a reference to the films made by Maurice Tourneur for Lasky-Paramount that starred Olga Petrova in 1917: *The Undying Flame, Exile, The Law of the Land*. (Ben Carré, formerly of Solax, worked as a production designer for Tourneur as well.) She then went on to found her own production company, Petrova Pictures, in the fall of 1917, with distribution by First National Exhibitors' Circuit Inc., with an initial contract for eight pictures, though only a few of those were made before Petrova retired from screen acting and returned to the stage.

"Intelligent, resourceful, self-supporting woman." Had this been written about many of Guy's Solax films it would have described them perfectly. It is even true of most of the films Guy directed starring Olga Petrova. Both *Tigress* and *Vampire* for example seem to be a combination of the one-reel melodramas—the "forgiveness" films—of the early Solax period, intent on showing how the social system was designed to penalize young women who lacked male financial and social protection, but with female heroes who assert

Figure 51. Alice directing *My Madonna*

themselves as the heroes of the action films such as *Two Little Rangers* did. And like the female heroes in the comedies of crossdressing (see next chapter), disguise and assumption of a whole new identity are usually involved, though unlike in the comedies, these changes are not based on switching gender roles. This much we can guess at, based on the documentation that is all that remains of these films.

Working as a director for hire did not stop Guy from making films like *The Tigress*, but it also meant that the scenarios, or at least the original stories on which the scenarios were based, were not always of her choosing. In her own memoirs, Guy describes how she was given ten lines of the poem "My Madonna" by R.W. Service and told to use it as the basis for a feature screenplay. She was provided with an office, a secretary, and 36 hours to write "your masterpiece." About this scenario Guy said, "I will not swear on my honor that the situation was entirely new, nor that I never plagiarized."[64] According to the reviewer for *Variety*, Guy co-wrote the script with Aaron Hoffman:

> Mr. Hoffman is one of vaudeville's foremost comedy writers, but somehow always seems to fall a bit shy on the drama stuff. And this is a werry, werry serious tragedy... in it Mme Petrova

places her left hand over her solar plexus to indicate undue
emotion and takes her bow at the finish with arms folded over
her chest, bending low, just as she did when in vaudeville she
gave imitations of parrots… Yet, despite its conventional melodramatic progression, it is very classily depicted and Mme
Petrova is not called upon to perform any undue chest heaving.[65]

In spite of the mixed critical reception (the review in *The Moving
Picture World* was more positive), the film garnered for Petrova a lot
of fan mail and was financially successful.

Painters painting models and corrupting them were at the heart
of the plots of *My Madonna* and *The Heart of a Painted Woman*.
It remained a steady theme in Guy's films throughout the late 1910s.[66]
As in *La Statue* (Gaumont, 1906) in which two clowns control a
wind-up statue that rebels against them, the control of a passive
figure (whether statue or young woman) seems to be a stand-in for
the process of filmmaking itself, and how subjectivity is constructed
in film. Guy was fully aware of how this mechanism worked, and
often highlighted the process in the form of her films in order to
make her viewers aware of it. These films show a certain consciousness of the control exercised by the person behind the camera,
the person who is immortalizing their gaze, and the relative weakness of the posing subject.

She extended this interrogation in her depiction of young actresses, especially in her last extant film that we have as of this
writing, *Her Great Adventure* or *The Spring of the Year*. It is hard to
say if this level of interrogation was there in all of her films, as many
may no longer exist. But the theme was consistently present in all of
her work from 1913 on. Perhaps her own awareness was heightened
because she herself was a center of media attention in the early
1910s, as the only woman to own her own studio in Fort Lee.

Guy's Extant Feature Films

AROUND AUGUST OF 1916 the Blachés decided to leave Popular Plays
and Players and return to independent production under the name
of the U.S. Amusement Corporation, which they had founded two
years previously, but under which rubric they had not produced
anything. They had made a dozen films for Popular Plays and Players,
but even though they owned their own studio they were not making
enough money.

As the U.S. Amusement Corporation they made about 10 films. These were distributed by Metro, Pathé, International Films, and especially United States Art Dramas. Distribution was negotiated on a film-by-film basis. As a result, the U.S. Amusement Corporation alternately tried to meet the program demands of each distributor, who had different subject and treatment guidelines. Though the list of films Guy described as co-produced with her husband ends in the summer of 1916, it appears that the close-knit collaboration continued, as there are various press pictures of them together from this period. For Art Dramas, which wanted films with a lot of action and punchy endings, Guy directed *The Adventurer* (6 reels, released February 16, 1917) based on an Upton Sinclair novel, with a screenplay by Harry Chandler and Lawrence McClosky.

However, the International Film Service stuck more closely to the Hearst agenda: a more romantic story, often based on the comic strips in his papers, with plenty of pathos but no brutality, with a likeable hero and even more importantly a "pure young woman," a suspenseful plot, and a dramatic and happy ending; as Bachy puts it, "the Mary Pickford school of narrative."[67] To meet these requirements,

Figure 52. Doris Kenyon haunts the house in *Ocean Waif*

Guy directed *The Ocean Waif* (5 reels, November 2, 1916, International Film Service).

The Ocean Waif still exists, in fragmented form, in the Library of Congress collection, one of only two of Guy's feature-length films to survive. It is clear from this film that Guy had completely adopted the use of point-of-view sequences and parallel editing that Griffith had popularized. What is interesting (if not unique) about this film is that it is a love story that gives equal screen time to each lover's point of view, with very few and limited sections that could be described as depicting an omniscient point of view. This is facilitated by the fact that for a large portion of the narrative the two lovers-to-be see signs of each other's presence but do not actually make contact. Millie (Doris Kenyon) is the "Ocean Waif" of the title, as she is found on the beach by a cruel fisherman who raises her. Sem is their not-so-bright neighbor, who loves Millie and tries to save her from the worst of her stepfather's abuse. When this abuse threatens to become incestuous, Millie escapes and hides in a large abandoned mansion. Meanwhile, Ronald Roberts (Carlyle Blackwell) sees the mansion from his yacht and decides to rent it for the time it takes him to write his next novel (his publishers are already sending him urgent telegrams for it). He discovers Millie in the house, and gradually the two fall in love, although Roberts is engaged to Beatrice (Dyne Donaldson), a society woman. When Millie's stepfather is found dead, Roberts is accused of murder and Beatrice breaks off the engagement. When Sem realizes that Millie loves Roberts, he confesses that he murdered her stepfather and then commits suicide, leaving the couple free to marry.

In this film, space is gendered in the same way that we saw in the Gaumont melodramas, but it is also defined by class. When Roberts enters the old mansion and fixes it up for himself he also finds love; but life in the hovel where Millie grows up is violent and cruel, in the mansion it is dark and scary until rich Roberts comes to the rescue. Millie spends several scenes entertaining herself by examining things like the support for hoop skirts and other such upper-class symbols in the house, until Roberts arrives on his yacht to make her play-acting at being the lady of the manor into reality. Roberts favors Millie and her wildflowers over the society woman in her white dress with her motorcar and her courtier-like friends. Here the plot of a painter corrupting an innocent young woman is given something of a turn: Roberts is saved from an empty marriage to a domineering society woman (who quickly consoles herself with a rich count) by Millie, who barely seems human. What she is, in fact, is an embodiment of his own muse. Like Pygmalion, he creates his perfect woman (the ghost that haunts the old house in clothes that are at least 100 years out of date) and marries her. How the two will reconcile the extreme differences in their backgrounds is not confronted. As soon as she enters the protection of "his" mansion, it is as if her lower-class background is completely stripped away. In fact, the two representatives of her past, her stepfather and Sem, die violent deaths. For Millie, finding a male protector is necessary for survival. To find one who objectifies her and puts her on a pedestal is treated like icing on the cake. The film is novel in the way that Millie and Roberts are given almost equal screen weight (she dominates the first half of the narrative, he the second, but the point of view alternates throughout), but it was not commercially successful.

Guy went on to make *A Man and a Woman* (5 reels, released March 19, 1917, adapted by Guy from Zola's novel *Nana*, distributed by Art Dramas). Critical reaction was tepid. The Blachés, in financial straits, sold their nice house on the edge of the woods and moved into a modest bungalow near the Solax studio. By May of 1917, the accumulated debts called for more drastic action, and it was at this point that the Blachés approached the Seligmans, who bought 51% of their shares with the stipulation that they make their protegee, Catherine Calvert, into a star. Guy directed Calvert in two films, *House of Cards* (U.S. Amusement Corporation, June 1917) and *Behind the Mask* (U.S. Amusement Corporation, September 1917). Blaché directed her in *Think it Over* (U.S. Amusement Corporation, August 1917) and *The Peddler* (U.S. Amusement Corporation, July 1917). Guy spends several pages in her memoirs describing the various machinations of Catrine Calvert to seduce her husband and Guy's own efforts to keep the two apart.[68]

It was at this time that Guy was invited to give two lectures at Columbia University, one on July 13, 1917 and a second on August 3, 1917, on "What themes to pick and how to handle dramatic situations, the rules of censorship in the different states and copyright laws," and "How to write the screenplay." About this engagement, Guy wrote:

> My husband and I often spent our evenings preparing the scenarios that we would direct, in turn. We complemented each

other very well. Perhaps I was the more imaginative, but he had a more critical, more realistic spirit.

We had taken as theme for one of our films the possibilities for understanding and happiness of a couple having the same career, a subject we knew well.... At that epoch, the public was very interested in the question of child labor in the factories. Children went to work at eight or ten years of age. This was the subject that I chose [to illustrate the advantages of a good marital and business partnership].

Goldilocks... made friends through the garden gate with a little black child, to whom she told her secrets. This child swore deep affection and he promised to help her escape [from kidnappers who used him to lure her away from her parents]. He tried his best and there was a whole series of elopement, of nights passed in houses under construction, of pilfering from bakery shelves, finally engagement in a factory, where the parents and the police, after days of anguish, found them.

On this occasion the professors at Columbia University paid me the great honor of an invitation to give a talk about the cinema to their students.

I objected, my English was faulty. I was no lecturer. But my husband, being English, spoke the language perfectly, he understood the business as well as I did and it would please him to satisfy the request.

"No, I beg you, it's you we want!"

"But why?"

"Because you're a woman."

I ended up by agreeing, with what apprehension you can imagine....

I chose to illustrate [the screenwriting lecture] by the film which I have just described. The conference over, I was surrounded and complimented very politely, but many professors asked me why, when treating so interesting a subject, I had thought it necessary to weaken the theme by the trite little children as intermediaries. There you are![69]

Guy goes on to recount that there was some talk of Columbia University starting "a little cinematography college" (she had been invited to speak by the school of journalism) "and if my stay in the

States had been longer we would certainly have tried to do something of the sort."[70]

It is ironic that Guy wrote *House of Cards* in order to reflect on "the possibilities for understanding and happiness of a couple having the same career," and that this was the first film in which she directed Catherine Calvert. It is not hard to understand that having Calvert forced on her by the Seligmans and then watching Calvert throw herself at her husband would have made Guy a little less than enthusiastic in the direction of her films. In any case, the reception of all four of the films starring Calvert was ambivalent at best. *Behind the Mask* also suffered when its New York City premiere—greatly built up in the press—was canceled in order to make room for the premiere of *The Lesson*, starring Lewis J. Selznick's protegé, Constance Talmadge.

Blaché again tried to regain control of the situation. The couple agreed to become directors for hire, and they rented the studio plant to Apollo Pictures. Guy was 44, and her last few films had been flops. Herbert Blaché was 35 and pretty starlets were throwing themselves at him. And then the United States entered the war.

Blaché sent his family to North Carolina, where Guy nursed both her children through a severe bout of rougeola and did volunteer work for the Red Cross. Blaché called her back to Fort Lee when he had found her work, directing *The Great Adventure* for Marcus Loew of Pathé Players.

The Great Adventure

A 28MM. VERSION of *The Great Adventure* was found in the UK and restored by the NFTVA. Fragments of the film are missing, but with assistance of photographs that Guy herself kept, we can reconstruct the plot. For the most part, except for one episode, the film is intelligible even with the missing portions.

Bessie Love stars as Milly Abbot, a young and very pretty *artiste* from a small country village who, "deceived by her drawing room successes, believes herself to be a second Isadora Duncan" (film intertitle). Milly lives with her Aunt Betty (played by Flora Finch, an English comedienne), a spinster whose primary concern is to find herself a husband, to which end she has been saving money for her dowry and putting together a *trousseau* for her wedding. The film's opening is intact; we see Milly and Aunt Betty at home and then we

Figure 53. Bessie with her hometown beau in *Her Great Adventure*

Figure 54. Is she famous for her dancing, or infamous for her
scanty attire? Bessie Love in *Her Great Adventure*

see Milly impress the members of her community at a revue staged in the local town hall. The most impressive feature of her act is that by the end of it she has (accidentally, but the audience does not understand this) shed some her clothing, leaving her legs bare. One rotund young man is especially impressed and brings her flowers. Milly is sweet to him but it is clear she has no strong attachment for him. After the impressive performance Aunt Betty decides to sacrifice her dowry and *trousseau* money to take Milly to New York and help her become a star. The film once had an elaborate departure sequence, with the entire town turning out to see Milly off, including the overweight suitor who is completely heartbroken at her departure. Only the very end of this sequence remains, but stills show some of the shots that are missing.

Milly and Aunt Betty next find themselves in the big city, where Milly is surprised to see that "her popularity has not followed her to the great town," as when she first visits the casting office even the secretaries (one male, one female) laugh at her behind their hands. Milly returns dejectedly to the lodging house. She cannot bring herself to face Aunt Betty with the bad news so she sits on the stairs, where she meets Harry Blake (Chester Barnett), a handsome and struggling young actor, when he trips over her. They are instantly attracted to each other. Harry tells her he is in a musical called "Spring of the Year." The next sequence is the one that is missing key footage and so the action is not clear. It appears that Milly takes a gun that Aunt Betty keeps for self-defense and climbs up the fire escape leading to the casting office (this shot is missing but a still of it exists) where she convinces the casting director to give her a bit part in "Spring of the Year." The film resumes as Milly leaves the casting office, now swaggering in front of the secretaries who laughed at her earlier, who cannot figure out how she got there. Back in her boarding house room she returns the gun to Aunt Betty who says "I told you that you would become a great artiste."[71]

From here on the film follows a fairly standard *42nd Street* plot, although it pre-dates that musical play by several decades. Milly is noticed by the handsome older male star, Mr. Sheen (Donald Hall), and when the leading female star leaves in a huff after several arguments with Sheen, he convinces the director to cast Milly in the starring role. (As she leaves, the star tells Harry: "I've had enough of that ghastly play, I'm going in for cinema where true talent is appreciated!"). Milly is a quick success, in a role which requires her to

Figure 55. Saying goodbye to the hometown beau in
Her Great Adventure

Figure 56. Saying goodbye to the hometown itself in
Her Great Adventure

dress as a soldier (there appears to be some intertextual reference to films such as *Girl Spy At Vicksburg* (Kalem, 1910); part of Gene Gauntier's "Girl Spy" series). When she takes her first solo bow the director comments to the producer: "She has no voice.... Nor can she dance.... But she has life and takes with the public... that's everything." Clearly we are meant to understand that in spite of her success, mostly brought about by her youth and energy, Milly has no future in the theatre. The real "adventure" is not onstage, but off.

Milly and Harry are continuing their courtship on the set, but Milly is soon distracted by Mr. Sheen who wines and dines both Milly and her aunt. Sheen pretends that his attentions are principally for the aunt but no one is really fooled by this. The set-piece of the film is the dinner where the Ziegfield Follies perform. Harry has followed Milly to this dinner even though he cannot afford it; he is escorted by Hazel (Florence Short), a comedienne who becomes very protective of Milly. Harry is concerned about Sheen's courthsip of Milly because he is jealous; but Hazel is interested in protecting Milly's innocence and youth. Hazel at first suggests that Harry pretend to court her in order to make Milly jealous, but Milly is so dazzled by the Ziegfield dancers and the entire atmosphere, as well as Sheen's star persona, that she does not even notice. When Sheen tries to kiss Milly on the dance floor Harry assaults him and pandemonium ensues. Milly and Aunt Betty flee back to their hotel, only to find that they have no key, as Milly had entrusted it to Sheen while they were dancing. It takes them a long time to wake up the porter, and as a result Aunt Betty catches a serious cold. This means she cannot perform her duties as chaperone for a week and opens up an opportunity for Sheen, who sends her allergenic flowers that make her sneeze even more (this sequence is no longer in the film, but stills survive). He also makes sure that Harry gets fired, but Harry manages to see Milly long enough to win her forgiveness for his behavior at the restaurant.

It is up to Hazel to help Milly prepare for her next date with Sheen, and she warns her explicitly that Sheen is trouble. Milly ignores her and leaves, though she stops guiltily when she runs into Harry who asks her to spend a day with friends at the beach. Milly explains she has promised to spend the day with Sheen but she will ask Sheen to take her to the beach and she will see Harry and their friends then. Harry interprets this as a brushoff. Hazel joins him and they watch Milly and Sheen drive off, then Hazel says she is sure that Sheen will take Milly to a certain very romantic "Red Rose Inn" and they must get there quickly to prevent the worst from happening.

Sure enough, in the car, Sheen promises Milly that they will do anything she wants, but he suggests they start with lunch at the very romantic Red Rose Inn. Milly says that it sounds fine, but first she wants to go to the zoo. Sheen acquiesces.

What ensues is a clear reversal and commentary on the D.W. Griffith style of cross-cutting between young woman menaced by would-be rapists and rescuers coming to the rescue. The movie cuts between Sheen and Milly and Harry and Hazel who are looking for Milly in order to protect her person and her virtue; but in fact, though we do not realize this until the end, it is Milly who is playing Sheen and Sheen who will eventually need rescuing. It begins at the zoo, with a montage of images where Milly is behaving as the child she still is, annoying the rhinocerous and teasing the monkeys. She insists that they go on an elephant ride together. Sheen keeps trying to get her to go to the inn, but every time he suggests it Milly comes up with some other adventure they must have first. As soon as Sheen mentions the inn we cut to Harry and Hazel at the inn, waiting for them to arrive, and Hazel muttering, "I was sure that he would bring her here." It is at this point that we know for sure that Hazel was once seduced (and her reputation ruined) by Sheen in just such a manner.

Meanwhile, Milly has convinced Sheen that they absolutely must go horseback riding. Sheen has been bragging about his various accomplishments, and now Milly wants him to show off for her. His reluctance makes it clear that he cannot live up to his own claims, but Milly would not take no for an answer, and so they rent riding clothes and end up on horses galloping towards the beach. By now Harry and Hazel have realized Sheen would not bring Milly to the inn, and Harry remembers that Milly said she would meet him at the beach, so they decide to go there. As they get closer they see the pair on horseback, Sheen bouncing uncomfortably, Milly riding expertly like the country girl that she is. Milly does not see Harry and Hazel, because she is too busy convincing Sheen to go swimming with her. Sheen refuses to swim in a rented bathing suit, so Milly settles for having him take her out in a canoe. Harry watches this anxiously from the shore, afraid that Sheen will take liberties again.

Milly is getting Sheen to regale her with stories of his exploits, and then proposes that she jump into the water and pretend to be

Figure 57. Bessie Love getting into the talent agency via the
back door in *Her Great Adventure*

Figure 58. Bessie Love gets her first job with a gun in
Her Great Adventure

drowning so that he can save her, as the publicity would be good for the play. Sheen does not think this is a good idea though he says, "My little Milly, I should love to be a hero in your eyes." Clearly, he swims about as well as he can ride. But Milly does not listen, she simply dives into the water. Sheen holds out a paddle for her but Milly rocks the boat so that he also falls into the water. Milly can clearly swim quite well but Sheen is immediately in trouble; lifeguards run into the water with a catamaran but Harry, believing Milly is really drowning, is ahead of them. Harry manages to push Sheen's head underwater and then swims over to Milly, who allows Harry to rescue her (and become a hero in her eyes) while the lifeguards get Sheen. It is only the spectator who sees clearly that Milly has staged everything in order to humiliate Sheen for having fired Harry and to put an end to Sheen's unwanted attentions.

Once Harry and Milly are both on the beach they notice that Sheen, having finally understood the message, leaves in the car without even looking for Milly. Milly and Harry decide to ride the horses home and Hazel advises them to find a preacher as soon as possible, as "he will marry you and that will be the best ending to the great adventure of our little Milly." Milly and Harry ride off together as Hazel watches.

One of the myths about Alice Guy's career is that she could no longer get work because she had lost her touch. As late as the Spring of 2000, Anthony Slide said as much in a documentary on early women filmmakers made by the American Movie Channel which includes a long section on Alice Guy. It is an understandable conclusion when *Ocean Waif* was the only one of Guy's features available for viewing. The way Guy conforms to the Hearst agenda in that film makes it seem as if she had lost sight of her own. By May of 2000, Slide had completely changed his opinion on the matter, as by then he had a chance to view *Her Great Adventure*. Even in its fragmented condition, the film has wonderful performances from Love, with Flora Finch, who does an incredible turn as the "redoubtable chaperone" who is herself smitten with the movie star, and Florence Short, who plays Hazel, the reformed vamp. Though she has the least amount of screen time, Hazel's character is complex in its counterpoint to various current discourses: she was once a vamp, as we understand from her appearance and her past history with Sheen; but she is still virtuous, in the sense that she behaves morally toward Milly and ensures Milly and Harry's happiness. In fact, it could be argued that Hazel is a continuation of Jean Lefarge, the character played by Olga Petrova in *The Vampire*, who is corrupted by a bigamist and then becomes an international spy. The image of the female vamp had originated with Philip Burne-Jones' painting, *The Vampire*, shown in 1897 in London, of a threateningly beautiful and ghostly woman who appears to have just killed the lover lying at her feet. The painting inspired a poem, play and novel, the latter two entitled *A Fool There Was* (1906 and 1909 respectively). This, of course, became the film that made Theda Bara a star, as the morally worthless, beautiful woman who sucked the life out of her lovers, directed by Frank Powell for Fox and released in January of 1915. Theda Bara spent most of her career reprising this role in various forms,[72] and the character of the vamp appeared in many other films, clearly an indirect response to the effort for suffrage. Though none of Guy's films featuring fallen women remain, the archival evidence makes it clear that Alice Guy tried, in all of her films that featured vamp characters, to undercut the classic misogynistic construct and humanize it, as well as pointing out the aspects of the system that led to women being corrupted to begin with.[73]

This is just as true in *Her Great Adventure* as it was in the films starring Olga Petrova. Hazel, the reformed vamp, does end up alone while Milly gets her man, but Hazel is a real actress whereas Milly, though lucky, is not talented enough to sustain a career. The opposition here is clear: women may still have to choose between marriage and career, but it is they who do the choosing, and arrange the pattern of their lives, and not men who choose for them. If a younger woman cannot plot out her own life wisely then older women should help them.

Clearly, Guy had neither lost sight of her own agenda nor had she lost her comic touch or her ability to undercut filmic styles. In this film alone she uses the traditional parallel cutting in a race to the rescue to satirize such "rescue films." More importantly she completely undermines the general conception of young girls as completely helpless, and skillfully and subtly turns the then-popular conception of the vamp as aggressive and destructive completely on its head.

The satire of the parallel-cutting race-to-the-rescue popularized by D.W. Griffith recalls a similar stylistic satire Guy made in 1913 that lampooned Griffith's *Lonely Villa*.[74] The film is *Napoleon* (Solax, 1913). *Napoleon* was neither synopsized in *Moving Picture World* nor reviewed, although its release was advertised. The nitrate print in the John E. Allen Collection is incomplete. There is a woman (Fannie Simpson), and her two daughters (Blanche Cornwall and Marion Swayne), who have locked themselves up in a house; it seems that they have heard that a madman, thinking himself Napoleon, is on the loose. Parallel cut to the madman (Billy Quirck), who is roaming the countryside in complete Napoleon regalia, with a wooden sword and a toy drum which he beats rhythmically. When he runs into a workman he uses his sword to convince the man to drop his work, "take up an arm" (bough from a tree), and follow him.

Back at the house the women receive a visit from a handsome young man (Darwin Karr), a college friend of the woman's son, who has sent his buddy along with a letter of introduction. The women think he is the madman and flee by running up the stairs (insert shot of their retreating feet—the entire sequence is designed as a parody of films like *Suspense* and *The Lonely Villa*) and hiding behind curtains. When he finally gets them to come out he thinks they are mad and tries to communicate with them by making faces and gestures and then initiates a game of Simple Simon. In an effort to humor him, the women follow all of his ridiculous antics while Karr laughs behind his hand. Meanwhile, the real madman has picked up a second follower, but the two workmen finally work up enough courage to escape from him. At the house Karr finally reaches into his jacket pocket (another Napoleon-like gesture that alarms the women), to withdraw his letter of introduction. At that moment the real madman arrives, closely followed by two policemen, who assure the women that Karr is sane and then get the madman to leave the premises by pretending to be his footsoldiers.

Napoleon is clearly looking back to films like *The Lonely Villa* where helpless women wait for men to rescue them, and films like Lois Weber's *Suspense* (1913) with a very similar theme. But the suspense in this parody hinges on how long it will take for the women to figure out that the man is the long-awaited guest, and for the man to figure out that the women are sane. *Napoleon* is a very early critique of the "women's-worst-nightmare" film that is still with us today. Even the madman, with his Napoleon complex, does not seem so bad from Guy's point of view. What is bad is hiding, not looking at the situation squarely, not taking steps to defend oneself.

Her Great Adventure proves that Guy had lost none of her skill, but had in fact, matured into a masterful director. However, she had lost sight of this herself. By her own account, she was weary of the additional stress of working for hire and the constant wheeling and dealing that was part of film production under those conditions. For example, parts of *Her Great Adventure* were shot on location in the Florida Everglades. Guy was given a set decorator and a crew with little experience, as well as a long list of do's and dont's in terms of the scenery. Guy herself said: "I had lost confidence in my own abilities… I was not too sure of myself; comedy is much more difficult than drama."[75] It seems unbelievable that these words were spoken by the same woman who directed all those comedies at Gaumont and all those one-reel romantic comedies, broad farces, and satires in the early Solax period. The going was getting more difficult. However, the film was a success, and Pathé Players was ready to negotiate with Guy to direct another film with Bessie Love, which for some reason never happened. Part of Guy's distress may have come from health problems she was starting to experience and which would plague her for the rest of her life. At this point she had lost the mobility in one arm and repeated surgeries did not help. Further distress was caused by her marriage, which had long been rocky, and now finally crumbled for good. As Guy finished directing *Her Great Adventure*, her husband and one of his actresses left together for California. Guy, nearly penniless, left her bungalow in Fort Lee and

Figure 59. Alice and her children

Figure 60. Alice and her children with the Capellanis

moved into a small apartment in the Bretton Hall Hotel in New York City. All of the documentation indicates that the end of her marriage, which for so long had been a successful partnership in every sense of the word, was a severe emotional as well as financial blow.

Léonce Perret, a former Gaumont comic actor who had come to the U.S. and started his own independent production company, Perret Pictures, with distribution by Pathé, was looking for a vehicle for Dolores Casinelli, his favorite star. Perret offered Guy a mere $2,000 a week for 6 weeks work, and she would have to contribute $100 a week to Osso, the film's publicity agent. The film went four weeks over schedule. Perret was slow in coming up with a scenario, and Guy ended up locked up in his apartment in an effort to help him finish it, which did not make Perret's wife happy.

Guy continued the process of interrogation in her films that featured painters' models (always female) and their relationship to the painters (always male) that painted them. She had featured them in films like *My Madonna*, *Heart of a Painted Woman*, and in her last film, *Tarnished Reputations or A Soul Adrift*, which was released in 1920. In this story, an innocent girl is seduced by a man who gets her to model for his painting. After he abandons her she has to leave her little town, as her reputation is ruined. Her reputation is further damaged by a corrupt judge and she ends up in jail. However, she is rescued by an intelligent benefactor who pays for her education and enables her to become a celebrated actress. Now that she is famous (and wiser to the ways of the world) the painter comes back a-courting. Though she still loves him, she plays hard-to-get long enough to extract her revenge. Again, it is her benefactor (who, of course, is in love with her too but is himself a Good Man) who reunites the couple. The review makes it quite clear that Perret's old-fashioned story was no longer suitable to American tastes, and between the lines we can see that Guy might have been able to do more with the material had she had an actress like Olga Petrova to work with:

> What should be done with Dolores Cassinelli at this stage of the picture game is to make a vamp of her. Properly handled, she should clean up the market right now in that sort of thing, but Pathe is intent on presenting her in parts in which she impersonates injured and abused young women who do everything to keep their virtue intact.... "Tarnished Reputations,"...

> Has a French melodramatic slant to it that is a little off the average of good American market stuff. Mme Alice Blache directed. Neither of these experts are naturally adapted to bringing out in Miss Casinelli those qualities that would put her at the top.[76]

At the end of filming Guy caught the Spanish influenza, which killed four of her colleagues. Perret's wife set aside her jealousy and nursed Guy through her illness.

Blaché, who happened to be passing through New York at this time, was horrified by both the mess his wife was in professionally and her wasted appearance, and out of pity invited her and the children to come to California.

Guy in Hollywood

BY THE SUMMER of 1919, Guy and her children were on the West Coast. The Perret film was not released until March of 1920, and Bachy doubts that Guy directed all of it, although her name appeared in lights when it opened on Broadway on March 14, 1920, with the title of *Tarnished Reputations or A Soul Adrift* (March 1920, Perret Pictures).

In Los Angeles, Guy and her children first stayed in a hotel, then rented a little bungalow. Herbert Blaché did not live with them. He directed Ethel Barrymore in *The Divorcée* (January 1919, screen-play by June Mathis, distributed by Metro). At the time his wife and children arrived he was engaged by Nazimova productions and directed Nazimova herself in *The Brat* (September 1919, Nazimova Productions) and *Stronger Than Death* (January 1920, Nazimova Productions). Guy worked as his assistant on these pictures, but she had long periods of inactivity. She developed a strong friendship with Nazimova.

However, this limbo-like existence was ruptured by a letter from Joseph Borrie, the plant manager at Solax, who asked her to return to the studio immediately. Their creditors were beating down on the doors and the Seligmans were about to seize their assets. Herbert Blaché had sublet the studio to a small photographic company, Apollo Pictures, and to another company, which had set it on fire. The insurers refused to pay. Meanwhile, a polio epidemic was sweep-ing the country. Guy, along with her countrymen, the Capellanis, fled with her two children to St. Marguerite in Canada.

In California she had come to accept that her marriage was over. Now Herbert Blaché had left her to deal with the task of deal-ing with the bankruptcy proceedings, including auctioning off the studio at a tremendous loss. She sued for divorce and won minimal alimony. The purchasers knocked down most of the studio in 1922. Now calling herself Alice Guy Blaché (having taken back her maiden name without letting go of her husband's surname, under which she had become known), Guy took her children, now 14 and 10, back to France with her.

It is unclear to me why Guy did not try to make it as a director for hire in Hollywood, as Blaché did. Perhaps the town was too small for both of them. In the spring of 1995, Regine Blaché arranged for some of her grandmother's mementos to be included in an exhibit at the Eiffel Tower in honor of the Centenary. These mementos consisted of a pair of long white opera gloves and a little silver pistol, among other things. Roberta Blaché said that Guy had originally bought the pistol after her children were kidnapped for a few hours in Chicago. Later she pulled it on Blaché in Hollywood, in a melo-dramatic effort to get him to live with her and his children.

Another problem in Hollywood could have been that her English was never very good, as she had insisted when she tried to refuse the invitation to lecture at Columbia. Olga Petrova also said that when Guy directed her she preferred to speak to her in French. Roberta Blaché has said that when the children were growing up and Blaché was not home, the family spoke French and when Blaché returned they switched to English. She also noted that Guy, in her later years, refused to speak English unless it was absolutely necessary, even during her final years in the United States.

Although her children were American citizens, Guy always remained French. After twenty-eight years in the film business, a brush with death, and a humiliating ending to a marriage that for many years she had spoken of as a model for equal partnership, it seems likely that she needed the solace and succor of her native country more than anything else. We can only wonder what might have been had she been able to stay in the United States.

6 MADAME A DES ENVIES (MADAM HAS HER CRAVINGS): CROSSDRESSING IN THE COMEDIES OF ALICE GUY

IN HIS 1992 article on Alice Guy's Solax films in the Library of Congress collection, Wheeler Winston Dixon stated that Guy was a "master at observed comment upon the role of dress and presentation in the creation of one's sexual identity." He also states that Guy "neatly skirted any serious issues of gender-identification and sexual placement that her stories of crossdressing and mixed identities might raise" and ascribes this skirting to "innocence."[1] [2]

My position, based on a larger body of films than Dixon had at his disposal, differs significantly from his. In this chapter I will show that Guy's comedies of crossdressing address the spectator in a different way at each level of narration, and that these differences show that she was very aware of what she was representing when it came to gender identification and sexual placement. Furthermore, for her these issues were part of a larger discourse on female social agency.

To return to the questions that started me on the search for Alice Guy to begin with: what does Alice Guy have to say to film viewers today? Was she a feminist? Can she, in fact, serve as a guide for feminist filmmakers?

In Alice Guy's films, especially in her comedies of crossdressing, it is possible to distinguish multiple modes of address within a single film. Each mode of address is identified with a specific level of narration, that is, it can originate diegetically, with the characters themselves in the world of the story; it can be detected in the narration in counterpoint to the address of the characters; or it is represented extra-diegetically, by details available to the viewer but not to the characters.

In this chapter I will argue that feminist modes of address do not necessarily imply a female speaking subject. But to make this point adequately I must begin by showing how multiplicitous (to use De Lauretis's term) modes of address operate in a film. I will show that feminist modes of address, homoerotic address, and patriarchal modes of address can co-exist in a single film (as Modleski argues in relation to Hitchcock's film *Rebecca*)[3], thus making it almost impossible to establish definitive criteria that would allow us to define a feminist aesthetic. This does not mean, however, that it is impossible to make feminist films.

My focus here will be on the comedies of crossdressing produced and directed by Alice Guy Blaché, especially those made at Solax between 1910 and 1914, the period when she had almost complete control. In other words, the films for which we can clearly point to her as historical author.

The choice of films is dictated by the following criteria: 1) recognizable address to female spectators in the diegesis; 2) recognizable female address outside of the film's diegesis; and 3) a "dialogue" or "counterpoint discourse" between the film's discourses and between the discourses of the film and cultural discourses outside of the film to which the film refers (insofar as these can be determined through historical research); 4) and finally, the accessibility of these discourses to present-day audiences. A key question here is: in what ways can early cinema be used to engage modern audiences in a "productive look," as Kaja Silverman[4] has defined it?

My aim is to show that the connection between the diegetic and extra-diegetic discourses in Alice Guy's films is a feminist mode of address. In my analysis I will focus on how character agency (especially female agency) is articulated in Guy's films, how friendships between female characters are handled, and how crossdressing is used by characters both as a means to develop agency and for homoerotic content. Not much information is available on how contemporary audiences engaged with these films,[5] but in this chapter I will begin to explore issues of engagement of contemporary audiences raised by multiplicitous address.

Many critics have pointed out how the method of discourse of classical Hollywood cinema separates protagonist from subject, specifically, the female subject, and makes the role of protagonist inaccessible for viewing females. The voyeuristic spectator is invited into a position of internal focalization, incriminating the spectator, though she be female and feminist, into a site of "interpretants shaped by a male habit."[6]

The process of "incriminating" the female into a narrative process that simultaneously denies her subjectivity and reduces the effects of the actions she has taken, or will take, to the role they play in a narrative where only males are the protagonists, is quite similar to the way Todorov describes the process of enunciation in dirty jokes:

> A (the man) addresses B (the woman) seeking to satisfy his sexual desire; the intervention of C (the rival) makes the satisfaction of desire impossible. Hence, a second situation develops: frustrated in his desire, A addresses aggressive remarks to B and appeals to C as an ally. A new transformation occurs, provoked by the absence of the woman or by the need to observe a social code: instead of addressing B, [the woman], A addresses C by telling him a rude joke; B may well be absent, but instead of being the addressee she has become (implicitly) the object of what is said; C derives pleasure from A's joke.[7]

In other words, one of the key mechanisms for eliminating the subjectivity of the female in dirty jokes, and in most myths and myth representations (specifically, in films), is the mode of address. B's (the woman's) agency is erased by the mode of address of the joke; whether she is present or not, she has been relegated to the third person.

The "you" that the "I" of the narrative addresses is a constructed "you"; narratologists writing about the circuit of narrative communication refer to this constructed "you" as the "narratee," the person the story is being told to. So the mode of address of a narrative or a film is inextricably bound up with the construction of the "narratee", a mask that the viewer or spectator is forced to wear.

Branigan, in his analysis of levels of narration, has identified nine levels at which a single narrative is operating at any given point; not all of these levels are always applicable in a given text, especially to texts from early cinema. Branigan defines narrative as a circle of communication that begins at each level with narration and ends with the narratee, the receiver of the narrative, a receptive position which has been determined by the text, though the spectator may or may not fit into that position. Though Branigan did not thoroughly explore the different levels of the narratee, his levels-of-narration tool does gives us a way of identifying the multiplicitous—and often conflicting—ways in which a narratee is constructed in a single text. Whether the actual spectator of the film engages or identifies with every level of address aimed at her is a question for reception studies; I will isolate my analysis here to how the narratee position is constructed in various crossdressing films.

Branigan's levels of analysis begin with the historical author, the actual writer(s) or creator(s) of the text. The basic assumption is that we cannot really know anything about the historical author's intent based on the text alone, we can only presuppose that one existed. In this case we know that Alice Guy had almost total control over the subject of her comedies of crossdressing made at Solax.

What stands out in Guy's comedies of crossdressing, unlike films featuring crossdressing made by other filmmakers, is that they are addressed primarily to women and that all of them, beginning with her very first films, require "productive looking" as Kaja Silverman describes it.[8] In other words, her films require a constant and conscious reworking of the terms under which we look at objects that make up our visual landscape. Guy's films encourage this "productive look" through the use of transvestism, crossdressing and even transbodiment and role-reversal.

Guy used crossdressing and role reversal in different ways in the films she made for Gaumont and Solax. The difference between her Solax films and her later Gaumont films reflects not just the change in narrative strategies that had just occurred, but also the difference between French and American tastes. She had had three years to see what American audiences liked and what they did not, and her own filmmaking reflected the tastes of her new audience.

French melodramas—especially those in the Grand Guignol tradition—and French comedies distributed in the U.S. often provoked responses of outrage and call for censorship. Richard Abel specifically describes a gag film about a man with an urgent need who mistakes a telephone booth for a bathroom. Another man then goes into the booth to use the phone and exits hurriedly, holding his nose in disgust. This film features what Abel describes as "...the kind of French humor, sensitive to tastes and smells, that prim and proper American reviewers, waving their own figurative handkerchiefs, would later find so excruciatingly unbearable."[9]

Ironically, the calls for censorship in the United States often came in the name of protecting women and children. Because films were marketed under the name of their production houses, and film directors were not publicized, no one realized that the brazen Gaumont comedies were made by a woman. Consider La Glu, also

Figure 61. Feeding soup to the women stuck in a humiliating position in *La Glu*

Figure 62. Tommy gets stuck in the glue-bucket in *La Glu*

known as *Tommy and the Gluepot* (Gaumont 1906). A little boy has
come upon a bucket of paste and a brush and proceeds to paint
glue on everything in sight, including the steps leading up to a house
and the garden bench set right in front of it. Two ladies sit on the
bench for a nice long conversation and then discover that though they
can get up and walk around, the bench goes everywhere with them.
They then try to crawl up the stoop on their hands and knees, only
to become stuck there. A man comes out of the house and spoon-
feeds them soup and wine, then spreads out a newspaper for them
to read, while the two women are forced to remain on their hands
and knees before him. I do not know if it was enough to satisfy
the American demand that films end happily, i.e., that bourgeois
values be restored, but in the end of *La Glu*, Tommy gets stuck in
the glue-bucket himself.[10]

Once in the United States, Guy adapted easily to the demand of
American audiences for the restoration of bourgeois values at the end
of a film. However, she did not completely abandon the ironic tone
so apparent in her French comedies. To the contrary, the effect of
American censorship and the more prudish American mores was to
push her to higher levels of sophistication.

Dance Films

AS WE SAW in Chapter One, Guy's earliest comedies were remakes of
Lumière *scènes comiques* usually directed by Georges Hatot, films
which reflected the male homosocial working world of the men who
made them, such as *Les Joueurs de cartes* and *Chez le photographe*
in which one man takes pictures of another.

Guy's own brand of comedy apparently evolved out of a more
"feminine" genre: dance films. Richard Abel points out that these
dance performances were descended from the "transformation scenes"
of Méliès, which usually included dance scenes. He also notes that
Lacassin's filmography[11] of Guy suggests that Gaumont specialized
in dance performances from 1900 to 1902, and that nearly half of
Gaumont's fiction production was given over to dance films.[12]

The earliest dance films listed in the Gaumont catalogue (No. 69,
Danse du soleil, de la lune et des étoiles, No. 71 *Danse des papillons*,
No. 72 *Danse fleur de lotus* and Nos. 73 and 74a *Ballet libella*)
are all described, as "dances of the genre of Loïe Fuller;" the woman's
diaphanous silk costume and the amazing ways she manipulates it

with her body are the object of spectacle. But at whom was the spectacle aimed? Does the nature of the film (sold in three parts, listed in the catalogue as No. 68a, 68b and 68c), listed just before these dance films, *Coucher d'Yvette*, which depicted a woman disrobing and getting into bed, support Abel's thesis that these films were mostly aimed at a male audience?

One of the unidentified early films in the NFTVA collection, listed simply as "*Gavotte*," is of interest in this regard. The film features two women dancing a gavotte on a stage in front of a painted flat. One woman is dressed in 18th-century style gown, the other in 18th-century men's clothing. Dance quickly turns into courtship. The "man" kneels at the woman's feet, lays a trail of kisses along her bare arm, and declares his love. The woman listens and reacts; the pair end in an embrace. The purpose of the film is clearly the eroticism of seeing two women kiss. This is clearly an example of what Chris Straayer has called "the paradoxical bivalent kiss," common to temporary transvestite films which "often support heterosexual desire at the narrative level and challenge it at a more ambiguous level where other desires are suggested."[13] Like all the dance films discussed here, the crossdressing in this film seems designed to heighten the spectacle for masculine eyes.

Pantomime Films

GUY HERSELF CROSSDRESSED as a "peasant husband" when she remade *La Fée aux choux* as *Sage-femme de première classe* (First Class Midwife) in 1902.[14] But in *Sage-femme*, having a woman play the husband signals that this is a children's story. (Guy's costume resembles a Pierrot costume, and Germaine Serrand, who plays the wife, is dressed like Columbine.) *Sage-femme* pokes fun at the way men use romance to coax women into producing children, but also at the way women insist that their babies meet certain class standards.

The story involves a husband (Guy), who uses every loving word, gesture, and kiss in his repertoire to persuade his wife to buy a baby. Finally, she agrees and they go together to the midwife's window and examine some of the baby dolls arrayed there. If the husband had been played by a man, such romantic coercion might have aligned it more with Pathé's *Danse des Apaches*, in which the man exhibits his control over the woman's body as a display of machismo.[15] In this film, the strong display of matrimonial affection also calls attention to the crossdressing practice, which highlights the satire which was probably aimed at the mothers in the audience (there is some evidence that film audiences before 1905 were comprised mainly of women and children).

Each of these films, and Vinnie Burns in her crossdressing role as Dick Whittington in the 1913 Solax film of the same name (discussed in Chapter 5), clearly indicate the roots of this type of crossdressing in *commedia dell'arte*, harlequinade, and traditional Christmas pantomimes (common in the UK and known in the U.S. principally through productions of *Peter Pan*). Marjorie Garber describes this type of crossdressing as follows:

> ...the pantomime was a traditional Christmas entertainment in which an actress, designated the Principal Boy, played the hero's part, and an actor (the Dame) played the comic female character, usually an old and/or ugly woman. Fairy tales often provided the foundation for the plot: Cinderella, Dick Whittington and His Cat, Mother Goose, the Babes in the Wood. The first Principal Boy(s)... dressed in the standard outfit of blond wig, short tunic, fleshings and high heels, the early Principal Boys were ample of figure. As the twentieth century wore on the Principal Boys became slimmer, more "boyish." The Ugly Sisters of Cinderella, the Cook in Dick Whittington, Mother Goose, and the Queen of Hearts are all classic Dame parts, played by... renowned actors.[16]

At an extra-diegetic level these films are addressing their narratees as aware of the pantomime tradition. Spectators who fit into that narratee position would therefore note that what is interesting about Alice Guy's "panto" films is that the Dame characters (the midwife in *Sage-femme*, the cook in *Dick Whittington*) are actually played by women (In *Madame a des envies* the character of principal boy and Dame appear to be combined in the figure of the abnormally tall pregnant woman). Like the earliest of Méliès *féerie* films, *Fée aux choux* and *Sage-femme* place a female figure in a position of power or take a woman's story as their subject. The way both films and other films like them (*La Fée printemps* (The Spring Fairy) for example[17]) place reproductive power in female hands is in direct contrast to other contemporary films by Méliès and Pathé. In *Lanterne magique* (1903), for example, Méliès depicted the camera apparatus as a magical phallus that generated infinitely reproducible images of women.[18]

This is not to say that the Dame figure was eliminated from early cinema. The "false woman" was a staple of the cinema of attractions, but these figures were more related to the male actors in drag that were a staple of the music hall. Leopoldo Fregoli was one such star who, in 1896, bought a Lumière camera and made dozens of comic films that involved men dressing as women. In *Fregoli amant* (Fregoli the lover), for example, he crossdresses in order to escape from a jealous husband. The highlight of these films is always the moment when Fregoli assumes his feminine disguise in real time.

The plot of *The Inquisitive Boots* (1905) is perhaps a better example of the function these films played in turn of the century French culture. A shoe-shiner in a hotel stops to peer through three keyholes. Through the first he sees a woman in the process of undressing, through the second a man, and through the third he sees a transvestite removing his costume. As Thierry Lefebvre has pointed out, the fact that he sees the transvestite through the third keyhole adds weight to the uneasiness men at the turn of the century had about "the third sex."[19]

As Guy's films became more sophisticated, with more elaborate slapstick and a larger number of characters, she began to exploit the comic potential of crossdressing more deliberately. Of her extant work, most of the films from the end of her Gaumont period (1905–06) that show crossdressing are chase films.

Another film from the NFTVA collection is a good example: *L'Âne récalcitrant* (Gaumont 1906), known in English as *Father Buys a Moke*. In the beginning of the film, a gypsy sells a little donkey to a rich man, who then tries to load his family into a cart and get the donkey to take them for a ride. The donkey, however, will not budge unless the cart is empty and it is led around by the bridle. The rich man resorts to a variety of ploys to get the donkey to move, and the members of an ever-larger crowd of observers drop what they are doing to help him. In one scene they attach firecrackers to the wheels of the cart. The husband is sitting in the driver's seat and his corpulent wife is sitting next to him. As the firecrackers are being loaded, she suddenly starts kissing her husband, for no apparent reason except that the wife is clearly played by a man in drag, and a paradoxical bivalent pleasure is to be derived from the sight. This moment seems like it might have been improvised or that it might have evolved spontaneously on the set. Having men crossdress as female characters when stunt work was involved was standard industry practice at the time (much as boys playing female roles was standard in Shakespeare's day). Could it be that the necessity to dress men as women in these slapstick films first inspired Alice Guy to start thinking about crossdressing and how dress affects behavior expectation?

In her analysis of the tradition of crossdressing the character of Peter Pan, Garber argues that:

> Peter is Wendy "unbound, "a regendered, not-quite-degendered alternative persona who can have adventures, fight pirates, smoke pipes, and cavort with redskins... Peter is a crossdressed version of Wendy—and Wendy as an unambivalent heterosexual. This reading would be a kind of progress narrative, in which the stage of believing in Peter became, in Neverland (or Freud's dream-work) the same as the stage of *being* him—while retaining the dreamer's prerogative of being herself at the same time.[20]

Garber is quick to point out that her analysis should not be read as a facile equation of the position of the crossdressed for "woman." Rather, Peter Pan is a "betwixt-and-between," a member

Figure 63. The bivalent kiss in *L'Âne récalcitrant*

of the third sex. It is the power of transvestism on western culture that has made Peter Pan (and Dick Whittington, and others like them) so enduring.

Alice Guy was not interested in the "nightmare" of transvestism, (as Garber refers to the Dame character) as evidenced by the "Dame" roles actually being played by women in her films, but she used the "dream" of transvestism—the "Principal Boy" roles being played by women—repeatedly in her films. In the Gaumont films these characters were actually crossdressed, but in her Solax films she keeps the "betwixt-and-between" characterization while dispensing with crossdressing. The resulting characters are clearly girls or young women, who usually appear in action films and are typed as tomboys. However, in her romantic comedies of the same period (1911–1913) adult women show similar characteristics without the tomboy personality. What is changing is the degree of agency these characters have; and their agency is always related in some way to the "betwixt-and-between" aspect of their characters, depicted here less through clothing than through behavior.

Behavioral Transvestism

IT IS EVIDENT that even in traditional cinema, female characters have been shown to have a degree of agency. They are even shown gazing upon and pursuing the objects of their desire. The difference is that they are routinely punished for it. Such female characters even have a name: transgressors. They are "transgressing" by breaking the cultural taboo that denies them agency. Susan Hayward defines agency as follows:

> Agency (see also subjectivity). Refers essentially to issues of control and operates both within and outside the film. Within the film, agency is often applied to a character in relation to desire. If that character has agency over desire it means that she or he (though predominantly in classic narrative cinema it is a 'he') is able to act upon that desire and fulfill it (a classic example is: boy meets girl, boy wants girl, boy gets girl). Agency also functions at the level of the narrative inside and outside the film. Whose narration is it? A character in the film? A character outside the film? The directors? Hollywood's? And finally, agency also applies to the spectator. In viewing the film, the spectator has agency over the text in that she or he produces a meaning and a reading of the filmic text.[21]

As this definition makes clear, an analysis that focuses on issues of agency in the various levels of a film text is a narratological one. In other words, it should not be necessary to construct films for women in a completely new or different cinematic language in order to address women as spectators. It is enough to include a feminist mode of address on at least one level of narration. For example, the character gaze could be female, and that of the camera male. This occurs often, especially in "women's films" though productive looking or reading against the grain is required for feminist enjoyment. Increased agency (usually read as "masculine"), could be described as behavioral transvestism; it is especially apparent in female heroes of action films. Scott Simmon has pointed out that in fact the image of a Southern Belle riding a horse and using a gun was not so far from reality, as women in the South were trained in these arts right alongside their brothers (Griffith apparently followed the same plot pattern in *Taming a Husband* and *Wilful Peggy*, both made in 1910); but L.R.H., the reviewer for *The Moving Picture World*, knows that "women do not love destruction."[22] This is a far cry from the gleeful destructiveness of the ten-year-old in *Two Little Rangers* and from Florence in *Greater Love Hath no Man* (both Solax, 1913) who whips out her pistol when she is sexually harassed.

In Guy's action films, the women are free to use their weapons without having to don a male disguise. A typical example is a film called *Two Little Rangers*, sometimes also known as *The Little Rangers* (Solax, 1912). The setting is the West (filmed in Fort Lee). Father is the postmaster, assisted by his two daughters and the male hero, Jim (Darwin Karr). Jim rescues and Father shelters the battered wife (played by Blanche Cornwall) of the villain, Grey, who gets revenge by throwing Father off a cliff (the famous Cliffhanger Point in Fort Lee, NJ) and then framing Jim for it by leaving Jim's knife stuck in a tree. The older of the two sisters (played by Vinnie Burns) uses her lasso to rescue her father from the ledge where he has fallen, pulling him up very unrealistically with a hand-over-hand move. But the real hero of this film is her ten-year-old sister, who protects Jim by waving her six-shooter around, helps her sister set the villain's cabin on fire with flaming arrows, and when he runs out, drives him over the cliff at gun point. Of course, Jim and Father and Grey's wife forgive Grey after the girls have reduced him to a trembling mass of contrition. The final triangular tableau, reminiscent of a pietà arrangement, is typical of Guy's endings for her action films;

Figure 64. An action scene from *Two Little Rangers*

Figure 65. *Pietà* ending from *Two Little Rangers*

we see a very similar tableau at the end of *Greater Love Hath No Man* (Solax, 1911).

A House Divided, Matrimony's Speed Limit, and *Burstop Holme's Murder Case* all deal with the balance of power between marriage partners. As we saw in Chapter Five, this was a theme of great interest to Guy, who wrote the feature *House of Cards* explicitly to show the pleasures of two spouses who also work together. The partners in *House Divided*, played by Billy Quirck and Marion Swayne, both of whom Guy made into stars, are depicted as equals in terms of their emotional power in the relationship. We see the husband at his office (Vinnie Burns does a hysterical send-up of the secretarial stereotype, complete with chewing gum and a typing style that looks more like jabbing the machine with her claws) where a perfume salesman sprays perfume all over his lapel. Meanwhile, back at the house, the wife catches her maid, Bridget, and the delivery man in an embrace. The man leaves but in his embarrassment forgets his gloves. When her husband returns home, she takes the perfume and he takes the gloves as signs of infidelity. Each then goes to their lawyer, who draws up a contract specifying that they will live "separately together" in the house in order to maintain appearances and will communicate only through notes. The separation quickly takes its toll on each partner; he cannot concentrate at work and she dissolves into tears in the kitchen. One night they throw a dinner party, and Bridget forgets her key, so she climbs into the house through the basement window. The wife hears the noise downstairs and tells her husband (in a note) that there is a burglar in the house, whom he must catch without alarming the guests. She also provides him with a gun, which neither of them know how to use. She follows him down to the basement, where he gives Bridget the fright of her life. In the humorous aftermath of this episode, they talk about their suspicions and clear up the misunderstanding. A final note of satire comes when the lawyer finds them embracing and shouts "Stop! You are breaking your agreement!"

Although the husband and wife in *House Divided* live in separate spheres, she at home and he at home and out in the world, they are depicted as equals in the relationship. She is shown commanding her household employees much the same way he deals with the people at his office (even if Vinnie Burns does upstage him with her foregrounded secretary send-up). This balance of power is shown as essential to the maintenance of the happy household. The balance of power emphasized in the plot is also maintained by the form: each character has almost equal screentime, and each is the focalizer for their own sequences. This early screwball comedy still gets audiences to laugh out loud.

The couple in *Matrimony's Speed Limit*, again played by Billy Quirck and Marion Swayne, exhibit this same emotional balance of power and share the focalization. In this story they are engaged; she is an heiress and he has a thriving business as a stockbroker. The film starts when he loses all in a crash and breaks off the engagement because of his poverty. She offers him all of her money, but he refuses and leaves. She then fakes a telegram from a law firm telling him that a distant uncle has just died and has left him a fortune, provided he is married by noon that day. This gives him about ten minutes to find a wife, and he runs out and proposes to the first woman he sees, and then the next, and the next, and the next. Curiously, he proposes to two strangers before he goes to the home of his former fiancée, who is out getting a preacher. After finding that Marian is not at home, he proposes to several more women, including one who is veiled; when she lifts her veil he sees that she

Figure 66. Steamrollered into marriage in *Matrimony's Speed Limit*

is black and flees. Finally Marian, preacher in tow, catches up to him, and the two are married in the time it takes a stop light to turn green, while a steamroller honks at them impatiently. Back at home he triumphantly shows her the telegram, and she confesses to the ruse. He wants to storm out angrily, but he cannot because she would not give him his hat. In the struggle to recover his hat they end up in each other's arms.

This film goes a little deeper into the issue of marital equality: is a man less of a man if he is not financially successful? Does it endanger the marriage partnership if the woman makes or has more money than the man? Since, as we saw in Chapter Two, it was Guy who made most of the money during her marriage, and later Herbert Blaché who lost money "playing the stock market" which contributed to the end of the Solax Company, it seems likely that these questions were of personal concern to her as well. Her answer in this comedy seems to be that the strength of marriage is (or should be) based on the emotional relationship and not the financial one.

However, she was not insensitive to the comic possibilities of a relationship where the balance of power is extremely skewed one way or the other. In *Burstop Holmes' Murder Case*, Blanche Cornwall, dressed in a suit jacket, tie, and skirt, with her hair slicked back (the suffragette garb is a non-diegetic reference to the suffrage movement and the then-current discourse around the effect of giving women the vote), runs her husband's life with an iron hand. Her husband, played by Darwin Karr, just wants to climb out the window and go play cards with the boys, so he puts a dummy in the bed and covers its head with one of his own wigs. When he climbs out the window, he cuts himself and stains the bedsheets with blood. When his wife comes up to his room looking for him, she believes he has been murdered. She then hires Burstop Holmes (Billy Quirck doing a Sherlock Holmes send-up) to find the killer. Burstop misses all the obvious clues and spends much time following up false leads. Meanwhile, the wife realizes the body in the bed is a dummy and goes to the site of the card game. There is a lovely tableau in which all of her husband's buddies note her silent, disapproving presence and leave the room one by one, (one of them actually crawls out on his hands and knees) while hubby, caught up in a winning streak, does not notice their disappearance until he is alone with his wife's dark, stern, and disapproving figure. He stands up fearfully, but suddenly she throws herself into his arms and sobs out her relief that he is alive. He pats her on the back with one hand while stuffing his winnings into his pocket with the other.

Burstop Holmes, made two weeks after *Officer Henderson,* shows similar thematic concerns: what are the "proper" roles for each marriage partner, and how are these roles tied into social constructions of gender, which is depicted in the films by attire. Henderson assumes woman's dress as a costume, while the wife in *Burstop Holmes* dresses in a masculine way normally. Her mannish clothes are signs of the role-reversal that characterizes her marriage. The point of *Burstop Holmes* is that such role-reversal is unimportant, as long as the emotional balance remains satisfactory.

Guy also explored the idea of men taking on women's roles using role-reversal without cross-dressing. One of the best examples of this is *Algie the Miner* (Solax, 1912), directed by Edward Warren and Harry Shenck, with Guy credited as "producer and directing supervision."[23] The Solax ad[24] summarizes it as follows:

> A Billy Quirck comedy. Algie is a "sissy boy" who has as much backbone as a jelly fish. When Algie falls in love and finds that his sweetheart objects to his "personality" he goes West and after several ludicrous experiences and hard struggles he becomes a "man." A comedy with strong character portrayals.

What is interesting about this summary is that it is actually fairly different from the film. In fact, Algie's sweetheart appears to be quite attached to him, no matter how foppish he is (his sissiness is indicated by white-face make-up and white gloves). It is her Father who objects, and when Algie asks for his daughter's hand, her father writes a note promising that Algie can marry his daughter if he can prove himself a man by going West for a year. Dad thinks this will get rid of Algie for sure, but Algie signs the note in great seriousness. The daughter is clearly bereft when he leaves. Next we see Algie packing in his over-decorated room. Among other things, he packs a lace doily and a tiny silver pistol, which he stuffs into his belt so that it is pointing directly at his groin.

Out West we see him getting off a train in some remote location and approaching two hard-bitten characters and asking them for directions. When they answer, he kisses one of them in gratitude, which makes the man's hat fall off, and then impels him to pull his (very large) gun. Algie, frightened, falls to his knees, and the second

Figure 67. Algie kisses a cowboy in gratitude in *Algie the Miner*

man stops the first from shooting Algie, so Algie kisses him too. This is too much for the men, so they lift Algie up, and carry him to a train trestle, and perch him there while they decide what to do with him. Algie tries pulling his little pistol, which amuses them, so they carry him off to the saloon for the entertainment of their friends. In the saloon he is introduced to Big Jim, the biggest ruffian of all with, of course, the largest pistol. Algie's education is "entrusted" to Big Jim.

In other words, at the diegetic level of narration the movie is about Algie becoming more virile, skilled and confident, but at the extra-diegetic level the film is a love story between two men. Big Jim gradually breaks Algie in to the realities of Gold Rush life and Algie nurses Big Jim through a bout with the DTs and finally helps him quit drinking altogether. Several moments, such as the moment when Big Jim throws Algie on the bed to put an end to his whining, are clearly meant to read as a sort of "taming of the shrew" scene. Finally, the two strike gold and Algie gets to show his mettle defending both Big Jim and the gold. The year is up and Algie and Big Jim go back East so Algie can claim his sweetheart. He no longer wears the pancake makeup, the suit or the gloves, and he rings the doorbell "western style" by shooting in the air.

Again, he deals not with his sweetheart, but with her father, who agrees to allow the two to marry under the watchful eye of Big Jim's gun.

It seems clear from this film as well as the two Solax crossdressing films discussed below that Guy was aware of the homosexual subtext implicit in her crossdressing films and deliberately chose to exploit it in this film. For the sake of (deceptive) closure, to satisfy American mores, she added the sweetheart subplot, but as we have seen the sweetheart is barely a presence: the whole story is about the three men. This film does not appear to have been studied by others but it is a sensitive portrayal of male bonding, the difficulties of living up to a "masculine ideal" (imposed by a powerful father figure), and an exploration of the all-male society of the Gold Rush camp, to which Guy would return again, although not so successfully, in such films as *Greater Love Hath No Man*. This film reverses the familiar triangle of two women loving one man into two men loving a gun-toting woman who pans her own gold dust. When the camp supervisor, the object of Florence's affection, is threatened by Mexicans in the camp, Jake warns his rival and then defends him from the Mexicans to the death, winning himself one kiss from Florence as he dies in her arms.[25]

Guy also uses role-reversal in some Solax films that are no longer extant, such as *Hubby Does the Washing*, another comedy starring Billy Quirck as the male housewife.

Other film companies also used role reversal. Centaur produced a film in 1910 entitled *She Would be a Business Man*.[26] The wife, after watching her husband fail at business, insists that she can do better, so the two agree to trade places as well as clothes. However, she does not pretend to be a man; she simply wishes to do business, but all the men with whom she wants to do business keep making passes at her, so she never has a chance to put her ideas into practice. Meanwhile, her husband is having no luck running the household, and the two wearily agree to return to their own spheres.

What stands out about these films? They are not crossdressing *per se*, but rather a form of behavioral transvestism; what Judith Mayne says in her analysis of Dorothy Arzner's films applies equally to Alice Guy: both directors are intent on making codes of behaviour based on conventions associated with gender "strange." Mayne repeats Judith Butler's assertion that:

> Gender ought not to be construed as a stable identity or locus of agency from which various acts follow; rather gender is an identity tenuously constituted in time, instituted in an exterior space through a stylized repetition of acts."[27]

Mayne's theory about Arzner is that her films show a preoccupation with behavioral transvestism and that greater degrees of agency can be associated with tomboyish personas. Mayne associates this with Arzner's own lesbianism and her relationship to Marion Morgan, whose choreography and persona influences Arzner's staging and characterizations.

For the most part, in these films Guy dispenses with transvestite or tomboyish dress, (with the exception of the wife's jacket and tie in *Burstop Holmes*, also associated with suffragettes of her day) and focuses on tomboyish behaviour: twirling lassoes, shooting flaming arrows, conducting chases of villains at a full gallop, straight shooting, making her own living panning gold dust, running a business, rescuing recalcitrant suitors, and wooing the man of her choice. Whether focalized through the perspective of the hapless male villain or love object or through the female action hero or comic hero, the equation is always the same: the conventions of the genre are pushed to the limit as these female characters assume the degree of agency that they, and the other characters around them, naturally assume is their due. It is no wonder then, that most of these films are stylized comedies.

Many of Guy's films that actually show characters crossdressing are still comedies, but are often more serious in tone, or at least contain more serious elements, and more sophisticated themes. Guy appears to be making a deliberate effort to achieve something different from the sometimes campy and almost burlesque tone of the films that depict greater female agency through behavioural transvestism by actually resorting to crossdressing.

Cross Dressing and Gender Identity

CROSSDRESSING WAS A staple of the cinema in Guy's day, although no other single film producer seems to have used it as consistently, and to such effect, as she did. A standard drama in literature as well as film was the young woman who dons a soldier's uniform and identity in order to: a) rescue her lover, b) be with her lover, c) do a job her lover cannot do because of a wound or cowardice or, d) all of the above. In these films (almost always dramas), for the woman to don a man's clothing and identity is seen as proof of great love: for a woman to behave in a masculine way is seen as a great sacrifice, performed temporarily under duress, and finished with as quickly as possible.

In *The House with the Closed Shutters* (Biograph 1910), D.W. Griffith carries this plot a little further, as the girl and her soldier brother trade places. The reviewer in *The Moving Picture World* commented on her action thus:

> With noble self-forgetfulness, the spirit to bear up against misfortune and an almost superhuman power to dare, to achieve and to suffer, she dons her brother's uniform and rides forth to do his duty. She delivers the despatches and becomes involved in a fierce battle. At times she falters, the scene is a horrible one, women do not love destruction, but she dashes in, the iron is in her blood, she attempts to save the flag and falls mortally wounded facing the enemy. Her brother's name is listed among the honored dead. Her brother really lives behind closed doors and shutters. A drunken decadent, he lives on and on through weary years. It is given out that he bravely died and his sister, with disordered mind, overturned by his supposed death, is behind those shutters. Year after year the faithful suitors leave their tributes of affection at the door of the old Southern house. The family honor is preserved, while somewhere in the unmarked trenches are the bones of the Southern rose.[28]

In western culture identity is essentially gendered. Clothes embody gender-specific meanings, but they are as changeable as any semiotic convention. In other words, it is very easy to undress, and very easy for men and women to trade clothes with each other, in other words, to crossdress. If the markers of our gender identity are so easily changeable, what does that say about identity itself?[29] This is the question Alice guy asked over and over again in her comedies of crossdressing, and in many of her other comedies too.

A Comedy of Errors (Solax, 1912) is structurally a mirror image to *Burstop Holmes' Murder Case*. The three lead actors are the same: Darwin Karr plays Greeneyes, the husband prone to fits of jealousy; Blanche Cornwall plays the faithful but misunderstood wife;

and Billy Quirck plays the neighbor in the apartment across the street who is smitten with her. The film plot bears no relation to the play by Shakespeare of the same title. The initial misunderstanding is very simple: Billy sees Blanche blowing kisses to her departing husband as she leans out the window, and he assumes the kisses are meant for him. When Blanche accidentally drops her book out of the window he takes this as an invitation, retrieves the book, and delivers it to her. He then tries to make love to Blanche, who pushes him away and then hastily hides him in the closet when her husband unexpectedly returns.

The "comedy of errors" then develops around clothes, and the husband and would-be lover gradually trade identities by exchanging their clothes. First Greeneyes finds Billy's umbrella on the chair, and in a quickly concocted lie, Blanche says it is a birthday present for him. Greeneyes goes out with the umbrella and Blanche gets Billy out of the house, but he returns when he realizes his umbrella is missing. Greeneyes returns unexpectedly again, and this time ends up with Billy's gloves, and then in a third go-round with Billy's coat. To make it up to Billy, Blanche gives him her husband's old coat (much too big for him), ripped umbrella, and worn gloves. But Greeneyes catches them together this time, pulls out a gun, and begins to tear the house apart in a furious search for Billy, who retrieves his own clothes and escapes. When Greeneyes collapses at the end of his unsuccessful murderous fit, his wife convinces him that "there were no birthday presents" that he imagined it all in a "fit of delirium." Greeneyes actually accepts this, as his wife caresses him and promises him that she will not forget his birthday. The film ends as it began, with Blanche blowing kisses to her husband out the window, Billy watching from his window, this time making a point not to get involved and caressing his own coat as if to make sure it is still there.

The motif of one person taking on the persona of their spouse's lover is repeated in *Officer Henderson*, in which the wife wilfully puts on the dress, hat, and veil that she believes belong to "the other woman." This is only one instance of how *Officer Henderson*, a very layered film, uses clothes in an exploration of identity. As Annette Kuhn observes:

> The truth lies under the clothing, and although it might well be
> expected that in ordinary circumstances it will not and should

not do so, *clothing can obscure rather than reveal the truth.* Dress constantly poses the possibility of distance between body and clothing, between "true" self, the fixed gender of (our) ideology, and assumed persona. Crossdressing as a realization of such a potential turns this distance to account, constructing sexual disguise as a play upon the fixity and the fluidity of gender identity.[30]

In other words, at the extra-diegetic level the film is pointing out that if males and females can trade clothes, then maybe what is male and what is female is not so unalterably fixed (as any transvestite knows). That, of course, is a profoundly disturbing idea. Filmmakers like to disturb people, but they do not want their films to be so disturbing as to alienate their audience. So, narrative devices emerged that were aimed at eliminating or reducing the viewers' potential discomfort with crossdressing. First, everything possible is done to make the viewer aware of the fluidity of the boundaries of masculinity and femininity, and then everything is returned to "normal."

This pattern is evident in *Officer Henderson* (Solax, 1911): Henderson and his partner, Williams, are police officers. They are told to dress like women so they can catch pickpockets who prey on lady shoppers. Henderson takes great pleasure in donning the disguise and showing that he "has it on Venus coming and going." We see Williams go shopping in a lace shop and promptly catch a pickpocket, but Henderson stops at a fancy bistro to eat lunch, where he is accosted by a masher. Henderson plays along from behind his veil while two real women (dainty ladies at lunch) watch with horror as Henderson invites the masher over to his table and flirts with him. This scene aptly illustrates Mary Anne Doane's statement:

At some level of the cultural ordering of the psychical, the horror or threat of that precariousness (of both sexuality and the visible) is attenuated by attributing it to the woman, over and against the purported stability and identity of the male. The veil is a mark of that precariousness.[31]

However, in Guy's universe, it is a *man* who wears a veil and illustrates that precariousness, and another man who is willingly duped; in the background we see two *real* women (no need of veils) whose reactions, shown in a point-of-view sequence, inform ours, the spectators'.

Henderson goes back to the police station where he re-enacts his exploits for his fellow officers (he tricked one of them into helping him cross a muddy street) and invites them all to the bistro the next day to watch him continue his flirtation with the masher.

Meanwhile, Mrs. Henderson, who has been visiting her mother, comes home early and finds Henderson's disguise hanging in the closet. She assumes he is having an affair and that the dress belongs to the other woman. She packs the whole thing up and runs back to mother, who advises her to put on the dress, approach Henderson, "and when he embraces you don't be afraid to use your knuckles." Once dressed, Mrs. Henderson decides to stop in at the bistro; the masher sees her and, thinking she is Henderson, starts caressing her. She jumps up and whips him soundly with her purse, while Henderson's fellow officers watch through the window, laughing hysterically. Mrs. Henderson runs out to the street, where she sees her husband, in his policeman's uniform, telling his partner, who is in his dress/disguise, that his women's clothes have disappeared. Assuming Williams is the other woman, Mrs. Henderson starts beating him about the head with her purse, so Henderson, not recognizing her, hauls her off to the police station, where all is revealed and the couple is reconciled.

It is interesting to note the double disguise here: the identity of the fictional "other woman" travels from Henderson, to Mrs. Henderson, to Henderson's partner, illuminating the process of projection: each character projects his or her fears and fantasies on this "other woman" figure, who is contained somehow in the clothes, and with the clothes passes from one character to the next as if she were playing musical chairs. But in the end, everything is restored to order under the watchful eye of the Chief of Police.

Cupid and the Comet (Solax, 1911) has some stylistic similarities to *What Happened to Officer Henderson*, which was made just a few months later. Together, the two films together clearly demonstrate the sophisticated nature of Guy's productive look.

The story starts with a father who has read about Haley's comet that is soon to appear and invites some of his friends over for a "comet party." When he finally gets his telescope focused through the window, he sees not the comet but his daughter in the arms of a "strange young man," as the plot summary describes him, sitting on a garden wall and silhouetted by moonlight. Father's reaction, after checking the telescope to see if it is working, is to run out to the

Figure 68. The image from *Cupid and the Comet*,
used to identify the film

garden, grab the unfortunate young man, and literally toss him out
with several well-aimed kicks to the derriere. Then he pulls his struggling daughter out of the garden by her hair and locks her in her
room. However, her lover, undaunted, appears beneath her window
and convinces her to elope. Dad catches her climbing out the window
and kicks the suitor away again; this time he spanks his daughter
before locking her up again, and to make doubly sure she cannot go
anywhere this time, he takes her clothes. Since one can never be
too sure about these things he tucks her clothes into bed with him.

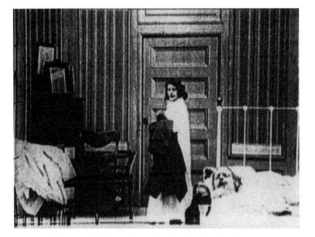

Figure 69. Stealing her father's clothes in
Cupid and the Comet

When her lover appears beneath her window a second time, she sneaks into her (now sleeping) father's room, but decides that pulling her clothes out of his bed is more than she can handle. So she takes his clothes and puts them on. She takes the added precaution of locking his closet and taking the key, which tells us that Father has a closet full of clothes, but she has only one set. Father wakes up and sees her climbing out the window, but this time he is delayed by the fact that his clothes are gone and his closet is locked. So, there is nothing to do but to put on her clothes. Meanwhile, back at the preacher's place, the young couple find the very effeminate minister unwilling to marry two young men to each other, at least until the bride's true identity is revealed—by the simple removal of her hat. The three of them, the "real" man, the woman dressed as a man, and the effeminate preacher, are watched closely by two "real women" reminiscent of the two women observers in *Officer Henderson*. Dad comes running in, dressed in his daughter's clothes, but it is too late, and he gets a lecture from the minister for both his anger and his odd habits of dress.

In *Cupid and the Comet*, Guy is deliberately using crossdressing as a source of comedy. In *Officer Henderson*, the way the narrative is resolved ultimately reinforces the fixity of sexual difference and the social/sexual hierarchies erected upon it. *Cupid and the Comet*, made earlier, is a little more daring. The young woman in this film adopts male clothes—and with them, apparently, the gumption to

Figure 70. Putting on his daughter's clothes in
Cupid and the Comet

Figure 71. The minister is reluctant to marry two young men
to each other in *Cupid and the Comet*

climb out a second story window and run off with her lover—in
order to escape her father, who is not only domineering and abusive,
but presumably incestuous as well. The final tableau presents us
with a "visionary multiplicity" of gender, an androgynous subversion
of gender fixity.[32] And even though the plot has a traditional resolution, with the two young people tied in a heterosexual marriage
knot, the fact that they are both dressed as men during the marriage
ceremony, that the minister is so glaringly effeminate, and that the

hulking and hirsute father arrives wearing his daughter's clothes undercuts even this narrative closure.

What Guy's crossdressing films focus on is not so much the conventions of femininity (which she problematized in her films of female transvestite behavior) but on gender conventions, gender as social more, social law. Judith Butler has pointed out that "Woman" can be taken as a category, as a signifier, as a site of new articulation.[33]

This is exactly what happens in Guy's films of crossdressing: Woman as a social construction is opened up as a site of political contest, by showing female characters crossdressing as males in order to achieve the degree of agency to which they are entitled, but to which the way is blocked (usually by a patriarchal figure). The contestation also occurs in Guy's films where male characters crossdress as females. In other words, whether men are crossdressing as women, or women as men, the crossdressing in these films points to a theme of resistance to the gender conventions as applied to Woman, and not to Man. This is achieved by having both sets of stories told from the perspective of a female character: by Winnie in *Cupid and the Comet* and by Mrs Henderson in *Officer Henderson*. Even though Mrs Henderson is introduced late in the film, the important duplicity of the disguise is the one worked on her; in her absence other female characters (the dissaproving women at the restaurant where Henderson flirts with the masher) focalize in her place.

Crossdressing and Role Reversal

As I INDICATED already, the temporary transvestite film *Officer Henderson* denaturalizes sexual difference and therefore threatens to disrupt an apparently natural order. For most of the film we experience the unsettling pleasures of the crossdressing narrative, and then the traditional narrative closure provides us with the satisfactions of completion as well as reassuring us that all is indeed well, that men are still men and women are still women.

The "justified crossdressing" or "closure" approach is basically the approach used in Hollywood films today, films such as *Tootsie* and *Victor/Victoria* and the classic *Some Like it Hot*. Annette Kuhn's analysis of a segment of *Some Like it Hot* makes a good starting point for discussing point-of-view in early cinema.

"To the extent that it denaturalizes sexual difference, crossdressing threatens to disrupt an apparently natural order,"[34] said Kuhn.

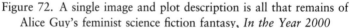

Figure 72. A single image and plot description is all that remains of
Alice Guy's feminist science fiction fantasy, *In the Year 2000*

This means that a more direct form of social critique is possible
with the crossdressing plot. This rarely occurs, but Alice Guy did
attempt it in two films, *Les Résultats du féminisme* (The Results of
Feminism), made for Gaumont in 1906, and remade as *In the Year
2000* for Solax in 1912 (Guy remade more than one of her Gaumont
films as Solax films). Both films, unfortunately, have been lost.

This is how *In the Year 2000* was summarized by the Solax
publicity department for *The Moving Picture World*:

> A great number of prognostications often terrify us with visions
> of what will be when women shall rule the earth and the time
> when men shall be subordinates and adjuncts. It is rather a fine
> question to decide—for chivalrous men, anyway. Today, with
> the multiplicity of feminine activities and the constant broadening

of feminine spheres, it is difficult to predict what heights women will achieve.

In the Solax production of "In the Year 2000," the release of Friday, May 17th, a serio-comic prognostication is unreeled on the screen with such magnetic force, charm and rich imaginative detail that one is compelled to accept the theories advanced on their face value.

The conditions are reversed. Women in this film are supreme, and man's destiny is presided over by woman. No attempt is made at burlesque—but the very seriousness of the purpose of the theme makes the situations ludicrous. This is one of the funniest comedies released by the Solax Company in some time, and that's saying a whole lot of this picture.[35]

Clearly, the Solax publicity man (H.Z. Levine), was ambivalent about the film. Apparently it was not reviewed.

Les Résultats du féminisme was advertised in the catalogue as "a humorous scene showing men reduced to doing their own washing, ironing, sewing, and even making hats for their wives!" The scenario for this film is in the Gaumont script collection at the Bibliothèque de l'Arsenal in Paris:

The first set is a hatmaking shop, where a group of elegant young men sew together hats. One of these young "seamstresses" walks out, carrying a hatbox.

On the street, an older, female "masher" catches sight of him, stops, and stares. She then accosts him and invites him to sit down with her. The young man pretends not to understand what she wants from him but as she blocks his way and prevents him from moving he gets angry and then begins to weep. A young woman passing by notices his predicament and saves him. She rebukes the old masher and sends her away after they exchange calling cards in the polite bourgeois fashion. The young woman then offers her arm to the young male hatmaker, sits him down on the bench, and comforts him. Their idyll begins. Other men walk by and turn their faces away and cover their eyes prudishly from the spectacle of the couple on the bench.

Now we see the young man at home, wearing a housecoat and working at a sewing machine. His father is ironing, and his mother sits in an easy chair, reading the paper and smoking. It is bedtime. Father and mother light a candle and go up to their room together. Left alone, our young hero pulls a portrait out of his pocket and covers it with kisses. Then he goes back to his sewing machine. There is a knock on the door—it's her! The young man opens the door, and the Doña Juana from the previous scene enters. Now she is here to convince him to elope with her; after much affectionate coaxing, she overcomes his resistance. He writes a note to his parents: "My dear parents, I am leaving with the one that I love, forgive me the pain I am causing you, but I know I cannot stay any longer in my beloved home when my heart is no longer pure. Goodbye."

Now we are in Doña Juana's bachelor pad, where Doña Juana is seducing our innocent young man. She has convinced him to take off his outer clothes, so that he is wearing just his trousers, shirt, and suspenders. Once he gets this far undressed he is overcome with shyness, and Doña Juana moves in for the score.

A few years later is the intertitle before the next scene. A construction site, women pavers and masons hard at work. Men walk by with their string shopping bags and milk bottles, ostensibly on their way to market, but really to flirt. The women show signs of exhaustion. One of them clumsily cuts herself and faints, the others all do too. The helpful men come to their aid, take up the tools, hand the women the shopping parcels, and take up the construction work.

New scene. A large square in front of a café. There are some (male) nannies breastfeeding babies; female soldiers walk up to them and flirt with them.

A group of women sit in the café smoking and talking; our Doña Juana is among them. Two attractive young men come in and the women start to flirt with them and tease them.

Some husbands come into the café, pulling young children by the hand. They are there to chase after their spouses, who prefer to stay at the bar rather than returning home. The women kick them out of the café.

Outside the café we see our young man coming back from the market loaded down with shopping parcels and pulling along a brood of children while pushing two additional babies in the baby carriage. He stops to give one baby (the actual term used in the script is "bastard") its bottle. Doña Juana walks by and the young man begs her to return home with him, not to neglect him anymore. Doña Juana ignores him, so the young man throws acid in her handsome face. Doña Juana runs away screaming. Other husbands surround our young man who tells his side of the story, melodramatically pointing to his brood of children. The neglected husbands swear vengeance and turn into a mob that breaks into the café and attack the drinking women. A fierce battle ensues. All the women are thrown out of the café, along with the broods of children, and the triumphant men remain in the café knowing justice has been served.[36]

The fact that men nurse babies means that these characters are not simply crossdressed, they are transbodied; the transbodiment is permanent and, indeed, the natural order; what is unnatural is the oppression exercised by women who are higher on the social scale than men. The story reaches a certain closure in the battle where the put-upon husbands give their neglectful wives a taste of their own medicine, but this closure fails to explain why the characters are transbodied and the social roles reversed. The film title "The Results of Feminism" suggests that the "normal" world of the film was not always this way. This could be read as a reactionary message: if women are given too many rights, this will be the dire result. And yet, for the women in the audience in 1906 this film could also have been read as a call to revolution, if they actually identified with the put-upon men.

It is interesting to consider *La Grève des bonnes* (*The Strike of the Housekeepers*, Pathé 1906, attributed to Lepine) in relation to *Les Résultats du féminisme*. It is difficult to determine which was made first, but it seems probable that *féminisme* owes a debt of inspiration to *Grève des bonnes*. In *bonnes*, a group of striking housekeepers convinces a cook to join them; she marches out to the dining room, whereupon the male head of the bourgeois family at dinner tries to complain about her cooking. She slaps him soundly. The striking housekeepers then go out onto the street, where they convince a group of housekeepers in line at a food market to join them. Next we see a rally of the striking housekeepers, which is broken up by a handful of policemen. Most of the housekeepers run away, but a couple of them tackle a policeman to the ground and beat him quite convincingly.

Now the film becomes a chase film, as the housekeepers run along the street with the policemen chasing them. Suddenly, the

Figure 73. Housekeepers on strike in Zecca's *La Grève des bonnes*

Figure 74. The (crossdressed) housekeepers help themselves
to soldiers in Zecca's *La Grève des bonnes*

housekeepers come upon a troop of soldiers with bayonets, all of them looking bored and desperate for amusement, some of them playing music. The housekeepers find the soldiers attractive, and "help themselves" to the ones that they like, simply picking them up and carrying them around, or embracing them tightly and beginning to dance, the pursuing police forgotten (and now nowhere in evidence.) What these women really needed, the film seems to say, was some male companionship, and once they have found that they will end their strike. The fact that all of the housekeepers are played by men in drag is pointed out in ironic ways. In crowd scenes, the housekeepers who are most obviously men are put in the foreground, and when the housekeepers beat policemen they hit them with straight, accurate punches. The director makes no effort to have these male actors behave like women, who generally do not have the opportunity to learn how to throw straight punches. In the final scene, no effort is made to conceal the housekeepers' male strength: they pick up the soldiers bodily as if they were children and cradle them lovingly on their hips. In other words, at no time in these films is crossdressing associated with the phenomenon that Claire Johnston, Joan Rivière and Mary Ann Doane have identified as "masquerade," a practice of adopting stereotypically feminine behaviours in order to accomplish a goal related to a higher degree of agency, such as climbing a career ladder.

Instead, crossdressing in these films is used to question, undermine, and subvert the socially delimited concept of gender, specifically, Woman. This is achieved through role-reversal: the highest degree of agency is for women to adopt the social roles of men.

It seems safe to say that Vitagraph's 1914 feature film, *A Florida Enchantment*, was influenced by the Solax approach to crossdressing, transbodiment, and role reversal.[37] Solax and Vitagraph were quite close to each other in Fort Lee and the various companies often hired from the same pool of actors. In *Enchantment*, a young woman and her black maid (played by a white actress in black-face), turn into men, while the woman's fiancé turns into a woman.

The change to the opposite sex is depicted almost entirely through performance. Edith Storey, who plays the young woman, gradually becomes more manly through changes in her behaviour: she likes to spit, she likes to smoke, she likes to travel, she chases after her own female cousin. She conceals the fact that she is now a man by wearing a dress through most of the film. The only physical change comes when she awakes with a slight mustache one morning, but she quickly shaves it off.

The changes in her fiancé (played by Sidney Drew) are shown in similar ways: as a woman (though still wearing male clothes), he becomes easily faint and fearful and likes to fawn on men s/he finds attractive. What is male and what is female, the film indicates, is hardly even tied to clothes; gender is almost reduced to an affectation depicted through behavior and attitude. In A Florida Enchantment, the gender switching is brought on by "African seeds," and the story is resolved when the female hero wakes up and realizes it has all been a dream; to her relief, her bumbling fiancé finally arrives to keep his date with her.

If we were to judge Guy by her crossdressing films alone, it would be easy to say that she was a feminist in the modern sense of the term, as she avowed later in her life. What stands out in her films of crossdressing, as with almost all of her films, is the preoccupation with female agency, the connection between agency and gender construction, and the obstacles facing the development of female agency in a patriarchal society. She was quite conscious of the fact that she herself had achieved an unprecedented degree of self-realization through her career of film producer and director; almost all of her films are addressed directly to women with the message "you too can do more—here's how". The "how" usually involved creative thinking, daring action, and a sense of humor: all three qualities required by the tomboyish persona and by crossdressers.

It is clear in public statements Guy made as a filmmaker that she believed every woman had a right to a career and that women were ideally suited to filmmaking. The following statement is among her most well-known:

> It has long been a source of wonder to me that many women have not seized upon the wonderful opportunities offered to them by the motion-picture art to make their way to fame and fortune as producers of photodramas. Of all the arts there is probably none in which they can make such a splendid use of talents so much more natural to a woman than to a man and so necessary to its perfection....[38]

It seems quite clear from all of Alice Guy's films, and especially her comedies of crossdressing, that Guy was a feminist. However, her feminist filmmaking did not take the form of a cinematic language that was radically different from that of the other filmmakers that surrounded the Solax studio at Fort Lee. Rather, her feminist aesthetic takes the form of multiple levels of address, all aimed primarily at female spectators. She accomplished this by telling her stories most often from the perspective of female characters; but even when this was not the case, a feminine narration (even if is not always feminist) is always in evidence. The address of these two levels is often reinforced or contradicted for humorous effect by the extra-diegetic narration, the details that call the spectator's attention from outside the story, such as indirect references to suffrage or communist revolution.

Finally, there is the complex figure of Alice Guy herself, the implied author who maintained a front of feminity and diffidence towards the press, either as a result of her French convent training, as a device for preserving her marriage, her business, or all three. At the same time she encouraged other women by example, public exhortation, and through her films, to follow her example, assert themselves in choice of marriage partner, in their relationships, and last but not least, in their choice of career. In one of her last films, *When You and I Were Young*, (5 reels, U.S. Amusement Corporation, July 1917), a young man and a young woman marry and both pursue their chosen artistic careers, though at first this gets them disowned by their respective families. The families come around eventually however; Guy's message here, as always, is to be true to oneself and everything else will work out. By that standard, she will always be young.

CONCLUSION

GUY'S LAST FILM was released in 1920. By 1922, the bankruptcy proceedings for the Solax plant and her divorce were concluded. The
court had awarded her a minimal alimony. At this point, Guy made
the decision to take her children and return to France.

She went to live in Nice with her sister. She approached the
Victorine Studios looking for work (Gaumont had sold or rented
the studios to an independent company, but later bought them back).
The French film industry was at a standstill in the aftermath of the
war, and the studio asked her to do an in-depth assessment of the
plant and its rentability. In her study, she concluded that a large
injection of cash would be necessary to really start up again. The
studio offered a joint development deal if she was willing to invest
a large amount of money,—money she did not have. This marked the
end of her film career.

She found other kinds of work, such as writing novelizations of
films and original stories for publication in women's magazines. She
gave lectures on filmmaking to students in schools in both France
and Switzerland. In her letters, Guy said over and over again that she
was sure she could not break back into the industry in France due
to sexism. She focused on getting her children established in their own
careers and surviving the vicissitudes of the depression of the 1930s
and World War II.

In 1936, she wrote to Gaumont and asked for a job, telling him
that her chronophone experience would stand her in good stead in
the new sound era. At this point, she was 63. Gaumont responded
by hiring her son Reginald and putting him to work in the developing
labs. Reginald lasted just a few months before migrating to the
United States to serve the war effort there.

She lived with her children, primarily Simone, until she died in
1968. Simone worked for the U.S. Diplomatic Corps and when
she retired in 1964 she took her mother with her back to New
Jersey, where Guy is buried. There was no obituary and there was
no indication on her tombstone that she was the first woman
filmmaker and the only woman filmmaker for the first decade of
the industry's history.

Figure 75. The Solax Studio in 1914, with additions being built

Figure 76. What was left of the Solax Studio in 1963

Why was Guy so completely forgotten? The reasons are complex and varied. Probably the main reason is that Léon Gaumont never thought film production was particularly important. He was an inventor and cultivated a variety of inventors within his firm. It was they who nominated him for the Legion of Honor award in 1924, and the invitation list read like a Who's Who of the Belle Époque's technical innovators. But Guy's name was not on the list.

Documentation attributing the direction of the Gaumont films made before 1905 is scarce. Gaumont did ask Guy to write up a list of films she directed and this list was deposited in the Gaumont archives without any contention from Léon Gaumont, a very detail-conscious man (remember, he had been careful not to donate money to a society that wanted to honor his colleague Demenÿ over his friends the Lumières as the inventors of the first motion picture camera). Léon Gaumont never did specifically recognize her, for example in his acceptance speeches when he received the Légion d'Honneur and again a few years later when he became an officer of the Légion d'Honneur, but neither did he acknowledge any other of the film producers in his employ, even Feuillade who at the time of the latter speech was still working for him. However, he did acknowledge Decaux and other inventors and technicians, most of whom were present when he gave the speeches (Feuillade and Guy were not). This oversight on his part seems to be more a reflection of his priorities (technical innovation over film production).

As a result, she was barely mentioned in any of the Gaumont company's official documents until Léon's son Louis began to write a history of the firm and asked Guy for information in the late forties and early fifties. It was inevitable, given the lack of documentation, that the film histories written from the 1920s until Guy's autiobiography appeared in the mid-1970s would not credit her for her accomplishments.

Another key reason for her "effacement" is that early films carried no credits, and until 1912, there was no copyright process for film scripts. At the time of her death it appeared that almost none of her films were still in existence.

Although we all recognize the need to alter and enlarge the scope of our investigations in cinematic meaning, the academy as a whole has yet to suggest a new coherent mode of study that would replace the auteur approach. A variety of possibilities are in the process of emerging, not all of them suitable to early cinema.

At the same time, the demands of the feminist project remain. We need to find and document the work of women artists. Much work like this has been done, but much remains to be done. Much work has been done on the analysis of female representation within patriarchal discourse, including cinema, but not enough on the work of more marginalized artists, such as women, who may or may not work in opposition to that tradition. The explosion of new forms for cinematic spectatorship, such as the multiplicity of modes for television viewing and new interactive technologies, brings new opportunities for telling stories that have not been told in ways that they have not been told before. But we cannot build on the work women before us have done unless we know their work. And so, while on the one hand in this work I did not treat Guy as an auteur, at the same time I felt a responsibility to the feminist project of bringing the work of the first woman filmmaker to light, making it accessible to an educated lay person, and to conduct an analysis of feminine voice as it can be discerned from the body of work we can legitimately think of as "hers."

I have tried to meet the requirements of modern scholarship by situating Guy's work in the context of the various discourses—both political and filmic—in which she took part. Much of my work has consisted of piecing together a filmography of the extant films on which she worked, whether her role was that of writer, director, or supervising producer. Even though Roberta Blaché confirmed some of the evidence of the films, namely Guy's feminism and her cultural Catholicism, my aim has not been to ascribe intent to Guy but to show, using her work as a sample, that the discourses in early cinema were infinitely richer and more varied, than previously supposed. Once we learn their language, these films have much to say to us.

Although it is not always possible to definitively attribute specific films to Guy, what I have tried to do in this book is show that she was an integral part of the birth of cinema in France as well as a leading force in the development of cinematic narrative. She developed the Gaumont house-style of shooting on locations, which foreshadowed the free-wheeling camera styles of the 1960s. She pioneered a hierarchical-but-still-cooperative system of studio management years before Thomas Ince did the same in the U.S. She trained Bossetti, Arnaud, Jasset and Feuillade who would later assume important places in the books of French cinema history, as well as set decorators

Figure 77. Alice with her Grecian hairdo

Menessier and Carré. And she trained her own husband, who went on to direct Buster Keaton in *The Saphead*, which made Keaton into a star. She made over 100 synchronized sound films when synchronized sound was still something of a dream.

But perhaps the most important quality of Guy's work is the way she spoke to women, her direct feminine address. She stated publicly that women were supremely suited for filmmaking, and in the films where she had creative control, and even in many of those where she did not, the women characters chose their own destinies. It is unfortunate that of the hundreds of films Guy directed and produced, only 111 are currently available for study, some of which still need to be preserved. But even these 111 films show us clearly that Guy made splendid use of all of her talents, talents so necessary to the perfection of the "art of the photodrama." In the surviving films, both halves of her career—the American and the French—are almost equally represented, and for this we can only be grateful.

Notes

INTRODUCTION

1. In the course of her life Guy had three names: Alice Guy (during the Gaumont period of her career) until she was married at the age of 34; Madame Blaché until she was divorced at the age of 50; and Alice Guy Blaché until she died at the age of 95. In France she is known as Alice Guy. In the U.S., the Library of Congress has filed her memoirs under Guy. For those reasons and for the sake of simplicity, I will call her Alice Guy, and I will refer to her husband, Herbert Blaché, as Blaché.

   An earlier, abridged version of this introduction was given as a paper entitled "Voice and Voyeurism in Early Cinema," at the *Before the Auteur: Text, Filmmaking, Authorship From Early Cinema to the Thirties*, International Conference on Film Studies, Udine, Italy, March 23, 1996.

2. Slide, Anthony, *Lois Weber: The Director Who Lost Her Way in History*, Westport, Ct.: Greenwood Press, 1996.

3. There is some controversy about whether Henri Gallet also directed some of the early Gaumont films. For more on this, see Chapters One and Three.

4. Brownlow, Kevin *The Parade's Gone By. . . .* Berkeley: University of California Press, 1968. Fell, John L. ed., *Film Before Griffith*, Berkeley, Los Angeles, London: University of California Press, 1983. Mast, Gerald, *A Short History of the Movies*, Indianapolis: Bobbs-Merrill Educational Publishing, 1971. Roud, Richard ed. *Cinema, A Critical Dictionary: The Major Filmmakers*, Vols. I & II, 1980.

5. Mitry, Jean *Filmographie universelle* t. II Paris: IDHEC 1964, *Histoire du cinéma* t. 1: *1895–1914* t. 2: *1915–1925* Paris: Editions Universitaires, 1969. Sadoul, Georges, *Histoire générale du cinéma Tome I: L'Invention du cinéma (1893–1897)*, Paris: Denoël 1946 re-edited, with corrections, in 1947, *Histoire du cinema mondial des origines à nos jours*, Flammarion, 1949.

6. Langlois, Henri "French Cinema: Origins" in Richard Roud, *Cinema: A Critical Dictionary of the Major Film-makers*, Vol. I, Aldrich to King, New York: Viking Press, 1980, pp. 394–401.

7. Ford, Charles "The First Female Film Producer," *Films in Review* 15, 3 (March 1964): 141. Lacassin, Francis, "Out of Oblivion: Alice Guy-Blaché," *Sight and Sound*, 40, 3 (Summer, 1971): 151–54. Peary, Gerald, "Czarina of the Silent Screen: Solax's Alice Blaché," *Velvet Light Trap* 6 (Fall, 1972): 2–7. Smith, F.L., "Alice Guy-Blaché," *Films in Review* 15, 4 (April, 1964): 254.

8. Guy, Alice, *Autobiographie d'une pionnière du cinéma (1873–1968)*, Collection Femme, Paris: Denoël/Gonthier, 1976.

9. Slide, Anthony, ed., *The Memoirs of Alice Guy Blaché*, transl. Roberta & Simone Blaché, Filmmakers, No. 12, Metuchen, N.J.: The Scarecrow Press, Inc. 1986, Revised and re-released, 1996.

10. Mitry, Jean: "À propos d'Alice Guy' in *Écran*, no. 49, 15 juillet, 1976 p. 5. Deslandes, Jacques: "Sur Alice Guy-Blaché: polémique" in *Écran* no. 50, 5 septembre 1976, p. 4. Wanamaker, Marc: "Alice Guy-Blaché in *Cinema*, no. 35, Beverly Hills, 1976, pp. 10–13. Koehler M.:" Die Filmpionerin Alice Guy in *Medien und Erziehung* no. 2, Munich, 1983. Bachy, Victor: "Un oublié de l'Histoire: Alice Guy, première femme cinéaste du monde" in *J.M. Peters, Liber Americorum*, Leuven, CeCoWe, 1984 pp. 47-58. Heck-Rabi, Louise: "Guy Alice" in *The MacMillan Dictionary*, vol. II, Directors (MacMillan Publications, 1984, pp. 239–241.

11. Slide, Anthony *Early Women Directors, Their Role in the Development of the Silent Cinema*, South Brunswick and New York, A.S. Barnes and Company, London Thomas Yoseloff Ltd. 1977, pp. 15–33.
    Reprint: New York: Da Capo Press, 1984.
    Re-issued (and extensively rewritten) as *The Silent Feminists: America's First Women Directors*, Lanham, Md.: Scarecrow Press, 1996.

12. MacCann, Richard Dyer, *The First Filmmakers*, American Movies: The First Thirty Years Metuchen, N.J. & London: The ScareCrow Press Iowa city, Iowa: Image and Idea, Inc. 1989.

13. Marchessault, Jovette, "Mon héroïne," *Les Lundis de l'histoire des femmes an 1*, Conférences du théâtre expérimental des femmes, Montréal: Les Éditions Remue-Ménage, Quebec, 1981, pp. 150–187.

14. Breton, Emile, *Femmes d'images* Paris: Éditions Messidor, Octobre 1984 pp. 10–17.

15. Guibbert, Pierre, ed., *Les Premiers ans du cinéma français*, Perpignan, Institut Jean Vigo, collection des Cahiers de la Cinémathèque, décembre 1985, 319 p. Contains: Bachy, Victor "Les Raisons d'un effacement," pp. 27-30, "Entretiens avec Alice Guy" pp. 31–42. Spehr, Paul C. "Influences françaises sur la production américaine d'avant 1914," pp. 105–115.

16. Acker, Ally *Reel Women: Pioneers of the Cinema* New York: Continuum, 1991. Foster, Gwendolyn Audrey *Women Film Directors: An International Bio-Critical Dictionary* Wesport, CT: Greenwood Press 1995. Foster and Wheeler Winston Dixon, *The Women Who Made the Movies*. New York: Women Make Movies, Inc. 1991. Video. Heck-Rabi, Louise *Women Filmmakers: A Critical Reception* Metuchen, N.J. & London: The Scarecrow Press, Inc. 1984. Quart, Barbara Koenig *Women Directors: The Emergence of a New Cinema* New York, Wesport CT., London: Praeger 1988. Smith, Sharon *Women Who Make Movies* Cinema Studies Series, Lewis Jacobs, Consulting Ed. New York: Hopkinson & Blake 1975.

17. Viscenzi, Lisa, *Alice Guy Blaché's Solax Company*, unpublished Master's Thesis, Film Division Library, Columbia University, c. 1984.

18. Abel, Richard, *The Ciné Goes to Town: French Cinema 1896–1914*, Berkeley: University of California Press, 1994. As ed., *Silent Film*, Depth of Field, New Brunswick, NJ: Rutgers University Press, 1996. Bowser, Eileen, *The Transformation Of Cinema, 1907-1915*, History of the American Cinema Series, Vol. 2, New York: Charles Scribner's Sons, 1990. Burch, Noël, *Life to Those*

Shadows, Ben Brewster, transl. Berkeley: University of California Press, 1990. Fernett, Gene, *American Film Studios: An Historical Encyclopedia*, Jefferson, NC: McFarland & Co., Inc. 1988. Hayward, Susan, *French National Cinema*, National Cinemas Series, New York: Routledge, 1993. Herbert, Stephen and Luke McKernan, *Who's Who of Victorian Cinema*, London: BFI Publishing, 1996. Koszarski, Richard, *An Evening's Entertainment: The Age of the Silent Feature Picture, 1915–1928*, History of the American Cinema Series, Vol. 3, New York: Charles Scribner's Sons, 1990. *Hollywood Directors 1914–1940*, London: Oxford University Press, 1976. Sklar, Robert, *Films: An International History of the Medium*, New York: Harry N. Abrams, 1993. Slide, Anthony, *The American Film Industry: A Historical Dictionary*, New York: Limelight Editions, 1990. Vincendeau, Ginette, ed., *Encyclopedia of European Cinema*, New York: Facts on File Inc., 1995. Williams, Alan, *Republic of Images: A History of French Filmmaking*, Cambridge: Harvard University Press, 1992.

19. Bachy, Victor, *Alice Guy Blaché (1873–1968) La Première femme cinéaste du monde*, Collec. "Les Cahiers de la Cinémathèque," Perpignan, France: Inst. Jean Vigo, 1993.

20. See complete list of films with distribution information in appendix.

21. *The Silent Feminists*, produced by Anthony Slide (documentary on early women filmmakers). Distributed on video by Direct Cinema, P.O. Box 10003, Santa Monica, CA. 90410–9003.

22. *Qui est Alice Guy?*, documentary produced by Nicole-Lise Bernheim, 1975.

23. See principally, Francis Lacassin's comments in *The Memoirs of Alice Guy Blaché*, Anthony Slide, ed., translated by Roberta and Simone Blaché, Filmmakers no. 12, Lanham, Md. and London: The Scarecrow Press, 1996 (1986), p. 28 and 136.

24. *Elle voulait faire du cinéma*, Tele-film. Co-production: Cinémas (Mag Bodard), Antenne 2, R.T.B.F., R.A.I. II, S.F.P., Ministère de la Culture, 1985. Scénario et réalisation: Caroline Huppert.

25. See for example Acker, Ally *Reel Women: Pioneers of the Cinema 1896 to the Present*, New York: Continuum, 1996, p. xix.

26. For more on the Brighton Conference of 1978, see *Cinema 1900–1906: An Analytical Study by the National Film Archive (London) and the International Federation of Film Archives*, compiled by Roger Holman, Brussels: FIAF 1982 and *Cinema 1900–1906: An Analytical Study by the National Film Archive (London) and the International Federation of Film Archives*, Vol. 2, "Analytical Filmography," under the supervision of André Gaudreault, Brussels: FIAF 1982.

27. Elsaesser, Thomas, ed., *Early Cinema: Space, Frame, Narrative*, London: BFI Publishing, 1990.

28. "Enigmas, Understanding, and Further Questions: Early Cinema Research in Its Second Decade Since Brighton" by Tom Gunning in *Persistance of Vision*, The Journal of the Film Faculty of the City University of New York, No. 9, 1992, pp. 4–10.

29. Jane Gaines at Duke University maintains a database on researchers working

on women filmmakers and has started an organization, the *Women Film Pioneers*, to support research and film preservation in this area.

30. Blaché, *Memoirs*, pp. 1–2.
31. From a personal interview with Gabriel Allignet in Paris in 1995.
32. Blaché, *Memoirs*, p. 3.
33. *Ibid.*, p. 3.
34. *Ibid.*, p. 5.
35. *Ibid.*, pp. 9–10.
36. *Ibid.*, p. 11.
37. Though Anthonly Slide believes it might have been March of 1894. Blaché, *Memoirs*, p. 15.
38. Blaché, *Memoirs*, p. 16.
39. *Ibid.*, p. 17.
40. Mannoni, Laurent, "Le Quatrième Centenaire du Cinéma," in *Théorème: Cinéma des premiers temps, nouvelles contributions françaises*, No. 4, Paris: Presses de la Sorbonne Nouvelle, 1996, pp. 32–33. This information is repeated with some minor updating in a biography by Mannoni, Marc de Ferrière le Vayer and Paul Demenÿ, *Georges Demenÿ: Pionnier du cinéma*, Douai: Pagine Éditions, 1997, pp. 83–84.

1. THE BIRTH OF FILM NARRATIVE

1. Acker, Ally, *Reel Women: Pioneers of the Cinema 1896 to the Present*, New York: Continuum, 1991, p. xxiv.
2. Katz, Ephraim, *The Film Encyclopedia*, Third Edition, Revised by Fred Klein and Ronald Dean Nolen, New Yok: Harper Perennial, 1998, p. 575.
3. A section of this chapter was previously published as a paper, "The Quest for Motion: Moving Pictures and Flight," in *Visual Delights: Essays on the Popular and Projected Image in the Nineteenth Century*, edited by Simon Popple and Vanessa Toulmin, Trowbridge, U.K: Flicks Books, 2000, pp. 93–104.
4. Nadar, *Revendication de la propriété exclusive du pseudonyme Nadar (Felix Tournachon-Nadar contre A. Tournachon jeune et Compagnie)*. 5 parts. Includes court documents. Paris, 1857, part 2, pp. 0–p. Quoted in "A Portrait of Nadar" by Maria Morris Hambourg, *Nadar*, New York: The Metropolitan Museum of Art, distributed by Harry N. Abrams, Inc. 1990, p. 25.
5. Dillaye, Frédéric, *La Théorie, la pratique et l'art en photographie*, New York: Arno Press, 1979, reprint of the 1891 ed. Published by À la librairie illustrée, Paris, p. 189, 193.
6. Hambourg, *Nadar*, p. 118. The two books are *Mémoires du Géant* (1864) and *Le Droit au Vol.* (1865).
7. *Ibid.*, 29–30.
8. Mannoni, Laurent, *Le grand art de la lumière et de l'ombre*, Paris: Université Nathan, series archéologie du cinéma, 1994, p. 282. This book was translated by Richard Crangle into *The Great Art of Light and Shadow: Archeology of*

the Cinema, with an introduction by Tom Gunning and a Preface by David Robinson, Exeter Studies in Film History, Exeter: University of Exeter Press, 2000, pp. 299–303.

9. The best source of information on Marey in English is Marta Braun's *Picturing Time: The Work of Étienne-Jules Marey (1830–1904)* Chicago and London: University of Chicago Press 1994. Nothing comparable exists on Demenÿ or Reynaud.

10. Marey, Étienne-Jules *Du mouvement dans les fonctions de la vie*, Paris, 1868, quoted in Laurent Mannoni, *Le Grand Art de la lumière et de l'ombre— archéologie du cinéma*, p. 300, my translation. Crangle translates this as "I have given a greater importance to movement, and I believe with Claude Bernard that movement is the most important action, in that all bodily functions derive their pattern from its accomplishment," on page 322 of the English version.

11. Braun, Marta, *Picturing Time: the Work of Étienne-Jules Marey (1830–1904)*, (Chicago: University of Chicago Press, 1992, p. xvii).

12. From *Webster's Third New International Dictionary*, quoted in John D. Anderson Jr., *A History of Aerodynamics*, Cambridge: Cambridge University Press, Cambridge Aerospace Series 8, Michael J. Rycroft and Robert F. Stengel, gen. Eds., 1998, p. 3.

13. *Ibid.*, p. 6.

14. Braun, p. 37.

15. Mannoni, p. 307 (French), pp. 329–331, (English).

16. Celluloid was first discovered by the Hyatt brothers in New Jersey in 1869, distributed in France by the French Celluloid company from 1876 on and by Planchon's factory, which supplied the Lumières and Gaumont, from 1894 on.

17. The footage of Raynaly still exists and can be seen on the video *Georges Demenÿ et les origines "sportives" du cinéma* from Le Groupe de recherche et d'essais cinématographiques (GREC) Réalisation: André Drevon Production: GREC 25 min/1995.

18. The Musée Grévin was a focus point for proto-cinematic and early cinematic exhibition. This aspect of its history has not been well examined. For example, Méliès performed his magic act there before 1888. (Georges Méliès, in a letter to Paul Gilson dated August 9, 1929. Reprinted in Georges Sadoul's *Lumière et Méliès*, Paris: Lherminier 1985, p. 227).

19. Loiperdinger, Martin and Roland Cosandey, "L'Introduction du cinématographe en Allemagne: de la case Demenÿ à la Case Lumière: Stollwerck, Lavanchy-Clarke et al., 1892–1896" in *Archives* No. 51, November 1992, published by Institut Jean Vigo, Cinémathèque de Toulouse.

20. Laurent Mannoni, Marc de Ferrière le Vayer and Paul Demenÿ, *Georges Demenÿ: Pionnier du cinéma*, Douai: Pagine Éditions, 1997, p. 82.

21. Blaché, *Memoirs*, p. 25.

22. *Ibid.*, p. xiv.

23. For more background on this, see the letter from Louis Lumière to the *Ciné-Tribune* dated June 30, 1920, which quotes, extensively from correspondence

between Demenÿ and the Lumières in 1894. Published in Lumière, Auguste and Louis, *Correspondances 1890–1953*, Librairie du premier siècle du cinéma Series, Paris: Cahiers du cinéma, 1994, pp. 221–228.

24. Blaché, *Memoirs*, pp. 27-8.

25. See also the interview with Alice Guy in *The New Jersey Star*, August 8, 1914.

26. Venhard, Gilles, "De la naissance à la puissance: les vertes années de la marguerite, 1896–1924," in *Gaumont: 90 ans du cinéma*, edited by Philippe de Hugues et Dominique Muller. Ramsay: La Cinémathèque Française p. 18.

27. Rittaud-Hutinet, Jacques *Les Frères Lumière: L'Invention du cinéma*, Flammarion, 1995, p. 372.

28. Blaché, *Memoirs*, p. 25.

29. Chardère, Bernard, *Lumières sur Lumière*, Lyon: Institut Lumière Presses Universitaires de Lyon 1987. Chardère reprints a letter from Demenÿ to L. Lumière dated March 27, 1895, in which Demenÿ apologized for not having been able to attend the screening.

30. Dureau, Georges, obituary for Jules Carpentier in *Ciné-Journal*, 9 July 1921, reprinted in *Lumières sur Lumière*, by Bernard Chardère, Institut Lumière/Presses Universitaires de Lyon, 1987, p. 270.

31. *Ibid.*

32. Blaché, *Memoirs*, pp. 26–27.

33. *Ibid.*, pp. 59–60.

34. Laurent Mannoni, Marc de Ferrière le Vayer and Paul Demenÿ, *Georges Demenÿ: Pionnier du cinéma*, Douai: Pagine Editions, 1997, p. 99.

35. Sadoul, Georges, *Lumière-Méliès*, Paris: Lherminier, 1985, p. 251.

36. Lacassin, Francis, *Pour une contre-histoire du cinéma*, Lyon: Institut Lumière Series: Premier Siècle du cinéma, Actes Sud, Hubert Nyssen, éd., pp. 30–31.

37. Bachy, Victor, *Alice Guy-Blaché (1873–1968): La Première femme cinéaste du monde*, Perpignan: Institut Jean Vigo, 1994, pp. 34–35.

38. The catalogue is *Comptoir Général de la Cinématographie chrono de poche pour prise et projection de vues de 15mm*. Description et instruction L. Gaumont et Cie N. 508 (after 1900). This film also appears to be an imitation of the Lumière film *Joueurs de cartes arrosés* no. 115.

39. Laurent Mannoni, Marc de Ferrière le vayer and Paul Demenÿ, *Georges Demenÿ: Pionnier du cinéma*, Douai: Pagine Editions, 1997, p. 105.

40. Mannoni, Laurent, "Une féerie de 1896: *La Biche au bois*," *Cinémathèque*, No. 10, automne 1996, p. 117.

41. "Des milliers de personnes, à Paris, sur la route et à Meulan, ont vu circuler les voitures automobiles (autant de bouches qui vont rapporter la bonne impression produite). Des centaines les on photographiées au repos et en marche; parmi elles, citons surtout M. Clément Maurice, l'habile photographe du boulevard des Italiens, et M. Gaumont, le directeur du Comptoir photographique de la rue St-Roch, qui ont reproduit le départ du boulevard Maillot, celui-ci avec l'appareil de Ménie (sic), celui-là avec le Cinématographe Lumière. Nous avons donc de bonnes et intéressantes projections animées en perspective." (Thousands of spectators in Paris on the road towards Meulan watched the circulating

automobiles (every spectator voiced his or her pleasure). Hundreds photographed the autos on the move and in repose, among them, Mr. Clément Maurice whose shop is on the boulevard des Italiens, and Mr. Gaumont, the head of the Comptoir Photographique on St-Roch Street, who filmed the departure of the autos, the latter with the Demenÿ apparatus, the former with a Lumière Cinématographe. We look forward to excellent animated projections.)

L.D. "L'Excursion de Meulan" in *La France Automobile: Organe de l'automobilisme et des industries qui s'y rattachent*, No. 17, Samedi 23 mai, 1896 p. 130. I am grateful to Anne Gautier for familiarizing me with this article and for first pointing out the resemblance between *Poursuite sur les toits* and *Les Cambrioleurs*. I am also grateful to Frank Kessler and Sabine Lenk for pointing out the error in my previous translation of this piece.

42. Mannoni, "Une féerie de 1896", *Cinémathèque*, pp. 122–123.

43. *Ibid.*, p. 123.

44. *Ibid.*, p. 119.

45. *Ibid.*, pp. 118–119.

46. Chardère, *Ibid.*, pp. 142–145. Chardère thinks the 1894 date is more likely (1894 would also be more in keeping with Alice Guy's memoirs) and that when Ducom mentions M. Lumière he must mean Lumière père, Antoine, because Louis Lumière left documentation showing that he and his brother only had one meeting in person with Demenÿ, and that much later.

47. Bachy, Blaché, p. 39.

48. "Deux attelages, de chacun quatre pairs de bœufs, trainent une charrue." 202 m. *Collection "Elge", Liste de vues animées*, N. 162, mai 1900.

49. Blaché, *Memoirs*, pp. 17-20.

50. If Guy was correct when she said she made *La Fée aux choux* in 1896, there must be three versions of the film. The version in the Sieurin film collection would then be the second one, made between 1897-1900. For my speculations on the first version, see below. If there was a first version, that version and the 35mm. version were probably almost identical.

51. See articles by Sabine Lenk and Alison McMahan in "À la recherche d'objets filmiques non identifiés: Autour de l'œuvre d'Alice Guy-Blaché" *Archives*, 81: août 1999 (entire double issue).

52. I am grateful to Professor Jan Olsson, Chair of Cinema Studies, Stockholm University, for providing me with this information and for enabling me to study the films themselves.

53. Alice Guy interviewed by *The New Jersey Star*, 1914.

54. *L'Arroseur arrosé*, Gaumont *Vues Animées* no. 90, Gaumont Catalogue no. 90. "Un gamin met son pied sur un tuyau d'arrosage. Arrêt de l'eau. Le jardinier examine sa lance. Le gamin lâche le pied. Sortie brusque de l'eau. Le jardinier poursuit le gamin et l'arrose à son tour." The Gaumont version of this film is lost, but two stills in the Mai 1899 Liste des vues animées and the catalogue photo and description show that it was a very exact copy of the Lumière version.

55. Gaumont catalogue no. 316, Lumière catalogue no. 107.

56. Gaumont catalogue no. 120, Lumière catalogue no. 118. The Lumière film can be seen on the Kino Video Series, *The Movies Begin*, Vol. I.

57. The same is true of Georges Méliès, whose first few films were close copies of Lumière films.

58. My source for attributing these films to Hatot is Georges Sadoul, *Lumière et Méliès*, Paris: Lherminier 1985 pp. 136–142.

59. Lumière catalogue number 677, Gaumont Vues Animées number 175, Gaumont catalogue 175.

60. *Vues Animées* 93.

61. Lumière catalogue number 962, Gaumont catalogue no. 129, dated 1898. The latter two Gaumont films are part of the Alan Roberts collection recently found in New Zealand and preserved by the Cinémathèque Royale de Belgique. Sabine Lenk identified these two films with my assistance.

62. Gaumont catalogue no. 118 dated 1898.

63. Lumière no. 682, Gaumont catalogue no. 708 dated 1904.

64. Lumière no. 952, Gaumont catalogue no. 116 dated 1898.

65. Williams, Alan, *The Republic of Images: A History of French Filmmaking*, Cambridge: Harvard University Press, 1992, p. 57.

66. It was Anne Gautier who told me that Jambon did the set for *Poursuite sur les toits*, which I have not yet been able to confirm. Guy describes Jambon in her memoirs as "a decorator celebrated for his scenes of Paris" and says that "we became a pair of friends." Slide, *Memoirs* p. 39.

67. Georges Méliès also made a similar film entitled *Sur les Toits*, Star film 1897. Dir. by Georges Méliès, 35mm, 20m. This film can be seen at the Archives du Film at Bois d'Arcy. I am grateful to Sabine Lenk for bringing this film to my attention.

68. Lumière catalogue no. 102.

69. Lumière catalogue no. 103.

70. Lumière catalogue no. 675.

71. Lumière catalogue no. 874.

72. Lumière catalogue no. 875.

73. Gaumont catalogue no. 841.

74. Gaumont catalogue no. 1545.

75. Felicity Sparrow first identified most of the Gaumont films directed by Alice Guy at the NFTVA. This is one of the few identifications that had to be corrected.

76. Gaumont catalogue no. 1550.

77. Lumière catalogue no. 948.

78. This film still exists but has suffered so much from the ravages of decomposition that it is probably not salvageable.

79. Lumière catalogue no. 1350.

80. Blaché, *Memoirs*, p. 46.

81. Letter to Louis Lumière, dated 8 March 1918 in the BIFI collection at the Cinémathèque Française.

82. See letters between Léon Gaumont and Louis Lumière in May and June of 1934, BIFI.

83. See correspondance between Léon Gaumont and Louis Lumière in August of 1930 and again in 1934, Lumière/Gaumont correspondance file, BIFI.

84. Musser, Charles, *Before the Nickelodeon: Edwin S. Porter and the Edison Manufacturing Company* Berkeley: University of California Press, 1991, p. 68.

85. See for example, *Une partie de cartes* (Star Film 1896) apparently Méliès' first film, shot in May 1896 in the garden of his house in Montreuil and featuring Méliès himself. (Le Giornate del Cinema Muto 2000, 19th Pordenone Silent Film Festival Catalogue, XVIII edizione Sacile 14–21 ottobre 2000, pp. 107-108).

86. Lumière catalogue nos. 51 and 62 respectively.

87. Musser, *Before the Nickelodeon* pp. 42–43.

88. Gunning, Tom, "The Cinema of Attractions: Early Film, Its Spectator and the Avant-Garde," in *Early Cinema: Space, Frame, Narrative*, Thomas Elsaesser, ed., with Adam Barker, London: BFI Publishing, 1990, pp. 56–61. Gunning refers to Eisenstein's 'How I Became a Film Director', in *Notes of a Film Director*, Moscow: Foreign Language Publishing House, n.d., p. 16.

89. *Ibid.*, p. 57.

90. *Ibid.*, pp. 59–60, his emphasis.

91. See Thomas Elsaesser's assessment of Gaudreault's article in his Introduction to *Early Cinema: Space, Frame, Narrative*, p. 18.

92. Gaudreault, André, "Film, Narrative, Narration: The Cinema of the Lumière Brothers" in *Early Cinema: Space, Frame, Narrative*, p. 72. In a footnote, Gaudreault notes that his thinking on this subject has changed. I have not had access to the more recent text, but Musser summarizes it as follows: "[Gaudreault] in fact, concludes that we should distinguish between 'narrative fragments'" on one hand and complete, if short, narratives (such as *L'Arroseur arrosé*) on the other (André Gaudreault, *Du littéraire au filmique: système du récit* [Librarie des Méridiens, 1988]). Cited in Musser, Charles, "Rethinking Early cinema: Cinema of Attractions and Narrativity," *The Yale Journal of Criticism*, volume 7, number 2, c 1994 by Yale University. Oxford: Blackwell Publishers, 1994, footnote number 33, page 230.

93. Gaudreault, André, "Film, Narrative, Narration," p. 73.

94. Musser, Charles, "Rethinking Early Cinema," p. 213.

95. *Ibid.*, p. 205.

96. *Ibid.*, p. 209.

97. *Ibid.*, pp. 210–1.

98. *Ibid.*, pp. 221–2.

99. Ezra, Elizabeth, *Georges Méliès*, French Film Directors Series, Manchester and New York: Manchester University Press, 2000, especially Chapter One. For other descriptions of alternatives to the attractions aesthetic in early fiction films see, Brewster, Ben and Lea Jacobs, *Theatre to Cinema*, Oxford: Oxford University Press, 1997.

100. Gunning, Tom, "'Now You See It, Now You Don't': The Temporality of the Cinema of Attractions," in *Silent Film*, edited by Richard Abel, New Brunswick: Rutgers University Press, 1996, p. 80 and 81.

101. Branigan, Edward, *Narrative Comprehension and Film*, London and New York: Routledge, 1992, p. 147.

102. Branigan, Edward, *Narrative Comprehension and Film*, footnote 15 on page 261.

103. "...off-screen space is divided into six 'segments': the immediate confines of the first four of these areas are determined by the four borders of the frame, and correspond to the four faces of an imaginary truncated pyramid projected into the surrounding space... A fifth segment... [is] 'behind the camera'... the characters in the film generally reach this space by passing just to the right or left of the camera. There is a sixth segment, finally, encompassing the space existing behind the set or some object in it. A character reaches it by going out a door, going around a street corner, disappearing behind a pillar or behind another person... or performing some similar act. The outer limit of this sixth space is just beyond the horizon." Noël Burch, *Theory of Film Practice*, Princeton: Princeton University Press, 1969, p. 17.

104. An apotheosis is a final, non-diegetic shot where all the fairies and other characters of the films would arrange themselves in an elaborate tableaux formation.

105. Elizabeth Ezra calls shots like these "subjective inserts", see Ezra, 2000, p. 38.

106. Charles Musser in his liner notes for the video series *The Movies Begin*.

107. Edison, 1903, directed by Edwin Porter.

108. Burch, Noël *Life to Those Shadows* Berkeley: University of California Press 1990 p. 193.

109. Arvidson, Linda *When the Movies were Young*, p. 66.

110. Musser, *Before the Nickelodeon*, p. 319. *The Whole Dam Family and the Dam Dog* can be seen on the Kino Video Series, *The Movies Begin*, Volume I.

111. *The Moving Picture World* Vol. VII No. 3 July 16, 1910 p. 142.

112. See also the plot summary in *The Moving Picture World* Vol. VII No. 1 July 2, 1910 p. 43.

113. The plot and images were based on a well known cartoon and the woman was understood to be a prostitute.

2. SOUND REWRITES SILENTS: ALICE GUY AND THE GAUMONT CHRONOPHONE

1. Richard Koszarski alludes to Herbert promoting himself over his wife in a caption under a reproduction of an ad that pictured both of them in *Hollywood Directors 1914–1940*, London, Oxford, New York: Oxford University Press, 1976, p. 9. Lisa Vincenzi also alludes to differences between the Blachés towards the end of the Solax company's existence, in her unpublished Master's Thesis, *Alice Guy Blaché's Solax Company*, Columbia University, 1984, pp. 6–9 and 83–84. Both of these scholars point to certain evidence and make hypotheses; but others took the hypotheses as evidence, especially some documentary filmmakers.

2. Gerry Gibson, who is now in the Library's Preservation Office, made the arrange-

ments. Sam Brylawski, head of the Recorded Sound Section of the MBRS has the documentation.

3. Altman, Rick, *Sound Theory/Sound Practice*, New York and London: Routledge, 1992, p. 113.

4. Altman, Rick, "The Silence of the Silents", *Musical Quarterly*, 80, no. 4 (1997), pp. 648–718.

5. Thompson, Kristin, and David Bordwell, *Film History: An Introduction*, New York: McGraw Hill, 1994, from the table of contents.

6. Martin Koerber, "Oskar Messter—Stationen einer Karriere", in: Martin Loiperdinger (ed.), *Oskar Messter—Filmpionnier der Kaiserzeit* (Ausstellungskatalog), *KINtop Schriften* 2, Stroemfeld Verlag, Basel, Franfurt am Main 1994, S. 35–36; Jeanpaul Goergen, "Der Kinematograph Unter den Lindern 21. Das Erste Berliner 'Kino' 1896/97", *KINtop 6* (1997), S. 155–158.

7. See "Wie singende Bilder (Tonbilder) entstehen", *Der Kinematograph*, Nr. 65, 25.3.1908.

8. The *Dickson Experimental Sound Film* was shown to film scholars and archivists at the 19th Pordenone Silent Film Festival in Sacile, Italy, October, 2000. See also, Pat Loughney, "Domitor Witnesses the 'Dickson Experimental Sound Film', Special DOMITOR issue of *Film History*, Vol. 11, no. 4, 1999, pp. 400–403.

9. Quote of Edison taken from *History of the Kinetograph, Kinetoscope and Kineto-phonograph* by W.K.L. Dickson and Antonia New York, Albert Dunn, 1895, Reprinted in a Facsimile Edition by the Museum of Modern Art, New York, 2000, p. 3.

10. Harald, Jossé, "*Die Entstehung des Tonfilms. Beiträge zu einer faktenorienterten Mediengeschichtsschreibung*, Verlag Karl Alber, Freiburg, München 1984, S. 82F. und 90F.

11. Wedel, Michael, "Schizophrene Technik, Sinnliches Glück: Die Filmoperette und der synchrone Musikfilm 1914–1929", in *MusikspektakelFilm, Musiktheater und Tanzkultur im deutschen Film 1922–1937*, redaktion: Katja Uhlenbrok, Munich: edition text + kritik, 1998, pp. 85–104.

12. Williams, Alan, "Historical and Theoretical Issues in the Coming of Recorded Sound to the Cinema" in *Sound Theory/Sound Practice*, p. 127.

13. Williams, Alan, "Historical and Theoretical Issues in the Coming of Recorded Sound to the Cinema" in *Sound Theory/Sound Practice*, pp. 126–137.

14. *Ibid.*, p. 128. His emphasis.

15. Williams makes the same case for color: "…most films had some form of color. At first, as in Reynaud's spectacle, color was hand-painted by brush onto individual copies, but soon stencil processes such as Pathècolor and the cheaper methods of tinting and toning became widely adopted. There remained great variability—even among individual copies of the "same" film—until the general adoption of "natural" (completely mechanized) color processes." Williams, Alan, "Historical and Theoretical Issues," p. 128.

16. Little Tich was a four-foot, six-inch tall music hall performer who specialized in energetic dances (especially parodies of serpentine dancers) and physical

comedy numbers and sang. He appeared in a handful of films around the turn of the century, including three early sound films made by Clément Maurice for the Phono-Cinéma-Théâtre in 1900.

17. For example, artists like Dranem and Little Tich appeared in both sound and silent films made by Gaumont and Pathé.

18. Raynauld, Isabelle, "Georges Méliès avait un vœu: 'Rendre l'imaginaire, l'impossible même, visibles," paper for the Colloque de Cerisy-La-Salle on Georges Méliès, unpublished, p. 4. My translation.

19. Raynauld, Isabelle, "Georges Méliès avait un voeu," p. 4.

20. *Collection "Elgé": Liste de vues animées* No. 137 May 1899
    Collection "Elgé": Liste de vues animées No. 162 Jan. 1900
    Collection "Elgé": Liste de vues animées No. 182 June 1900
    Comptoir général de cinématographie Tarif Général des appareils cínématographiques No. 501 Jan. 1901
    Comptoir général de cinématographie Chrono de Poche pour prise et projection de vues de 15 mm No. 508 1901
    Collection "Elgé": Liste de vues animées généralement en magasin (1901).

21. Richard Abel, *The Ciné Goes to Town: French Cinema 1896–1914* pp. 61–62.

22. *Ibid.*, p. 78.

23. Laurent Mannoni believes that Georges Demenÿ may have directed the serpentine dancers filmed with the 58mm. camera, as the dancers were from the Moulin Rouge, a venue Demenÿ was familiar with. Laurent Mannoni, Marc de Ferrière le Vayer and Paul Demeny, *Georges Demenÿ: Pionnier du cinéma*, Douai: Pagine Editions, 1997, pp. 105–6.

24. For more about serpentine dances, see Naomia Backer, "Reconfiguring Annabelle's *Serpentine* and *Butterfly* Dance Films in Early Cinema History," *Visual Delights: Essays on the Popular and Projected Image in the Nineteenth Century*, edited by Simon Popple and Vanessa Toulmin, Trowbridge, U.K: Flicks Books, 2000, pp. 93–104.

25. See Figure 7 on page 21.

26. De Vries, Tjitte, "Sound-on-Disc-Films 1900–1929 and the Possibilities of Video Transfer," *Cinema 1900–1906: An Analytical Study*, Brussels: FIAF, 1982, pp. 340–341.

27. Harald, Jossé, *Die Entstehung des Tonfilms: Beitrag zu einer faktenorientierten Mediengeschichtsschreibung.* Freiburg/München: Verlag Karee Alber, 1984, p. 72.

28. Dickson described the kinetophone coupling that he demonstrated to Edison upon his return from Europe on Oct. 6, 1889, as follows:

> "A rough description of the method adopted to synchronize the [kinetograph and phonograph] might be useful. The only modification made to the kinetograph, was to place a ratchet wheel at one end of the driving shaft. Thus one end of the shaft held the sprocket wheel which engaged the perforated film, and the the other end held a magnetic escapement device, which was controlled and timed through a relay and battery from an extra commutator collar on the phonograph motor shaft. The impulses electrically received through the ratchet wheel were spaced at 1/2–inch intervals for

each phase or picture." Dickson, W.K. Laurie, "A Brief History of the Kinetograph, the Kinetoscope and the Kineto-phonograph," in A *Technological History of Motion Pictures and Television*, Raymond Fielding, ed., Berkeley: University of California Press, 1967, p. 13.

29. Gaumont, Léon, *Établissements Gaumont (1895–1929)*, Paris: Imprimerie Gauthier-Villars, 1929, p. 30.
30. Harald, Jossé, *Die Entstehung des Tonfilms*, p. 75.
31. *Ibid.*, p. 76. See also Gaumont, Léon, *Établissements Gaumont (1895–1929)*, Paris: Imprimerie Gauthier-Villars, 1929, p. 82.
32. *Ibid.*, p. 73.
33. Gaumont, *Établissements Gaumont*, p. 59.
34. Gaumont, Léon, "Gaumont Chronochrome (sic) Process Described by the Inventor," (Jan. 1959), translated by the Historical and Museum Committee of SMPTE, reprinted in A *Technological history of Motion Pictures and Television* by Raymond Fielding, ed., Berkeley: University of California Press, 1967, p. 65.
35. Gaumont, *Établissements Gaumont*, p. 71.
36. *Ibid.*, p. 71.
37. "Notice pour l'emploi du chronophone," p. 1, in Gaumont catalogue, *Phonoscènes pour chronophone*, 1912. See also Gaumont, Léon, *Établissements Gaumont (1895–1929)*, Paris: Imprimerie Gauthier-Villars, 1929, p. 66.
38. "A Forty-Five minute Talking Picture," *The Moving Picture World*, Vol. XVI, No. 8, May 24, 1913, p. 801.
39. Blaché, *Memoirs*, p. 55.
40. Gaumont, *Établissements Gaumont*, p. 71.
41. Blaché, *Memoirs*, p. 48.
42. Honoré, F., "Le Cinématographe parlant: Un spectacle inédit à l'Académie des Sciences," originally printed in *L'illustration*, 31 December 1910, reprinted in *Établissements*, p. 82.
43. Gaumont, Léon, "Historique: Notice sur les Établissements Gaumont," in *Établissements*, p. 2.
44. Blaché, *Memoirs*, pp. 48–49.
45. *Ibid.*, p. 49.
46. I am grateful to Koszarski (and his research assistant) for sharing this information with me.
47. Records for the Gaumont Flushing Studio at 48–64 Congress Avenue & Park Place (now 137th Street and Latimer Place, Flushing). Block #4952, Lot 32, Queens Borough Records Department.
48. I am grateful to Tony Slide for this information.
49. Both scripts were reprinted in Ciezar, Valeria "Bibliothèque Nationale: Les Scénarios Gaumont" in *Cinémathèque: revue semestrielle d'esthétique et d'histoire du cinéma*, Paris: Cinémathèque Française & Musée du Cinéma, No. 2, November, 1992, pp. 130–132.
50. Pearson, Roberta, *Eloquent Gestures: The Transformation of Performance Style in the Griffith Biograph Films*, Berkeley/Los Angeles/Oxford: University of California Press, 1992, p. 21.

51. Pearson, *Eloquent Gestures*, p. 24.

52. Smith, Leon in *Films in Review*, Vol. XV, No. 4, april 1964, pp. 254–55. Cited in Bachy, *Alice Guy Blaché*, p. 277.

53. Note: Gaumont founded Gaumont-British in London in 1898; the first releases included *An Attack on a Chinese Mission Station*, *Terrible Railway Disaster*, and *Queen Victoria's Visit to London*. In 1902, Gaumont opened an open-air studio on the cricket ground at Dulwich. Herbert Blaché-Bolton, (he was the illegitimate son of a Frenchman and an Englishwoman, hence the double name) was working for Gaumont-British as a cameraman by 1904, as indicated by several film registrations forms from that year archived at the NFTVA. One of these films, *Electric Bell*, is preserved at the NFTVA in its entirety.

54. Blaché, *Memoirs*, p. 56.

55. Letter from Alice Guy to the Marquis de Baroncelli, May 15, 1906, published in *Archives*, No. 56, November, November, 1993, Perpignan: Institut Jean Vigo, p. 4.

56. Blaché, *Memoirs*, p. 53.

57. Comptoir Général de Cinématographie, *Projections parlantes*, July, 1908, pp. 54–55.

58. Blaché, *Memoirs*, p. 59.

59. Ibid.

60. Hans Klepp, "Lebende Photographieen" in *Die Technik* 1987 Heft 1, S.1. Reprinted in Loiperdinger, Martin, "Szenen des früen Kinos," *Kintop* Schriften 2, *Oskar Messter: Filmpionier der Kaiserzeit*, 1994, p. 48. I am grateful to Malte Hagener for his translation.

61. Loiperdinger, Martin, "Szenen des früen Kinos," *Kintop* Schriften 2, *Oskar Messter: Filmpionier der Kaiserzeit*, 1994, pp. 8–26.12.

62. See "Annonce der Messters Projektion" in *Der Kinematograph*, No. 162, February 2, 1910. Reprinted in Loiperdinger, Martin, "Szenen des früen Kinos," *Kintop* Schriften 2, *Oskar Messter: Filmpionier der Kaiserzeit*, 1994, p. 48. I am grateful to Malte Hagener for his translation.

63. All of my materials on Messter is from *Kintop: Oskar Messter: Filmpionier der Kaiserzeit*. The translations are by Rolland Westreich.

64. From the press material which circulated with the Gaumont Centenary retrospective, which came to New York in 1994.

65. From the Gaumont file, Edison National Historic Site.

66. Gaumont was not singled out for such treatment. Other foreign companies, such as Urban-Eclipse, Great Northern were also excluded from the AEL-FSA (the first incarnation of the Motion Picture Patents Company). See Richard Abel's *The Red Rooster Scare: Making Cinema American, 1900–1910*, Berkeley, Los Angeles, London: University of California Press, 1999, especially pp. 88–91 where he shows how Edison used similar tactics to weaken Pathé's dominant market position.

67. In 1907 the Cleveland city directory listed: "Blaché, H. technician, 315 Electric Building, Gaumont Chronophone Co., George B. Pettingill, Pres., Max Faetkenheur, Mgr." In 1908, Blaché is not listed, but Pettingill is still listed as

president, with R.E. McKisson as Secretary, and the address is changed to 312 High Ave. SE. I am grateful to Tony Slide for this information.

68. Letter from Gaumont to Edison in the Gaumont File at the Edison National Historic Site. See also "The Gaumont 'Chronophone': New Talking-Moving Picture Machine Now Ready with Supply of Films and Records," *The New York Dramatic Mirror*, September 5, 1908, p. 8.

69. See "The Truth of the Gaumont Rumors,", *The Moving Picture World*, vol. 6, No. 25, June 25, 1910.

70. "Gaumont Talking Pictures," *The New York Dramatic Mirror*, October 31, 1908.

71. Abel, *Red Rooster Scare*, p. 114.

72. Blaché, *Memoirs*, p. 67.

73. *Ibid.*, p. 79.

74. Gaumont file, Edison National Historic Site.

75. See "The Truth of the Gaumont Rumors,", *The Moving Picture World*, vol. 6, No. 25, June 25, 1910.

76. See "Important Gaumont Letter," in which Gaumont notified Mr. Saunders, the editor of the *News*, that the Gaumont Company is ending its relationship with Kleine and joining the ranks of the independents. *The Moving Pictures News*, Vol. IV, No. 43, October 28, 1911, p. 8.

77. Many of the dates in "Gaumont Chronochrome (sic) Process Described by the Inventor," by Léon Gaumont, Jan. 1959 translated by the Historical and Museum Committee of SMPTE, reprinted in *A Technological History of Motion Pictures and Television* by Raymond Fielding, ed. Berkely: University of California Press 1967 p. 65 are erroneous. I have the originals in French and the dates are clearly stated in the original. I have relied on Fielding to assist me with the translation of the more technical portions, but used the dates from the French documents.

78. Gaumont, Leon, *"Synchronisme du cinématographe et du phonographe"* Communication à la Société française de photographie, 7 novembre 1902, reprinted in *Établissements*, pp. 60–63.

79. Program, *Films parlants (Talking pictures) and Chronochrome*, 39th Street Theatre, New York, June, 1913.

80. *The Moving Picture World*, Vol. 15, No. 13, Mar. 29, 1913, p. 1318.

81. For background on this company, see "The First Danish Film with Photographic Sound Restoaured" (sic) by Uffe Lomholt Madsen, *Griffithiana*, May-September 1992, Issue nos. 44/45, p. 231.

82. Blaché, *Memoirs*, p. 67.

83. *The Moving Picture World*, Vol. VII, No. 5, October 8, 1910, p. 812.

84. Dixon, Wheeler Winston, "Alice Guy: Forgotten Pioneer of the Narrative Cinema," *New Orleans Review*, 19 nos. 3&4, Fall-Winter 1992, p. 9.

85. Wanamaker, Marc, "Alice Guy Blaché," *Cinema Magazine* 35, 1976, p. 12.

86. *A Child's Sacrifice* was distributed as Gaumont number 7005, *Le Sacrifice d'une enfant*, *A Fateful Gift* was released as Gaumont number 7001 *Le Pourboire fatal*, *A Widow and her Child*as Gaumont number 7002 *La Veuve et Son*

enfant, *Her Father's Sin* as *Le Péché d'un père*, and *What is to Be Will Be* as Gaumont number 7003, *Ce qui doit être, sera*.

87. Conversation with Roberta Blaché, fall, 1995.
88. Correspondence between Guy and Léon Gaumont, Gaumont Archives, BIFI collection, Cinémathèque française
89. Abel, *The Red Rooster Scare*, p. 91.
90. In a letter to Richard Dyer, Director of the Edison Co., dated January 12, 1909, Gaumont wrote: "According to a letter which I have just received from Mr. Kleine and to certain passages of a contract between you, and which concerns us, I understand that you insist that we discontinue the manufacture of moving picture films in the United States. I should like to know exactly if such is the situation.

I can hardly believe after all my efforts to bring you together with the Biograph Co. that yourself and Mr. Kennedy can have come to such a decision and I should like to know what I could do with installation and stock which we have in New York and which were established exclusively for the American tastes, if I were to accept such a pretension.

We have already expanded our New York affair more than $20,000, and we thought ourselves all the more justified in going ahead as on several occasions you gave me your formal assurances that the chronophone would in no way injure you.

Naturally our patents will permit us to protect our interests. Do you not think it will be to our common interests to join them to those of your combination? Naturally in exchange we should require a licence to continue our exploitation." From the Edison National Historic Site, Gaumont file.

3. THE GROWTH OF NARRATIVE: ALICE GUY'S SILENT FILM PRODUCTION AT GAUMONT, 1902–1907

1. Lacassin first argued that *La Fée aux choux* could not date from 1896 in *Pour une contre-histoire du cinéma*, Paris:U.G.E., 1972, the in *Louis Feuillade*, Paris: Bordas, 1995, p. 54 he said the film was made around Easter of 1896.
2. Blaché, *Memoirs*, p. 45.
3. *Ibid.*, p. 37.
4. Moreau, Frédérique and Henri Bousquet, *Les Premiers ans du cinéma français*, Perpignan: Institut Jean Vigo, 1985, p. 301.
5. Blaché, *Memoirs*, p. 39.
6. Crafton, Donald, *Emil Cohl, Caricature, and Film*, Princeton: Princeton University Press, 1990.
7. Williams, Alan, *The Republic of Images: A History of French Filmmaking*, Cambridge: Harvard University Press, 1992, p. 57.
8. Blaché, *Memoirs*, p. 40.
9. This film is in the George Eastman House collection.
10. Abel, Richard, *The Ciné Goes to Town: French cinema 1896–1914*, Berkeley: University of California Press, 1994, pp. 131–132.

11. "DOMITOR" is an international organization promoting the study and preservation of early cinema. http://cri.histart.umontreal.ca/Domitor/en

12. Katz, Ephraim, *The Film Encyclopedia*, New York: Thomas Y. Crowell, Publishers, 1979, p. 1262.

13. Bousquet, Henri, "L'Age d'Or," in *Pathé: premier empire du cinéma*, Jacques Kermabon, supervising ed. Premier Siècle du Cinéma series, Paris: Editions du Centre Pompidou, 1994, pp. 51–52.

14. Abel, Richard, *The Ciné Goes to Town: French Cinema 1896–1914*, Berkeley: University of California Press, 1994, p. 19.

15. Williams, Alan, *The Republic of Images: A History of French Filmmaking*, Cambridge: Harvard University Press, 1992, p. 44.

16. *Ibid.*, p. 45.

17. Lacassin, Francis, *Pour une contre-histoire du cinéma*, Institut Lumière/Actes Sud, 1994, p. 32. See also Blaché, *Memoirs*, pp. 31, 36 and 43.

18. Étienne Arnaud in *Le Cinéma pour tous*, his memoirs of his time working in the film industry, published in 1922.

19. d'Hugues, Philippe and Dominique Muller, supervising eds. *Gaumont: 90 ans de cinéma*, Paris: Ramsay, La Cinémathèque Française, 1986, p. 218.

20. Comptoir Général de Cinématographie, *Liste de vues animées*, 1903. My translation.

21. It is a pity that the Gaumont Company has not published even a simple facsimile of their silent film catalogues, as such a publication would help avoid confusion, such as we have seen around the attribution of *Les Méfaits d'une tête de veau*.

22. Sadoul, Georges, *Histoire générale du cinéma: L'invention du cinéma 1832–1897*, Paris: Éditions Denoël, 1948, pp. 380–381.

23. Bachy, Victor, "Alice Guy, les raisons d'un effacement," in *Les Premières années du cinéma français*, Actes du Ve Colloque International de l'Institut Jean Vigo, Paris, 1985, p. 32.

24. Abel, Richard, *The Ciné Goes to Town: French Cinema 1896–1914*, Berkeley, Los Angeles, London: The University of California Press, 1994, p. 102.

25. Gaudreault, André, editor, *Ce que je vois de mon ciné... la représentation du regard dans le cinéma des premiers temps*, Quebec: Université Laval, Meridiens Klincksieck, 1988, p. 13.

26. Williams, *The Republic of Images*, p. 55.

27. Ezra, Elizabeth, *George Méliès*, p. 38.

28. Abel, *The Ciné Goes to Town*, pp. 102–103.

29. Abel, *The Ciné Goes to Town*, p. 104.

30. *Ibid.*, pp. 102–178.

31. Abel, *The Ciné Goes to Town*, p. 109. Musser, *The Nickelodeon Era Begins*, pp. 5–6.

32. Abel, *The Ciné Goes To Town*, p. 109.

33. *Ibid.*, p. 117. Abel refers to Emily Apter, *Feminizing the Fetish: Psychoanalysis and Narrative Obsession in Turn-of-the-Century France*, Ithaca: Cornell University Press, 1991.

34. *Ibid.*, p. 121.

35. Abel also applies this model to the following Gaumont films: *Le Matelas alcoolique* (discussed above), *un homme aimanté* (1907), *La Bombe* (1907), *Le Frotteur* (1907). Abel, *The Ciné Goes to Town,* pp. 141–45.
36. Williams, *The Republic of Images,* pp. 55–56.
37. Menessier worked for Guy at Solax, and when that company was plagued with financial difficulties, found work with Jasset at Éclair. Ben Carré joined him later, to find Arnaud already working there as a director. See Ben Carré, "My First Visit to the Éclair Studio", *Griffithiana* 44/45, May-Sept. 1992, p. 25.
38. Blaché, *Memoirs,* p. 46.
39. Personal Communication, 1995.
40. Blaché, *Memoirs,* pp. 33–34.
41. *Ibid.,* p. 46.
42. Blaché, *Memoirs,* p. 33.
43. Ciezar, Valeria "Bibliothèque Nationale: les Scénarios Gaumont" in *Cinémathèque: revue semestrielle d'esthétique et d'histoire du cinéma,* Paris: Cinémathèque Française & Musée du Cinéma, No. 2, November 1992, p. 130.
44. Gaumont Scenario collection, 1906 folder, Bibliothèque Nationale, Paris.
45. Ibid.
46. Conversation with Roberta Blaché, April 1996.
47. Bachy, Victor "Alice Guy, les raisons d'un effacement" in *Les Premiers ans du cinéma français,* Actes du Vᵉ Colloque International de l'Institut Jean Vigo, Paris, 1985, p. 41.
48. Abel, Richard *The Ciné Goes to Town: French Cinema 1896–1914,* Berkeley: University of California Press, 1994, p. 166.
49. Blaché, *Memoirs,* pp. 45–46.
50. Tissot, James, *The Life of our Saviour Jesus Christ,* i, p. ix.
51. Blaché, *Memoirs,* p. 47.
52. Reynolds, "From Palette to the Screen," p. 277.
53. Williams, *The Republic of Images,* p. 57.
54. Gunning, Tom, *D.W. Griffith and the Origins of American Narrative Film: The Early Years at Biograph,* Urbana and Chicago: University of Illinois Press, pp. 59–60.

4. SOLAX: AN AMERICAN FILM COMPANY

1. See "The Solax Company", The Moving Picture World, Vol. 7, No. 15, October 8, 1910, p. 812.
2. *The Moving Picture News,* Vol. IV, No. 24, June 17, 1911, pp. 8–9.
3. "Solax at Fort Meyer", *The Moving Picture News,* Vol. IV, No. 26, July 1, 1911, p. 10 and "Solax Fort Meyer Pictures", *The Moving Picture News,* Vol. IV, No. 27, July 8, 1911.
4. "Solax Company", *The Moving Picture News,* Vol. IV, No. 29, July 22, 1911, p. 10.
5. "A Crack Shot", *The Moving Picture News,* Vol. IV, No. 31, August 5, 1911, p. 16.

6. See "Solax Scoop of Atlantic Squadron Mobilization," *The Moving Picture News*, Vol. IV, No. 31, August 5, 1911, p. 16.

7. "Studio Efficiency: Scientific Management as Applied to the Lubin Western Branch by Wilbert Melville," *The Moving Picture World*, July 1913, p. 624.

8. "Herbert Blache (sic) Sails for Europe", *The Moving Picture News*, Vol. IV, No. 43, October 28, 1911, p. 7, and Solax Ad entitled "Naval Review" on p. 19.

9. "Mr. H. Blache (sic)", *The Moving Picture News*, Vol. IV, No. 37, Sept. 16, 1911, p. 9.

10. "The Solax Company," *The Moving Picture News*, Vol. IV, No. 49, Sept. 9, 1911, pp. 16–18.

11. "Reorganization of the Solax Company", *The Moving Picture News*, Vol. IV, No. 38, Sept. 23, 1911.

12. "Solax Engages Prominent Comedian," *The Moving Picture News*, Vol. IV, No. 47, November 25, 1911, p. 14.

13. "Levine, Publicity Manager for Solax," *The Moving Picture News*, Vol. IV, No. 47, November 25, 1911, p. 36.

14. Solax Ad, "Postponed," *The Moving Picture News*, Vol. IV, No. 48, December 2, 1911.

15. "The Solax Company," *The Moving Picture News*, Vol. IV, No. 49, Sept. 9, 1911, p. 16.

16. "Magie Joins Universal", *The Moving Picture World, Feb or March 1913*.

17. "Marian Swayne, Sold Programs," *The Moving Picture World, April 1913*.

18. "The Solax Company," *The Moving Picture News*, Vol. IV, No. 49, Sept. 9, 1911, p. 16.

19. "Solax Engaged Billy Quirck," *The Moving Picture News*, Vol. IV, No. 51, Dec. 23, 1911, p. 38

20. "Mace Greenleaf with Solax," *The Moving Picture News*, Vol. V. No. 5, February 3, 1912, p. 23.

21. See "In Memoriam: Mace Greenleaf", *The Moving Picture World*, Vol. V., No. 14, April 6, 1912, p. 7.

22. "The New Solax Plant: A Modern Structure Representing the Last Word in Moving Picture Plant Architecture," *The Moving Picture News*, Vol. VI, No. 12, September 21, 1912.

23. Gunning, Tom, *D.W. Griffith and the Origins of the American Narrative Film: The Early Years at Biograph*, Urbana and Chicago: University of Illinois Press, 1991, especially p. 59.

24. David Bordwell, Kristin Thompson, and Janet Staiger, *The Classical Hollywood Cinema*, New York: Columbia University Press, 1985, pp. 113–141.

25. Musser, Charles, "Pre-Classical merican Cinema: Its Changing Modes of Film Production," in *Silent Film*, edited by Richard Abel, New Brunswick, NJ: Rutgers University Press, 1996, pp. 85–108. The article was originally printed in *Persistence of Vision* No. 9, New York: The City University of New York, 1991.

26. Bordwell, Staiger and Thompson, *The Classical Hollywood Cinema*, pp. 113–141.

27. Laurent Mannoni, Marc de Ferrière le Vayer and Paul Demenÿ, *Georges Demenÿ: Pionnier du cinéma*, Douai: Pagine Editions, 1997, p. 105. The fact that she

would address a letter to Demenÿ at all also supports the theory that she may have shot her first few films on the Demenÿ camera.

28. Blaché, *Memoirs*, p. 27.
29. *Ibid.*, pp. 28–31.
30. *Ibid.*, p. 34.
31. Blaché, *Memoirs*, pp. 36–37.
32. Musser, "Pre-Classical American Cinema" in *Silent Film*, p. 91.
33. Gunning describes the first exhibitors as businessmen who owned their own projectors and films and traveled around screening their wares, following a circuit of vaudeville theaters, lyceums, or on fairgrounds, and occassionally setting up their own exhibition tents: "[Usually they] edited together their one-shot films into sequences and programs, often accompanying them with narration, music and sound effects. This individual creation of programs meant that each exhibitor's show could be a unique event, outside the control of production companies." Gunning, Tom, *D.W. Griffith and the Origins of the American Narrative Film: The Early Years at the Biograph*, Urbana and Chicago: University of Illinois Press, 1991, p. 59.
34. Musser, "Pre-Classical American Cinema," in *Silent Film*, p. 104.
35. *Motion Pictures 1912–1939 Catalogue of Copyright Entries—Cumulative Series*, Washington DC: Copyright Office, Library of Congress, 1951.
36. Bachy, Victor, *Alice Guy Blaché: La Première femme cinéaste du monde*, Perpignan, Institut Jean Vigo, 1993, p. 345.
37. Letter from Alice Guy Blaché to Louis Gaumont, undated typed letter, annotated in Guy's handwriting, a response to Louis Gaumont's letter of January 19, 1954. He answers March 3, 1954, so this letter was probably written in late January or early February of 1954. Guy Blaché/Louis Gaumont correspondence file at the Cinémathèque Française.
38. The film exists in fragmented form in the Library of Congress Collection.
39. Brooks, Peter, *The Melodramatic Imagination*, pp. 14–15, quoted in Lang, *American Film Melodrama*, p. 5.
40. Bachy, Victor, *Alice Guy Blaché*, p. 345.
41. Blaché, *Memoirs*, p.
42. *The Moving Picture World*, Vol. V., No. 4, Jan. 27, 1912. p.
43. Green, J. Ronald, *Straight Lick: The Cinema of Oscar Micheaux* by J. Ronald Green, Bloomington and Indianapolic: Indiana University Press, 2000, p. 29.
44. Green, p. 23.
45. This section was first given in the form of a paper, first at the 1997 *Back in the Saddle* Conference in Utrecht, which was entitled "1911: The Year of the Western" and then at the SCS Conference in San Diego in 1998.
46. Everson, William K. in the introduction to the section on western films in *Before Hollywood: Turn-of-the-Century Film from American Archives*, New York: The American Federation of Arts, 1986, p. 154.
47. See Steve Neale's "Questions of Genre," in *Film Genre Reader II*, Barry Keith Grant, ed., Austin: University of Texas Press, 1995, p. 167.
48. Bowser, Eileen, *The Transformation of Cinema, 1907-1915*, History of the

American Cinema Series, Charles Harpole, gen. Ed., New York: Charles Scribner's Sons, 1990, p. 154.

49. As Eileen Bowser has noted, some filmmakers, such as Selig, went out to California as early as 1909 specifically to find better locations for westerns. See Bowser, *The Transformation of Cinema, 1907-1915*, pp. 177-179.

50. Riley, Glenda, *The Life and Legacy of Annie Oakley*, Norman and London: University of Oklahoma Press, pp. 46–49.

51. A partial list of "western" elements would include: alcoholism, the army, firearms, attacks, attacks by Indians, bullets, headbands, banks, buffalo, desperados, sheriffs, caravans, horses, horse tack, cemeteries, fist fights, ranch hands, duels, ambush, the Woman, forge, train stations, general stores, holdups, man-on-a-horse, hotels, Indian, trails, long trips, the Young Man, The Gambler, The Journalists, isolated homes, merchant-class homes, murder, Mexicans, pioneers, politicians, sylvan glades, main streets, barber shops, old men, Indian villages, ghost towns, new settlements, rape, fathers, food.

52. Bowser, Eileen, *The Transformation of Cinema* pp. 177-179.

53. G. Méliès produced a film in 1910 with a similar theme entitled *His Sergeant's Stripes*, about a sergeant who bravely delivers a message in enemy territory in order to earn the sergeant's stripe that will allow him to marry. However, the effort costs him his life and his fiancee sews the stripe on his uniform just to bury him in it.

54. See Nanna Verhoeff, "Early Westerns: How to Trace a Family," unpublished Master's Thesis, Film and TV Studies, University of Utrecht, August 1996. Also Peter Stanfield, "The Western 1909–14: A Cast of Villains," *Film History*, 1987, Vol. 1, no. 2, pp. 97-112.

55. The Archive (and Magliozzi) had listed it as *Cowboy Streiche* and estimated the date as 'Solax 1919'.

56. "The Solax Company," *The Moving Picture News*, Vol. IV, No. 28, July 15, 1911, p. 14.

57. Bernardi, Daniel, ed., *The Birth of Whiteness: Race and the Emergence of U.S. Cinema*, New Brunswick: Rutgers University Press, 1996, p. 5.

58. The review is quoted in a Solax ad in The Moving Picture News, Vol. IV, No. 24, June 17, 1911.

59. This film was broadcast on German television. Annette Forster identified the film, but we do not know where the actual film itself is archived. Guy mentioned this film specifically as one she directed in her interview with Gerald Ford, *Films in Review*.

60. Ruth Ann Baldwin was a society journalist and publicist, and started writing serials such as *The Black Box* for Universal in 1915. She also wrote numerous screenplays for Rex, but records are insufficient to establish even a filmography; we do not even know the years of her birth and death, though it appears that her career ended around 1921. Except for a portrait originally published in Moving Pictures Stories in November 1915 there is no known photograph of her. Baldwin's very modern approach to screenwriting can be discerned in the following quote from that article: "It has always been my aim to construct

photoplays with as few subtitles as possible, compelling the action to tell the story, without any more inserts than are absolutely necessary."

61. Both *Ocean Waif* and *'49 to 17* are available from Kino Video in New York City.

62. *The Moving Picture News*, Vol. V., No. 3, Jan 20, 1912, p. 42.

63. This section was previously published on the *SilentsMajority* website, at http:// www.mdle.com/ClassicFilms/Guest/mcmahan2.htm

64. Abel, Richard, *The Red Rooster Scare: Making Cinema American 1900–1910*, 1999, p. xiii.

65. *Ibid.*, p. xiv.

66. Thanhouser, an independent film company based in New Rochelle, made a similar film called *An American in the Making* in which an Italian immigrant goes to work in an American factory. The emphasis in this film is on The Great American Industrial Way: the many devices used to protect workmen, such as goggles to protect the eyes in the steel works and guards attached to saws. Instead of better working conditions, the Solax films focus on the difference in social mores, especially as they pertain to women.

67. *The Moving Picture News*, Vol. V., No. 1, Jan 6, 1912, p. 7.

68. *The Moving Picture News*, Vol. V., No. 1, Jan 6, 1912, p. 8.

69. www.mdle.com/ClassicFilms/SpecialFeature/theaters.htm. The figures listed there are taken from *Film Daily*, 1929. The 1919 figure from *Midnight Rambles: Oscar Micheaux and the Story of Race Movies*, "The American Experience" WGBH, 1994.

70. Joseph Young's *Black Novelist as White Racist: The Myth of Black Inferiority in the Novels of Oscar Micheaux* (Westport, Conn.: Greenwood Press, 1989) which focuses on his novels.
    Writing Himself Into History: Oscar Micheaux, His Silent Films, and His Audiences, by Pearl Bowser and Louise Spence, Forward by Thulani Davis, New Brunswick, New Jersey, and London: Rutgers University Press, 2000, 288 pages. Paper $20.00, 0–8135–2803; cloth: $52.00, 0–8135–2802–X; August 2000.
    Straight Lick: The Cinema of Oscar Micheaux by J. Ronald Green, Bloomington and Indianapolis: Indiana University Press, 2000, 316 pages. Cloth: $29.95, 0–253–33753.
    See also From *Midnight Rambles: Oscar Micheaux and the Story of Race Movies*, "The American Experience" WGBH, 1994 and www.mdle.com/ClassicFilms/ FeaturedVideo/birth.htm#midnight and http://www.mdle.com/ClassicFilms/ SpecialFeature/feb597.htm

71. See http://www.cinemedia.net/NLA/black.html and http://www.mdle.com/ ClassicFilms/FeaturedBook/MustReads/book59.htm
    See also Bernstein, Arnold, *Hollywood on Lake Michigan*, Chicago: Lake Claremont Press, 1998, and http://www.mdle.com/ClassicFilms/FeaturedBook/ sfbiblio.htm

72. Bernstein, Arnold, *Hollywood on Lake Michigan*, pp. 53–54.

73. *Blacks n Black and White: A Source Book on Black Films*, by Henry T. Sampson (Scarecrow Press, 1995, p. 202)

74. *MPW* October 5, 1912, p. 11

75. Information and photos about the discovery of *A Fool and his Money* can be found on The Silents Majority Website at the following URL:

   http://www.mdle.com/ClassicFilms/SpecialFeature/fool.htm

76. *MPW* October 5th p. 82.

77. Cripps, p. 28.

78. Anonymous review of *A Fool and his Money*, *The Moving Picture World*, Vol. 14, No. 4, October 26, 1912, p. 344.

79. Walton, *New York Age*, August 26, 1909 p. 6. See Anna Everett's account of Lester Walton's career as a film critic in "Lester Walton's *Écriture noire*: Black Spectatorial Transcodings of 'Cinematic Excess'" *Cinema Journal* 39, No. 3, Spring 2000, pp. 30–50. A more extended treatment is now available in her book, *Returning the Gaze: A Genealogy of Black Film Criticism, 1909–1949*, Durham and London, Duke University Press, 2001, especially pp. 12–58.

80. Hansen, Miriam, Babel and Babylon: Spectatorship in American Silent Film, Cambridge, Mass. And London: Harvard University Press, 1991, p. 65.

81. This statement is based on a comparison of the stills with Guy family pictures.

82. Green, p. 5.

5. FEATURE-LENGTH FILMS AND THE END OF THE SOLAX COMPANY

1. Robinson, David, "The Year 1913," *Griffithiana*, No. 50, May 1994, p. 25.

2. Humouda, Angelo R., "Preface," *Griffithiana*, No. 50, May 1994, p. 5.

3. Robinson, "The Year 1913," p. 9.

4. *The Moving Picture News*, Vol. V, No. 24, June 15, 1912, page 3, and Vol. V., No. 25, June 22, 1912, p. 3, and cover.

5. *The Moving Picture World*, Vol. V, No. 25, June 22, 1912, p. 13.

6. Plot description is from *The Moving Picture News*, Vol. V, No. 24, June 15, 1912, p. 13.

7. M.I. MacDonald, "Madame Blaché's Production of Auber's Fra Diavolo," *The Moving Picture News*, Vol. V, No. 24, June 15, 1912, p. 18.

8. Bachy, Victor, *Alice Guy Blaché: La Première femme cinéaste du monde*, Perpignan: Institut Jean Vigo, 1993, p. 241.

9. Cooper, Courtney Ryley," Dublin Dan (Solax) A Tale of the Underworld," *Motion Picture Story*, Vol. IV, No. 10, Nov. 1912, pp. 81–90.

10. Bachy, *Alice Guy Blaché*, pp. 234–235.

11. "Edward Warren Leaves Solax," *The Moving Picture World*, Vol. XVII, No. 7, Aug. 16, 1913, p. 725.

12. Cooper, Courtney Ryley, "Dublin Dan (Solax) A Tale of the Underworld," in *Motion Picture Story*, Vol. IV, No. 10, Nov. 1912, pp. 81–90.

13. *Motion Pictures 1912–1939 Catalogue of Copyright Entries—Cumulative Series*, Washington D.C.: Copyright Office, Library of Congress, 1951.

14. *The Moving Picture World*, Vol. XVI, No. 7, May 17, 1913 p. 711.

15. Anthony Slide notes: "Paul Bourgeois was a Belgian cameraman, actor and director, whose real name was Paul Sablon. He worked with French director Alfred Machin. For reasons unknown, and it has been suggested perhaps because he was a bit of a rogue, he used the pseudonym in the U.S. Alice Guy does not appear to be aware of his correct name or background. (Personal correspondence from Anthony Slide dated December 20, 1996). In 1915 Bourgeois played the lead role in Herbert Blaché's feature film *The Prisoner of the Harem*, in which a tiger, an elephant, and a lion played key roles. (See "The Prisoner in the Harem, A Royal Bengal Tiger Helps the Hero in the Latest Four-Part Offering of the Blache Feature Film Company" by H.C. Judson, *The Moving Picture World*, October 25, 1915.)

16. Blaché, *Memoirs*, p. 71.

17. *Ibid.*, p. 69.

18. *Ibid.*, p. 244.

19. Judson, J.K., *"Kelly from the Emerald Isle*: Barney Gilmore Plays His Well Known Role, 'Kelly' for the Solax Camera," *The Moving Picture World*, Vol. XVI, No. 9, May 31, 1913, p. 925.

20. *The Moving Picture World*, Vol. XVI, No. 10, June 7, 1913, p. 1034.

21. *Motion Pictures 1912–1939 Catalogue of Copyright Entries—Cumulative Series*, Copyright Office, Washington D.C.: Library of Congress, 1951.

22. Bachy, *Alice Guy-Blaché*, p. 246.

23. *The Moving Picture World*, Vol. XVI, No. 1, April 5, 1913, p. 60.

24. Blaché, *Memoirs*, p. 73.

25. Williams, Alan, *The Republic of Images*, Cambridge, Mass.: Harvard University Press, 1992, p. 57.

26. Blaché, *Memoirs*, pp. 72–3.

27. *Ibid.*, p. 72. The film could have been *The Woman of Mystery*, as the reviewer in *The Moving Picture World*, 30 May 1914, notes the naturalness with which Claire Whitney handles a box of snakes sent to her as a gift.

28. Advertisement, *The Pit and the Pendulum, The Moving Picture World*, Vol. XVII, No. 3, July 19, 1913, pp. 282–83.

29. *The Moving Picture World*, Vol. XVI, No. 11, June 14, 1913. p.

30. Blaché, *Memoirs*, p. 79.

31. *The Moving Picture World*, Vol. XVII, No. 7, Aug. 16, 1913, p. 725.

32. *The Moving Picture World*, Vol. XVII, No. 18, November 8, 1913, p. 20.

33. *The Moving Picture World*, Vol. XVII, No. 8, August 23, 1913, pp. 802–803. Blaché's press release is on p. 807.

34. Undated, typed letter from Alice Guy-Blaché to Louis Gaumont, annotated in Guy's handwriting; a response to Louis Gaumont's letter of January 19, 1954. He answers March 3, 1954, so this letter was probably written in late January or February of 1954. On file in the Gaumont Archives at the Cinémathèque Française.

35. See the ads in *The Moving Picture World* throughout 1913.

36. For the most lucid explanation available on the AEL-FSA, the MPPC, and the Sales Co., see Abel, *The Red Rooster Scare*, pp. 92–94.

37. "The Lure" to Blaché Studio, *Moving Picture World*, May 9, 1914.

38. Blaché, *Memoirs*, pp. 91–2. See also "Censors pass 'The Lure' Mme. Alice Blache's (sic) Adaptation of Famous George Scarborough Drama Beautifully Done," *The Moving Picture World*, July 4, 1914.

39. *The Moving Picture World*, Vol. XX, No. 6, May 9, 1914, p. 829.

40. Robinson, David, "The Year 1913," *Griffithiana*, No. 50, May 1994, p. 7.

41. Staiger, Janet, *Bad Women: Regulating Sexuality in Early American Cinema*, Minneapolis: University of Minnesota Press, 1995, p. 116.

42. *The Moving Picture World*, Vol. XVII, No. 2, July 1913, p. 189.

43. The Pathé footage of Davison's funeral can be found in the Museum of Modern Art's film collection in New York City.

44. Suffrage was hot copy even without stunts like Davison's. A film manufacturer, The Short Features exchange, distributed films made by the New York State Woman Suffrage League, most of them 1,000 feet in length, that were booked on the Loews circuit in 1917 as the pressure and interest in suffrage increased. *Moving Picture World*, October 13, 1917.

45. In the sound era this type of melodrama would be dubbed "the fallen woman film." I prefer to keep the title "redemption films" because in Guy's films, at least, the male character(s) need redemption as often as the female, though the females are usually the focus of the story.

46. Staiger, *Bad Women*, p. 177.

47. "Blache (sic) Forms New Company. Will Be Known as United States Amusement corporation and Will Make Big Features," *The Moving Picture World*, May 2, 1914, p. 653.

48. See "Blache (sic) Forms $500,000 Company", *Motography*, May 2, 1914, p. 317.

49. In the French version of Guy's *Memoirs* Nicolese Bernheim and Claire Clouzot confuse Popular Plays and Players with Famous Plays and Players. The two were distinct and separate entities.

50. "Will Pay $1,000 for Scenarios: Herbert Blache (sic) Says He will Give that Sum for First Choice of Writer's Output," *The Moving Picture World*, June 23, 1916.

51. "BLACHE (sic) ENLARGING STUDIO", *The Moving Picture World*, October 23, 1915.

52. Slide, Anthony, "ALCO FILM CORPORATION," in *The American Film Industry: A Historical Dictionary*, New York: Limelight Editions, pp. 6–7.

53. Gabler, Neal, *An Empire of Their Own: How the Jews Invented Hollywood*, New York: Doubleday, 1989, p. 91.

54. Review "The Tigress", *Variety*, 25 December 1914.

55. Reviews, "The Heart of a Painted Woman," *Variety*, 23 April 1915.

56. Petrova, Olga, *Butter with my Bread: The Memoirs of Olga Petrova*, Camden, N.J.: Bobbs-Merrill, 1942, p. 258.

57. Blaché, *Memoirs*, p. 86.

58. Petrova, Olga, "A Remembrance," Appendix A in *The Memoirs of Alice Guy Blaché*, edited by Anthony Slide, pp. 102–103.

59. Petrova, *Butter with My Bread*, p. 259.

60. Also listed as jointly produced by Guy and Blaché are *The Ragged Earl*, 5 reels, dir. Lloyd B. Carleton, September 1914; *The Lure of a Heart's Desire*, 5 reels, Dir. Francis J. Grandon, January 1916; *The Spell of the Yukon*, 5 reels, dir. Burton L. King, May 1916; *The Devil at his Elbow*, 5 reels, dir. Burton L. King, August 1916, *The Weakness of Strength*, 5 reels, dir. Harry Revier, August 1916, *The Iron Woman*, 6 reels, dir. Carl Harbaugh, October 1916; *When You and I Were Young*, dir. Alice Guy, July 1917.

61. See especially reviews in *Variety* of "The Soul Market", 10 March 1916, "Playing with Fire" on 28 April 1916, "Extravagance," *Variety*, 10 November 1916, and the "heart interest" quote is in the review of "The Secret of Eve," 2 March 1917.

62. Review "The Eternal Question", *Variety* 30 June 1916.

63. Petrova, *Butter with my Bread*, pp. 266–267.

64. Blaché, *Memoirs*, p. 86.

65. Review of "My Madonna," in *Variety*, 5 November 1915.

66. Herbert Blaché made a picture starring Mary Astor entitled *The Young Painter* (Realart 1922). Poor painter falls in love with a socialite who toys with him, then drops him. His masterpiece is her portrait, but his heartbreak is too much for his already delicate constitution and he dies. This film exists in its entirety at the George Eastman House.

67. Bachy, *Alice Guy Blaché*, p. 313.

68. Blaché, *Memoirs*, pp. 87-88.

69. *Ibid.*, pp. 74–75.

70. *Ibid.*, p. 75.

71. I am grateful to my former MA student Erin Hennessy for helping me piece together this sequence.

72. See Ronald Genini's *Theda Bara: A Biography of the Silent Screen Vamp, with a Filmography*, Jefferson, North Carolina and London: McFarland & Company, Inc., 1996.

73. That efforts like hers won out is clear from articles such as the one printed in *The Moving Picture World* on April 17, 1920, in which a prize of $500 was offered to the minister who could preach the best sermon on the "Modern Magdalene" in connection with a new film, *A Good Woman*.

74. This is not to say that Guy herself never produced such films. She made a version of these suspense-by-phone films called *At the Phone* (Solax, 1912). As in the melodramas, the woman's passivity is justified by a dangerous illness. She is in the hospital recovering from surgery, and her husband waits anxiously in the hall to hear whether she will survive. He calls home to check on the nanny and his children; the nanny forgets to hang up the phone and over the open wire he hears two thieves threatening his children's lives. He is tormented, not knowing whether to stay with his wife or whether to try to rescue his children. While he tries to decide, police save his children and his wife recovers. What is interesting here is the father's passivity and his inability to take action.

75. Blaché, *Memoirs*, p. 91.
76. Review of "Tarnished Reputations" in *Variety*, April 9, 1920.

6. MADAM A DES ENVIES (MADAM HAS HER CRAVINGS): CROSS-DRESSING IN THE COMEDIES OF ALICE GUY

1. Wheeler Winston Dixon "Alice Guy: Forgotten Pioneer of the Narrative Cinema" *New Orleans Review* 19 Nos. 3 & 4 (Fall-Winter 1992) p. 12.
2. Much of the content of this article is repeated in Dixon's book *It Looks at You: The Returned Gaze of the Cinema* Albany: State University of New York Press 1995 pp. 12–13.
3. Modleski, T. (1988) *The Women Who Knew Too Much: Hitchcock and Feminist Theory*, New York and London, Methuen.
4. Silverman, Kaja (1996) *The Threshold of the Visible World*, New York and London: Routledge, pp. 180–185.
5. If the mode of address is the part of the communication that travels from narration to narratee, the reception is the response from the spectator sent back to the source of the narrative address. For a reception study approach that parallels my approach of identifying separate modes of address at each level of analysis, see Janet Stagier's *Perverse Spectators: The Practices of Film Reception*, New York and London: New York University Press, 2000, especially her chart (figure 17) on pp. 34–35.
6. This quote is from Mieke Bal's book, *Reading "Rembrandt"*, in which she critiques the so-called universalism of the myth genre of storytelling because this claim to universalism conceals the split between "the subject who tells the story about itself and the subject it tells about." (Mieke Bal, "Visual Story-Telling: Father and Son and the Problem of Myth." From *Reading "Rembrandt": Beyond the Word-Image Opposition*, New York, Cambridge University Press, 1991, p. 123).
7. Todorov, *Théories du symbole*, Paris 1978, as quoted in Willemen, 1980, p. 62.
8. Silverman, Kaja, *The Threshold of the Visible World*, New York: Routledge, 1996, 180–5.
9. Abel, Richard, *The Ciné Goes to Town* p. 90.
10. Both Theo. Pathé and Pathé Frères imitated the films. See *The Moving Picture World*, vol. III No. 2 July 11, 1908, p. 38 for a summary of Theo. Pathé's *The Leaking Gluepot* and the same journal, vol. XVII No. 12 Sept 17, 1910, p. 647 for summary of Pathé Frères' *A Good Glue*.
11. Francis Lacassin, "Filmographie d'Alice Guy," in Guy, *Autobiographie d'une pionnière du cinéma*, pp. 173–177.
12. Abel, Richard, *The Ciné Goes to Town: French Cinema 1896–1914* p. 78.
13. Straayer, Chris, *Deviant eyes, Deviant Bodies: Sexual Re-orientation in Film and Video*, New York: Columbia University Press, 1996, p. 54.
14. Guy often acted in her Gaumont films. Gabriel Allignet and Roberta Blaché have both told me that she even had plastic surgery (paraffin wax injected

into her cheeks to make them fuller, which later caused health problems) so that she would look better on film. It appears that *Sage-femme* is the only one of the films in which she acted that still exists, although Roberta Blaché has pictures of her in costume for at least half a dozen other roles.

15. See Richard Abel, *The Ciné Goes to Town: French Cinema 1896—1914*, p. 78.

16. Garber, Marjorie, *Vested Interests: Cross-Dressing & Cultural Anxiety*, New York and London: Routledge, 1992, p. 176.

17. There is an unidentified film called *La Fée printemps* in the film collection at the Museum of Modern Art. Both Pathé and Gaumont made films with this title around the same time. The Pathé version is in the George Eastman House film collection. Although there are no identifying marks on the MOMA *Fée printemps*, the possibility that it is the Gaumont version of this film cannot be eliminated. I have compared both prints and it is clear that the MOMA version is different from the Pathé version at George Eastman. The films are quite similar, one is probably a "plagiarism" of the other (see my discussion of Gaumont/Pathé plagiarisms in Chapter Three). What matters in this discussion is that both endow a female fairy with the power to control the weather, make fields and countryside fertile, and produce children for a grateful peasant couple.

18. For an analysis of masculine generative power associated with the camera in Méliès, see Richard Abel's *The Ciné Goes to Town* pp. 66–67.

19. Thierry Lefebvre "Voyage autour d'une serrure, des clefs pour comprendre," in André Gaudreault, ed. *Ce que je vois de mon ciné....* Quebec: Meridiens Klincksieck, 1988, pp. 57–58.

20. *Ibid.*, pp. 167–8.

21. Hayward, Susan, *Key Concepts in Cinema Studies*, London and New York: Routledge, 1996, p. 4.

22. Simmon, Scott, *The Films of D.W. Griffith*, Cambridge Film Classics, Cambridge: The Cambridge University Press, 1993, p. 120.

23. Bachy, *Ibid.*, p. 217.

24. *The Moving Picture World*, Vol. V, No. 7, Feb 17, 1912, p.

25. Herbert Blaché remade Guy's one-reel treatment of this story as a five-reel feature in 1915.

26. *The Moving Picture World*, Vol. VII, No. 1, July 2, 1910 p. 49.

27. Butler, Judith, *Gender Trouble: Feminism and the Subversion of Identity*, New York and London: Routledge, 1990, p. 140, quoted in Judith Mayne, *Directed by Dorothy Arzner*, Bloomington and Indianapolis: Indiana University Press, 1994, p. 5.

28. *The Moving Picture World*, Vol. VII No. 8, Aug. 20, 1910, p. 402.

29. Kuhn, *Ibid.*, p. 52.

30. Kuhn, *Ibid.*, p. 54.

31. Doane, Mary Anne *Femmes Fatales: Feminism, Film Theory, Psychoanalysis* New York: Routledge 1991 p. 46.

32. Kuhn, *Ibid.*, p. 54.

33. Butler, Judith, *Bodies that Matter: On the Discursive Limits of Sex*, New York and London: Routledge, 1993, p. 222.

34. Kuhn, *Ibid.*, p. 56.

35. *The Moving Picture World*, Vol. V, No. 18, May 4, 1912, p. 34.

36. From the Gaumont Scenario Collection, 1906 folder, file G0010, no. 3811, 1906. My translation.

37. See Chris Straayer's discussion of this film in *Deviant Eyes, Deviant Bodies*, pp. 70–74.

38. *The Moving Picture World*, Vol. XXI, No. 2, July 11, 1914 p. 195.

Appendix A

PART ONE

A Standard Identification Process
or How the Work of Alice Guy
has benefitted from increased communication
between researchers

by Sabine Lenk
(translated from the French by
Alison McMahan)

THE ALAN ROBERTS COLLECTION belonging to the The New Zealand Film Archive, Wellington, was preserved and restored, for the most part, by the Cinémathèque Royale de Belgique (CRB - Bruxelles) in 1994–95. Among the ninety-four 35mm films sent to us from New Zealand, two stood out. Both were unidentified, their only titles being those provided by the New Zealand archive: 'Revolution. Soldiers Shooting' and 'Men on the Rooftop'. Both were in critical condition; the film was brittle, suffered from at least a 2 percent shrinkage, and was so fragile that it threatened to fall apart with the least handling. It was impossible to look at it even on an editing table. The beginning of 'Revolution. Soldiers Shooting' was in pieces in the can. Without any labelling or credits, either on the can or handwritten on the film leader, my colleague Claude Dusépulchre and I were just as much at a loss as to the identity of these films as our fellow archivists in New Zealand had been.

Claude and I subjected the films to the most intense examination. There was no trademark on the perforated edges (that would have been too easy!) which were solid black on each side. Both films were in black and white and each consisted of a fiction film with one camera set-up and shot on location. The camera maintained a sufficient distance from the action in order to make the entire set visible. The actors played their parts as they would after a curtain had gone up on a stage: they made their entrance, set up the action, encountered certain obstacles to their goals, a climactic moment was reached, then a resolution and a conclusion, which consisted of making an exit (given the short length of the films—21 and 15 meters—the spectacle did not always include the complete exit). All of these elements indicate that these films were from the very earliest days of the cinema. An analysis of the costumes gave us our first clue to the identity of 'Men on the Rooftop': some of the characters were dressed as policemen, typical of a certain kind of French farce that lovingly satirises authority. The characters in the second film, on the other hand, looked more like Russian soldiers. Unfortunately the flag flapping in the wind never spread out enough for us to pinpoint a nationality.

Another detail caught our attention: the black edges alongside each frame were perforated with four almost-square holes. By checking the book by Harold Brown[1] we were able to identify three possible production companies: the English film manufacturer Robert Paul, the Edison Company, and Pathé, all of which had black film edges at certain points in their history. However, none of them used perforations that were placed along the images in quite such a way as these.

In my efforts to find the exact titles, I combed through the catalogues of the various film manufacturers conserved by the CRB, but all in vain. Who the devil made this film—Edison, Lumière, Pathé, Gaumont, or a British or a German film manufacturer? Star Film was quickly excluded, as the aesthetic approach of our films was too different. The Edison Company was also excluded, as none of the titles in their catalogue even remotely evoked the action of 'Revolution. Soldiers Shooting', which played like a faux documentary. In addition, we knew that the Alan Roberts collection consisted almost entirely of European films. This film bore some similarity to some of Pathé's fake actuality films on the Russian-Japanese war. These were produced in 1904, which seemed a bit late for our films, but at least there was a similarity of subject matter. But this too, was a dead-end, as we found no image in the catalogue that matched our film.

Could we be dealing with a Lumière Company film, which, as everyone knows, used imported Edison footage with its four square perforations alongside its own system of round perforations? The book by Jacques Rittaud-Hutinet[2] gave us our initial clue: among the last titles mentioned in the book there was one of interest called 'Poursuite sur les toits' (no. 952) (Chase on the Rooftops). At first glance, the image from the catalogue looked like the sets were the same as those in 'Men on the Rooftop' and that the content of this comedy resembled that of our film. If we were correct, then what was the second film, which had the same type of perforated edges, indicating it had been made by the same company as the first? The description of another film, 'Surprise d'une maison au petit jour' (no. 962) (Surprise Attack on a House at Dawn) by Rittaud-Hutinet matched the action of the second film. Though the photo showed a cannon and soldiers in uniform as in our unidentified film, the whole was nonetheless filmed in front of exterior walls of a building and not in a courtyard as it was in 'Revolution. Soldiers Shooting'.

By examining individual frames of 'Men on the Rooftop' with a magnifying glass we discovered a key detail: the presence of the Gaumont logo, a daisy with the four letters ELGE. We then resorted to reading the book by Victor Bachy on Alice Guy.[3] Bachy mentioned a film of 1898, entitled 'Les cambrioleurs', (The Burglars) and described as follows: "Burglars

1. Harold Brown, *Physical Characteristics of Early Films as Aids to Identification*. Bruxelles: Fédération internationale des archives du film, 1990, p. 19.
2. Jacques Rittaud-Hutinet, *Auguste et Louis Lumière. Les 1000 premiers films*. Paris: Philippe Sers Éditeur, 1990, p. 218/219.
3. Victor Bachy, *Alice Guy Blaché: La Première femme cinéaste du monde*. Perpignan: Institut Jean Vigo, 1993, p. ???.

escape to a rooftop pursued by policemen. Chase and struggles between the two ending with some getting thrown off the roof." This is exactly the plot of 'Men on the Rooftop', except for the lack of someone getting thrown off the roof. Was our print incomplete? To add to our glee, the book mentioned a second film with the same title as the Lumière film 'Surprise d'une maison au petit jour', but unfortunately Bachy provided no description. Bachy mentioned a length of 25m for the first film and 20m for the second; the minor differences in length with our films could be explained by the neglected and extremely fragile state of our prints. In the absence of photos from Gaumont catalogues of either films, our trail towards definitive identification was dead-ended.

What we could do was ascertain that the Gaumont Company had actually made these films and had not simply bought and re-distributed films made by the Lumière Company. A trip to the Services du Film (Bois d'Arcy) gave us the occasion to show Éric Lonné and one of his colleagues pictures from our 'unidentified film objects.' Both of them were of the opinion that the black edges negated the chance that these were Lumière films, as at that period their films had clear edges, but agreed that the set of 'Men on the Rooftop' pointed to 'Poursuite sur les toits'.

When I returned to Brussels I met Alison McMahan who was researching the films of Alice Guy and who made me a generous gift of copies of many early Gaumont catalogues. One evening of reading and I finally found what I had been looking for: I had recognized the set of 'Revolution. Soldiers Shooting' on an image in the Gaumont Catalogue of May 1899 for a film entitled: 'Surprise d'une maison au petit jour (Épisode de la guerre de 1870)' (série C, no. 129). Clearly Alice Guy had imitated the Lumière film (which was made in 1897) and used the same title, a practice that was quite common at the time. 'Les Cambrioleurs', the 'comic scene' mentioned in Bachy's book, was listed as part of the same série C (no. 116), but unfortunately there was no photo along with it. So the final identification would not be achieved by comparing film to catalogue. In the end the final identification came from the print itself. Claude and I had repaired certain tears in the film; once repaired we saw some numbers, difficult to read, which we thought were 9II; after our other discoveries it became clear that the number must be 116, in other words, the same number as in the catalogue.

The next day, Alison McMahan and a mutual friend, Jeannine Baj (who at that time was studying the CRB's film holdings from 1895-1913), took it upon themselves to find the precise frame from the first film which matched the catalogue image. At the same time they did a frame-by-frame comparison of the CRB print of 'Poursuite sur les toits' (Lumière) with 'Les Cambrioleurs'. Thanks to their observations, we now know that Alice Guy did not make a simple imitation, but carefully copied the subject while making important improvements.

The two Alice Guy films have now been preserved. The archival team from the 'L'immagine ritrovata' of the Cineteca del commune di Bologna contributed enormousely to the effort by successfully preserving and conserving the extremely fragile print of 'Surprise d'une maison au petit jour'. Generally speaking, credit for the preservation of these films goes to all the archives mentioned, starting with New Zealand who did not hesitate to entrust their treasures to the CRB. None of this would have been possible if it had not been for the financial support of the European Union (Projet Lumière). Finally, the successful identification is the reward of a collaboration between researchers and archivists, without which we would have never known the true identity of our two mysterious film objects.

A short postscript to this ordinary tale of film identification: it looks like a casual conversation about black film edges with Jan Olsson has led to more film identifications in Sweden. Vive la communication!

PART TWO

Alice Guy in the NFTVA

BY GRAHAM MELVILLE
(Article dated 7.7.97, updated by
Alison McMahan August 2001)

IN 1978, A researcher asked the National Film Archive[1] of the British Film Institute if it had any film by Alice Guy. The answer was no. Did it have her *La Vie du Christ* (Gaumont, 1906)? The answer was yes, but that was made not by her, but by Victorin Jasset.

This article deals with some of the fiction films held by the National Film and Television Archive which are now linked to Alice Guy. It describes how they came to be in the Archive, how the production companies and the titles were established and how Guy's name was eventually linked to them.

Alice Guy and Gaumont

IN 1937 THE firm of Collingridge and Co., a firm of gold and silver refiners in Clerkenwell, London, gave a collection of films to the two-year-old National Film Library. One of them carried the English title *Father Buys A Moke* ('Moke' is English slang for donkey). It had no production company name, no intertitles, and, as it was shot entirely on location, no trade mark anywhere in the image. The architecture strongly suggested France. A search through several British trade journals held by the Archive found a review in *The Kinematograph and Lantern Weekly* for 4 July 1907 that listed it as a Gaumont film. The French title remained unknown.

The same year the Archive acquired an untitled Franco-Prussian war drama with four English intertitles each carrying the word ELGÉ. The word, derived from Léon Gaumont's initials, was used by him as a copyright name and, superimposed on a daisy, as a trade mark. Another search through the Kinematograph and Lantern Weekly found in the 22 August 1907 issue both a review and an advertisement for a title, *The Hand of the Enemy*, that echoed the film's second intertitle 'In the Enemy's Hands'. The plot summary more or less matched. The French title remained unknown. The donor of the film is not recorded.

Both films carried Gaumont production numbers. But the Archive had no French filmographies or Gaumont catalogues that would have led to the

---

1. The National Film Library was established in 1935, only two years after the British Film Institute was founded. It was called the National Film Archive from 1955 to 1993 and, since then, the National Film and Television Archive. This article refers to it as the Archive.

original French titles. Unknowingly, the Archive had acquired its first two Alice Guy films.

In 1937, when these two films were acquired, it is likely that nobody in the Archive even knew her name. Only with the notable publications of Sadoul in 1948,[2] Mitry in 1964,[3] Lacassin in 1971[4] and, above all, with the appearance of Alice Guy's 'Autobiographie' (1976)[5] which contained Lacassin's filmography of her Gaumont work, and the 1986 English translation which added Anthony Slide's Solax filmography, did she gradually become a familiar name in early film circles.

The two Gaumont films mentioned above are typical in that the production company could usually be quickly identified. Around 1906, all the Gaumonts shot at the studio had the ELGÉ trade mark hanging on the set. Films shot on location did not. Main titles, which survived on about half the films, and intertitles, where the film was long enough to have them, carried the trade name in the original French versions but not in all the English versions. The English titles were usually found but not the French titles. A search through the British trade press sometimes found a review or an advertisement that gave the British release date and the length. The individuals concerned were unknown.

Not until 1952 did the Archive acquire an Alice Guy film for which the French title was known. James Clark of Boston in Lincolnshire wrote to say "I have recently come across a veritable goldmine of ancient films from c. 1900 until about 1914... These films were found in two large wooden boxes behind the stage at the Regal Cinema, Boston. They were put there when the old Scala Theatre was sold. The owner of the Scala is a man called George Howden. He used to show these films in the Market Place during the May Fair, and it would appear that these films are the very copies he bought then..." Of the 33 films, four were newsreels (including the *Inundation of Paris* (1910)). The remainder were dramas and comedies. Several were suffering from rusty spools and sticky; at least three were beyond redemption. But a *Life of Christ* was immediately identifiable from the ELGÉ on the intertitles as Gaumont's 40-minute spectacular *La Vie du Christ* (1906). This was the film of which Alice Guy was most proud and which Léon Gaumont had, at the premiere, publicly and explicitly credited to her as auteur. The copy was not, alas, complete, containing only the first 12 of the 25 tableaux, taking the story up to 'Jésus avant Caiphé'. Sadoul's *Histoire générale du cinéma* (1948), the main source at the time for early French film information, credits the film to Victorin Jasset and this

2. Georges Sadoul: *Histoire générale du cinéma*. Tome 2. Les pionniers du cinéma 1897–1909. Paris, 1948. He mentions 24 of Alice Guy's titles.

3. Jean Mitry: *Filmographie universelle*. Tome 2. Paris, 1964. He lists 50 of her titles.

4. Francis Lacassin: *Alice Guy, la première femme réalisatrice de films du monde*. (In *Cinéma 71*, no. 152, janvier 1971, and in *Sight and Sound*, Summer 1971).

5. Alice Guy: *Autobiographie d'une pionnière du cinéma*. Paris, 1976, and, in English translation, 1986.

was copied into the Archive catalogue. At a later date "with Georges Hatot" was added.

About 30 years later, in 1981, the Archive acquired over 1500 films from Switzerland dating from 1896 to 1932. These had been accumulated by the Jesuit cinephile Abbé Joye for showing to his pupils at the Borromaeum in Basle. It included a longer *Vie du Christ* which, though still incomplete, carried the story as far as tableau 18, 'Jesus tombe pour le première fois'. This time, Alice Guy was credited in the Archive catalogue as the director. In 1994, a can labelled *Kriegsschau No. 15* was found to contain, not Messter's Great War newsreel, but fragments from four films. The fourth fragment was the last two tableaux, 24 and 25, of *La Vie du Christ*. The five scenes still missing, including 'La Crucifixion', were presumably among the material that had deteriorated too far to be rescued.

Another title was acquired from two separate sources. The brothers John and Bill Barnes, the founders of the Barnes Museum of Cinematograpy at St. Ives in Cornwall, sold a collection of films to the Archive in 1966. One, a comedy about a mischievous boy, bore the name *Stickphaste* and was identified as *Tommy and the Gluepot*, a Gaumont film released in Britain in 1907. In 1978 the Czech Film Archive gave the Archive a new print of a film with the Czech title *Lepidlo Na Ptaky*. The Archive catalogued it as a French film of c1907, production company unknown, and gave it the translated title of *Glue for Birds*.[6] Not till the 1990s did staff realise that they were, in fact, the same film, *La Glu* (1906).

This print from Prague had been among over 500 titles from 17 different archives lent for screening before the FIAF Conference on Cinema 1900/1906 held at Brighton in 1978. For the same conference, among the films provided by the Library of Congress was a 7-foot 16mm fragment of *(Pierrot Murderer)* (1904). Similarly, the Russian Film Archive Gosfilmofond lent (but subsequently gave in exchange) a number of films for the conference. These included *Madame a des envies* (1906) which still carried its main title. A second film from Gosfilmofond had no title, intertitles or trade marks, so was given the invented title of *The Maid and the Officers* (circa 1906).

Two other films arrived without titles. 'Archive' titles had to be invented by the staff. *A Living Mattress* (circa 1902) came from a private collector in 1954. The daisy trademark on the bedroom wall was not noticed at the time so no production company was recorded. A comedy about two thieves substituting an old boot for a ham, was identified as a Gaumont by a daisy on a fireplace and given the title *Too Many Cooks* (circa 1906). This title was donated in 1968 by, surprisingly, the newsreel company British Movietone News.

In 1993, the filmmaker Felicity Sparrow was researching for a documentary about Alice Guy. The Archive now attributed one Gaumont, four Solax shorts and one Pathé Players film to Alice Guy.[7]

6. When the title of a film is unknown, one is invented by the archive staff. It is always shown in brackets.

7. This documentary was never made, but an article did result, by Lis Rhodes

Sparrow searched Lacassin's and Bachy's[8] filmographies for likely French equivalents to the English titles held by the Archive. She matched the films she viewed against the descriptions in Gaumont catalogues. She found an illustrated advertisment for *L'Âne récalcitrant* (1906) which matched *Father Buys a Moke*. Her research found possible Gaumont titles in French for twelve of the films. Some of her identifications were later confirmed by Alison McMahan. The remaining titles remained stubbornly in English or German.

The film historian Alison McMahan contacted the Archive in 1995. Over the next two years, her viewings in archives in London and abroad, together with the descriptions and stills in Gaumont catalogues she had painstakingly gathered from various sources, and in the Moving Picture World, enabled her to confirm tentative identifications and to make new identifications among the Gaumonts.

She was able to confirm Sparrow's identifications of (*Pierrot Murderer*) as *Pierrot assassin* (1904); (*Too Many Cooks*) as *Un soulier pour un jambon* (1906); (*Tommy and the Gluepot*) as *La Glu* (1906); (*The Stepmother*) as *La Marâtre* (1906) and (*A Living Mattress*), not previously known as a Gaumont, as *Le Matelas alcoolique* (1906).

She identified *The Hand of the Enemy* as *La Fiancée du volontaire* (1907) and The Inlaid Floor Polisher (1907) as *Le Frotteur* (1906). An untitled comedy in which a maid is courted by 4 soldiers of increasing rank had been dubbed *The Maid and the Officers* (circa 1906). The production company was unknown. Sparrow had suggested it might be Gaumont's *Militaire et Nourrice* (1904). It was positively identified by McMahan as *La Hiérarchie dans l'amour* (1906).

How many of these films could be linked to Alice Guy?

She can be credited as producer or, more precisely, as head of film production for all Gaumont fiction up to her departure in 1907, though her position was formalised only in 1905.

Which films did she direct herself?

According to Francis Lacassin, up to Autumn 1905, she was Gaumont's only fiction filmmaker and all their fictions, with a few known exceptions[9] can be attributed to her. The only Gaumont fiction held by the Archive from this period was *Pierrot assassin* (1904).

From autumn 1905 the picture is less clear. The opening of the newly built glass-roofed studio, the 'cathédrale de verre', at Buttes-Chaumont in late 1905 greatly speeded up the rate of production. Gaumont's aim was for

and Felicity Sparrow, "Her Image Fades as Her Voice Rises," in *Multiple Voices in Feminist Film Criticism, edited by Diane Carson, Linda Dittmar, and Janice R. Welsch*, Minneapolis and London: University of Minnesota Press, 1994, pp. 421–431.

8. Victor Bachy: *Alice Guy-Blaché (1873–1968)) La Première femme cinéaste du monde*. Perpignan, 1993.

9. For example: Ferdinand Zecca c. 1899; René Decaux—some *phonoscènes* in 1905; Roméo Bosetti 1905.

an output of one title per day! Guy needed assistants. She continued to make films but she also engaged, trained and supervised several collaborators to assist and to make films themselves. These included her assistant on *La Vie du Christ*, Victorin Jasset, Roméo Bossetti, Etienne Arnaud and the man whom she was to recommend as her successor in 1907, Louis Feuillade.

Of the Gaumonts held by the Archive, she herself mentions only three as her works. One was, of course, the prestigious *La Vie du Christ*. She described the street incident that had inspired her *Matelas Alcoolique* (1906). The third was *La Marâtre* (1906) with the most unsympathetic of all her women characters.

Of the remaining Gaumonts in the Archive, *Monsieur qui a mangé du taureau* (1906) is probably by Jasset, and *Un coup de vent* (1906) by Feuillade. The Archive's remaining seven Gaumonts from this period cannot be firmly attributed to any individual. Nevertheless, all have motifs that can be parallelled in Guy's confirmed titles. Films like *La Hiérarchie dans l'amour*, *La Fiancée du volontaire*, and, above all, *Madame a des envies*, about the cravings of a pregnant wife, suggest the input of a feminine mind. (*Envies* has been attributed to Guy by the Gaumont Co.).[10] The newly married Alice and Herbert Blaché left for the USA in March 1907.

Alice Guy Blaché and Solax

IN 1938, TOWNLEY SEARLE, an artist who had once run a cinema, lent to the Archive his collection of films, magic lantern strips, loops of animated drawings, books, bills, programmes and "three early machines." "I am pleased to let your Society have these on loan, and if you can see your way to purchase I will let you have the entire collection for 100...". Most of the films were actualities and newsreels c. 1903–c. 1918 (with particular emphasis on Paris fashions) but the seven fiction films included "two scraps of film, broken, marked SOLAX 256–9". They came from the Solax production *The Thief*. The Bioscope (7.8.13) and Kine Monthly (August 1913) both carried reviews.

The films of Solax, the American firm founded and run by Alice Guy Blaché from 1910 to 1914, rarely gave the problems that dogged the Gaumonts. Even when the main title was missing, they were all long enough to have intertitles and these usually carried the title of the film, the rising sun trademark incorporating the word Solax, and a catalogue number. As 'President' of the company, Alice Guy Blaché can be credited as producer for the entire Solax output. Initially she directed all the films. From 1911, she wrote and directed many one-reelers and all of the more ambitious films, such as the 3-reeler *Dick Whittington and His Cat* (1913), acquired by the Archive in 1980 from the widow of a Whitley Bay collector. She also

10. The Archive has three other Gaumonts tentatively dated as 1906. Neither the English nor the French titles are known and they are ignored in this article. They have been catalogued as (*Saucy Magazine*), (*Interrupted Wedding Breakfast*) and (*Fanatische Seilt-nzerin*). Identifications would be welcome.

employed Edgar Lewis and Edward Warren as directors and there is some evidence that her husband, Herbert Blaché, directed some of the Solax films.

One private collection yielded two Solax titles. Daniel Hanbury of Hampshire, a keen amateur cinematographer, had, from circa 1910 to circa 1918, accumulated almost 200 films. After his death, the collection was offered to the Archive in 1949 by his daughter Dorothea and her husband, Air Chief Marshall Sir Alec Coryton "as it is no longer possible to privately run 35mm films". It was accompanied by Hanbury's own handwritten catalogue. The dramas included two Solax titles. For *A Comedy of Errors* (1912), two references were found in the British trade press for 1913. In the second film, a western with a pair of typically feisty heroines, the surviving intertitles carried a title, *The Little Rangers*, which did not appear in the British trade press nor in Library of Congress copyright records. References were eventually found in both the British trade press and in Lauritzen and Lundquist[11] under the title *Two Little Rangers* (1912).

In 1972 the Distribution Division of the British Film Institute acquired three Solax titles. They made 16mm copies for distribution purposes and passed the original 35mm copies to the Archive. These were *Broken Oaths,* (1912), *The Strike* (1912), and *Dublin Dan* (1912).

In 1977 the Archive bought a chaotic collection of around 4000 items from Normans Film Services, a Soho stock shot library. It included the Mexican western *The Fight in the Dark* (1912) from which all the action sequences had been cut out for use as stock shots. It arrived in over 30 separate fragments.

Channel 4 Television was an unexpected source. In January 1985 it transmitted three programmes devoted to the work of woman directors put together by Felicity Sparrow. She included *A House Divided* (1913), a comedy about infidelity, which Sparrow had bought for from an American company. An agreement negotiated with Channel 4 allows the Archive to record off-air 25% of the channel's output for permanent preservation.[12]

Alice Guy Blaché at Pathé Players

THE FIVE-REEL SHOW business drama *The Great Adventure*, also known as *Her Great Adventure*, (1918) starring Bessie Love, is the only example of her freelance work held by the Archive. A seven-reel 28mm copy, together with six later 28mm films and a Pathe 28mm projector, was bought for 100 from the daughter of a Swansea collector in 1990. The credits in Lauritzen included Alice Guy Blaché as director. The format presented a problem: the Archive had no equipment for copying 28mm in order to make a 35mm viewing copy. This was especially unfortunate as it appeared to be a unique

---

11. Einar Lauritzen & Gunnar Lundquist: Film-Index 1908–1915. Sweden, 1976. Although Swedish, this became the Archive's most used source of information in its field.

12. The Archive has one other Solax, dated as c1914 and lacking a title. It has been catalogued as *(Mr. Bruce Wins at Cards)*. Identification would be welcome.

copy, was her penultimate film, the feature starring Bessie Love, *Her Great Adventure or The Spring of the Year*, and her last to survive. Not until 1997 did the engineers adapt an existing printer making it possible to print up the Archive's 28mm holdings on to 35mm.

An aspect of archiving that emerges from this account is the arbitrary way in which these films were acquired. They never arrived as individual films, always as part of a mixed collection. The existence of these collections only became known when the collector or his heirs approached the Archive. As the Archive became recognised as the national depository for films and as the best place to preserve the volatile nitrate films and to make them accessible, so more material surfaced.

It also illustrates the input of other archives and of independent researchers for building and identifying the collection.

In 1995 the National Film Theatre held a day-long 'special event' on 'The Silent Pioneers: Women in the Early Film Industry'. The Munich Archive supplied a VHS copy of *Cupid and the Comet* (Solax 1911) identified previously by Alison McMahan and shown as part of her lecture on Guy's work. After this 'premiere,' it was passed to the Archive. The Archive had another Alice Guy.

THE EXTANT FILMS OF ALICE GUY
AND HERBERT BLACHÉ
and where to find them

COMPILED BY ALISON McMAHAN
August 2001

Fiaf Archives

BELGIUM
Cinémathèque Royale de Belgique
23 Rue Ravenstein
B-1000 Bruxelles
Tel: 32-2-507-8370
FAX: 32-2-513-12-62

> *Les Cambrioleurs* 1898 dir. Guy P. Gaumont
> *Surprise d'une maison au petit jour* 1898 dir. Guy P. Gaumont
> *Les Maçons* 1905 dir. Guy P. Gaumont A. The O'Mers
> *La Statue* 1905 dir. Guy P. Gaumont
> *Course à la saucisse* 1906 dir. Guy P. Gaumont
> *Le Fils du garde-chasse* 1906 dir. Guy P. Gaumont
> *Le Noël de monsieur le curé* 1906 dir. Guy P. Gaumont
> *La Vie du Christ* (2 scènes: le Sommeil de Jesus; les Rameaux) 1906 d.
> Guy P. Gaumont Asst. Jasset Sets Menessier, Garnier

> Unattributed
> *Bonsoir (La Fée aux fleurs)* 1905 P. Gaumont

CANADA
Audio-Visual Sector
National Archives of Canada
395, Wellington Street
Ottawa K1A ON3
Tel: (613)996-6009
Fax: (613) 995-6575

> *The Pit and the Pendulum*, dir. Guy, P. Solax 1913

GERMANY
Bundesarchiv—Filmarchiv
Postbox 310667
10636 Berlin
(offices: Fehrbelliner Platz 3)
Tel: 49-30-86-81-1
Fax: 49-30-86-81-310

Outwitted by Horse and Lariat (Cowboystreiche) 1911 Solax dir: Guy
L'Enfant de la barricade 1906 dir: Guy P: Gaumont (nitrate only)
Le tonneau 1904 dir. Guy P: Gaumont (nitrate only)

Filmmuseum/Münchner Stadtmuseum
St. Jakobs-Platz 1
D-80331 München
Bundesrepublik Deutschland
Tel: +49-89-233-223-48
Fax: 49-89-233-239-31

> *Cupid and the Comet* 1911 dir. Guy P. Solax
> *La Vie du Christ* 1906 dir. Guy Asst. Jasset P. Gaumont (Incomplete:
> ends after episode 11, where Jesus is presented to Pilate).

Stiftung Deutsche Kinemathek
Pommernallee 1
D-14052 Berlin
Tel. 49-30-307235/4
FAX: 49-30-3029294

> *La Marâtre [Die Stiefmutter]* 1906 dir: Guy P: Gaumont
> *Le Frotteur (Der fleissige Oskar)* 1906 dir: Guy P: Gaumont
> *L'Enfant de la barricade (Der Heldenmut eines Jungenr)* 1906 dir:
> Guy P: Gaumont
> *Le Jaloux puni (Bestrafte Heifersucht)* 1906 dir: Guy P: Gaumont
> *La Vie du Christ (Das Schweisstuch der heiligen Veronika)* (The
> Veronica's Veil episode) 1906 dir: Guy P: Gaumont Asst: Jasset Sets:
> Menessier, Garnier.

> Attribution refuted:
> *Déménagement à la cloche de bois*
> A print by this title at the archive is credited to Alice Guy, but by com-
> paring this film to the Gaumont script of the same title deposited in the
> Gaumont script collection at the Bibliothèque Nationale in Paris, I
> have established that this film is not hers.

THE NETHERLANDS
Nederlands Filmmuseum
Postbox 74808
1070 BV Amsterdam
(office: Vandelpark 3)
Tel: 31-20-58-91-400
Fax: 68-33-401

> *Brennan of the Moor (Brennan de Straatover)* 1913 3 reels dir. Edward
> Warren P: Solax
> *Two Little Rangers* 1912 dir: Guy P: Solax

NEW ZEALAND
The New Zealand Film Archive
P.O. Box 11445 Wellington
New Zealand
Tel: +64-4-384-7647
Fax: 382-9595

> *Whoso Findeth a Wife* 5 reels 1916 dir: by Frank Crane, Prod: Herbert Blaché P: US Amusement Corp.

SPAIN
Arxiu d'Audiovisuals
de la Generalitat
de Catalunya
(Filmoteca)
Gran Via de les Cortes Catalanes, 184
08004 Barcelona
Spain
Tel: 34-3- 331-35-50
Fax: 34-3- 432-23-22

> Attribution doubtful:
> *Le Pêcheur dans le torrent* 1896 or 1897 P: Gaumont
> *Baignade dans le torrent* 1897 P: Gaumont
> *Retour des champs* 1899-1900 P: Gaumont

U.K.
British Film Institute
NFTVA—Viewing Services
21 Stephen St.
London WIP IPL

> *Dick Whittington and his Cat* 3 reels 1913 Dir: Guy P: Solax
> *The Thief* 1913 Dir: Guy P: Solax
> *Pierrot Assassin* 1904 Dir: Guy P: Gaumont (fragment)
> *L'Âne récalcitrant [Father Buys a Moke]* 1 reel 1906 Dir: Guy P: Gaumont
> *La Marâtre [The Stepmother]* 1906 Dir: Guy P: Gaumont
> *La Glu [Tommy and the Gluepot] [Stickphaste]* 1906 1 reel Dir: Guy P: Gaumont
> *Fiancée du volontaire [The Hand of the Enemy]* 1907 Dir: Guy P: Gaumont
> *Le Frotteur [The Inlaid Floor Polisher]* 1907 Dir: Guy P: Gaumont
> *La Hiérarchie dans l'amour [The Maid and the Officers]* 1906 P: Gaumont
> *Madame a des envies [Madame in Nöten]* 1906 dir: Guy P: Gaumont
> *The Little Rangers [Two Little Rangers]* 1912 dir: Guy P: Solax
> *La Vie du Christ* 1906 dir: Guy P: Gaumont (Incomplete: 11 first scenes are there)

Dublin Dan Solax 1912
La Vie du Christ 1906 dir: Guy P: Gaumont (more complete version, up to the Carrying of the Cross, from the Joye collection, with German intertitles).
Matelas alcoolique 1906 dir: Guy P: Gaumont (fragment)
Un Soulier pour un jambon [Too Many Cooks] 1906 dir: Guy P: Gaumont
A Comedy of Errors 1912 dir: Guy P: Solax
Across the Mexican Line 1911 dir: Guy P: Solax (neg. only)

The Great Adventure 1918 7 reels
Sc: Agnes Christine Johnston, based on the novel *The Painted Scene* by Henry Kitchell Webster dir: Guy
P: Pathe Players for Marcus Loew

Solax Films listed in the NFTVA holdings which I have not been able to verify:
Mr. Bruce Wins at Cards 1914
The Strike Solax 1912
Broken Oaths Solax 1912

by Herbert Blaché
Electric Shock 1904 Gaumont (British) Camera: Herbert Blaché
New York Idea (After Divorce, What?) 1920 dir: Herbert Blaché P: Realart Pictures

Unnatributed Gaumont films at the NFTVA:

The Gavotte 1898 This could be *Gavotte Directoire*
An Interrupted Wedding Breakfast Gaumont 1906
Saucy Magazine Gaumont 1906
Fanatische Seiltanzerin Gaumont 1906 some think this is *Danse Fantousiste* with Lina Esbrand 35 mm. 299 ft. from Czech film archive but it does not match the catalogue description.
Reue Edler Kinderherzen Gaumont 1906
Les Débuts d'un ténor (Eine Tenorstimme) Gaumont 1907
Im gluck Vergiss Die Eltern Nicht Gaumont 1905
Harlequin and the Gendarmes Gaumont 1908?
Concours de grimaces Gaumont 1901
L'Amie Uncertain 1908 (This is not *L'Ami Fidele*)
The Cripple and the Cyclists 1906 This is not *Cul-de-jatte amoureaux*

U.S.A.

THE GEORGE EASTMAN HOUSE
900, East Avenue
Rochester, NY 14607
Tel: (716)271-3361
Fax: (916)271-3970

A Man's a Man 1912 Dir: Guy P: Solax
The Beasts of the Jungle 1913 dir. Edward Warren P: Solax
Le Matelas alcoolique (The Drunken Mattress) 1906 Dir: Guy
P: Gaumont

by Herbert Blaché
The Young Painter 1922 dir. Herbert Blaché P: Realart

The Motion Picture, Broadcasting and Recorded Sound Division
THE LIBRARY OF CONGRESS
Washington, D.C. 20540
Tel: (202)707-5840
Fax: (202)707-2371

All Solax films, and all directed by Guy unless otherwise
indicated:
Falling Leaves 1912
The Detective and His Dog 1912
Algie the Miner 1912 dir. by Edward Warren and Harry Shenk
The Sewer 1912 dir: Menessier
Greater Love Hath No Man 1913
Canned Harmony 1913
House Divided 1913
The Girl in the Armchair 1913
Brennan of the Moor 3 reels 1913 dir: Edward Warren
Matrimony's Speed Limit 1913
The Pit and the Pendulum 1913
The Ocean Waif 5 reels 1916 P: U.S. Amusement Corporation
A Fool and His Money Solax 1912

Dept. of Film and Video
MUSEUM OF MODERN ART
11 West 53rd Street
New York, NY 10019
Tel: (212)708-9600
Fax: (212)708-9531

La Fée printemps Uncertain: Gaumont 1906?
A House Divided 1913 dir: Guy P: Solax
Someone's Luck Society (neg. only) 1912 dir: Guy P: Solax
The Pit and the Pendulum 1913 dir: Guy P: Solax (incomplete)

UCLA FILM AND TELEVISION ARCHIVE
University of California, Los Angeles
302 East Melnitz, 405 Hilgard Ave.
Los Angeles, CA 90224-1323
Tel: +1-310-80-13
Fax: 206-3129

His Mother's Hymn 1911 dir: Guy P: Solax
The Making of An American Citizen 1912 dir: Guy P: Solax
The High Cost of Living 1912 dir. Edward Warren P: Solax

Private Archives

FRANCE
Serge Bromberg
Red Lobster Films
13 Rue Lacharrière
75011 Paris
Tel.: 33-1-43-38-69-69
FAX: 33-1-43-57-26-05

All films directed by Guy and produced by Gaumont unless otherwise indicated:

One shot films:
Ballet Libella 1897
Danse du papillon 1897
Danse fleur de Lotus, 1897
Chez le magnétiseur 1898
Scène d'escamotage 1898
L'Utilité des rayons X 1898
La Petite Magicienne, 1900
Chirurgie fin de siècle 1900
Guillaume Tell 1900
Les Chiens savants, 1902 (two films joined together)
Les Malabars 1902
Faust et Mephistophélès, 1903
Intervention malencontreuse 1902.

Phonoscène
Mayol singing *Questions indiscrètes* 1906
(Preserved and hand-colored to approximate the original)

The Making of An American Citizen 1913 dir: Guy P: Solax (Sepia toned (original tint) with French intertitles)
Cakewalk de la pendule 1903–04 P: Gaumont
a seriously desintegrated print, probably not salvageable
Une histoire roulante P: Gaumont
Not verified.

CINÉMATHÈQUE GAUMONT
30, av. Charles de Gaulle
92200 Neuilly sur Seine
Tel: +33-1-46-43-20-00

Phonoscènes (all 1906)

Mayol singing
Questions indiscrètes
La Matchiche
Lilas blancs
La Polka des trottins
La Paimpolaise
À la cabane bambou
C'est une ingénue

Elval singing
Chemineau, chemine!
Anna, qu'est-ce que tu attends?

Mercadier singing
L'Amant de la Lune

Dranem singing
Le Vrai Jiu Jitsu
Bonsoir M'Sieurs, Dames

Artist not named (picture only):
Dame de pique, je vous aime
Eugène, où êtes-vous parti?
Viens

Silent Films
Sage-femme de première classe 1902 dir: Guy P: Gaumont
L'Enfant de la barricade 1906 dir: Guy P: Gaumont
La Vie du Christ 1906 dir: Guy P: Gaumont (complete)

Alice Guy tournant une phonoscène documentary clip of Guy directing
a phonoscène

SWEDEN

Swedish Television Institute
(address needed)

All films Sieurin French Film Collection, all directed by Guy and all produced by Gaumont. The dates are from the catalogues in which the films
first appear.

Chez le photographe 1899
L'Aveugle fin de siècle 1899
Les Joueurs de cartes 1900
La Bonne Absinthe 1900
La Concierge 1901
Chez le maréchal-ferrant 1901
Chapellerie et Charcuterie mécaniques 1901
L'Hiver: danse de la neige 1901
La Fée aux choux ou la Naissance des enfants 1901

GERMANY

Exact Location uncertain: the following film has been shown on various German Television channels.
Playing Trumps 1912 dir: Guy P: Solax

U.S.A.
Emgee Film Library
6924 Canby Avenue, Suite 103
Reseda CA 91335 USA
Tel: (818)881-8110

All directed by Guy and all Solax unless otherwise indicated:
Canned Harmony 1913
His Double Solax 1913
What Happened to Officer Henderson (Officer Henderson) 1913
A House Divided 1913
Matrimony's Speed Limit 1913
Burstop Holme's Murder Case 1913
The Girl in the Armchair 1913
Pierrot Assassin 1903 or 1904 P: Gaumont (fragment)

all except *Pierrot Assassin* available for purchase or rental in 16mm. and VHS (NTSC) video

John E. Allen
P.O. Box 452
Newfoundland, PA 18445
(201)391-3299
Fax: (201)391-6335

The following are all nitrate only, not preserved and not viewable:

Napoleon 1913 dir: Guy P: Solax
The Roads that Lead Home 1913 dir: Guy P: Solax
For the Love of the Flag 1912 dir: Guy P: Solax
When Marion was Little 1911 dir: Guy P: Solax
Old Love and New 1912 dir: Guy P: Solax

Viewing copy:
Le Matelas alcoolique Gaumont 1906

Fragment:
Unidentified film, possibly *Blood and Water* badly decomposed

Kino Video
333 W 39th St. Suite 503
New York, NY 10018
FAX: (212)714-0871

The Making of an American Citizen Solax 1913 is on *The Movies Begin Vol. 5: Comedy, Spectacle and New Horizons* released 1994. (This is a black and white version of the tinted nitrate original from the Red Lobster collection)

The Ocean Waif 1915 dir: Guy P: U.S. Amusement Corporation (video of the Library of Congress Print)

National Fulfillment Services
Haddon Craftsmen
c/o Smithsonian Institute
1205 O'Neill Hwy
Dumore PA 18512
(610)532-4700

Matrimony's Speed Limit Solax 1913 and *House Divided* Solax 1913 (both dir. by Guy) are on the *Origins of American Film Vol. 6: America's First Women Filmmakers, Alice Guy Blaché and Lois Weber* $34.95 each

Other

New York Public Library—Donnell Branch
A House Divided Solax 1913

Films About Alice Guy Blaché

Alice Guy ou l'enfance du cinéma Documentary by Florida Sadki, 30 mins. (1997). Cine-Cinefil/Centre Georges Pompidou/Les Films de la Passerelle/Triangle Productions/Lobster Films/Zeaux Production. Avec la collaboration de R.T.B.F.

Le Jardin oublié: La Vie et l'Œuvre d'Alice Guy Blaché 60 mins. documentary by Marquise Lepage for the National Film Board of Canada (1996). Also available in English as *The Forgotten Garden: The Life and Work of Alice Guy Blaché.*

The Silent Feminists Produced by Anthony Slide (documentary on early women filmmakers) Producers Library Service 1051 N. Cole Ave Hollywood CA 90038 (213)465-0572

Before Hollywood There was Fort Lee documentary produced by Tom Hanlon, distributed by Tom Hanlon.

Le Retour de L'Historiographe is a "home movie." André Gaudreault (University of Quebec) specializes in recreating the texts of "bonimenteurs" or early film narrators that told stories along with silent films, sometimes in keeping with the nature of the film, sometimes in counterpoint to the film. This video is a recreation of what an early film session might have looked like, complete with pianist and "bonimenteur" in costume. Two of the films included are the Pathe 1905 *La Passion* and the Gaumont (Alice Guy's) *Vie du Christ* (1905).

Qui est Alice Guy? documentary produced by Nicolese Bernheim 1975
Alice Guy tournant une phonoscène Documentary clip
Cinémathèque Gaumont, Paris, 1906

Alice Guy
A 15-minute interview filmed for the television show *Hiéroglyphes* by
I.N.A. Paris. Most of this footage is included in *Le Jardin Oublié.*

Elle Voulait Faire du Cinéma 90 minute fiction film for television
Co-production fy Cinemas (Mag Bodard), Antenne 2, R.T.B.F., R.A.I.
II, S.F.P., Ministère de la Culture. 1985
Screenplay and direction: Caroline Huppert
Focuses on the French portion of Guy's film career, until she met Herbert. The film is based on a comment of Jasset's to the effect that the only
way Guy could have ended up as head of Gaumont's production arm was
if she was Léon Gaumont's mistress, a relationship for which there is no
other support. The film is otherwise faithful to the atmosphere at the time
of the birth of cinema.

   Mein Traumprinz war der Kinematograph Ein Film von Katja Raganelli
& Konrad Wickler.

   Alice Guy, film by Paul Seban; introduced by Charles Ford. Emission
T.V. du lundi 1er juillet 1963 à 22h35.

   Émission *Cinépanorama* du 25 avril 1957.

Other Films of Interest

   Georges Demenÿ et les origines "sportives" du cinéma, video documentary, from Le Groupe de recherche et d'essais cinématographiques (GREC)
Réalisation: André Drevon Production: GREC 25 min/1995.

APPENDIX C

COMPLETE FILMOGRAPHY

ALICE GUY FILMOGRAPHY (GAUMONT)
Compiled by Alison McMahan

THIS LIST IS an updated version of François Lacassin's and Bachy's. Instead of using Lacassin's personal numbering system, I have reverted to the Gaumont catalogue numbers. I have followed the grouping by periods done by Frédérique Moreau, with one significant difference (indicated when it occurs). For reasons of space, I have only included the catalogue description when the film exists. When a film has been attributed to a director other than Alice Guy by Moreau, I give the name of the director. Names of actors and screenwriters are included when known. I have also included genre-indications when they are available. *Comique* means slapstick, *humoristique* or variation thereof refers to a comic situation.

58mm. Gaumont-Demenÿ (1896–1897) It is unkown who directed these; they could have also been directed by Georges Demenÿ. I have numbers 7–103 listed below because these films were apparently reprinted as 35mm. prints later.[1]

    7. *Avenue de l'Opéra*. (Walking Backwards).
  12. *Serpentine Danse: Loïe Fuller*.
  19. *Scène à la terrasse d'un café*.
  24. *Duel de dames*.
  72. *La Partie de cartes*.
  74. *Mauvais joueurs*.
  82. *Cygnes et Cigognes (vue prise au Jardin d'Acclimatation)*.
  96. *Leçon de bicyclette*.
102. *Surprise désagréable*.
103. *La Servante maladroite*.

In November of 1897 a new list with a new numbering system was released.[2] Bachy credits the following films (the rest are military exercise and documentary films) to Guy:

  42. *Une nuit agitée*.
143. *Transformation d'un chapeau*.
144. *France et Russie*.
145. *Chez le barbier*.

    1. The list is taken from Laurent Mannoni's compilation of the various holdings of 58mm. films around the world, published in Mannoni's *Georges Demenÿ, Pionnier du cinéma*, Douai: Éditions Pagine, 1997, pp. 129–131. Mannoni vehemently denies Guy any involvement in filmmaking at Gaumont before 1897.
    2. *La Mise au point, Revue photographique trimestrielle*, number 1, novembre 1897. "Liste des nouvelles vues animées généralement en magasin pour le chronophotographe G. Demenÿ. Tirées sur bandes de 60mm. de largeur." As quoted in Mannoni's list.

35mm films:
From Catalogue Number 182, L. Gaumont & Cie, Juin 1900.

Série A
(The films in this series, the first list of films published by Gaumont for the 35mm. gauge, are almost all identical to those on the lists for the 60mm. production, which makes it clear that they were originally shot for that camera and then reprinted as 35mm. Because they are the few obviously narrative titles from the 60mm. list, Bachy attributes them to Alice Guy.)

1. *Une nuit agitée*
2. *Leçon de bicyclette*
3. *Batteuse mécanique*
4. *Transformation d'un chapeau*
5. *Chez le barbier.*

From Catalogue Number 137, Collection "ELGÉ", Liste de Vues Animées, May 1899, 35mm.
(If a length is not given then the film is 20m or under).

Série N[3]
1. *La Sortie du bain.*
2. *Peintres et Modèles*
3. *L'Indiscret*
4. *Le Tub*

Série B
Before May 1897:
3. *Le Pêcheur dans le torrent.* Comique et très mouvementé. 16,50 m.
4. *Rentrée joyeuse.* 16,50m
12. *Leçon de danse.* Scène comique. 16,50 m.
13. *La Baignade en mer.*
15. *Arrivée d'un train en gare d'Auteuil.*
20. *Baignade dans le torrent.* Plein air. 16,50m.
21. *Les Concierges.* Scène comique.

From June 1897 to May 1898:
52. *Une nuit agitée.* Scène comique, 26m.
68a, b, and c. *Coucher d'Yvette.* Three reels of 20m each.
69. *Danse du Soleil, de la Lune et des Étoiles.* Danse genre Loïe Fuller, d'un trés bel effet. Étoiles, lune et soleil sont peints sur la robe de la danseuse.
70. *Danse espagnole.* 26m.
71. *Danse des papillons.* Danse genre Loïe Fuller. De grands papillons sont peints sur la robe de la danseuse.
72. *Danse fleur de lotus.* Danse genre Loïe Fuller, très mouvementée. 25 m.

3. Bachy does not include these in his filmography of Alice Guy because he believes their *risqué* nature is against Guy's conservative personality. However other films that he does attribute to her are similarly erotic, so I have put the Série N back on the list.

73. *Ballet Libella*. Danse. 20m. Danse de caractère exécutée par deux danseuses.
74a. *Ballet Libella*. Danse. 22m.

75. *Le Planton du colonel*. Très comique. 40m. (1898)
76. *Idylle*. 22m. (1898)
77. *Baignade en Seine*. 28m. (1898)
78. *Comme papa*. Très comique. 25m. (1898)
79. *À confesse*. 25m. (1898)
81. *Pioupiou et Nounou*. Comique. (1898)
83. *Tuyau d'arrosage*. Comique. (1898)
84. *L'Aveugle*. Comique. 25m.
85. *Danse du chalet du Cycle*.
86. *Les Suites fâcheuses d'une maladresse*. Comique (1898)
87. *Farce de caserne*. Comique. (1898)

90. *L'Arroseur arrosé*. Comique. 20m.
91a(20m) and b(24m). *Au réfectoire*.
92a and b. *En classe*.
93. *Les Dernières Cartouches*. 25m. Reproduction de l'épisode célèbre de la guerre de 1870 pendant le combat de Bazeilles.
113. *Les Petits Soldats*. Comique. (1898)
114. *Le Saut-de-mouton*. (1898)

Série C
115. *L'Ours et la Sentinelle*. Scène comique.
116. *Les Cambrioleurs*. Scène comique. (Available in 20 or 25 m length). Cambrioleurs réfugiés sur un toit et poursuivis par des gendarmes. Luttes, péripéties, chutes dans l'espace.
117. *Don Quichotte*. Scène comique.
118. *Le Cocher de fiacre endormi*. 26m.
119. *Les Tribulations de Mme Pipelet*. Scène comique. Des gamins attachent un caniche au cordon de la sonnette. Le facteur survenant à ce moment reçoit un seau d'eau destiné aux enfants. Mêlée générale.
120. *Chez le photographe*. (Available in 20 or 25 m length). Le photographe ne pouvant arriver à faire poser ses clients, leur présente comme résultats deux toiles qu'il leur crève à la fin sur la tête.
121. *Les Métamorphoses de Satan*. 40m.
122. *Chez le dentiste*. Scène comique.
123. *Marchande de frites et Cocher de fiacre*. Scène comique.
124. *Les Surprises d'un perruquier*. Scène comique.
125. *Barbe bleue*.
126. *Querelle de soudards*. Scène de Duel.
127. *Noce comique*.
128. *Guet-apens sous François Ier* (20 or 27m length)
129. *Surprise d'une maison au petit jour*. Épisode de la guerre de 1870.
130. *Explosion du Merrimac*. (20 or 23 m). Scène d'actualité.
131. *Bonaparte au pont d'Arcole*. Scène historique.

132. *Duel de clowns.* (20 or 25m)
135. *Épisode de la guerre hispano-américaine.* Scène de combat. Les soldats espagnols surprenant des insurgés dans une maison en font l'attaque.
136. *Quatre jours de clou.* (28m). Scène comique.
137. *Combat sur la voie ferrée.* (20 or 25m).
138. *Pioupiou et Nounou.* Scène comique.
139. *L'Aveugle fin de siècle.* Scène comique. Expulsé d'un square, un aveugle revient, change ses guenilles contre le vêtements d'un bourgeois endormi, qui est expulsé à son tour.
140. *La Mort de Lannes.* Scène historique.
141. *Gendarmes au vert peints.* Scène comique.
142. *Un duel néfaste.*
143. *En conciliation.*
144. *Pêche miraculeuse.* Scène comique.
145. *Idylle interrompue.* Scène comique.
146. *Chez le magnétiseur.* Scène comique. Une dame se trouvant chez un magnétiseur est déshabillée et se rhabille avec une partie des vêtements d'un gendarme qui, lui-même, met ceux de la dame.
147. *Les Farces de Jocko.* Scène comique de transformation.
148. *Scène d'escamotage.* Une dame couchée sur un divan et recouverte d'un voile est métamorphosée en singe. Le tout disparait. Réapparition de la dame.
149. *Déménagement à la Cloche de bois.* (Remade in 1907 see Gaumont number 1617).
150. *Je vous y prrrends!*
151. *Entre deux vins.*
154. *Le Nègre et les Maçons.*
155. *L'utilité des rayons X.* À l'octroi une dame se présente; son embonpoint parait suspect. Les douaniers la soumettent aux rayons X. De nombreux produits de contrebande sont découverts et la délinquante est déshabillée malgré sa résistance.
156. *Horribles grimaces.*
157. *Rouget de l'Isle chantant la Marseillaise.*
158. *Mariage forcé.*
173. *Leçon de boxe.* Comique.

175. *Les Colleurs d'affiches.*
181. *Déjeuner de bébé.*

LA VIE DU CHRIST
Série de onze tableaux inspirés de tableaux de grands Maîtres
(scenes could be sold separately; each segment was about 20m).

182. *1er Tableau: La Crèche à Bethléem*
183. *2e Tableau: La Fuite en Égypte.*
185. *3e Tableau: L'Entrée à Jérusalem.*
186. *4e Tableau: La Cène*
187. *5e Tableau: Le Jardin des Oliviers.*

188. *6ᵉ Tableau: Jésus devant Pilate.*
189. *7ᵉ Tableau: La Flagellation.*
190. *8ᵉ Tableau: Le Chemin de croix.*
191. *9ᵉ Tableau: Le Crucifiement.*
192. *10ᵉ Tableau: La Descente de croix.*
193. *11ᵉ Tableau: La Résurrection.*

202. *Le Laboureur.* Deux attelages, de chacun quatre paires de bœufs, traînent une charrue.
203. *Le Laboureur.* Même sujet que le No. 202, mais aller et retour.

From Catalogue Number 162, Collection "ELGÉ", Liste de vues animées, janvier 1900. 35mm
(If a length is not given then the film is 20m or under).

March 1899-March 1900
Guy has noted on the catalogue (BIFI copy) that she personally made the following films. The idea of the series was to show people from all walks of life.

207. *L'Avenue de l'Opéra à Paris*
208. *Le Tondeur de chiens.* Amusant.
209a, b, c. *Panorama de la Seine.* Le spectateur a la sensation d'être placé à l'avant d'une bateau. Il voit se dérouler le paysage si accidenté des environs de Paris et poursuit sa course jusque dans la capitale, où il traverse les différents ponts, apercevant au delà les édifices de Paris.
210. *Au pont de Suresnes*
211. *Avenue du Bois-de-Boulogne*
212. *Le Déjeuner des enfants* (Amusant)
213. *Un coin de Paris* (le matin aux Halles)

Guy has noted on the catalogue (BIFI copy) that she commissioned an inventor Mr. C. Rumailho, to make the following six films:

Écoles à feu:
217. *Pièce de 5 se chargeant par la bouche*
218. *Tir de siège.* Canon de 24.
219. *Tir de siège.* Pièce de 120.
220. *Tir de siège.* Canon de 138.
221. *Tir de siège et de place.* Pièce de 155 court.
222. *Tir de siège et de place.* Mortier de 220.

223. *Cortège historique.* Promenade d'Étienne Marcel et des Corporations dans Paris.
224. *Course de Taureaux: Entrée du quadrille*
225. *Les Banderilles*
226. *La Mort et l'enlèvement*

229. *Au cabaret.* Comique.
232. *La Mauvaise Soupe.* Comique.
234. *Scène d'ivrognes.* Comique.

235. *Scène d'arrosage*

236. *Un lunch.* Amusant.

237. *En été.*

238. *La Toilette de bébé*

244. *Les Méfaits d'une tête de veau.* Comique et à transformation.[4] Une tête de veau s'échappe du plat où elle était déposée et va se remettre à un clou. Le boucher la replace dans son plat et la nettoie avec rage. La tête enchantée va alors se fixer sur les épaules du boucher, dont la tête prend place au milieu du plat. La tête de veau, devenue boucher à son tour, se venge en la grattant, en l'étouffant à moitié avec le persil et en la coiffant du récipient où elle baignait précédemment et qu'elle lui appuie avec force sur le crâne.

246. *Erreur judiciaire*

247. *L'Aveugle*

248. *La Bonne Absinthe*

250. *Danse serpentine par Mme Bob-Walter*

251. *Mésaventure d'un charbonnier.* Comique.

252. *Monnaie de lapin.* Comique.

253. *La Fille mal et bien gardée.*

254. *La Marchande des quatre saisons.* Comique.

256. *La Toilette du marié*

257. *Les Dangers de l'alcoolisme.* 30m.

258. *La Mouche d'or*

259. *Le Tonnelier.* Comique

260. *Bal d'enfants*

261. *À la pêche au pain d'épice*

262. *Chanteurs des cours.* Comique.

263. *Transformations*

266. *Le Chiffonier.* Comique.

267. *Retour des champs.* Voici midi, les paysans se dirigent vers la ferme, les vaches conduites par leurs gardiennes s'abreuvent avant de rentrer et les charretiers, pour arriver plus vite, poussent leurs chevaux.

268. *Chez le maréchal-ferrant.* Au premier plan, un homme soulevant péniblement le pied d'un cheval en présente le sabot au maréchal-ferrant qui y adapte un fer, pendant que des enfants jouent et que de robustes forgerons martèlent le fer sur l'enclume.

270. *Courte-échelle.*

271. *L'Angelus.*

272. *Bataille d'oreillers.*

---

4. In Guy's copy of this catalogue, she wrote Zecca's name next to this title. As discussed in Chapter Three, this either means that Zecca worked has her assistant for two weeks in 1901 instead of 1904 as various French scholars believe, or that Guy is confusing the 1901 version of the film with the 1904, longer version, and Zecca worked for her in 1904.

282. *Bataille de boules de neige.*
285. *La Première Pipe.*
286. *Le Marchand de coco.*
287. *Peinture interrompue.*
288. *Boulanger at Charbonnière.*

April–September 1900
314. *Jeunes apprentis en récréation.* 16,5m.
315. *Le Déjeuner précipité.* 20m.
316. *Chapellerie et Charcuterie mécaniques.* 16,5m. La machine est sous pression, lapins, chats, chiens son précipités vivants dans les engrenages. D'un côté, la machine rend de la charcuterie et de l'autre des chapeaux.
317. *Avenue de l'Opéra.* 16,5. Marche en arrière. Vue drôlatique des véhicules et des gens qui se démènent au milieu de l'avenue.
318. *Boulevard des Italiens.* 16,5. Marche en arrière. Comme le n° 317.
319. *Boulevard des Italiens.*
320. *La Petite Magicienne.* 16,5m. D'une étincelle, une gentille petite magicienne surgit et se livre à une grande scène de prestidigitation, pour disparaître après dans une grande flambée.
321. *Leçon de danse.* 16,5m.
327. *Chez le photographe.*
328. *Sydney's Joujoux: Le Bébé.* 16,5m.
329. *L'Arlequine.* 16,5m.
330. *Le Matelot.* 16,5m.
331. *Le Lapin.* 16,5
332. *La Paysanne.* 16,5
333. *L'Écossaise.* 16,5
334. *La Poupée noire.* 16,5
335. *Le Polichinelle.* 16,5
336. *La Reine des Jouets.* 16,5
337. *Derrière les coulisses.* 16,5
338. *Au Bal de FLORE.* Ballet Directoire de G. de Dubor, Musique de Mlle Jane Vieur, dansé par Mlles Lally et Julyett, de l'Olympia. Valse Directoire. 20m.
339. *Au Bal de FLORE.* Ballet Directoire de G. de Dubor, Musique de Mlle Jane Vieur, dansé par Mlles Lally et Julyett, de l'Olympia. Déclaration d'Amour. 20m.
340. *Au Bal de FLORE.* Ballet Directoire de G. de Dubor, Musique de Mlle Jane Vieur, dansé par Mlles Lally et Julyett, de l'Olympia. Gavotte Directoire. 20m.
341. *Ballet japonais.* De G. de Dubor, Musique de Gaston Lemaire, Dansé par Mlles Barbier et Gillet, de l'Opéra. Pas Japonais. 20m.
342. *Ballet japonais.* De G. de Dubor, Musique de Gaston Lemaire, Dansé par Mlles Barbier et Gillet, de l'Opéra. Pas de Grâce. Japonais. 20m.
343. *Ballet japonais.* De G. de Dubor, Musique de Gaston Lemaire, Dansé par Mlles Barbier et Gillet, de l'Opéra. Pas d'Éventails. 20m.

356. *Danse serpentine.* 16,5
357. *Danse du pas des foulards, par des Almées.* 16,5
358. *Danse de l'ivresse.* 16,5
359a. *Coucher d'une Parisienne.* 20.
359b. *Coucher d'une Parisienne.* 20.

Series: Les Fredaines de Pierrette.
359. *Complet.* 20m.
360a. *Arrivée de Pierrette et de Pierrot.* 20m.
360b. *Arrivée d'Arlequin.* 20m.
360c. *Suite de la danse.* 20m.
360d. *Départ d'Arlequin et de Pierrette.* 20m.

Series: Vénus et Adonis. Ballet de M.G. de Dubor, Musique de M. Mestres, dansé par Mlles Boos et Meunier, de l'Opéra.
361. *Badinage.* 20m.
362. *Valse lente.* 20m.
363. *Danse du voile.* 20m.
364. *Mort d'Adonis.* 20m.
365. *Le sang d'Adonis donnant naissance à la rose rouge.* 20m.
366. *La Tarentelle.* 16,5m

Series: Danse des Saisons.
367. *Le Printemps: danse des roses.* 16,5m
368. *L'Eté: danse de la moisson.* 16,5m
369. *L'Automne: danse des vendanges.* 16,5m
370. *L'Hiver: danse de la neige.* 16,5m
371. *Danse excentrique.* 16,5m
372. *Danse excentrique.* 16,5m
373. *La Source.* 60m.
374a. *Danse du papillon.* 16,5m.
374b. *Danse du papillon.* 16,5m.
379. *La Fée aux choux ou la Naissance des enfants.* Une fée dépose des bébés vivants qu'elle retire de choux. Très gros Succès.
383. *La Concierge.* Une personne venue pour louer n'accepte pas le logement proposé en raison de l'étage et d'une inscription placée sur la maison; après son départ des enfants tirent la sonnette. La concierge sort et les poursuit. Rentrée de celle-ci et nouveau coup de sonnette. La concierge revient avec un seau d'eau qu'elle jette croyant arroser les enfants; c'est le locataire, revenu après réflexion pour retenir l'appartement, qui est arrosé. Dispute et bataille. 16,5
384a. *La Bourse ou la Lettre.* 20m.
384b. *La Bourse ou la Lettre.* 20m
386. *Pêche aux fruits.* 20m.

October 1900 and 1901.
393. *Concours de grimaces enfantines.* 16,5

Series: Danses, par Mlle Valentine Brouat.
394. *L'Habanera.* 16,5
395. *Pas du poignard.* 16,5
396. *Pas de l'éventail.* 16,5
397a. *Chirurgie fin de siècle.* 20m.
397b. *Chirurgie fin de siècle.* 20m.
  Dans une salle d'hôpital. Un malade, soumis à l'action du chloro-forme, est livré au chirurgien qui lui enlève un bras et une jambe et laisse aux internes les soins du pansement. Ceux-ci s'avisent de cher-cher dans une tourie renfermant des bras et jambes, de quoi rem-placer les membres enlevés par le chirurgien et recomplètent tant bien que mal l'amputé qui, réveillé par une taloche et des soufflets, s'abandonne à une joie folle en voyant ses membres au complet.
398. *Une rage de dents.* 16,5m. Comique.
399. *Le Saut humidifié de M. Plick.* 16,5m
400. *Guillaume Tell.* 16,5m.

From the Collection "ELGÉ", *Liste des vues animées généralement en magasin*, 1901.
403. *La Danse du ventre.* 16,5m.
404. *Lavatory moderne.* 16,5m.
408. *Lecture quotidienne* (Scène à transformation). 16,5

Series: Folies Masquées
469. *Scène d'amour.* 35m.
470. *Pas de Colombine.* 30m.
471. *Scène d'ivresse.* 35m.

473. *Hussard et Grisette* (Frivolité). 60m. Divertissement-Pantomime de Mlle Jeanne Vieu. Le Hussard: Mlle Julie Soufflet, de l'Opéra; La Grisette: Mlle Geneviève Koch, de l'Opéra. 60m.
476. *Le Dompteur List, ses fauves et ses chiens.* 200m.
477. *Les Vagues.* Divertissement-Pantomime de Mlle Jeanne Vieu. Mlle Julie Soufflet, de l'Opéra. Mlle Geneviève Koch, de l'Opéra. 32,m.
478. *Danse Basque.* Divertissement-Pantomime de Mlle Jeanne Vieu. Mlle Julie Soufflet, de l'Opéra; Mlle Geneviève Koch, de l'Opéra. 32m

1902
539. *En faction.* 30m. Comique.
540. *La Première gamelle.* 30m. Comique.
541. *La Dent récalcitrante.* 25m.
542. *Le Marchand de ballons.* 30m. Comique.
543. *La Femme caoutchouc.* 50m. Comique.
544. *Les Chiens savants.* 120m. Présentés par une jeune et charmante artiste, Miss Dundee.
587. *Danse fantaisiste.* 20m.
588. *Danse serpentine.* 25m.
589. *Danse excentrique.* 20m.
590. *La Gigue.* 25m.

Series: Les Malabares
Grâce à une faveur exceptionnelle de la direction du Jardin d'Acclimatation de Paris, nous avons cinématographié une tribu des plus intéressantes de l'Inde venue en exhibition sur les pelouses du Jardin. Nous voulons parler des Malabares.

591. *Défilé de la tribu.* 20m.
592. *Les Acrobates.* 50m.
593. *L'Escamotage d'une femme.* 100m.
594. *Les Charmeurs de serpents.* 20m.
595. *Les Danses.* 50m.
596. *Les Clowns.* 50m. Comique.

626. *Sage-femme de première classe.* 102m.
627. *Quadrille réaliste.* 40m.
628. *Une scène en cabinet particulière vue a travers le trou de la serrure.* 60m.
629. *Farces de cuisinier.* 55m.
630. *Valse acrobatique.* 25m.
631. *Idylle paysanne.* 50m.
632. *Danse Mauresque.* 30m.
633. *Danseuse comique.* 32m.
634. *Le Lion savant.* 41m. Comique.
635. *Le Boucher.* 40m. Comique.
636. *Intervention malencontreuse.* 25m. Comique. Une femme, suivie de son mari, entre en colère dans sa chambre. Pendant que ce dernier s'efforce de la calmer elle se retourne pour lui envoyer un coup d'ombrelle qui n'atteint que le chapeau et le casse en deux. Le cercle seul reste sur la tête du mari. Celui-ci l'enlève, le regarde d'un air consterné, puis le brosse du revers de sa manche. Il fait un pas vers sa femme qui, véritable furie, le secoue au point de lui arracher les manches de son veston. Alors elle demeure un moment ahurie, tandis que le mari furieux lève la main sur elle, puis finalement se venge sur le mobilier, casse les assiettes, imité en cela par sa femme.
La concierge, attirée par le vacarme, apparaît au moment où la femme brandit encore une assiette. Comme la concierge l'invective, elle lui casse l'assiette sur la tête, puis elles s'attrapent par les cheveux. La concierge reste le crâne nu tandis que le mari, pour rétablir le calme, est allé chercher la vase de nuit dont il renverse le contenu sur la tête de la concierge qui s'enfuit en se retroussant et coiffée du vase, pendant que le mari et la femme se réconcilient.

637. *Les Tribulations d'un vieux beau.* 41m. Comique.
640. *Trompé mais content.* 75m. Comique.
641. *Le Pommier.* 30m.
642. *La Cour des Miracles.* 52m.
643. *La Gavotte.* 52m.

February to July 1903
655. *Potage indigeste.* 20m. Comique.
656. *Illusioniste renversant.* 25m.
657. *Le Fiancé ensorcelé.* 50m.
658. *Les Apaches pas veinards.* Comique. 20m.
659. *Mésaventures d'un voyageur trop pressé.* 50m.
660. *Ne bougeons plus.* 20m.
661. *Comment Monsieur prend son bain.* 40m.
664. *La Main du Professeur Hamilston ou le Roi des dollars.* 25m.
699. *Service précipité.* 25m.
700. *La Poule fantaisiste.* 30m.
706. *Pierrette et son pot au lait.* 40m.
707. *Modelage express.* 37m.
708. *Faust et Méphistophélès.* 44m.
709. *Lutteurs américains.* Comique. 20m.
710. *La Valise enchantée.* Comique. 34m.
711. *Compagnons de voyage encombrants.* Comique.30m.
712. *Cake-Walk de la pendule.* 30m.
714. *Répétition dans un cirque.* 40m.

August to October 1903
715. *Jocko musicien.* 40m.
718. *Chez la modiste.* 40m.
721. *Phroso ou la Poupée mystérieuse.* 37m.
723. *Les Braconniers.* 69m. (Guy attributes this film to C. Bromhead).
725. *La Liqueur du couvent.* 40m.
728. *Le Pharmacien.* 87m.
729. *Chez le patissier.* Comique.
741. *Le Voleur sacrilège.* Comique. 30m.
743. *L'Enlèvement en automobile, mariage précipité.* 90m.
744. *Le Secours aux naufragés.* 200m.
771. *La Mouche.* 24m.
772 *La Chasse au cambrioleur.* 50m.
773. *Le Poulet récalcitrant.*
774. *Nos bons étudiants.* 30m.
776. *Les Surprises de l'Affichage.* 34m.
777. *Comme on fait son lit on se couche.* 30m.
778. *Le Pompon malencontreux.* 21m.
779. *Comment on disperse les foules.* 38m.
780. *Les Enfants du miracle.* 47m.
781. *Pierrot assassin.* 80m. 1ère scène.- Pierrot, à la chasse, aperçoit un lièvre, tire dessus et le tue; au même moment apparaît un garde-chasse qui veut lui dresser procès-verbal. Pierrot le supplie; le garde, inflexible, refuse; Pierrot veut reprendre son fusil, le garde l'en empèche, et, dans la bousculade, reçoit un coup de fusil et tombe raide mort. Pierrot reprend son lièvre et s'en va.

2ᵉ scène.—Arlequin et Colombine sont à table, ils attendent Pierrot, en retard; deux gendarmes à la recherche de l'assassin du garde se présentent; Arlequin les fait se cacher dans une pièce voisine. Arrivée de Pierrot; son carnier est vide, il se met à table. Au moment où il passe un plat à Colombine, il voit un gendarme, bientôt remplacé par Colombine: ce n'était qu'une hallucination. Le même fait se produit avec Arlequin. Les deux gendarmes remplacent les convives. Affolé, Pierrot va chercher la servante; disparition des gendarmes. Enfin, ceux-ci réapparaissent, et Pierrot, avouant son crime, part avec eux.

783. *Les Deux rivaux.* 76m.
787. *L'Assassinat du courrier de Lyon.* 122m.
788. *L'Enterré récalcitrant.* 50m. Comique.
789. *Vieilles estampes.* 80m. 4 episodes of 20m each.
790. *Mauvais cœur puni.* 50m. Comique.
791. *Magie noire.* 60m.
792. *Trahison japonaise.* 50m.
793. *Bombardement de Wladiwostock.* 16,5m.
794. *Rafle de chiens.* Comique. 17m.
795. *Cambrioleur et Agent.* Comique. 35.
796. *Scènes directoire.* 92m.
797. *Duel tragique.* 35m.
799. *L'Explosion de grisou.* 105m.

May 1904
808. *Le Vieux Mari.* Comique. 39m.
809. *La Cible.* 32m.
812. *Transformations.* 22m.
813. *Le Jour du terme.* 97m.
815. *Rapt d'enfants.* 92m.
818. *Endroit réservé.* Comique. 14m.
819. *Électrocutée.* Comique. 27m.
824. *Le Rêve du chasseur.* 30m.
825. *Nos souverains.* 35m.
828. *Amour et Faction.* 35m.
829. *Le Monolutteur.* 23m.
830. *Les Petits Coupeurs de bois vert.* 82m.
831. *Clown en sac.* Comique. 43m.
832. *Les Débuts d'un amateur photographe.* 34m.
833. *Casseur d'assiettes.* 54m.
834. *Triste fin d'un vieux savant.*
835. *Le Testament de Pierrot.* 35m.
836. *Les Secrets de la prestidigitation dévoilés.* 69m.
838. *Nourrice et Bébé.* 35m.
839. *Lavandiers et Marquis.* 21m.
840. *La Faim... L'Occasion... L'Herbe tendre....* 70m.
841. *Militaire et Nourrice.* 45m.
842. *Le Tonneau.*

843. *La Première Cigarette.* 62m.
844. *Départ pour les vacances.* 112m.
845. *Habillage de femme impossible.* 90m.
846. *Tout en morceaux.* 21m.
847. *Tentative d'assassinat en chemin de fer.*

September–December 1904
849. *Le Baptème de la poupée.* 52m.
850. *Les Petits Peintres.* 55m.
851. *Paris la nuit.* 95m.
852. *Le Concours de bébés.* 47m.
853. *Erreur de poivrot.* Comique. 23m.

October 1904
854. *Volée par les Bohémiens.* 225m.
856. *Les Bienfaits du cinématographe.* Comique. 40m.
857. *Patissier et Ramoneur.* 34m.
858. *Gage d'amour.* 35m.
859. *Assassinat de la rue du Temple.* 200m.
860. *Le Réveil du jardinier.* Comique. 30m.
861. *Les Cambrioleurs de Paris.* 83m.

1905
886. *Les Plaisirs de l'automobilisme.* 86m.
887. *Voleur de chien.* 50m.
888. *Lecture passionnante.* 55m.
889. *Aventures de carnaval.* Comique. 100m.
890. *Les jongleurs "Omers".* 34m.
891. *Le Cliché révélateur.* 60m.
892. *À propos de Bottes.* 24m.
893. *Cambrioleur par amour.* 44m.
895. *Les Souliers du cambrioleur.* 55m.
896. *Farces de Rapin.* 64m.
897. *Les Expressions photographiques.* 60m. Directed by Roméo Bosetti.
898. *Les Amours au village.* 98m.
899. *Le Pochard amoureux.* 25m. Directed by Roméo Bosetti.
900. *Réhabilitation.* 250m. A single story in ten scenes.
1111. *Les Dangers de suivre un jolie femme.* 62m.
1112. *Le Papier tue-mouches.* 48m.
1113. *Le Galant commissaire.* 58m.
1114. *Comment on vend ses œuvres.* 50m.
1115. *Lecture et Sommeil.* 30m.
1116. *Les Abeilles.* 165m. Bachy does not credit Guy for this film, but Guy herself mentions helping scientists film difficult views, including one about bees.

1135. *Douaniers et Contrebandiers.* 79m. Also known as La Guérite.
1137. *Le Mort qui ressuscite.* 58m.
1138. *Un Drame à Séville.* 118m.

1148. *Comment on dort à Paris*. 93m.
1149. *Le Sculpteur et le Mannequin*. 73m.
1150. *Le Lorgnon accusateur*. Comique. 20m.
1152. *Pour une fleur*. 60m.
1153. *Les Œufs de la crémière*. Comique. 25m.
1154. *Le Képi*. 49m.
1155. *La Charité du prestidigitateur*. 65m.
1169. *Sérénade humide*. 27m.
1170. *Le Chat de la Mère Michel*. 40m.
1172. *Les "Flegmatics" Acrobates*. 89m.
1181. *Le Pot de fleurs*. 103m.
1182. *Une Noce au lac Saint-Fargeau*. Comique. 137m.
1183. *Évasion et Mort de Robert Macaire et Bertrand*. 163m.
1184. *Le Pantalon coupé*.
1185. *Ballet de singes*. Comique. 19m.
1189. *Gendarmes et Cambrioleurs*. 125m.
1191. *Les Acrobates "Flegmatics"* (À l'envers)
1192. *Le Plateau*. Comique. 50m.
1193. *Le Fantassin guignard*. Comique. 96m. Directed by Roméo Bosetti.
1194. *Roméo pris au piège*. 58m. Screenplay by Feuillade, directed by Roméo Bosetti.
1197. *L'Éclipse*. 50m.

1300. *La Esmeralda*. Based on the novel *Notre-Dame de Paris* by Victor Hugo. 8 scenes, 290m.[5]
1301. *Le Pavé*. 20m.
1302. *Chien jouant à la balle*. 25m.
1303. *Âne récalcitrant*. 18m.
1304. *Le Baromètre*. Comique.
1305. *Le Petit Peintre*. 19m.
1306. *Les Maçons*. Comique. 40m. Starring the O'Mers (acrobat troupe). Des maçons construisent une maison. Deux agents surviennent et sont en butte aux plaisanteries des ouvriers, qui leur font de nombreuses farces. Il s'ensuit une lutte comique dans laquelle les représentants de l'autorité sont très houspillés.
1308. *La Statue*. 120m.
1309. *La Colère de l'aveugle*. 30m.
1311. *Ivrogne et Photographe*. 28m.
1312. *Mésaventures d'un petit patissier*. Comique. 20m.
1313. *Magnétisme*. 40m.
1314. *Déjeuner sur l'herbe*.

5. This was advertised as September, 1905, in the *Revue Mensuelle des Nouveautés Cinématographiques*. As a result, I date all the proceeding films as 1905 and through to number 1320, all included in the same issue of the revue, as produced before September 1905, though Bachy, following Moreau, starts 1906 at catalogue number 1135.

From the *Tarif Général de Cinématographie*, October 1907, Société des Établissements Gaumont

1315. *Villa dévalisée.* Comique. 80m.
1316. *Peintre et Ivrogne.* Comique. 20m.
1317. *On est poivrot, mais on a du cœur.* Comique. 80m.
1320. *Au poulailler.* Comique. 47m.

1906
1321. *Les Rêves du fumeur d'opium.* 177m.
1322. *Une barbe au village.* Comique. 50m.
1323. *Un fromage qui s'envole.* Comique. 25m.
1326. *Arrêtez mon chapeau.* Comique. 58.
1328. *Les Clowns chanteurs.* Comique. 60m.
1329. *La Fée printemps.* 32m.
1330. *La Fève enchantée.* 275m. Féerie in 18 scenes.
1331. *Les Clowns boxeurs.* Comique. 41m.
1332. *La Politique chez le coiffeur.* Comique. 68m.
1333. *Danse cinghalaise.* 38m.
1334. *La Vie du marin.* 160m.
1335. *Duel à l'américaine.* 43m.
1336. *Vols ingénieux.* Comique. 38m.
1337. *La Chaussette.* Comique. 36m.
1338. *La Chauve-souris.* Comique. 15m.
1339. *Mauvais gardien.* Comique. 40m.
1341. *La Messe de minuit.* 127m.
1342. *Pauvre pompier!* Comique. 107m.
1343. *Le Dîner de fiançailles.* Comique. 110m.
1344. *Auguste est pris pour un cambrioleur.* Comique. 70m.
1345. *Algésiras.* 50m. Views of the town.
1346. *Le Régiment moderne.* Comique. 142m.
1350. *Les Druides.* 96m.
1351. *Le Fils de Lagardère.* 194m.
1352. *Une intrigue aux bains de mer.* Comique. 62m.
1353. *Monsieur Purgeon.* Comique. 64m.
1354. *Un bon apéritif.* Comique. 49m.
1355. *Dispute de mendiants.* Comique. 20m.
1356. *Clowns excentriques.* Comique. 59m.
1359. *Clowns toréadors.* Comique. 56m.
1360. *Clowns et Policeman.* Comique. 61m.
1362. *Devant Guignol.* Comique. 32m.

1364. *Le Dimanche de Pitou.* 72m.
1365. *Pâques fleuries.* 37m.
1366. *La Tentation de Colombine.* 146m.
1367. *La Nouvelle Bonne.* Comique. 102m.
1369. *Transformations du Sphinx.* 38m.
1370. *Mauvais arrangement vaut mieux que bon procès.* 100m.

Voyage en Espagne[6]
1371. *Monastère de Montserrat.* 16m.
1372. *Madrid.* 72m.
1373. *Madrid.* 90m.
1374. *Madrid. Panorama de Las Ventas.* 56m.
1375. *Madrid. Panorama de Las Ventas.* 44m.
1376. *Cordoue.* 64m.
1377. *Séville.* 51m.
1378. *Séville.* 27m.
1379. *Grenade.* 31m.
1380. *Grenade. Panorama.* 50m.
1381. *Danses gitanes.—Marengaro.* 49m.
1382. *Danses gitanes.—Sévillane.* 47m.
1383. *Danses gitanes.* 42m.
1384. *Danses gitanes.* 63m.
1385. *La Malle de l'Arménien.* 107m.

1387. *Les Clowns tireurs.* Comique. 91m.
1388. *Danseuse étoile.* 33m.
1389. *Effets de mer.* 50m.

1406. *Conscience de prêtre.* 150m.
1407. *L'Honneur du Corse.* 107m. Un père tue son fils d'un coup de fusil parce que ce dernier, séduit par l'offre d'une montre, a révélé aux gendarmes l'endroit où son père avait caché des contrebandiers venus lui demander l'hospitalité.

La Vie du Christ
1410. *Arrivée à Bethléem.* 41m.
1411. *La Nativité.* 43m.
1412. *Le Sommeil de Jésus.* 30m.
1413. *La Samaritaine.* 18m.
1414. *Miracle de la fille de Jaïre.* 30m.
1415. *Marie-Magdeleine.* 22m.
1416. *Les Rameaux.* 16m.
1417. *La Cène.* 26m.
1418. *Au jardin des Oliviers.* 20m.
1419. *La Veillée.* 12m.

6. From mid-October to the end of November, 1905, Alice Guy travelled through Spain (Barcelona, Zaragoza, Madrid, Cordoba, Seville, the Sierra Nevada, and Algeciras) with her cameraman, Anatole Thiberville. They made silent films (catalogue numbers 1371 to 1384) and sound films. Many of the sound films (numbers 340 to 352 in the 1908 Chronophone catalogue) were found to be unuseable due to a technical glitch on their return, but those that did come out where eventually exhibited at the opening of the Gaumont Hippodrome. According to Bachy, one reason Guy was sent to Spain was so René Decaux could be given the opportunity to make some films himself at the Paris studio.

1420. *La Trahison et l'Arrestation.* 22m.
1421. *Jésus devant Caïphe.* 41m.
1422. *Le Reniement de saint Pierre.* 32m.
1423. *Jésus devant Pilate.* 30m.
1424. *La Flagellation.* 32m.
1425. *Ecce Homo.* 18m.
1426. *Chargement de la croix.* 15m.
1427. *Jésus tombe pour la 1re fois.* 31m.
1428. *Sainte Véronique.* 25m.
1429. *La Montée au Golgotha.* 40m.
1430. *La Crucifixion.* 25m.
1431. *L'Agonie.* 16m.
1432. *Descente de croix.* 30m.
1433. *La Mise au tombeau.* 15m.
1434. *La Résurrection.* 32m.

1435. *J'ai un hanneton dans mon pantalon.* 68m.
1436. *La Conquête du Trottin.* 49m.
1437. *Le Cochon de lait.* Comique. 117m.
1438. *La Femme au masque.* 40m.
1439. *Amour et Hypnotisme.* Comique. 42m.
1440. *Le Cadeau du mari.* 17m.
1441. *Un complot anarchiste.* Comique. 67m.
1442. *Une course d'obstacles.* 147m.
1443. *Cul-de-jatte amoureux.* 18m.
1444. *Le Galant Jardinier.* 30m.
1445. *Le Conte de Saint-Nicolas*, also known as *La Légende de Saint-Nicolas.* 170m.
1446. *Le Sommeil du juste.* 44m.
1447. *L'Ardoisière.* Dramatique. 112m.
1448. *Le Restaurant du Lapin Sauté.* Comique. 85m.

1477. *La Fée Mélusine.* Féerie. 120m.
1478. *Crime affreux.* Comique. 62m.
1479. *Victime de l'interview.* 83m.
1480. *Un fil à la patte.* Comique. 28m.
1482. *Le Pardon de l'aïeul.* Dramatique. 67m.
1483. *Les Tziganes.* Dramatique. 117m.
1484. *Contrebandier!* Dramatique. 78m. Screenplay by Louis Feuillade, directed by Bosetti.

1486. *Un cas de divorce.* 57m.
1487. *La Cuiller d'argent.* Comique. 97m.
1488. *Bébé veut écrire.* Directed by Feuillade.
1489. *La Loi de lynch.* Drame. 83m.
1490. *La Tentation d'Antoinette.* Period piece in 5 scenes. 100m.
1491. *Drame d'amour.* Drame. 105m.
1492. *Rencontre d'amis.* Comique. 93m.

316 ALICE GUY BLACHÉ: LOST VISIONARY OF THE CINEMA

1493. *Titi se venge.* 103m.
1494. *Le Fils du garde-chasse.* Dramatique. 83m.
1495. *Course de taureaux à Nîmes.* (Of the bullfighter Machaquito). 161m.
1496. *La Quittance de loyer.* Comique. 81m.
1497. *La Fête au village.* 160m.
1498. *Ta pièce est fausse!* 50m.
1499. *Sauve maman.* 35mm.

1500. *Rêve d'artiste.* 28m.
1510. *Ami fidèle.* 50m.
1511. *Un soulier pour un jambon.* 58m.
1512. *La Douche des amoureux.* Comique. 20m.
1513. *Ils s'en décrochent la mâchoire.* Comique. 26m.
1514. *Le Satyre du bois de Boulogne.* Comique. 50m.
1515. *C'est papa qui prend la purge!* 107m. Directed either by Bosetti or Feuillade.
1516. *La Leçon de bicyclette.* 76m. Comique.
1517. *Madame a des envies.* 102m. Comique. Madame se trouve dans une position intéressante, et ses envies les plus bizarres doivent immédiatement être satisfaites: ainsi son mari la voit avec terreur voler un sucre d'orge à des enfants, des fruits à un marchand, boire la consommation d'un Monsieur à la terrasse d'un café, manger un hareng saur et fumer la pipe d'un ouvrier.
1518. *Farces de pages.* 122m.
1519. *La Jalousie du marin.* Dramatique. 76m.
1520. *Jack, le mauvais sujet.* 53m.
1521. *Pitou lutteur.* Comique. 72m.
1522. *La Pègre de Paris.* 260m. Drama in 9 scenes.
1523. *Le Nègre amoureux.* 56m.
1524. *Le Rêve du sculpteur.* 66m.
1525. *On demande une jeune fille.* 152m.
1526. *Le Pion.* 150m.
1527. *L'Ouverture de la chasse.* 140m.
1528. *Le Gendarme a une idée.* Comique. 52m.
1529. *Le Brésilien à Paris.* 300m.
1530. *Un nouveau Guillaume Tell.* Comique. 48m.
1531. *Voyage ministériel.* Comique. 91m.
1532. *Le Fromage dénonciateur.* 56m.
1533. *Le Petit Robinson.* 127m.
1534. *Le Portrait de Mme X...* 75m.

September 1906
1535. *Lèvres closes.* 77m.
1536. *Medor douche son maître.* Comique. 16m.
1537. *Madame Ducordon, concierge.* Comique. 66m. Starring the O'Mers.
1538. *L'Avare et son neveu.* Comique. 77m. Starring the O'Mers.
1539. *Le Songe du pêcheur.* 96m.
1541. *Le Bon Écraseur.* Comique.38m.

1542. *La Crinoline.* Comique. 37m.

1543. *La Voiture cellulaire.* Comique. 37m.

1544. *La Femme collante.* 50m.

1544. *La Hiérarchie dans l'amour.* Un soldat, un sergent, un adjudant, un capitaine et un colonel, courtisent successivement la même femme, et hiérarchiquement jaloux recueillent hiérarchiquement d'injustes punitions, du moins les quatre premiers.

1546. *Les gendarmes sont sans pitié.* 130m.

1547. *La Marâtre.* Dramatique. 175m.

1548. *Une histoire roulante.* 53m.

1549. *Nos bons docteurs.* Screenplay by Feuillade, directed by Bosetti.

1550. *Le Matelas alcoolique.* 218m. Une pauvre matelassière s'aperçoit bien tard, après combien de péripéties, qu'un ivrogne s'est couché dans le matelas qu'elle était en train de remettre à neuf.

1551. *Un coup de vent.* 110m. Directed by Étienne Arnaud.

1552. *Fou!* 110m.

1556. *Le Noël du petit Savoyard.* 146m.

1557. *Le Noël de M. le curé.* 128m. Un miracle apporte au curé d'un pauvre village le petit Jésus qu'il n'avait pu se procurer pour la crèche.

1558. *Noël de la fille perdue.* 142m. Screenplay by Feuillade, directed by Bosetti.

1559. *Les Souliers de bal.* 132m.

1560. *Le Noël du pauvre hère.* 60m.

1561. *Concours de fumeurs.* 28m.

1562. *Le Pendu.*

1563. *Padoubny et Aimable de la Calmette.* 100m.

1565. *À la recherche d'une appartement.* 120m.

1566. *Ma bonne est une perle.* 152m.

1568. *Les Lunettes du Père Noël.* 136m.

1570. *La Vérité sur l'homme-singe.* 160m.

1571. *La Fugitive.* 150m.

1572. *Casimir fait la bombe.* 145m.

1573. *Les Résultats du féminisme.* 140m.

1574. *L'Assassin.* 141m.

1576. *Le Toboggan moderne.* 82m.

1579. *Histoire d'un vieil habit.* 151m.

1580. *Le Docteur Coupe-Toujours.* Comique. 118m.

1581. *La Dame de Pèzenas.* 142m.

1582. *Il pleut, bergère....* Comique. 82m.

1583. *L'Enfant bien gardée.* 146m.

1584. *La Ceinture électrique.* 200m.

1586. *Le Bilboquet homéopathique.* Comique. 120m.

1587. *Course à la saucisse.* 93m. Un chien vole, à la porte du charcutier, tout un chapelet de saucisses, d'où poursuite très mouvementée à travers les rues de la ville, les bois, etc. 93m.

1588. *Le Thé chez la concierge.* 140m. Directed by Feuillade.

1590. *La Terroriste.* 240m.

1591. *La Fille du faux-monnayeur.* 200m.

1597. *Salomé.* 160m.

1598. *Le Verglas.* 105m.

1599. *L'Homme-sandwich.* 170m.

1610. *L'Échelle.* 181m. Screenplay by Feuillade, directed by Étienne Arnaud.

1611. *Orpheline!* 214m.

1612. *Chien et Chemineau.* 86m.

1613. *Isidore ne sera plus en retard!* 160m.

1614. *Le Gêneur.* 177m.

1615. *La Bonne Pharmacie.* 186m.

1616. *Le Billet de banque.* 235m.

1617. *Déménagement à la cloche de bois.* 92m.

1618. *Le Mannequin est sans pitié.* 140m.

1619. *Le Cul-de-jatte emballé.* 105m. Screenplay by Feuillade, directed by Roméo Bosetti.

1620. *Histoire d'un mari et d'une chapeau.* 114m.

1621. *La Puce.* 81m.

1626. *Un facteur trop ferré.* 165m. Screenplay by Feuillade, directed by Roméo Bosetti.

1627. *Belle-maman n'ira plus à la fête.* 170m. Screenplay by Feuillade, directed by Roméo Bosetti.

1628. *Le Cavalier novice.* 70m.

1629. *Le Tic.* Screenplay by Feuillade, directed by Roméo Bosetti.

1630. *La colle était bonne!* 172m.

1631. *L'Évadé.* 130m.

1632. *La Bienfaitrice.* 234m.

1633. *Le Bonnet à poil.* 114m.

1636. *L'Âne récalcitrant.* 192m. Pensant faire plaisir à toute sa famille, un brave rentier fit l'acquisition d'un joli petit âne attelé à une belle voiturette. Mais l'animal était dressé: Une fois acheté il ne voulut ni tirer la charrette, ni se laisser monter! On finit par allumer despétards aux roues de son véhicule: Il s'emballe et retourne chez... le marchand!

1637. *Un bon hôtel.* 200m.

1640. *La Vengeance du derviche.* 153m. Directed by Arnaud.

1641. *Le Bien pour le mal.* Drame. 131m.

1642. *Le Mauvais Vin.* 71m.

1643. *L'Oncle à héritage.* 227m.

1645. *Le Fauteuil.* 170m. Directed by Arnaud.

1646. *Un Monsieur aimanté.* 135m. Screenplay by Feuillade, directed by Roméo Bosetti.
Un Monsieur, ayant peur des Apaches, décide de porter une 'cotte de mailles', mais dès sa première sortie il constate que son 'armure'a été aimantée. Tous les objets métalliques sont attirés par notre promeneur: plaques d'égout, étalages, etc.

1647. *Essuyez vos pieds.*

1648. *Toujours tout droit!* 217m.

1648. *Le Frotteur.* 70m. Voilà un homme qui a conscience de sa vocation: il frotte avec ardeur, avec plaisir. Le parquet luit et reluit, les gens glissent, tombent sur le plancher usé par l'astiquage: celui-ci se défonce et la dégringolade continue d'étages en étages.

1652. *Sportsman par amour.* 150m.

1653. *La Fiancée du volontaire.* 205m. Une jeune fille devait se marier avec le soldat tué par l'officier allemand qu'elle soigne. Quand elle apprend la nouvelle, la malheureuse a bien envie de se venger... Mais elle préfère rendre le bien pour le mal!

1654. *La Fontaine de jouvence.* Screenplay by Feuillade, directed by Roméo Bosetti.

1655. *Le Nettoyage par le vide.* 110m. Directed by Louis Feuillade.

1657. *Un sale coup pour la fanfare!* 165m.

1658. *Les Gendarmes.* 104m.

1659. *Fumée sans feu!* 77m.

1660. *Le Jaloux puni.* 78m.

1661. *Le Bon Parapluie.* 122m.

1663. *La Bombe.* 94m. Directed by Arnaud.

1664. *Une héroïne de 4 ans.* 128m.

1665. *Le Lit à roulettes.* 102m. Screenplay by Feuillade, directed by Roméo Bosetti.

1666. *La Glu.* 140m. Une gamin, mauvais plaisant comme tous ses congénères, s'amuse à enduire de glu les escaliers d'une maison, un banc, la selle et le guidon d'une bicyclette. Chacune de ces farces aura des conséquences irrésistiblement comiques. Finalement le petit coupable sera lui-même victime du fameux pot de glu qui adhérera trop solidement à son postérieur.

1667. *Le Mari modèle.* 98m.

1668. *Faux départ.* 125m.

1669. *Le Témoignage de l'enfant.* 214m.

1670. *Le Piano irrésistible.* 126m.

1671. *Grand-père et le Petit Chat.* 68m.

1672. *La Revanche du sorcier.* 93m.

1673. *On a volé mon vélo.* 77m.

1674. *L'Auto-remorque.* 122m.

1675. *Un noyé.* 125m.

1676. *L'Estafette.* 180m.

1677. *Le Colonial.* 195m.

1679. *Sur la barricade.* 88m. Pendant la Commune un jeune garçon, sorti pour aller aux provisions, est pris pour un émeutier, dans une escarmouche avec la troupe. On se préparait à le fusiller au moment où sa grand'mère, venue, inquiète, à l'aperçoit et lui fait un rempart de son corps. L'officier, ému, laisse partir le prisonnier.

1680 *Les Souliers blancs.* 95m. This might be Les Souliers du bal, Screenplay by Feuillade, directed by Roméo Bosetti.

SOUND FILMS DIRECTED
BY ALICE GUY
COMPILED BY VICTOR BACHY

IN 1905 AND 1906, Guy directed synchronized sound films, called *phono-scènes*, for the Gaumont Chronophone. Gaumont listed them separately, with a separate numbering system, so they are listed in the same way here. Missing numbers indicate gaps in the catalogues available to us.

2. *Ave Maria.* 47m.
4. *Le Couteau*, sung by M. Ribière, 63m.
5. *Celle que j'aime*, sung by M. Morton. 63m.
6. *Un monsieur qui sait ce qu'il fait*, sung my M. Morton. 55m.
7. *Cake-walk du Nouveau-Cirque.* 60m.
8. *Joyeux cake-walk.* 40m.
9. *Aubade au concierge.* 48m.
10. *Las dos Princesas.* 55m.
18. *Viens, poupoule.* Sung by Charlus. 50m.
19. *Cinémato parisien.* 60m.
20. *Peau d'Espagne.* 60m.
21. *Twin Duet.* 58m.
22. *Il Bacio.* 47m.
23. *Swing Song.* 55m.
24. *Le Médecin rigolo.* Sung by Charlus. 54m.
25. *J'ai quelque chose qui plaît.* Sung by Charlus. 54m.
27. *Derrière la musique militaire.* 27m.
29. *Le Fanchon.* 66m.
30. *La Chanson des tire-laines.* 71m.
31. *Funicoli-Funicola.* 57m.
32. *Ernani.* 62m.
33. *Paillasse.* 58m.
34. *I due Foscari.* 64m.
35. *Le Barbe de Seville.* 68m.
36. *A Marechiare.* 61m.
37. *Solo de piston.* From *Les Dragons de Villars*, sung by M. Le Barbier. 57m.
38. *Solo de piston.* From *Faust*, sung by M. Le Barbier. 56m.
39. *Solo de piston.* From *Faust.* Sung by M. Le Barbier. 39m.
40. *Le Jour et la Nuit.* Sung by Mlle Demoulins. 63m.
41. *La Mascotte.* Sung by Mlle Demoulins and M. Dambrine. 41m.
42. *Enlèvement à la Toledad.* Sung by Mlle Demoulins and M. Dambrine. 50m.
43. *Enlèvement à la Toledad.* Sung by Mlle Demoulins and M. Dambrine. 63m.
44. *Carmen.* "Je vais danser," 63m.
45. *Carmen.* "La Fleur que tu m'avais jetée. 60m.
46. *Carmen.* "Non, tu ne m'aimes pas. 63m.

47. *Carmen.* Air des cartes. 56m.
48. *Mireille.* "O Magali". 57m.
49. *Mireille.* "Anges du Parais." 60m.
50. *Manon.* "Le Rêve". 40m.
51. *Manon.* "N'est-ce plus ma main," sung by M. Dambrine. 48m.
52. *Boccace.* Air des tonneliers. Sung by M. Dambrine. 75m.
53. *Ma vie Rosette.* Sung by M. Dambrine. 81m.
54. *Miss Helyett.* Sung by Mlle Demoulins and M. Dambrine. 67m.
55. *Les Cloches de Corneville.* "Je regardais en l'air." 56m.
56. *Véronique.* 50m.
57. *Barbe-Bleu.* 75m.
58. *La Fille de Madame Angot.* "Pour être forte." 86m.
59. *La Fille de Madame Angot.* "La République". 77m.
60. *Les Mousquetaires au couvent.* 72m.
61. *La Fille du tambour-major.* Sung by Mlle Demoulins and M. Dambrine. 61m.
62. *La Perichola.* Sung by Mlle Demoulins and M. Dambrine. 75m.
63. *Mamzelle Nitouche.* Sung by Mlle Demoulins and M. Dambrine. 75m.
64. *Les Saltimbanques.* Sung by Mlle Demoulins and M. Dambrine. 90m.
65. *Le Cœur et la Main.* Sung by Mlle Demoulins and M. Dambrine. 80m.
66. *Le Jour et la Nuit.* "La Portuguaise". Sung by Mlle Demoulins and M. Dambrine. 72m.
67. *La Belle Hélène.* "Le Rêve." Sung by Mlle Demoulins and M. Dambrine. 105m.
68. *La Belle Hélène.* Air de Cythère. Sung by Mlle Demoulins and M. Dambrine. 82m.
69. *Miss Helyett.* Air du portrait. 55m.
70. *Les Noces de Jeannette.* Air du rossignol. 62m.
71. *Mireille.* "Trahir Vincent." 59m.
72. *Mireille.* "Heureux petit berger". 43m.
73. *Mireille.* Valse. 39m.
74. *Rip.* Air des enfants. 48m.
75. *Carmen.* "Ma mère, je la vois". 70m.
76. *Carmen.* Habanera. 57m.
77. *Carmen.* "Près des remparts". 36m.
78. *Carmen.* "Les Tringles." 58m.
79. *Carmen.* Air du toréador. 82m.
80. *Carmen.* "Le Duel". 59m.
81. *Carmen.* Duo du 4e acte, 1ère partie. 60m.
82. *Carmen.* La Mort (4e acte, 1ère partie). 70m.
83. *Dragons de Villars.* "Ne parle pas.". 55m.
84. *Dragons de Villars.* "Couplets de l'ermite" 55m.
85. *Dragons de Villars.* "Quand le dragon". 55m.
86. *Dragons de Villars.* " Eh bien! Sylvain." 55m.
87. *Dragons de Villars.* "Chanson provençale". 61m.
88. *Dragons de Villars.* "Le Sage qui s'éveille. 55m.
89. *Dragons de Villars.* "Espoirs charmants". 69m.

90. *Dragons de Villars*. Duo "Moi, jolie". 66m.
91. *Dragons de Villars*. *Air des mules*. 66m.
92. *Mignon*. "Connais-tu le pays." 66m.
93. *Mignon*. "Légères hirondelles". 56m.
94. *Mignon*. "Styrienne" 59m.
95. *Mignon*. "Adieu, mignon". 44m.
96. *Mignon*. "Je suis Titania". 60m.
97. *Mignon*. "As-tu souffert?" 66m.
98. *Mignon*. "Elle ne croyait pas." 68m.
99. *Mignon*. *Berceuse*. 61m.
100. *Mignon*. "Prière". 44m.
101. *Faust*. "Salut, ô mon dernier matin". 72m.
102. *Faust*. Duo du 1er acte, 1ère partie. 70m.
103. *Faust*. Duo du 1er acte, 2e partie.
104. *Faust*. Duo du 1er acte, 3e partie. 42m.
105. *Faust*. "Faites-lui mes aveux." 56m.
106. *Faust*. "Salut, demeure chaste et pure". 69m.
107. *Faust*. " La Coupe du roi de Thulé. 64m.
108. *Faust*. Air des bijoux. 75m.
109. *Faust*. "Quatuor du jardin" 62m.
110. *Faust*. Évocation. 54m.
111. *Faust*. "Laisse-moi contempler ton visage. 57m.
112. *Faust*. "Ô nuit d'amour" 60m.
113. *Faust*. "Il m'aime". 47m.
114. *Faust*. "Divine pureté". 40m.
115. *Faust*. Scène de l'église (1ère partie). 58m.
116. *Faust*. Scène de l'église (2e partie). 78m.
117. *Faust*. La Sérénade. 61m.
118. *Faust*. Trio du duel. (1ère partie). 54m.
119. *Faust*. Trio du duel. (2e partie).
120. *Faust*. (La prison). " Le Jour va luire". 65m.
121. *Faust*. (La prison). "Mon cœur est pénétré. 60m.
122. *Faust*. (La prison). Trio final. 62m.
123. *Les Cornemuseux*. 61m.
124. *Ballet égyptien*. (1ère partie). 56m.
125. *Ballet égyptien*. (2e partie). 56m.
126. *Fiançailles*. 57m.
127. *Ballet de Sylvia*. 46m.
128. *Espana*. 65m.

Phonoscènes starring Polin: (all songs unless otherwise noted)
129. *Le Portrait de Léda*. Monologue. 52m.
130. *Le Gosse du commandant*. Monologue. 62m.
131. *La Balance automatique*. 57m.
132. *La Vénus du Luxembourg*. 50m.
133. *Les Questions de Louise*. 47m.
134. *Le Frotteur de la colonelle*. 44m.

135. *L'Auto du colon.* 39m.
136. *L'Anatomie du conscrit.* 50m.
137. *Le Pépin de la dame.* 47m.
138. *Situation intéressante.* Monologue. 59m.
139. *Chez les lutteurs.* 48m.
140. *La Belle Cuisinière.* 52m.
141. *La Lecture du rapport.* Monologue. 76m.

142. *Scandinave.* Dance. 58m.

Phonoscènes starring Mayol:
143. *La Fifille à sa mère.* 48m.
144. *Le Petit Panier.* 54m.
145. *Le Petit Grégoire.* 54m.
146. *Viens, poupoule.* 55m.
147. *Lilas blanc.* 63m.
148. *Jeune homme et Trottin.* 62m.
149. *La Polka des trottins.* 52m.
150. *La Paimpolaise.* 56m.
151. *C'est une ingénue.* 56m.
152. *Si ça t'va.* 51m.
153. *À la cabane bambou.* 56m.
154. *Questions indiscrètes.* 56m.
155. *La Mattchiche.* 50m.

156. *Ballet d'Hamlet.* Dance. 60m.

Phonoscènes starring Dranem:
157. *Allumeur-Marche.* 45m.
158. *Le Trou de mon quai.* 49m.
159. *Valsons.* 46m.
160. *V'la le rétameur.* 51m.
161. *Les P'tits Pois.* 41m.
162. *L'Enfant du cordonnier.* 45m.
163. *Être légume.* 38m.
164. *La Cucurbitacée.* 44m.
165. *Le Boléro cosmopolite.* 49m.
166. *Le Vrai Jiu-Jitsu.* 48m.
167. *Five o'clock tea.* 57m.

Phonoscènes in a foreign language:
209. *Chez le dentiste.* In German. 49m.
211. *Le Rire du nègre.* In English. 43m.
212. *Cake-walk nègre.* 44m.
214. *Je siffle dessus.* 59m.
216. *Le Boléro.* Dance by Miss Saharet. 69m.
217. *L'Excentrique Anglais.* In English. 55m.
218. *Cavaleria Rusticana.* In Italian. 59m.

219. *La Juive*. In German. 54m.
220. *Il a été une fois*. In German. 53m.
221. *Carmen*. 1 acte, duo in German. 74m.

The sound films that Guy shot in Spain in 1905 were not released until 1906 and appeared in the catalogue as follows:

340. *La Gatita Blanca*. "Machicha". In Spanish. 49m.
341. *La Gatita Blanca*. "Couplet number 2" In Spanish. 46m.
342. *El Husar de la Guardia*. Duet in Spanish. 55m.
343. *Gigantes y Cabezudos*. Duet in Spanish. 64m.
344. *La Viejecita*. Duet in Spanish. 60m.
     El Amigo del Alma. Duet in Spanish. 60m.
347. *El arte de ser bonita*. In Spanish. 45m.
348. *Las Carceleras*. 69m. In Spanish.
349. *La Tempestad*. 60m. In Spanish.
350. *El Husar de la Guardia*. Number 2. In Spanish. 63m.
351. *Nina Pnacha*. Sung by Mme Lina Landi. In Spanish.
352. *El coro frigio*. 81m. In Spanish.

The following late-numbered films, listed as "the red series" have also been attributed to Alice Guy by the Gaumont Co.:

500. *La Dame de pique*.
552. *Eugène, où êtes-vous parti?*
562. *Viens*.

THE AMERICAN FILMS OF ALICE GUY BLACHÉ
FILMOGRAPHY BY ALISON McMAHAN

THIS FILMOGRAPHY USED those by Anthony Slide and Victor Bachy as a starting point. In addition, I have gone back to original sources (especially *The Moving Picture World*, *The Moving Picture News*, *Variety* and others as well as Alice Guy Blaché's papers in the Roberta Blaché Collection). We know that Alice Guy supervised the production of all the Solax films and that she directed the majority of them. She had three directors working under her supervision at Solax: Wilbert Melville, Edward Warren and Edgar Lewis. Herbert Blaché also contributed (for an extended discussion of this, see Chapter 5). When a different director is listed in any documentation, the name of the director is given here. Length is one reel unless stated otherwise.

1910

A Child's Sacrifice	October 21, 1910
The Sergeant's Daughter	October 28, 1910.
A Fateful Gift	November 4, 1910.
A Widow and Her Child	November 11, 1910.
Her Father's Sin	November 18, 1910.
One Touch of Nature	November 25, 1910.
What is to Be, Will Be	December 2, 1910.
Lady Betty's Strategy	December 9, 1910.
Two Suits	December 16, 1910.
The Pawnshop	December 23, 1910.
Mrs Richard Dare	December 30, 1910.

1911

The Nightcap	January 6, 1911. Split reel with
Salmon Fishing in Canada	January 6, 1911. (Commissioned scenic).
The Girl and the Burglar	January 13, 1911.
A Reporter's Romance	January 20, 1911.
His Best Friend	January 27, 1911.
Ring of Love	February 3, 1911.
Mixed Pets	February 10, 1911.
Corinne in Dollyland	February 17, 1911.
Love's Test	February 24, 1911.
A Costly Pledge	March 3, 1911
Out of the Arctic	March 8, 1911.
Put Out	March 10, 1911.
Caribou Hunting	March 10, 1911. (Commissioned scenic).
A Midnight Visitor	March 15, 1911. Split reel with
Highlands of New Brunswick, Canada	March 15, 1911. (Commissioned scenic).
A Hindu Prince	March 17, 1911.
Cupid's Victory	March 22, 1911.
Out of the Depths	March 24, 1911.

A Package of Trouble	March 29, 1911.
She Was Not Afraid	March 29, 1911.
The Mill of the Gods	March 31, 1911.
The Bachelor's Housekeeper	April 2, 1911.(Listed in *Motography*, vol. IX, No. 7 April 1911, p. 240 but not in *Motion Picture News*. Different plot from next film).
A Maid's Revenge	April 5, 1911.
The Rose of the Circus	April 7, 1911.
Tramp Strategy	April 12, 1911. Split reel with
The Scheme That Failed	April 12, 1911.
The Little Flower Girl	April 14, 1911.
The Old Excuse	April 19, 1911.
The Voice of His Conscience	April 21, 1911.
The Count of No Account	April 26, 1911.
Across the Mexican Line	April 28, 1911. Starring Miss Frances Gibson as the Senorita Juanita.
Sensible (also listed as "Susceptible") *Dad*	May 3, 1911.
Their First Baby	May 10, 1911.
The Somnambulist	May 5, 1911.
Nearly a Hero	May 10, 1911. Split reel with
Beneath the Moon	May 10, 1911.
Between Life and Duty (also listed as *Between Life and Death*)	May 12, 1911. (Military)
Deaf and Dumb. Later listed as *His Dumb Wife*	May 17, 1911.
In the Nick of Time	May 19, 1911. (Military)
The Devil in a Tin Cup	May 24, 1911. Split reel with
The House of Peace	May 24, 1911.
An Officer and a Gentleman	May 26, 1911. (Military)
A Marvelous Cow	May 31, 1911.
Never Too Late to Mend	June 2, 1911. (Military)
Bridget the Flirt	June 7, 1911.
A Mexican's Girl's Love	June 9, 1911. (Military)
A Bad Egg	June 14, 1911.
A Daughter of the Navajo	June 16, 1911. (Military)
Cupid and the Comet	June 21, 1911.
Marked for Life	June 23, 1911.
The Fascinating Widow	June 28, 1911. Split reel with
Johnnie Waters the Garden	June 28, 1911.
A Terrible Catastrophe	June 28, 1911.
Greater Love Hath No Man	June 30, 1911. (Military)
Starting Something	July 5, 1911.
The Silent Signal	July 7, 1911.(Military)

Baby's Rattle	July 12, 1911.
That June Bug	July 12, 1911.
The Girl and the Bronco Buster	July 14, 1911.
All Aboard for Reno	July 19, 1911.
Sergeant Dillon's Bravery	July 21, 1911. (Military)
The Double Elopement	July 26, 1911.
Outwitted by Horse and Lariat	July 28, 1911.
When Reuben Came to Town	August 2, 1911.
The Mascot of Troop "C"	August 4, 1911. Advertised as the "First of the 15th U.S. Cavalry Pictures Taken at Fort. Meyer, VA." (Solax Ad, *The Moving Picture News*, Vol. IV, No. 29, July 22, 1911, p. 4.) (Military). Directed by Wilbert Melville.
His Wife's Insurance	August 9, 1911. Split reel with
A Bum and a Bomb	August 9, 1911.
An Enlisted Man's Honor	August 11, 1911. (Military) Directed by Wilbert Melville.
Sergeant Mann's Bravery	August 11, 1911. (Military).
The Phony Ring	August 16, 1911.
Let No Man Put Asunder	August 18, 1911.
A Gay Bachelor	August 23, 1911.
The Stampede	August 25, 1911. (Military) Directed by Wilbert Melville.
The Patched Shoe	August 30, 1911. (Military)
The Hold-Up	September 1, 1911.
Hector's Inheritance	September 6, 1911.
The Best Policy	September 8, 1911.
Her Uncle's Will	September 13, 1911.
The Altered Message	September 15, 1911. (Military, filmed at Fort Meyer)
Oh! You Stenographer!	September 20, 1911.
Nellie's Soldier	September 22, 1911. (Military)
How Hopkins Raised the Rent	September 27, 1911.
An Italian's Gratitude	September 29, 1911.
A Breezy Morning	October 4, 1911.
His Sister's Sweetheart	October 6, 1911. (Military).
He Was a Millionaire	October 11, 1911.
His Mother's Hymn	October 13, 1911.
A Corner in Criminals	October 18, 1911. Split reel with
A Lover's Ruse	October 18, 1911.
His Better Self	October 20, 1911. (Military filmed at Ft. Meyer).
Percy and His Squaw	October 25, 1911.
For Big Brother's Sake	October 27, 1911.
Following Cousin's Footsteps	November 1, 1911.

A Heroine of the Revolution	November 3, 1911. (Military)
Naval Review	Special Release advertised on November 4, 1911.
An Interrupted Elopement	November 8, 1911.
Baby Needs Medicine	November 8, 1911
Grandmother Love	November 10, 1911.
Only a Squaw	November 17, 1911.
Husbands Wanted	November 22, 1911.
The Will of Providence	November 24, 1911.
A Troublesome Picture	November 29, 1911. Split reel with
Life on Board a Battleship (also advertised as *Fun on board U.S.S. Vermont*)	November 29, 1911.
A Revolutionary Romance	December 1, 1911. (Military).
Baby's Choice	December 6, 1911. Split reel with
The Paper Making Industry	December 6, 1911.
The Little Shoe	December 8, 1911.
The Violin Maker of Nuremberg	December 9, 1911. (Maximized the length limit for a 1-reel production, that is, went to 1,000 feet, as the market for 2 reels was not yet there). Scr, prod. and dir by Alice Blaché ("The Solax Production of the Violin Makers of Nuremberg," *The Moving Picture News*, Vol. IV, No. 48, December 2, 1911, p. 10.). Starred Berkeley Barrington as Gottlieb, Gladden James as Fritz, Blanche Cornwall as Gretzel, and Edgar Lewis as her father.
Fickle Bridget	December 13, 1911.
The Little Kiddie Mine	December 15, 1911.
Love, Whiskers, and Letters	December 20, 1911.
Christmas Presents	(First announced December 24, 1911, then re-announced December 31st, then finally released on January 7, 1912.)
When Marian was Married (also listed as *When Marian was Little*)	December 27, 1911.
The Divided Ring	December 29, 1911.

1912

His Musical Soul	January 3, 1912. Directed by Alice Guy Blaché, used stop-motion animation to make objects move. Starring Lee Beggs.
Our Poor Relations	January 5, 1912.
Economical Brown	January 10, 1912.
Black Sheep	January 12, 1912.
By the Hand of a Child	January 14, 1912.

Parson Sue	January 17, 1912. (First Solax film to star Billy Quirck).
A Man's a Man	January 19, 1912.
The Legend of the Balanced Rock	January 21, 1912.
The Little Soldier	January 24, 1912.
Memories of '49	January 26, 1912.
Frozen on Love's Trail	January 28, 1912.
The Wonderful Oswego Falls	January 31, 1912. (Commissioned scenic).
The Fixer Fixed	January 31, 1912.
Mignon	February 2, 1912. (1,000 ft in length, released as a one-reeler, played in 16 to 18 minutes) Adapted from the opera, staged and directed by Madame Alice Blaché. With Marion Swayne as Mignon, Blanche Cornwall as Filina, Darwin Karr as Guglielino, Gladden James as Laerte, Edgar Lewis as Lothario, Lee Beggs as Giarno, and Billy Quirck as Federico.[1]
The Snowman	February 4, 1912.
A Guilty Conscience	February 7, 1912.
Mrs Cranston's Jewels	February 9, 1912.
Lend Me Your Wife	February 11, 1912.
Bessie's Suitors	February 14, 1912.
A Terrible Lesson	February 16, 1912.
The Wise Witch of Fairyland	February 18, 1912.
Hubby Does the Washing	February 21, 1912.
God Disposes	February 23, 1912.
His Lordship's White Feather	February 25, 1912.
Algie the Miner	February 28, 1912.
Blighted Lives	March 1, 1912.
Sealed Lips	March 6, 1912.
The Animated Bathtub	March 8, 1912. Directed Madame Blaché
The Detective's Dog	March 10, 1912
The Boarding House Heiress	March 13, 1912.
Falling Leaves	March 15,1912. Directed By Madame Alice Blaché[2]
Count Henri, the Hunter	March 20, 1912. Split reel with

1. "Mignon," *The Moving Picture News,* Vol. IV, No. 52, Dec. 30, 1911, p. 23. The Solax Ad in the same issue indicates that "the picture moves with the rhythmic action and inspiring harmony of the opera. Indeed, the production has been so arranged that all the important pieces from the opera may accompany the exhibition."

2. "Falling Leaves," *The Moving Picture World,* Vol. V, No. 14, April 6, 1912, p. 22

The Bachelor's Club	March 20, 1912.
The Child of the Tenements	March 22, 1912.
Billy's Shoes	March 27, 1912.
Handle with Care	March 29, 1912.
The Witch's Necklace	April 3, 1912.
Billy's Troubelsome Grip	April 5, 1912.
The Detective's Dog	April 10, 1912.
Billy's Nurse	April 12, 1912.
Saved by a Cat	April 17, 1912.
Billy, the Detective	April 19, 1912
The Sewer	April 24, 1912. 2 reels. Directed by Edward Warren.[3]
Billy's Insomnia	April 26, 1912.
The Reformation of Mary	May 1, 1912.
A Question of Hair	May 3, 1912.
The Wooing of Alice	May 8, 1912.
Auto-Suggestion	May 10, 1912.
Souls in the Shadow	May 15, 1912.
In the Year 2000	May 17, 1912.
The Glory of Light	May 22, 1912.
The Knight in Armor	May 24, 1912.
A Message from Beyond	May 29, 1912.
Just a Boy	May 31, 1912.
The Old Violin	June 5, 1912.
The Dog-Gone Question	June 7, 1912. Split reel with
Billy Boy	June 7, 1912.
Mickey's Pal	June 12, 1912. Directed by Edward Warren; they burned a car for this film.[4]
The Great Discovery	June 14, 1912.
Four Friends	June 19, 1912.
Indian Summer	June 21, 1912.
Planting Time	June 26, 1912. Split reel with
Love's Railroad	June 26, 1912.
The Call of the Rose	June 28, 1912.
Father and the Boys	July 3, 1912.
Between Two Fires	July 5, 1912.
Winsome but Wise	July 10, 1912.
Fra Diavolo	July 12, 1912. 3 reels. Directed and screenplay by Alice Guy Blaché, based on the opera by d'Aubert, starring Billy Quirck, George Paxton, Fanny Simpson, Darwin Karr, and Blanche Cornwall.

3. *The Moving Picture World*, Vol. XVI, No. 11 June 14, 1913.

4. "Solax Burns Auto for Realism," *The Moving Picture World*, Vol. V, No. 20, May 18, 1912, p. 29.

Hotel Honeymoon	July 12, 1912.
Slippery Jim	July 17, 1912.
The Four Flush Actor	July 19, 1912.
Broken Oaths	July 24, 1912.
The Requital	July 26, 1912.
Bottles	July 31, 1912. Split reel with
Imagination	July 31, 1912
Buddy and His Dog	August 3, 1912.
Two Little Rangers	August 7, 1912.
The Pink Garters	August 9, 1912.
The Blood Stain	August 14, 1912.
The Strike	August 16, 1912.
His Double	August 28, 1912.
The Equine Spy	August 23, 1912. 2 reels. Directed by Edward Warren.
Phantom Paradise	August 28, 1912.
Playing Trumps	August 30, 1912.
The Fight in the Dark	September 4, 1912.
Open to Proposals	September 6, 1912.
Treasures on the Wing	September 11, 1912.
The Soul of the Violin	September 13, 1912.
The Spry Spinsters	September 18, 1912.
The Life of a Rose	September 20, 1912.
The Love of the Flag	September 25, 1912.
The Fugitive	September 27, 1912.
Si's Surprise Party	October 2, 1912.
The Report from Eden	October 4, 1912.
Riding Feats of the 15th Cavalry	October 4, 1912. (Military)
Dublin Dan	August or October 9, 1912. 3 reels. Directed by Edward Warren, or possibly Herbert Blaché (see discussion in Chapter 5).
Canned Harmony	October 9, 1912.
A Fool and His Money	October 11, 1912.
The Gold Brick	October 16, 1912.
The Maverick	October 18, 1912.
The High Cost of Living	October 23, 1912.
The Idol Worshipper	October 25, 1912.
Making an American Citizen	October 30, 1912.
At the Phone	November 1, 1912.
The New Love and the Old	November 6, 1912.
Just Hats	November 8, 1912.
The Prodigal Wife	November 13, 1912.
Flesh and Blood	November 15, 1912.
A Comedy of Errors	November 20, 1912.

The Power of Money	November 22, 1912.
The Paralytic	November 27, 1912.
The Jenkins-Perkins War	November 29, 1912.
The Raffle	December 4, 1912.
The Face at the Window	December 6, 1912.
The Hater of Women	December 11, 1912.
The Girl in the Armchair	December 13, 1912.
Hearts Unkown	December 18, 1912.
Five Evenings	December 20, 1912.
The Finger Prints	December 25, 1912.
The Woman Behind the Man	December 27, 1912.

1913

Cousins of Sherlock Holmes	January 1, 1913.
Canine Rivals	January 3, 1913.
A Million Dollars	January 8, 1913.
Beasts of the Jungle	January 11, 1913. 3 reels. Directed by Edward Warren.[5]
The Mutiny of Mr. Henpeck	January 10, 1913.
Mother and Daughter	January 15, 1913.
The Quarrellers	January 17, 1913.
The Coming of Sunbeam	January 22, 1913.
The Roads That Lead Home	January 24, 1913.
The Wrong Box	January 29, 1913.
The Scheming Woman	January 31, 1913.
Overcoats	February 5, 1913.
The Monkey Accomplice	February 7, 1913.
The Eyes of Satan	February 12, 1913.
The Thief	February 14, 1913.
Burstop Holmes, Detective	February 19, 1913.
Till the Day Breaks	February 21, 1913.
The Veteran's Mascot	February 26, 1913
The Bashful Boy	Feburary 28, 1913.
Dick Whittington and His Cat	March 1, 1913. 3 reels. Directed by Alice Guy Blaché
Napoleon	March 5, 1913.
The Kiss of Judas	March 7, 1913
What Happened to Henderson	March 12, 1913.

5. See footnote 22.

The Plan of the House	March 14, 1913.
In the Wrong Flat	March 19, 1913.
The Way of the Transgressor	March 21, 1913.
Burstop Holmes' Murder Case	March 26, 1913.
The Climax	March 28, 1913.
The Bachelor's Houskeeper	April 2, 1913.
The Ogres	April 4, 1913.
The Lady Doctor	April 9, 1913.
His Son-in-Law	April 11, 1913.
The Mystery of the Lost Cat	April 16, 1913. (A Burstop Homes Burlesque— comic character played by Billy Quirck).
Where Love Dwells	April 18, 1913.
His Wife's Affinity	April 23, 1913.
A Severe Test	April 25, 1913.
The Silver Cross	April 30, 1913.
A House Divided	May 2, 1913.
The Case of the Missing Girl	May 7, 1913.
The Past Forgiven	May 9, 1913.
Dad's Orders	May 14, 1913.
The Man in the Sick Room	May 16, 1913.
Kelly from the Emerald Isle	May 17, 1913. 3 reels. Directed by Edward Warren.
The Amateur Highwayman	May 21, 1913.
The Man who Failed	May 23, 1913.
The Henpecked Burglar	May 28, 1913.
The King's Messenger	May 30, 1913.
The Hopes of Belinda	June 4, 1913
Blood and Water	June 4, 1913. 2 reels
Gregory's Shadow	June 6, 1913.
Matrimony's Speed Limit	June 11, 1913.
Her Mother's Picture	June 13, 1913.
Romeo In Pajamas	June 18, 1913.
Strangers from Nowhere	June 20, 1013.
The Merry Widow	June 25, 1913. Split reel with
The Dynamited Dog	June 25, 1913.
The Message to Heaven	June 27, 1913.
An Unexpected Meeting	July 2, 1913.
True Hearts	July 4, 1913.
The Flea Circus	July 9, 1913.
As the Bell Rings	July 11, 1913.

Cooking for Trouble	July 16, 1913.
Brennan of the Moor	August. 3 reels. Directed by Edward Warren, or possibly by Herbert Blaché (see discussion in Chapter 5).
The Intruder	July 18, 1913.
That Dog	July 23, 1913.
As Ye Sow	July 25, 1913.
The Coat that Came Back	July 30, 1913.
When the Tide Turns	August 1, 1913.
The Heavenly Widow	August 6, 1913
Falsely Accused	August 8, 1913.
Four Fools and A Maid	August 13, 1913.
A Drop of Blood	August 15, 1913.
The Pit and the Pendulum	August 18, 1913. 3 reels. Directed By Alice Guy
The Smuggler's Child	August 22, 1913.
A Terrible Night	August 27, 1913.
A Child's Intuition	August 29, 1913.
A Fight for Millions	September, 1913, 4 reels. Directed Herbert Blaché.
Men and Muslin	September 3, 1913.
Retribution	September 5, 1913.
Dooley and His Dog	September 10, 1913.
Gratitude	September 12, 1913.
Invisible Ink	September 17, 1913.
Western Love	September 19, 1913.
The Quality of Mercy	September 24, 1913.
The Soul of Man	September 24, 1913.
A Prisoner in the Harem	October 1913, Herbert Blaché.
Tale of a Cat	October 1, 1913.
The Lame Man	October 3, 1913.
Blood and Water	October 4, 1913. 2 reels.
The Little Hunchback	October 8, 1913.
Handcuffed for Life	October 10, 1913.
Ish Ga Bibble	October 15, 1913.
Fisherman's Luck	October 17, 1913.

The Rogues of Paris. October 20, 1913. 4 reels. Produced and directed by Alice Guy Blaché. Starring Claire Whitney. Filmed at Lake Hopatong and at a castle on the Russell Sage Estate.[6]

Shadows of the Moulin Rouge. December 26, 1913. 4 reels. Written and directed by Alice Guy Blaché.

6. See notice in *Moving Picture World*, September 20, 1913 and Solax Ad on Nov. 1, 1913.

The Star of India. Blaché Features, Inc. Released November 17, 1913. 4 reels. Although usually credited to Alice Guy Blaché, this film appears to have been directed by Herbert Blaché. (Slide)

The Fortune Hunters. Blaché Features, Inc. Released December 15, 1913. 4 reels. Although usually credited to Alice Guy Blaché, this film appears to have been directed by Herbert Blaché. (Slide)

1914

Beneath the Czar. Solax. Released February 1914. 4 reels. Direction and Screenplay: Alice Guy Blaché. Starring Claire Whitney and Fraunie Fraunholz.

The Dream Woman. Blaché Features, Inc./Box Office Attraction Film Rental Company. Released March 1914. 4 reels. Direction and Screenplay: Alice Guy Blaché, based on the novel by Wilkie Collins. With Claire Whitney and Fraunie Fraunholz.

The Prisoner in the Harem. Blaché Features, Inc./Box Office Attraction Film Rental Company. Released October 1913. 4 reels. Directed by Herbert Blaché. Starring Paul Bourgeois, Countess de Marstini, Darwin Karr and Fraunie Fraunholz.

The Monster and the Girl. Solax. Released March 25, 1914. 4 reels. Directed By Alice Guy Blaché, starring Vinnie Burns, Joseph Levering and Fraunie Fraunholz.

The Million Dollar Robbery. Solax/Blaché Features, Inc. Released May 1914. 4 reels. With Claire Whitney, Vinnie Burns, Fraunie Fraunholz, and James O'Neill.

The Woman of Mystery. Blaché Features, Inc. Released May 13, 1914. 4 reels. Screenplay and directed by Alice Guy Blaché. With Vinnie Burns, Claire Whitney and Fraunie Fraunholz.

The Lure. Blaché Features, Inc. /World Film Corporation. Released August 24, 1914. 6 reels. Screenplay: Alice Guy Blaché, based on the play by George Scarborough, directed by Alice Guy Blaché. Starring Bernard Daly, Kirah Markham, Lucia More, Lola May, Claire Whitney, Fraunie Fraunholz, James O'Neil, and Wallace Scott.

The Ragged Earl. Popular Plays and Players/ALCO, Released September 1914, 5 reels. Co-produced by Alice Guy Blaché and Herbert Blaché directed Lloyd B. Carleton, starring Andrew Mack, William Conklin, Ormi Hawley, Eleanor Dunn, and Edward J. Pell.

The Tigress. Popular Plays and Players/Alco. Released December 7, 1914. 4 reels. Directed by Alice Guy Blaché, screenplay: Aaron Hoffman, starring Olga Petrova.

1915

The Heart of a Painted Woman. Popular Plays and Players/Metro Film Corporation. Released April 19, 1915. 5 reels. Screenplay: Aaron Hoffman. Directed by Alice Guy Blaché. Photography: Alfred Ortlieb. Starring Olga Petrova.

The Shooting of Dan McGrew. Popular Plays and Players/Metro Film Corporation. Released May 2, 1915. 5 reels. Co-produced by Alice Guy Blaché and Herbert Blaché, directed by Herbert Blaché, based on Robert W. Service's poem of the same title, starring Edmund Breese, Katheryn Adams, Audrine Stark, Betty Riggs, Wallace Stopp, and William A. Morse.

The Vampire. Popular Plays and Players/Metro Film Corporation. Released August 9, 1915. 5 reels. Screenplay: Aaron Hoffman, based on the play by Edgar Allan Woolf and George Sylvester Viereck. With Olga Petrova, Vernon Steele, William A. Morse, and Wallace Scott.

The Song of the Wage Slave. Popular Plays and Players/Metro Film Corporation. Released October 4, 1915. 5 reels. Co-produced by Alice Guy Blaché and Herbert Blaché, directed by Herbert Blaché. Screenplay by Herbert Blaché and Aaron Hoffman based on the poem by Robert W. Service. Starring Edmund Breese, Helen Martin, I. Byrnes, Pranio Fromholz, Albert Broom, George Macintyre, Wallace Scott, Mabel Wright, claire Hillier, Kitty Helenert, and William Morse.

My Madonna. Popular Plays and Players/Metro Film Corporation. Released October 25, 1915. 5 reels. Screenplay: Aaron Hoffman, based on the poem in "The Spell of the Yukon," by Robert W. Service. Directed by Alice Guy Blaché. Photography: John William Boyle. Starring Olga Petrova, Guy Coombs, Evelyn Dumo, Albert Howson.

Barbara Frietchie. Popular Plays and Players/Metro Film Corporation. Released November 24, 1915. 5 reels. Co-produced with Alice Guy Blaché and directed by Herbert Blaché. Based on poem by Whittier and stageplay by Clyde Fitch. Starring Mary Miles Minter, Mrs. Thomas W. Whiffen, Guy Coombs, Fraunie Fraunholz, Louis Sealy, Frederick Heck, Wallace Scott, Ann Q. Nilsson, Myra Brooks, Charles Hartley, William A. Morse, and Jack Burns.

1916

What Will People Say? Popular Plays and Players/Metro Film Corporation. Released January 3, 1916. 5 reels. Screenplay: Aaron Hoffman, based on the play by Rupert Hughes. Directed by Alice Guy Blaché. Starring Olga Petrova, Fraunie Fraunholz, Fritz de Lint, Charles Dugan, John Dudley, Zadee Burbank, Marilyn Reid, William Morse, Elenore Sutter, and Jean Thomas.

The Soul Market. Popular Plays and Players/Metro Film Corporation, January 1916, 5 reels. Co-produced by Alice Guy Blaché and Herbert Blaché, directed Francis J. Grandon, , screenplay by Aaron Hoffman. Starring Olga Petrova.

The Spell of the Yukon. Popular Plays and Players/Metro Film Corporation, January 1916, 5 reels. Co-produced by Alice Guy Blaché and Herbert Blaché, directed Burton L. King, based on the poem of the same name by Robert W. Service, starring Edmund Breese, Arthur Hoops, Christine Mayo, "Billy" Sherwood, Evelyn Brent, Frank McArthur, Joseph S. Chaillee, Jacques Suzanne, Mary Reed, Harry Morevelle, and Baby Volare.

The Lure of a Heart's Desire. Popular Plays and Players/Metro Pictures Corporation, January 17, 1916, 5 reels. Co-produced by Alice Guy Blaché and Herbert Blaché, directed by Francis J. Grandon, starring Edmund Breese, Jeannette Horton, Arthur Hoops, Evelyn Brent, John Mahon.

Playing with Fire. Popular Plays and Players/Metro Film Corporation, April 1916, 5 reels. Co-produced by Alice Guy Blaché and Herbert Blaché, directed by Francis J. Grandon, screenplay by Aaron Hoffman. Starring Olga Petrova, Arthur Hoops, Evelyn Brent, Pierre Le May, and Catherine Calhoun.

The Girl with the Green Eyes. Popular Plays and Players/Pathé. Released May 15, 1916. Directed by Herbert Blaché. Based on the story by Clyde Fitch. Starring Katherine Kaelred, Julian L'Estrange and Edith Lyle.

The Scarlet Woman. Popular Plays and Players/Metro Film Corporation, May 1916, 5 reels. Co-produced by Alice Guy Blaché and Herbert Blaché, directed by Edmund Lawrence, screenplay by Aaron Hoffman. Starring Olga Petrova.

The Eternal Question. Popular Plays and Players/Metro Film Corporation, July 1916, 5 reels. Co-produced by Alice Guy Blaché and Herbert Blaché, directed by Burton L. King under the supervision of Harry Revier (sic), story Aaron Hoffman, screenplay by Burton L. King and Wallace O. Clifton. Starring Olga Petrova, Mahlom Hamilton, Arthur Hoops, Warren Oland, Edward Martindel, Henry Leone, Howard Messimer and Evelyn Dumo.

The Devil at his Elbow. August 1916, 5 reels, directed by Burton L. King. Co-produced by Alice Guy Blaché and Herbert Blaché.

The Weakness of Strength. August 1916, 5 reels, directed by Harry Revier. Co-produced by Alice Guy Blaché and Herbert Blaché.

The Iron Woman. Popular Plays and Players/Metro Film Corporation, October 1916, 6 reels. Co-produced by Alice Guy Blaché and Herbert Blaché, directed by Carl Harbaugh, starring Nance O'Neil, Elnar Linden, Alfred Hickman, Evelyn brent, Vera Sisson, William Postance, and Christine Mayo.

The Ocean Waif. Golden Egle/International Film Service. Released November 2, 1916, 5 reels. Screenplay: Frederick Chapin. Photography: John G. Hass. With Carlyle Blackwell, Doris Kenyon, William Morse, Fraunie Fraunholz, Lynn Donaldson, Augsut Bermeister, and Edgar Norton.

Extravagance. Popular Plays and Players/Metro Film Corporation, November 1916, 5 reels. Co-produced by Alice Guy Blaché and Herbert Blaché, directed by Burton L. King, story by Aaron Hoffman, screenplay by Wallace C. Clifton, photographed by Andre Barletier. Starring Olga Petrova, H. Cooper Cliffe, Mahlon Hamilton, Arthur Hoops, J.W. Hartman, Edward Martindel and Tom Cameron.

The Black Butterfly. Popular Plays and Players/Metro Film Corporation, December 1916, 5 reels. Co-produced by Alice Guy Blaché and Herbert Blaché, directed by Burton L. King, screenplay by L. Case Russell, photography by Andre Barletier. Starring Olga Petrova (playing two roles), Mahlon Hamilton, Anthony Merlo, Count Zewenhesso, Edward Brennan, Violet B. Reed, John Hopkins, Morgan Jones, Norman Kaiser, Roy Pilcher, and Evelyn Dumo.

1917

Bridges Burned. Popular Plays and Players/Metro Film Corporation, January 1917, 5 reels. Co-produced by Alice Guy Blaché and Herbert Blaché. Directed by Perry N. Verkroff, story by Olga Petrova, screenplay by Wallace Clifton, photography by Neil Bergman. Starring Olga Petrova, Mahlon Hamilton, Arthur Hoops, Meury Steuart, Robert Broderick, Mathilde Brandage, Louis Stern, and Thomas Cameron.

The Secret of Eve. Popular Plays and Players/Metro Film Corporation, February 26, 1917, 5 reels. Co-produced by Alice Guy Blaché and Herbert Blaché. Directed by Perry N. Vekroff, story by Aaron Hoffman, screenplay by Wallace Clifton. Starring Olga Petrova in three roles, Arthur Hooper William Hinkley, Edward Roseman, Laurie Mackin, Florence Moore and George Morrell.

The Adventurer. U.S. Amusement Corporation/Art Dramas, Inc. Released February 15, 1917, 5 reels. Directed by Alice Guy Blaché. Screenplay by Harry Chandlee and Lawrence McCloskey, based on the story by Upton Sinclair. With Marion Swayne, Pell Trenton, Charles Halton, Kirke Brown, Ethel Stanard, Yolande Doquette, and Martin Hayden.

The Empress. Popular Plays and Players/Pathé. Relased March 11, 1917, 5 reels. Directed and screenplay by Alice Guy Blaché and Holbrook Blinn, William Morse, and Lynn Donaldson.

A Man and the Woman. U.S. Amusement Corporation/Art Dramas, Inc. Released March 22, 1917, 5 reels. Directed and screenplay by Alice Blaché, based on the novel *Nana*, by Emile Zola. Photography: John G. Hass. With Edith Hallor, Leslie Austen, Krike Brown, H. Bradley Barker, Yolande Douquette, Zadee Burbank, and Lorna Volare.

House of Cards. U.S. Amusement Corporation/Art Dramas, Inc. Released May 31, 1917, 5 reels. Directed and screenplay by Alice Guy Blaché. Starring Catherine Calvert, Frank Mills, James O'Neill and Kittens Reichert as the girl.

When You and I Were Young. Apollo Pictures, Inc., U.S. Amusement Corporation/Art Dramas, Inc. Released August 1917, 5 reels. Based on a story by Frederick Rath. Produced by Harry Raver. Photography: John G. Hass. Starring Alma Hanlon, Harry Benham, Florence Short, Robert Mantell Jr., Louis Thiel, and Al Stearn.

Behind the Mask. U.S. Amusement Corporation/Art Dramas, Inc. Released September 3, 1917, 5 reels. Directed Alice Guy Blaché Screenplay: Charles T. Dazey. Photography: John G. Hass. With Catherine Calvert, Richard Tucker, Kirke Brown, Charles Dungan, Flora Nason, and Charles Holton.

1918

The Great Adventure. Pathé. Released March 10, 1918, 5 reels. Directed by
Alice Guy Blaché. Screenplay: Agnes Christine Johnston, based on a
short story "The Painted Scene" by Henry Kitchell Webster. Photo-
graphy: George K. Hollister and John G. Haas. Starring Bessie Love,
Chester Barnett, Flora Finch, Donald Hall, Florence Short, John W.
Dunn, and Walter Craven.

1919

The Divorcée. Metro Pictures Corporation, January 1919. Directed by
Herbert Blaché under the supervision of Maxwell Karges, assisted by
Alice Guy Blaché. Screenplay by June Mathis and Katharine Kava-
naugh, based on the play *Lady Frederick* by Somerset Maugham.
Starring Ethel Barrymore, E.J. Ratcliff, Naomi Childers, John Gold-
sworthy, Jos Kilgour, and Herbert Blaché.

The Brat. September 14, 1919. Nazimova Productions/Metro Pictures
Corporation. Directed by Herbert Blaché assisted by Alice Guy Blaché,
based on the play by Maud Fulton, starring Alla Nazimova.

1920

Stronger than Death. January 1920. Nazimova Productions/Metro Pictures
Corporation. Herbert Blaché assisted by Alice Guy Blaché. Screenplay
by Charles Bryant, based on the novel *The Hermit Doctor of Gaya* by
I.A.R. Wylie., starring Alla Nazimova, Charles W. French, Charles
Bryant, Margaret McWade, Herbert Pryor, W.H. Orlamond, Millie
Davenport, Bhogwan Singh and Henry Harmon.

Tarnished Reputations. Perret/Pathé. Released March 14, 1920. Producer
and Screenplay: Leonce Perret. Director and co-screenwriter: Alice Guy
Blaché. Photography: Harry Forbes and Alfred Ortlieb. With Dolores
Cassinelli, Albert Roscoe, George Deneubourg, and Ned Burton.

BIBLIOGRAPHY

Abel, Richard, *The Ciné Goes to Town: French Cinema 1896–1914*, Berkeley: University of California Press, 1994.

Abel, Richard, ed., *Silent Film*, New Brunswick, NJ: Rutgers University Press, 1996.

Abel, Richard, *The Red Rooster Scare: Making Cinema American 1900–1910*, 1999.

Acker, Ally, *Reel Women: Pioneers of the Cinema from 1896 to the Present*, New York: Continuum, 1991.

Arnaud, Étienne, *Le Cinéma pour tous*, 1922.

Bachy, Victor, *Alice Guy-Blaché (1873–1968): La Première femme cinéaste du monde*, Perpignan: Institut Jean Vigo, 1993, p. 390.

Barteche, Maurice & Robert Brassilach, *Histoire du cinéma*, Paris: Andre Martel, 1948, p. 21.

Barthes, Roland, *The Pleasure of the Text*, Richard Miller, trans. New York: Hill and Wang, the Noonday Press, 1975.

Beck, Calvin Thomas, *Scream Queens: Heroines of the Horrors*, New York: Collier Books, London: Collier MacMillan Publishers, 1978, pp. 1, 5, 8, 24, 31, 33–40.

Beylie, Claude and Philippe Carrasonne, *Le Cinéma*, Paris: Bordas Spectacle, 1988, pp. 15, 19, 111 (Preface by Daniel Toscan, Postface by Elia Kazan).

Bordwell, David, Kristin Thompson, and Janet Staiger, *The Classical Hollywood Cinema*, New York: Columbia University Press, 1985.

Boussinot, Roger, *L'Encyclopédie du cinéma*, Paris: Bordas, 1980, pp. 584–585.

Bratton, Jacky, Jim Cook, and Christine Gledhill, *Melodrama: Stage, Picture, Screen*, London: British Film Institute, 1994.

Breton, Emile, *Femmes d'images*, Paris: Messidor, 1984, pp. 11–17.

Brownlow, Kevin, *The Parade's Gone By....* Berkeley: University of California Press, 1968.

Burch, Noël, *Life to those Shadows*, translated and edited by Ben Brewster, Berkeley and Los Angeles: University of California Press, 1990, pp. 17, 27, 64, 66, 138, 159 n. 3, 237, 242 n. 2.

Original version:

Burch, Noël, *La Lucarne de l'infini: Naissance du langage cinématographique*, Paris: Nathan, 1991, pp. 23, 31, 67, 69, 136, 141, 226.

Bushnell, Brooks, *Directors and Their Films: A Comprehensive Reference: 1895–1990*, North Carolina: London: Jefferson: McFarland, 1993, pp. 143–144.

Charensol, Georges, *Le Cinéma*, Paris: Larousse, 1986, pp. 78, 333.

Cinema 1900–1906: An Analytical Study, Brussels: FIAF, 1982.

Crafton, Donald, *Emile Cohl, Caricature, and Film*, Princeton: Princeton University Press, 1990.

Deslandes, Jacques & Jacques Richard, *Histoire comparée du cinéma*, Paris: Casterman, 1968, Tome 2, pp. 331–332.

Dixon, Wheeler Winston, *It Looks at You: The Returned Gaze of the Cinema*, Albany: State University of New York Press, 1995.

Doane, Mary Anne, *Femmes fatales: Feminism, Film Theory, Psychoanalysis*, New York: Routledge, 1991.

Elsaesser, Thomas, ed., *Early Cinema: Space, Frame, Narrative*, London: British Film Institute, 1990.

Fernandez Cuenca, Carlos, *Historia del cinema*, Madrid: Afrodisio, 1948, pp. 356–358, 359.

Fielding, Raymond, ed., *A Technological History of Motion Pictures and Television*, Berkeley: University of California Press, 1967.

Filmlexicon degli autori e delle Opere, Rome: Eidzioni de Bianco e Nero, 1958, Tome 1, p. 675.

Ford, Charles, *Femmes cinéastes ou le Triomphe de la volonté*, Paris: Denoël-Gonthier, 1972, pp. 9–23, 25, 28, 87, 101, 129, 240.

Ford, Charles, *Histoire moderne du cinéma*, Alleur: Marabout, 1987, pp. 22–25, 42.

Gabler, Neal, *An Empire of Their Own: How the Jews Invented Hollywood*, New York: Doubleday, 1989.

Garçon, François, *Gaumont: Un siècle de cinéma*, Paris: Gallimard, 1994, pp. 16–17.

Gaumont, Léon, "Historique: Notice sur Les Etablissements Gaumont" in *Etablissements Gaumont (1895–1929)*, Paris, 1924.

Grand dictionnaire illustré du cinéma, Paris: Ed. Atlas, 1985, Tome 2, p. 310 (Bib. André Malraux).

Griffith, Mrs. D.W. (Linda Arvidson), *When the Movies Were Young*, Introduction by Edward Wagenknecht, New York: Dover Publications, Inc., 1969.

Gunning, Tom, *D.W. Griffith and the Origins of the American Narrative Film: The Early Years at the Biograph*, Urbana and Chicago: University of Illinois Press, 1991.

Guy, Alice, *Autobiographie d'une pionnière du cinéma: 1873–1968*, Paris: Denoël-Gonthier, 1976, p. 236.

Harald, José, *Die Enstehung des Tonfilms: Beitrag zu einer Faktenorientierten Mediengeschichteschreibung*, Freiburg/München: Verlagkare Alber, 1984.

Hayward, Susan, *French National Cinema*, London: Routledge, 1993.

Heck-Rabi, Louise, *Women Filmmakers: A Critical Reception*, Metuchen, N.J. & London: The Scarecrow Press, Inc., 1984.

Heck-Rabi, Louise, "Alice Guy" in the *MacMillan Dictionary: Directors*, S.1: MacMillan Publications, 1984, Vol. 2, pp. 239–241.

Hugues, Philippe d' et Dominique Muller, *Gaumont: 90 ans de cinéma*, Paris: Ramsay, Cinémathèque Française, 1986, pp. 42–45.

Hugues, Philippe d' et Michel, Marmin, *Le Cinéma français: le muet*, Paris: Ed. Atlas, 1986, pp. 33–34, 48–49, 64, 69–70, 78, 81–82.

Jeanne, René & Charles Ford, *Histoire encyclopédique du cinéma*, Paris: R. Laffont, 1965, Tome 1, pp. 53–54, 76, 113, 141.

Jeanne, René & Charles Ford, *Histoire illustrée du cinéma: le cinéma muet*, Verviers (Belgique): Ed. Gérard (Collection Marabout), 1966, Tome 1, pp. 22–23, 31, 34.

Katz, Ephraim, *The International Film Encyclopedia*, S.l: Papermac, 1979, p. 519.

Kermabon, Jacques, ed., *Pathé: premier empire du cinéma*, Premier Siècle du Cinéma series, Paris: Editions du Centre Pompidou, 1994.

Koszarski, Richard, *Hollywood Directors: 1914–1940*, London: New York: Oxford University Press, 1976, pp. 7–11, 42.

Kuhn, Annette, *The Power of the Image: Essays on Representation and Sexuality*, New York: Routledge, 1985.

Lacassin, Francis, *Pour une contre-histoire du cinéma*, Paris: Union Générale d'Éditions, 1972, pp. 11–22.

Le Cinéma: Grande histoire illustrée du 7e art, Paris: Ed. Atlas, 1984, Tome 9, pp. 2296–2297.

Leyda, Jay and Charles Musser, *Before Hollywood: Turn-of-the-Century Film from American Archives*, New York: American Federation of Arts, 1986.

Lumière, Auguste and Louis, *Correspondances 1890–1953*, Librairie du Premier Siècle du Cinéma Series, Paris: Cahiers du Cinéma, 1994.

MacCann, Richard Dyer, *The First Filmmakers*, American Movies: The First Thirty Years, Metuchen, N.J.: The ScareCrow Press, Iowa City, Iowa: Image & Idea, Inc., 1989.

Marchessault, Josette, *Mon héroïne*, les lundis de l'histoire des femmes: an 1. Conférence du théâtre expérimental de femmes, Montreal: Ed. du Remue-Ménage, 1981, Texte par Josette Marchessault sur Alice Guy, pp. 149–187.

Marey, Étienne-Jules, *Du mouvement dans les fonctions de la vie*, Paris, 1868.

Mast, Gerald, *A Short History of the Movies 3rd Edition*, Indianapolis: Bobbs-Merrill Educational Publishing, 1981 (1971).

Mitry, Jean, *Filmographie universelle: 1895–1914*, Paris: Ed. Universitaires, 1969, Tome 1, p. 155.

Mitry, Jean, *Filmographie Universelle: 1895–1914*, Paris: Ed. Universitaires, 1969, Tome 2.

Moreau, Frédérique and Henri Bousquet, *Les Premiers ans du cinéma français*, Perpignan: Institut Jean Vigo, 1985.

Musser, Charles, *Before the Nickelodeon: Edwin S. Porter and the Edison Manufacturing Company*, Berkeley: University of California Press, 1991.

Passek, Jean-Louis, *Dictionnaire du cinéma*, Paris: Librairie Larousse, 1986, pp. 303–304.

Passek, Jean-Louis, assisté de Michel Ciment, Claude-Michel Cluny, and Jean-Pierre Frouard, *Dictionnaire du cinéma français*, Paris: Larousse, 1987, p. 187.

Pearson, Roberta, *Eloquent Gestures: The Transformation of Performance Style in the Griffith Biograph Films*, Berkeley/Los Angeles/Oxford: University of California Press, 1992.

Petrova, Olga, *Butter with my Bread: The Memoirs of Olga Petrova*, Camden, N.J.: Bobbs-Merrill, 1942.

Pinel, Vincent, *Un siècle de cinéma*, Paris: Bordas, 1994, pp. 21, 39, 40, 53, 323.

Quart, Barbara Koenig, *Women Directors: The Emergence of a New Cinema*, New York, Wesport CT., London: Praeger, 1988.

Rittaud-Hutinet, Jacques, *Les Frères Lumière: L'Invention du cinéma*, Flammarion, 1995, p. 372.

Roud, Richard, *Cinema: A Critical Dictionary, The Major Filmmakers*, Vol. I Aldrich to King, Vol. II Kinugasa to Zanussi, New York: Viking Press, 1980.

Sadoul, Georges, *Histoire générale du cinéma: L'invention du cinéma 1832–1897*, Paris: Éditions Denoël, 1948.

Sadoul, Georges, *Histoire du cinéma mondial: des origines à nos jours*, Paris: Flammarion, 1972 (9ᵉ éd. rev. et Augmentee), p. 59.

Sadoul, Georges, *Histoire générale du cinéma*, Paris: Denoël, 1978, Tome 2, pp. 74, 78–79, 201, 291–293, 348, 352, 395.

Sadoul, Georges, Remise à jour par Émile Breton et Michel Marie en 1981, *Dictionnaire des cinéastes*, Paris: Microcosme/Éd. du Seuil, 1982, p. 126.

Sadoul, Georges, *Lumière et Méliès*, Paris: Lherminier, 1985.

Sklar, Robert, *Film: An International History of the Medium*, New York: Harry N. Abrams, Inc., 1993.

Slide, Anthony, *Early Women Directors: Their Role in the Development of the Silent Cinéma*, New York: Barnes-Yoseloff, 1977, pp. 15–33.

Slide, Anthony, ed., *The Memoirs of Alice Guy Blaché*, transl. Roberta & Simone Blaché, Filmmakers, No. 12, Metuchen, N.J.: The Scarecrow Press, Inc., 1986.

Slide, Anthony, *The American Film Industry: A Historical Dictionary*, New York: Limelight Editions, 1990.

Smith, Sharon, *Women Who Make Movies*, Cinema Studies Series, New York: Hopkinson and Blake, 1975, pp. 2–10.

Spehr, Paul C., *The Movies Begin: Making Movies in New Jersey, 1887–1920*, Newark, N.J.: The Newark Museum in cooperation with Morgan and Morgan, Inc., 1977.

Staiger, Janet, *Bad Women: Regulating Sexuality in Early American Cinema*, Minneapolis: University of Minnesota Press, 1995, p. 116.

Tulard, Jean, *Dictionnaire du cinéma: les réalisateurs*, Paris: R. Laffont, 1992.

Vincendeau, Ginette, ed., *Encyclopedia of European Cinema*, New York: Facts on File, Inc., 1995.

Williams, Alan, *Republic of Images: a History of French Filmmaking*, Cambridge: London: Harvard University Press, 1992, pp. 54, 57, 67, 396.

Women in Film: A Bibliography, Women in the Arts, Albany Area NOW, Box 6064, Albany, NY, 11568.

Periodicals in the Bifi Collection

"Alice Guy-Blaché fut en France et aux États-Unis la première femme metteur-sen-scène de cinéma" In: *Films et Documents*, number 119, août 1957.

"Alice Guy" In: *Télérama*, number 702, 30 juin, 1963.

"Alice Guy" In: Fiches de Monsieur Cinéma, 1982.

"Alice Guy Premièr(e) Cinéaste" In: *Le Monde Arts et Spectacles*, 15 décembre, 1994, p. 111.

"Autobiographie d'une pionnière du cinéma: Alice Guy" In: *France Soir*, 29 juin, 1976.

Blaché, Alice, "Woman's Place in Photoplay Production," In: *The Moving Picture World*, Vol. XXI, No. 2, July 11, 1914, p. 195.

Brady, David, Untitled, In: The New York Dramatic Mirror, 1912.

Bulletin de l'Association française des ingénieurs et techniciens de cinéma, 6ᵉ année, 1952: "Alice Guy."

Chanot, Régine & Paul Green, Entretien avec Jackie Buet, "Un Regard de femme" sur le festival international de films de femmes. In: *Villages*, March 1994, p. 21.

Chanot, Régine, "16ᵉ festival du film de femmes: quelques impressions," In: *Villages*, Mars 1994, p. 27.

Chanot, Régine, "À l'aube naissante du cinéma, une Pionnière."

Chanot, Régine, "Créteil, présentation du 16ᵉ éme festival international de films de femmes: regards doux-amers sur le cinéma féminin," In: *Villages*, février 1994, p. 18.

Chardère, Bernard, *Lumières sur Lumière,* Lyon: Institut Lumière Presses Universitaires de Lyon, 1987.

"Demain, à 20 heures, sur France culture, qui est Alice Guy," In: *Le Figaro*, 1ᵉ juillet, 1975.

Deslandes, Jacques, "Sur Alice Guy: polémique," In: *Ecran*, no. 50, 15 septembre, 1976, p. 6.

Elisabeth, Jenny, "Pionnière d'hier," In: Programme du 16ᵉ festival international de films de femmes de Créteil du 18–27 mars, 1994, pp. 75, 86.

"Elle fut la seule metteur-en-scène de la Belle-Époque. Pionnière du Cinéma," In: *L'Aurore*, 11 juin, 1976.

"Elle fut pendant 17 ans la seule femme réalisatrice et dirigea plus de 500 films: Alice Guy, la première oubliée du cinéma," In: *Le Figaro*, 11 mai, 1976.

Ford, Charles, "The First Female Producer," In: *Films in Review*, March 1964, pp. 129–145.

FrauenFilmFest, Köln, 6–11 Juli, 1988, Cologne: Feminale'88, 1988, pp. 155–160.

French, Harriet, "Memories of Early Movie Days: First Woman Director Lives Quietly in D.C.," In: *The Sunday Star*, 26 June, 1955.

"Gaumont de A" à "Z et en bobines" In: *Le Figaroscope*, 8 au 24 janvier, 1995, p. 5.

Gaumont, Léon, "Alice Guy. Première femme 'metteur-en-scène'," In: *Dimanche Matin*, 11 juillet, 1917.

Gaumont, Léon, "Quelques souvenirs sur Madame Alice Guy Blaché, la première femme 'metteur-en-scène'," In: *La Technique cinématographique*, sans date, pp. 66–68.

Gaumont, Louis, "Quelques souvenirs sur Madame Alice Guy-Blaché," In: *Bulletin de l'Association française des ingénieurs et techniciens du cinéma*, n° Hors-Série, 8 décembre, 1954, pp. 23–28.

Guy, Alice, sans titre, In: *Moving Picture World*, 11 juillet, 1914.

"Here is a woman who works with husband in the same business but spurns his help," In: *Evening Sun*, 8 October, 1915.

Heymann, Danièle, "Léon Gaumont, le pionnier: le cinéma célébrera bientôt ses cent ans: avant-première à New-York," In: *Le Monde*, 26 janvier, 1994, p. 1.

"Il y a soixante ans, le cinéma comptait déjà une femme metteur-en-scène," In: *La Presse*, 11 juin 1957.

Jeanne, René, "Soixante ans après ses débuts, la doyenne des auteurs de films évoque la préhistoire du cinéma," In: *Les Nouvelles littéraires*, 24 janvier, 1957.

"La Naissance du cinéma par Alice Guy," In: *La Revue du cinéma/Image et son*, no. 283, avril 1974, pp. 42–53.

Lacassin, Francis, "Alice Guy, la première femme réalisatrice au monde," In: *Cinéma*, number 152, janvier 1971, pp. 47–56.

Lacassin, Francis, "Out of Oblivion: Alice Guy Blaché," In: *Sight and Sound*, Summer, 1971, pp. 151–154.

Lacassin, Francis, Sans titre, In: *Cinéma 71*, number 152, janvier 1971, pp. 47–56.

"Le Paléocinéma féminin: le premier carré (Alice Guy, Musidora, Germaine Dulac, Jacqueline Audry)," In: *Cinémaction*, no. 9, automne 1979, p. 44.

Lebesque, Morran, "Le Troisième Œil," In: *L'express*, 4 juillet, 1963.

"Les Cent Ans de la marguerite: le style Gaumont. De Léon Gaumont à Léon," In: *Le Film français*, no. 2533, 18 novembre, 1994, pp. 32–33.

Levine, H.Z., "Madame Alice Guy," In: *Photoplay*, March 1972.

Loiseau, Jean-Claude, "Alice Guy, la première cinéaste," In: *L'Express*, 24 mai, 1976.

"Mademoiselle Alice et les méfaits d'une tête de veau," In: Sans titre, 29 juin, 1963.

Martin-Chauffier, Gilles, "Les femmes de notre siècle: Alice Guy," In: *Paris Match*, 4 novembre, 1983, pp. 158–163.

Mérigeau, Pascal, Sans titre, In: *Le Monde*, janvier 1995.

Mitry, Jean, "À propos d'Alice Guy," In: *Écran*, no. 49, 15 juillet, 1976, p. 5.

Mitry, Jean, "Polémique sur Alice Guy (suite)," In: *Écran*, no. 55, 15 février, 1977, p. 7.

"Première femme metteur en scène de cinéma, Madame Alice Guy-Blaché vient de fêter son quatre-vingt cinquième anniversaire," In: *Franc-Tireur*, 14 juin, 1957.

Professor William, Sans titre, In: *The New York Times*, January 1994.

Roche, France, "Le Cinéma, un travail de jeune fille!" In: *Le Journal du dimanche*, 24 mars, 1957.

Sans auteur, Sans Titre, In: *Films in Review*, mars 1964, pp. 224–265.

Sans auteur, Sans Titre, In: *Films in Review*, avril 1964, pp. 224–265.

Sans auteur, Sans titre, In: *The New York Dramatic Mirror*, 6 November, 1912.

Sans auteur, Sans titre, In: *The Velvet Light Trap*, number 6, sans date.

Sans nom, Sans titre, In: *Harvey Gates*, 1912.

Sans nom, Sans titre, In: *The New York Tribune*, 1913.

Sans nom, Sans titre, In: *Toledo News*, 1913.

Santacreu, Elisabeth, "Au nom de la marguerite," In: *Le Parisien*, 18 janvier, 1995.

Seydoux, Nicolas, Sans titre, In: *La Presse de Montréal*, 1994.

Silbermann, S., "Alice Guy (85 ans, 60 ans de cinéma) reçoit la légion d'honneur," In: *Paris Journal*, 22 décembre, 1958.

Tinazzi, Noël, "La Gaumont se montre à la Cinémathèque," In: *La Tribune Desfossés*, 20 janvier, 1995.

Toulet, Emmanuelle, en collaboration avec Philippe Coutant, "Entretien avec Nicolas Seydoux, PDG de Gaumont," In: *La Lettre du 1er siècle*, no. 3, janvier 1994.

Other Periodicals

Primary Sources:
The Moving Picture World, 1908–1917.
The Moving Picture News, 1908–1912.
Photoplay
Motion Picture Story
Billboard
New York Dramatic Mirror
Motography

Anonymous: "Wie singende Bilder (Tonbilder) entstehen," in *Der Kinematograph*, No. 65, March 25, 1908. Reprinted in *Kintop, Oskar Messter: Filmpionnier der Kaiserzeit*, pp. 50–52.

Anonymous: "The Gaumont 'Chronophone': New Talking-Moving Picture Machine Now Ready with Supply of Films and Records," *The New York Dramatic Mirror*, September 5, 1908.

Anonymous: "Gaumont Talking Pictures," *The New York Dramatic Mirror*, October 31, 1908.

Bachy, Victor, "Alice Guy, les raisons d'un effacement," in *Les Premières années du cinéma français*, Actes du Ve Colloque International de l'Institut Jean Vigo, Paris, 1985.

Blaché, A.G., "Letter," *Films in Review*, Vol. 15, No. 5, May 1964, p. 317.

Ciezar, Valeria, "Bibliothèque Nationale: Les Scénarios Gaumont," in *Cinémathèque: revue semestrielle d'esthétique et d'histoire du cinéma*, Paris: Cinémathèque Française & Musée du Cinéma, No. 2, November 1992, pp. 130–132.

Interview with Alice Guy in *The New Jersey Star*, August 8, 1914.

Dixon, Wheeler Winston, "Alice Guy: Forgotten Pioneer of the Narrative Cinema," *New Orleans Review*, Vol. 19, Nos. 3 and 4, Fall-Winter 1992.

Ford, C., "The First Female Producer," *Films in Review*, Vol. 15, No. 3, May 1964, p. 141.

Klepp, Hans, "Lebende Photographieen," in *Die Technik*, 1987, Heft 1, S.1.

Letter from Alice Guy to the Marquis de Baroncelli, May 15, 1906, published in *Archives*, No. 56, November 1993, Perpignan: Institut Jean Vigo, p. 4.

Lacassin, F., "Out of Oblivion," *Sight and Sound*, Vol. 40, No. 3, Summer 1971, pp. 151–154. Taken from his book, *Le Septième Art au féminin: Les femmes et la mise-en-scène de 1895 à 1930*.

L.D., "L'Excursion de Meulan," in *La France automobile: Organie de l'auto-mobilisme et des industries qui s'y rattachent,* No. 17, Samedi 23 mai 1896, p. 130.

Lefebvre, Thierry, "Voyage autour d'une serrure, des clefs pour comprendre," in André Gaudreault, ed., *Ce que je vois de mon ciné....* Quebec: Meridiens Klincksieck, 1988, pp. 57–58.

Loiperdinger, Martin, "Szenen des früen Kinos," *Kintop* Schriften 2, *Oskar Messter: Filmpionier der Kaiserzeit,* 1994.

Mannoni, Laurent, "Une féerie de 1896: *La Biche au bois,*" *Cinémathèque,* No. 10, automne 1996.

Musser, Charles, "Pre-Classical American Cinema: Its Changing Modes of Film Production," in *Silent Film,* edited by Richard Abel, New Brunswick, NJ: Rutgers University Press, 1996, pp. 85–108. The article was originally printed in *Persistence of Vision,* No. 9, New York: The City University of New York, 1991.

Peary, G., "Czarina of the Silent Screen," *The Velvet Light Trap,* Vol. 6, No. 3, Fall 1972.

Petrova, Olga, "A Remembrance," Appendix A in *The Memoirs of Alice Guy Blaché,* edited by Anthony Slide, pp. 102–103.

Robinson, David, "The Year 1913," *Griffithiana,* No. 50, May 1994.

Smith, F.L., "Alice Guy Blaché," *Films in Review,* Vol. 15, No. 3, April 1964, p. 254. Letter.

Smith, Sharon, "Women Who Make Movies," *Women and Film,* Vol. 1, Nos. 3–4, 1973, p. 13. A condensed version of Smith's later book of the same title.

Tzvetan Todorov, "The Fantastic in Fiction," *Twentieth Century Studies,* No. 3, 1970, pp. 76–92.

Other Media
Audio Documents

Émission radio animée par Nicole Bernheim et Claire Clouzot.
Invités: Louise Lagrange, Henri Langlois, Charles Ford, Pierre Lherminier, Liliane de Kermadec et Francis Lacassin.

Photographs at the Musée Gaumont

Portraits of Alice Guy
* Alice Guy Blaché, aged (taken around 1955–1956) B&W
* Alice Guy (young) B&W
* Alice Guy directing in the U.S. B&W
* Alice Guy (young) B&W
* Alice Guy (young) B&W
* Alice Guy (young) B&W
* Alice Guy directing in Fort Lee, NJ (probably *My Madonna* in 1915) B&W
* Alice Guy directing a phonoscène (*Mignon,* 1906) B&W

Film Stills
Negative of a postcard of *L'Arroseur arrosé* (Gaumont version)
From *La Vie du Christ,* Negatives, B&W
* Le Sommeil de Jésus (Baby Jesus Naps)
* Jésus prêchant L'Évangile (Jesus Preaches the Gospel)
* Sainte Véronique
* Les Rameaux (Palm Sunday)

- Le Crucifiement (The Crucifixion)
- La Dernière cène (The Last Supper)
- Au jardin des oliviers (In the Garden of Olives)
- La Trahison de Judas (Judas' Betrayal)
- La Flagellation de Jésus (The Scourging of Jesus)
  Color Slides of postcards from *La Vie du Christ*
- Jésus prêchant L'Évangile (Jesus Preaches the Gospel)
- Sainte Véronique
- Les Rameaux (Palm Sunday)
- Le Crucifiement (The Crucifixion)
- La Dernière cène (The Last Supper)
- Au jardin des oliviers (In the Garden of Olives)
- La Trahison de Judas (Judas' Betrayal)
- La Flagellation de Jésus (The Scourging of Jesus)

Other Postcards
Clown en sac B&W
Le Testament de Pierrot B&W
La Première cigarette B&W
Les Petits Coupeurs de bois vert B&W
L'Électrocutée ou Les Secrets de la prestidigitation dévoilés B&W
Faust: divine pureté B&W

Postcard Images of Phonoscènes
Dranem 1 photo sur scène
Mayol in *Questions indiscrètes* B&W
Carmen 3 photos, B&W
Mignon:
Connais-tu le pays où fleurit l'oranger?
As-tu souffert, as-tu pleuré?
Légères hirondelles, oiseaux bénis de Dieu
Est-ce bien Mignon que voilà?

Gaumont Publications

Press Material
Press material which circulated with the Gaumont Centenary retrospective, which
    came to New York in 1994.
Program, *Films parlants (Talking pictures) and Chronochrome*, 39th Street Theatre,
    New York, June 1913.

Catalogues
*Comptoir Général de la Cinématographie chrono de poche pour prise et projection
    de vues de 15mm.* Description et Instruction L. Gaumont et Cie N. 508 (after
    1900).
Collection "Elgé": Liste de Vues Animées, No. 137, May 1899,
    Collection "Elgé": Liste de Vues Animées, No. 162, Jan. 1900.
Collection "Elgé": Nouvelle liste des vues animées of 35mm films, No. 181, June 1900.
Collection "Elgé": Liste de vues animées, No. 182, June 1900.
Comptoir général de cinématographie, Tarif Général des appareils ciné-
    matographiques, No. 501, Jan. 1901.
Comptoir général de cinématographie, Chrono de Poche pour prise et projection de
    vues de 15 m/m, No. 508, 1901.

Collection "Elgé": Liste de vues animées généralement en magasin (hand dated 1901 by the person who copied it from the École Louis Lumière).
Comptoir Général de Cinématographie, *Liste de vues animées*, 1903.

Chronophone Catalogues
Comptoir Général de Cinématographie, *Projections Parlantes*, July 1908.
Comptoir Général de Cinématographie, *Phono-scènes pour Chronophone*, July 1912.
Brochure, *Le Chronophone*.

Patents
Gaumont, Léon, "Automatic Clutch Running Kinematographs and Phonographs Synchronously," Specifications of Letters Patent No. 1,074,943, application filed March 14, 1911, serial No. 614,429, patented Oct. 7, 1913, U.S. Patent Office.
Gaumont, Léon, "Gaumont Chronochrome (sic) Process Described by the Inventor," (Jan. 1959), translated by the Historical and Museum Committee of SMPTE, reprinted in *A Technological history of Motion Pictures and Television* by Raymond Fielding, ed., Berkeley: University of California Press, 1967.

Other Collections

Edison National Historic Site: various files, especially the Gaumont file.

Motion Pictures 1912–1939 Catalogue of Copyright Entries—Cumulative Series, Washington D.C.: Copyright Office, Library of Congress, 1951.

The George Kleine Manuscript Collection, The Library of Congress.

Fonds Will Day
Fonds Georges Demenÿ
Fonds Louis Gaumont
Les collections consultables à la BIFI (Bibliothèque du Film), 100, rue du faubourg Saint-Antoine, 75012 Paris.

Roberta Blaché collection: letters, scenarios, legal documents, press clippings, photographs. Now at MOMA, NY.

INDEX